THE BUILDINGS OF ENGLAND
HEREFORDSHIRE
NIKOLAUS PEVSNER

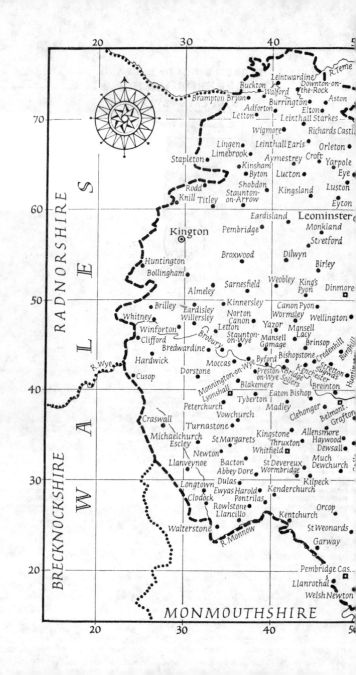

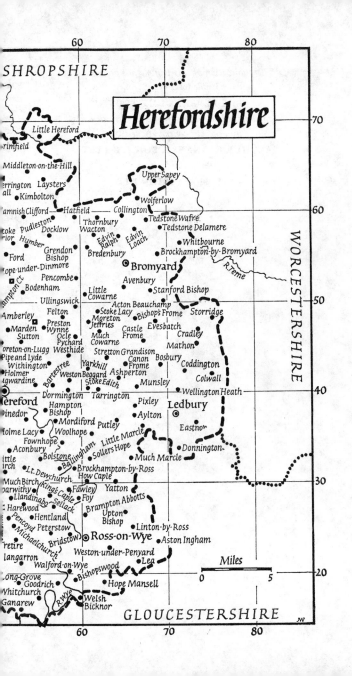

SHROPSHIRE

Herefordshire

WORCESTERSHIRE

Little Hereford

rimfield

Middleton-on-the-Hill

errington Laysters
all   Kimbolton

amnish Clifford Hatfield Collington

oke Pudleston Docklow
rior Humber

Upper Sapey

Wolferlow

Tedstone Wafre

Thornbury Wacton
Ford Grendon
Bishop
ope-under-Dinmore

Tedstone Delamere

Whitbourne

Edvin
Ralph
Bredenbury

Edvin
Loach
Brockhampton-by-Bromyard

R. Teme

Pencombe
ampton Ct. Bodenham

Bromyard

Avenbury

Stanford Bishop

Ullingswick

Amberley Felton
Marden Preston
Sutton Wynne Octe
Pychard Westhide

Little
Cowarne
Stoke Lacy
Moreton
Jeffries
Much
Cowarne

Acton Beauchamp
Bishop's Frome Storridge
Castle Evesbatch
Frome Cradley
Mathon

oreton-on-Lugg
Pipe and Lyde
Withington
Holmer
igwardine

Barts tree
Weston Beggard
Yarkhill
Stoke Edith

Stretton Grandison
Canon Bosbury
Frome
Ashperton
Munsley

Coddington

Colwall

Wellington Heath

ereford
inedor

Dormington Tarrington
Hampton
Bishop
Mordiford Putley

Pixley

Aylton

Ledbury

Eastnor

Holme Lacy
Fownhope Woolhope
Aconbury
ittle Bolstone Ballingham Little Marcle
irch Lt. Dewchurch Sollers Hope
Much Birch Brockhampton-by-Ross Much Marcle
arwithy Kings Caple Fawley Yatton
Llandinabo Sellack Foy
Harewood
Pencoyd Hentland Upton
Michaelchurch Peterstow Bishop
etire Bridstow Linton-by-Ross
langarron Ross-on-Wye Aston Ingham
ong Grove Weston-under-Penyard
Goodrich Walford-on-Wye Lea
Whitchurch Bishopswood
Ganarew Hope Mansell
Welsh
Bicknor

Donnington

R. Wye

GLOUCESTERSHIRE

Miles

0   5

JW

The publication of this volume has been made possible by a grant from
THE LEVERHULME TRUST
to cover all the necessary research work and by generous contributions from
ARTHUR GUINNESS, SON & CO LTD
and
ABC TELEVISION LTD

★

THE BUILDINGS OF ENGLAND

Herefordshire

BY

NIKOLAUS PEVSNER

*

PENGUIN BOOKS

PENGUIN BOOKS
Published by the Penguin Group
27 Wrights Lane, London W8 5TZ, England

Viking Penguin Inc., 40 West 23rd Street, New York, New York 10010, USA
Penguin Books Australia Ltd, Ringwood, Victoria, Australia
Penguin Books Canada Ltd, 2801 John Street, Markham, Ontario, Canada L3R 1B4
Penguin Books (NZ) Ltd, 182–190 Wairau Road, Auckland 10, New Zealand

Penguin Books Ltd, Registered Offices: Harmondsworth, Middlesex, England

—

First published 1963
Reprinted 1973, 1977, 1982, 1987, 1990

—

ISBN 0 14 071025 6

—

—

Made and printed in Great Britain
by Butler & Tanner Ltd, Frome and London
Set in Monotype Plantin

FOR
UTA AND IAN

CONTENTS

*

*

Map References

*

The numbers printed in italic type in the margin against the place names in the gazetteer of the book indicate the position of the place in question on the index map (pages 2-3), which is divided into sections by the 10-kilometre reference lines of the National Grid. The reference given here omits the two initial letters (formerly numbers) which in a full grid reference refer to the 100-kilometre squares into which the country is divided. The first two numbers indicate the *western* boundary, and the last two the *southern* boundary, of the 10-kilometre square in which the place in question is situated. For example Sollers Hope (reference 6030) will be found in the 10-kilometre square bounded by grid lines 60 and 70 on the *west* and 30 and 40 on the *south*; Broxwood (reference 3050) in the square bounded by grid lines 30 and 40 on the *west* and 50 and 60 on the *south*.

The map contains all those places, whether towns, villages, or isolated buildings, which are the subject of separate entries in the text.

FOREWORD

I have always reckoned that The Buildings of England *would total fifty volumes. As this is volume twenty-five, I can regard it as my halfway house and rest for a bit to look back. On the whole the series has found a very kind reception. Certain reservations have been made, rightly and wrongly, and I want to use this opportunity to comment on them. The first volume came out in 1951. The twenty-five have thus taken twelve years. The second twenty-five ought not to take more. So, D.V., the series may be complete by 1975. This is quick work, and it has all the disadvantages of quick work. I cannot do all the preparatory reading and extracting myself, and however well equipped and conscientious my assistants may be, it is a disadvantage that the reading person and the writing person are not the same. Also we cannot do first-hand research; we must rely (with few exceptions) on what has been published. And thirdly we cannot do anything like the checking and re-checking that takes place before the Royal Commission on Historical Monuments or the Victoria County History publishes a volume. But then, how many will be their final total and how often do they publish a volume? The prime* raison d'être *of* The Buildings of England *is in fact that completion of the country by the Royal Commission and the* VCH *cannot be expected for a century in the case of the latter, several centuries in the case of the former. So we go on working in a hurry. Admittedly, the hurry could be a little less if I distributed volumes to local authors. This, however, I have never wanted to do, because the outsider keeping in mind all the time the whole of England and perhaps even something of the Continent seems to me to have overriding advantages. But, on the other hand, counting on one man and his inordinately long life is perhaps taking an equally dangerous risk. The Surrey volume was in fact, as users may have noticed, largely the work of another topographer. So will be the Sussex, the Lincolnshire, and, I hope, the Gloucestershire volumes. So it is not that I want to hog the whole enterprise. On the contrary, I want to live to see it completed, and I am only anxious to preserve a certain unity of approach and treatment. Of any lack of the necessary fanaticism and readiness to accept discomforts among those who have joined in this crazy enterprise I cannot complain, and indeed I must, to complete this preamble to the Foreword, add the welcome fanaticism of Sir Allen*

Lane who has over all these years happily endowed – first alone, of late vigorously supported by the generosity of the Leverhulme Trust, of Arthur Guinness, Son and Company Ltd, and of ABC Television – a series which could not possibly support itself.

Now for Herefordshire.

The preparatory work for this volume was done by Mrs D. Irwin, and she did it so well that if there are actual mistakes in the book, they are more likely to be mine than hers. Readers will no doubt spot many, and I should be grateful for notification. This applies to omissions as well. Omissions are unlikely for buildings of before 1714, the date to which the Royal Commission on Historical Monuments carried until recently their job of inventorizing. So that far we could work from a virtually complete record. For the C18 and part of the C19 there were in addition the appropriate entries in the lists of buildings of architectural or historical interest which it is the statutory duty of the Ministry of Housing and Local Government to compile. As for previous volumes, I had the privilege of a full use of these lists, which cover the whole county. Where I have relied on the lists for information not otherwise available for use, I have added the abbreviation MHLG. The abbreviation RCHM means of course the Royal Commission; GR refers to the late H. S. Goodhart-Rendel's list of Victorian churches, TK to Sir Thomas Kendrick's list of Victorian stained glass, PF to the extensive card index of Victorian church restorations compiled by Mr Peter Ferriday. He most generously put this at the disposal of The Buildings of England.

My text is based on personal visits to all buildings mentioned. Where no visit was possible, the description of the building is placed in brackets. The entries on prehistoric and Roman antiquities were provided by Mr Derek Simpson, those on geology (in the Introduction) by Mr Terence Miller. Mr J. T. Smith gave Mrs Irwin the benefit of his great knowledge of timber-framed buildings. The National Buildings Record (NBR), represented by the Director and Miss Margaret Gossling, was as helpful as ever. In addition my thanks are due to Mr J. F. W. Sherwood, Miss V. E. Coleman, and Mr J. F. L. Norwood of the Hereford City Library and Museum, Mr Walter Gittens, Mr G. E. Spain, Mr Peter Newton, Mr Ivor Bulmer-Thomas, Mrs Pauline Beesly, Mrs Diane Uhlman, Mr J. Lucas-Scudamore, Major M. Munthe, Mr H. Garrett-Adams, and the many other owners or occupiers of houses who have courteously taken us round and patiently replied to letters, to the many rectors and vicars who have answered questions of mine, to my secretary Miss Margaret Tims who battled with letters and *answers, and, of course, to my wife who drove with me through the whole county notwithstanding the rains of the memorable autumn of 1960.*

My gazetteer will no doubt be faulty in certain ways. Reasons why this is bound to be so have been given earlier on, and corrections from users will be appreciated. One source of faults, peculiar to Herefordshire, is this. There are far more black and white cottages (and stone cottages in the parts bordering on Wales) and far more medieval roof trusses in houses and cottages than I could examine. My selection from the volumes of the RCHM and the lists of the MHLG may in certain cases have been ill-judged. Also features mentioned in them and taken over by me may have disappeared since, and others may have been found in the last ten or twenty years. So these parts of the present book ought to be used with some leniency.

As in all other volumes of The Buildings of England *no more than a selection of Victorian and post-Victorian buildings could be included, the selection being based on what seemed to me aesthetically most significant. In houses no paintings other than wall-paintings are referred to, and no furniture other than what can be regarded as fixtures. In churches timber roofs are mentioned only where they are of special merit, churchyard crosses only where more than steps and base survives, and coffin lids with foliated crosses, doors, chests, chairs, bells, plate of after 1837, and brasses after the Reformation only very exceptionally.*

INTRODUCTION

THERE are not many counties in England of which it can be said that, wherever one goes, there will not be a mile which is visually unrewarding or painful. The former is due mainly to natural, the latter to social reasons. Herefordshire is one of the least industrialized of all counties. Cider, yes; Herefordshire cattle, yes; hops, yes; but that is hardly industry. So there are no factory suburbs of Hereford, no factories along the country roads, no council housing noticeable for quantity or indeed quality. Nor – for better or worse – any big towns either. Hereford has 33,000 inhabitants. It is followed by Leominster with 6,000, Ross with 5,000, Ledbury with 4,500. Also, the population of the county altogether is only 127,000, the forty-first in the country, if one counts the Yorkshire Ridings singly, whereas in area Herefordshire comes twenty-eighth. As for natural characteristics, there is no flat land at all. Rolling country is the rule, though there are the little picture-book hills rising suddenly and isolatedly about the Pyons, and there are of course the Malverns, exquisite in their Italian outline – the Euganei are the nearest I can think of – and the mountains of the Welsh 1a border. Also, Herefordshire has an infinite number of rivers, streams, and brooks and unusually large areas still or again covered by woods – still, where the venerable oaks and elms and the tangled undergrowth line the serpentines of the river Wye from Ross down into Monmouthshire; again, where the Forestry Commission has planted its conifers which go so well with the calm outlines of the ancient hills towards Radnor and Brecknock. And how pleasant is the contrast of mood between them – the one picturesquely romantic, the other romantic in a deeper sense – and the orchards laden with fruit and the serried ranks of hop-poles with the joyous trails of the hops. No-one can say that variety is lacking in Herefordshire.

Geographical variety is founded on varied GEOLOGY, and buildings by their materials express the ground they stand on. In Herefordshire there is the great basic difference between building in stone and building in timber and plaster, with brick much later joining in. The stone is predominantly the Devonian Old Red Sandstone, and so in large areas the soil is red, and the churches and major houses are red, occasionally a rather hot red, but as a rule an attractive greyish pink. The stone and the timber express unmistakably the physiographic shape of the county. It is roughly a saucer, split by the Wye and its tributaries, with an almost continuous rim of hills. This shape is partly due to the relative softness of the rock, weathering down easily into a rich soil, to which has been added a generous spread of glacial and river-borne silt and loam, with mounds and ridges of coarser sand and gravel. This good agricultural foundation made for a bias towards building with materials from above the ground, leaving the land unscarred by quarries. But wherever stone was needed, as it was e.g. for castles, the geological structure ensured supplies. Round the rim of the saucer, the hard-rock basement of England comes to the surface in the Malvern Hills, and in the wooded shoulders of the hills on the NW side, from Bradnor Hill up to Bringewood Chase. Here also the lowest strata of the Devonian system, the Downton Stone, have been worked from very early times as a yellow-green freestone, and can be seen used all over Herefordshire. Moreover, when the main part of the 'Old Red' itself is hard and compact, as it is about Weobley and Eye, around Ross-on-Wye, and again over the county borders in the Black Mountains, it has been much quarried. In addition, close to Hereford itself, a geological dome-structure has brought to the surface Silurian limestones, and they are quarried near Woolhope. They have several local names, depending on colour and texture, and they occur again over the county border in the Black Mountains, either drab grey, red, or chocolate-coloured. Interbedded with these strong rock bands are occasional unimportant limestone patches (except that these often contain fossil fish), and layers of clay or shale, which are source-materials for brick-making.

Younger rocks appear only in the SE corner of the county. Here a gently-tilted slab of Carboniferous strata lies above the Old Red Sandstone, forming part of the 'underpinning' of the Forest of Dean coalfield. Of these rocks, the smooth, pale-grey Carboniferous Limestone – the 'Mountain Limestone' of Derbyshire and Yorkshire and the Avon Gorge – was formerly much quarried for the iron industry of the Forest, and is seen occasionally in old walls. The fine-grained, buff-coloured Drybrook Sandstone above the Limestone, somewhat resembling the finer parts of the Millstone Grit of the Pennines, is also a good building stone.

There remains only one geological curiosity that has a bearing on human use. This is perhaps one of the very youngest true rocks in Britain – the post-glacial calcareous tufa, or travertine, of Southstone Rock, just beyond the Herefordshire boundary, in the Teme valley, near Shelsley Walsh. Tufa of this kind is formed round the outlet of a spring whose waters are charged with lime in solution. This particular one derives its calcareous matter from one of the limestones in the Old Red Sandstone. It is a spongy, cavernous deposit, but relatively hard and resistant. The Normans used large blocks of it in their building work in Herefordshire.

In PREHISTORIC times, Hereford, with the rest of Britain N of a line roughly from the Severn to the Wash, was covered by ice during the last three principal glacial periods when evidence of Palaeolithic (Old Stone Age) man is represented in Europe.

With the retreat of the ice after the final glaciation and the gradual encroachment of forests, first of birch and pine and later of oak, there was a general movement of population to coastal regions and to sandy heathlands. Material remains of these Mesolithic (Middle Stone Age) settlers have been found in King Arthur's Cave near Ganarew. Their economy was based on hunting, fishing, and gathering, and their most characteristic flint form was a small blade, or microlith, employed singly as the tip of an arrow or collectively as the barbs in a bone fish spear.

Again in the Neolithic phase (New Stone Age) the heavy clay soils of the county must have supported thick oak forests, presenting a formidable barrier to the first farmers and necessitating the clearance of considerable tracts of woodland for their crops and herds. That small groups did penetrate the area is clear from the megalithic tomb known as Arthur's Stone 3b near Dorstone. This is an outlier of a group of chambered tombs centred on the lands bordering the Severn and the Cotswolds. Burial in these tombs appears to have occurred intermittently over a considerable period of time, the entrances to the burial chambers being carefully blocked up after each successive deposit. The passage and chamber were covered by a barrow of earth or stones, generally of wedge-shaped plan; in the case of Arthur's Stone all traces of this covering mound have vanished. A second megalithic tomb may have existed at St Margaret's Park (see p. 284) but was destroyed in the C19. A Neolithic working area at Frith Farm, Ledbury, is represented by numerous finds of flint flakes and artefacts scattered over a wide area; these include fragments of polished axes intended for forest clearance and the leaf-shaped arrow-heads characteristic of the period.

Evidence for Beaker and Early Bronze Age settlement is again slight. Two bell beakers were found in a pair of adjacent cists in the Olchon valley. Such vessels are typical products of the earliest of the three principal beaker-making groups in Britain and represent an initial invasion of the E and SE coasts from Holland c.1850 B.C. In lowland Britain, burial generally took the form of a crouched inhumation in a pit-grave, or on the old ground surface, beneath a round barrow. In the highland zone, contracted inhumations were again the rule, although the body was commonly placed in a cist, either as a flat grave (Olchon valley) or covered by a cairn or barrow. Another flat cist grave at Llangarron contained a crouched male skeleton without grave goods. Few of the round barrows in the county, which are probably monuments of this period, have been excavated. A bowl barrow near Brandon, opened in the C17, covered an urn containing a cremation. A second Early Bronze Age collared urn was found in the Mathon sandpits. These finds, bronze flat axes from Eaton Bishop and Newton, and stray barb-and-tang flint arrow-heads are the only evidence for occupation of the county at this period.

Material of the Middle and Late Bronze Age is equally scarce, and no field monuments can be attributed to these periods. For the former period one has the chance discoveries of bronze palstaves at Bucknell and Much Marcle and a dirk and rapier at Hereford and Aston Ingham respectively. Late Bronze Age objects include socketed axes and the upper part of an early type of bronze sword from Fairoaks, Hereford. The paucity of finds suggests that there was little actual settlement in the county throughout the duration of the Bronze Age, and the few recorded bronze objects may represent wares lost or buried by itinerant smiths and merchants plying between the settlements of North Wales and the downlands of Wessex. That the principal routes followed by these traders crossing the county were the valleys of the Wye and Lugg is apparent from the concentration of bronzes strung along the courses of these two rivers.

It is only in the Iron Age that one has for the first time evidence of a considerable prehistoric population in the county. Excavations at the hill-fort of Croft Ambrey, Aymestrey, suggest some slight penetration of the region by peoples of the first, Iron Age A culture, but the main influx of settlers came in the middle of the C1 B.C., when refugees from western France introduced a distinctive form of the Iron Age B culture to the region. These immigrants penetrated the county by the traditional routes of the Wye and Lugg, constructing hill-forts on 3a those scarps which overlook the rivers as they leave the mountains of the west and flow through relatively low-lying country. The forts are generally of multivallate plan with ramparts inturned at the entrances. This system of defensive architecture was conditioned by the introduction of sling warfare, which required defence in depth as a protection against sling bullets. The forts were probably occupied only in times of unrest, and the considerable quantity of occupation material immediately within the ramparts at Sutton Walls and Aconbury merely points to the generally unsettled conditions prevailing in this period. A textile industry is attested by bone weaving-combs and clay loom-weights and spindle whorls, and an anvil with considerable quantities of iron slag at Sutton Walls indicates the smelting of iron on the site. Iron sickles are the only evidence for farming, and the very large quantity of cattle bones at Sutton Walls suggests that pastoralism rather than cereal production was the mainstay of the economy – this was no doubt a primary consideration in hill-fort construction, as livestock can be more easily carried off by raiders than grain. The horse appears to have been in general use, and antler cheek-pieces from bridles as well as skeletal remains were found at Sutton Walls.

The third prehistoric Iron Age Culture, Iron Age C, was introduced to Britain by Belgic immigrants settling in South-East England in two main waves in the CI B.C. The second group, refugees from Caesar's campaigns in Gaul and consisting largely of Gaulish Atrebates, gradually moved westward until, c. A.D. 25, small bands settled in Herefordshire. They occupied the existing hill-forts and possibly constructed new ones, although this has not been confirmed by excavation. At Sutton Walls, the ramparts were raised and the revetment at the w entrance was probably in part re-built. Similar alterations were probably carried out on the other pre-existing forts of the area. Following the Roman invasion of South Britain the ditch w of the entrance just mentioned was hurriedly re-cut, but, very shortly afterwards, the Roman military occupation of the county is dramatically attested by the bodies of the defenders, some decapitated or showing wounds, which were hurled into the ditch and covered with a thin layer of soil. After the taking of the fort the ramparts were allowed to fall into decay.

The ROMAN occupation of the district probably took place during Governor Frontinus's campaign into South Wales *c*. A.D. 75. A sea-borne invasion of Glamorgan and the construction of forts at river mouths secured the coast. From there it was possible to use the river valleys to penetrate and outflank the Black Mountains. An important natural route in this campaign was undoubtedly the Wye valley, and Watling Street, which runs due N through the county connecting the legionary fortress at Caerleon with Wroxeter and Chester in the north, must have been constructed at this time. Following the conquest of Wales, Herefordshire, with the rest of southern Britain, appears to have enjoyed comparative peace for two centuries, and no purely military sites have been discovered in the county. The native economy must have altered little with the coming of the Romans. Within the fort at Sutton Walls, huts identical to those of the prehistoric occupation were constructed, the only difference in the finds from these huts being the appearance of Roman domestic wares. A small Roman town was established at 4a Kenchester (Magna), connected by a branch road with Watling Street. The only other site of the period worthy of the term town is Weston-under-Penyard (Ariconium), possibly founded on an existing Iron Age settlement. This appears to have been an industrial community engaged in the smelting of iron obtained from the ore deposits in the Forest of Dean. No villa in the county has been excavated in modern times, although foundations and floor mosaics at Bishopstone and portions of tessellated pavements at Whitchurch and Walterstone suggest the presence of these provincial Roman economic units. The date and circumstances of the Roman withdrawal from the area are obscure. Increasingly unsettled conditions and raids are reflected in the fortifications at Kenchester and the large hoard of coins buried at Walford, and a general withdrawal must have taken place at the end of the C4.

The native Celts continued to occupy the area, however, and may even have constructed hill-forts, although this has not been proved by excavation. Some of the strip lynchets and cultivation terraces too may belong to this immediately post-Roman period. It is only however with the westward expansion of the Saxons that one again finds dateable field monuments in the county. A bishopric was established at Hereford in the C7, and a number of the ditch systems in the county may date from this period (e.g. Yatton); but the great military monument of the Saxons belongs to the succeeding century, when Offa, king of Mercia (*c.* 757–96), constructed a massive earthwork which ran from the coast at Prestatyn, Flintshire, to the Severn at Sedbury, Gloucestershire, marking the western limits of his kingdom and serving as a bulwark against the Welsh principalities. In Hereford the course of the Dyke is erratic, and there are considerable gaps which appear never to have been artificially strengthened. Such gaps almost certainly mark densely wooded areas which would have formed a natural and impenetrable barrier. Although the dyke was conceived as a unitary design and dug over a period of ten or twelve years in the latter part of Offa's reign, the structural variations in the individual stretches probably mark changes in a gang engaged in its construction (a good example occurs in Kington Rural parish, where the Dyke on Rushock Hill has a s ditch but changes to a N ditch in Kennel Wood).

Considering the much more than local interest of Offa's Dyke, it is surprising that in ANGLO-SAXON STONE ARCHITECTURE Herefordshire has not a single building or part of a building that would qualify for mention here. The only possible exception is the fragment at Acton Beauchamp of an excellent c9 shaft with large scrolls 'inhabited' by a bird, a lion, and perhaps a goat,* and it is doubly surprising if one remembers that for NORMAN ARCHITECTURE Herefordshire has an outstanding record, outstanding for cathedral as well as monastic as well as parochial architecture, and – it must be added – outstanding among all English counties for architectural sculpture, sculpture as part of the building.

We had better start with the cathedral. Nothing of it goes back to beyond the time of Reynelm, called the *fundator* of the church, i.e. beyond *c.*1110. Then building must have gone on quickly; for the consecration of about 1145 seems to mark completion at the W end. Of the remaining parts the E wall of the s transept seems earliest, the completion of the transept and 6b the building of the chancel, originally with towers on the E bays of the aisles, came a little later, the crossing seems contemporary with the chancel, and the nave came a little later still. In the E 5 wall of the transept the forms are massive and the capitals elementary. Zigzag comes in only in the clerestory and then, a little lower down, the W wall. In the chancel it is in use, and indeed a favourite, from the start. That and the geometrical

---

* The two panels at Llanveynoe, one with a childishly primitive Crucifixus, the other with a cross and an inscription 'Haefdur fecit crucem', are the concern of archaeology, not of the history of art.

patterns of the tympana of the twin gallery openings are reminiscent of Peterborough, and Peterborough was begun in 1118.
But the gallery at Hereford also introduces a change of plan or
an adaptation to West Country custom. The piers of the arcade
below are compound, the responds of the gallery fat demi-
cylinders. Now the West Country had declared itself unmistakably in favour of massive columns at Tewkesbury and
Gloucester before 1100, and first perhaps at Evesham. Once
Hereford had accepted this fashion, the nave continued with it,
and though the piers are not as tall as those of Tewkesbury and
Gloucester, they have a diameter of well over 6 ft. The nave
gallery consequently was not so under-developed, and a more
balanced result was obtained. The gallery unfortunately was
not restored when the C14 W tower fell in 1786, but replaced by
one in another style. The details of the work of Reynelm and his
successors cannot be considered fully; for in the 1840s much
was restored and much removed. However, it is certain – for
original capitals are about in various places in the cathedral – that
the early capitals were lively, varied, and included apart from
8a foliage trails scenes done in an agitated, somewhat graphic
manner, influenced by Anglo-Saxon carving and draughtsmanship, whereas towards the end carvers had settled down to less
fantastic but also less imaginative many-scalloped capitals. The
W front cannot have been very imaginative either. There was
no dominant tower, only turrets, somewhat as at Rochester.

The other major building of the same time, the Priory of
Leominster, seems to have been started a little later, if, that is,
the assumption is true that the start followed the presentation
of the priory to Henry I's newly-founded favourite Reading
Abbey. So Leominster, like Reading, was Benedictine. So were
Kilpeck Priory, of which nothing survives, and four or five
others also completely gone. Cluniac Clifford and Titley of the
Order of Tiron have likewise disappeared. So has the later house
of the Greyfriars at Hereford, whereas of that of the Blackfriars
the range to the W of the cloisters stands up, though in a ruinous
state. What remains in addition of monastic houses is this:
a substantial and highly important part of the church of the
Cistercian Abbey Dore (which must be discussed later), part of
the early C13 church of the Augustinian Canonesses at Aconbury,
a single ruined C13 building of Limebrook Priory, also of the
Augustinian Canonesses, some overgrown early C13 ruins of
the aisleless and transeptless, but apsed church and the chapter
house at Craswall, one of the three houses in England of the

Order of Grandmont, the eminently interesting, but only excavated and not or hardly visible, round naves of St Giles's Hospital at Hereford and of Garway, the latter a house of the Knights Templars, the one C13 doorway at Clifford (which was a Cluniac Priory), the gable wall of the s transept, some more late C12 walling, and the C14 or C15 abbot's lodging of the Augustinian (or more precisely Victorine) Wigmore Abbey,* and one range of the Augustinian Flanesford (Goodrich), which is mid-C14 and contained the refectory, curiously enough on the upper floor.‡

The remains at Leominster are infinitely the most important. 6a They look extremely strange now, because the chancel has gone, and an E.E. second nave, an early C14 aisle, and a Perp tower have been added, but they must always have looked strange, because the system of the elevation inside was from the first unexpected and has become highly confusing by change of plan. The original idea seems to have been an alternation of narrow and wide bays, repeated three times, a rhythm reminiscent of the cathedral of Trier, where it has different reasons and looks very different.§ At Leominster they soon turned away from it, introduced round piers to break the system, and put a gallery over which has no logical connexion with the arcading below. The most successful piece at Leominster is the w portal, which has highly decorated capitals with quite a different sense 8b of sculptural form from those of the cathedral. They are inspired by Reading Abbey, Henry I's favourite foundation. Reading was established in 1121, Leominster from Reading in 1123. An altar in the E bay of the nave was consecrated in 1130. So the w portal will be of the mid C12.

But the best sculpture of mid-C12 Herefordshire appears in parish churches, and parish churches have not so far been mentioned. Many survive, and in a large number parts or fragments survive. We have evidence of early, mature, and late work, the early work characterized by herringbone masonry, the

* This had started at Shobdon between 1131 and 1148 (*see* below) and moved to three different sites and back to Shobdon before settling down between Adforton and Wigmore.

‡ Coningsby Hospital at Hereford stands on the site of a hospital administered by the Knights Hospitallers of Dinmore (of their establishment no more is visible than part of the N wall of the present church. This dates from the late C12), and some of the masonry of Coningsby Hospital may indeed be medieval. All traces are lost of the Augustinians (Victorines) of Wormsley, the Premonstratensians of Holme Lacy, and the Templars of Bosbury.

§ And of Périgueux, *see* p. 225

simplest mouldings, the use of tufa, and also by the use of very large blocks of stone (*see* e.g. Castle Frome). We have also sufficient evidence of very large parish churches such as Ledbury, which had heavy round piers and round clerestory windows (cf. Southwell), and Madley, which was cruciform, and we have 7 complete small parish churches, such as Moccas and Kilpeck. In fact none in the whole country can be more thrilling than Kilpeck. Kilpeck and Moccas consist of nave, lower and narrower chancel, and yet lower and narrower apse. Tarrington 4b and Mathon also had apses. Peterchurch has in addition a space between nave and chancel which must have carried a kind of tower. Fownhope still has a tower following after the nave, though we do not know what the E parts were like. As against such central towers, Eaton Bishop has a w tower with twin bell-openings and Bridge Sollers has a w tower too.

Of the churches mentioned, Fownhope and of course Kilpeck participate in the great achievement of the HEREFORDSHIRE SCHOOL OF NORMAN SCULPTURE, really not a school but a workshop, one is led to believe, travelling from place to place and working where commissions were given. The place where we first find the workshop in action is Shobdon. The church was consecrated before, probably shortly before, 1148, and shows the principal master of the group at his best. The sculpture is 9a not now *in situ*; it serves, ignominiously though charmingly, as a folly or eye-catcher in the former grounds of the former Shobdon Court and consists of two former doorways and the former chancel arch. The sculpture is ruined beyond redemption by being exposed to West Country weather. The style already has all the characteristics of the school and the principal master. 9b He must have gone from Shobdon to Kilpeck, where the s doorway is his, and his best remaining work. But the figures on the 9c chancel arch at Kilpeck are of a different kind and without doubt by a different hand. The principal master can be recognized at Fownhope too and, in addition, one of his Shobdon tympana was copied at St Giles's Hospital, Hereford. A much weaker 11b imitator certainly was responsible for the work at Rowlstone. 10 The tympana at Brinsop and Stretton Sugwas seem just a little 11a later,* and the fonts at Eardisley and Castle Frome so decidedly &, later that they are more likely by the successor of the Shobdon 12 master than by himself having grown older. The style of the workshop has a diversity of sources, as Dr Zarnecki has

---

* But as that of Stretton Sugwas was copied in the w portal at Leominster, which can hardly be later than *c.*1150, the difference must be small.

exemplarily demonstrated: Anglo-Saxon and Viking, Reading–Leominster–Benedictine, West French, and also – at least for the chancel arch at Kilpeck, or so it seems to me – North Italian. In detail the long trails and the figures entwined in them are Anglo-Saxon, the long winding dragons and snakes and the dragon-heads as corbels Viking, the beak-heads of Kilpeck depend on Reading, the tympana of Brinsop and Stretton Sugwas are almost copied from Parthenay-le-Vieux, and the radial arrangement of figures and ornament on the voussoirs is also a West French motif (Aulnay, Saintes, etc.). The figures placed one on top of the other in the chancel arch of Kilpeck are North Italian in origin (Modena, Ferrara) rather than inspired by the Puerta de las Platerias at Santiago de Compostela, although it is known that the founder of Shobdon went on a pilgrimage to Compostela before the church was built. The style of the principal master as it finally emerges out of such varied inspiration is characterized by the wire-like quality of the parallel, curvy drapery folds, the intensity of gestures, and the delight in improbable attitudes (angels flying upside down) and in such details as the long claws of birds and beasts. The claws have the same character as the folds, and the folds the same intensity as the gestures – in short this is an accomplished art in which ruthless stylizing is done for a purpose.

In the later works, especially the two fonts, figures are shorter and heavier, the wire-like folds become rope-like, but the intensity never slackens. The school is also represented by work outside Herefordshire: Ruardean in Gloucestershire, Rock and Chaddesley Corbett in Worcestershire, and, at its very end, the *lavatorium* at Much Wenlock Priory in Shropshire, which can hardly be earlier than about 1180.

There is of course, apart from this so-called Herefordshire School, other NORMAN SCULPTURE in Herefordshire as well, and some of it is lacking in just those qualities which distinguish the 'school', i.e. it displays confused motifs got together without any system. Such is the case in the tympana of Willersley, Moccas, and Aston,* the fonts at How Caple and Michaelchurch, and the lintel at Bredwardine with figures described as oriental deities. Who are they, what did the sculptor mean by them, and

* The centre here is a Lamb and Cross in a circle, as it is also in the tympanum at Byton. Other tympana have geometrical decoration only (two at Bromyard; also Tretire), and geometrical, i.e. zigzags etc., are also the motifs in the arches of the doorways of Ledbury and Leominster and the chancel arch of Garway.

where did he get his knowledge of them from? Sources and the use made of them are a baffling problem in the earlier Middle Ages.

A striking example is the last purely Norman building to be referred to here: Bishop Losinga's Chapel at Hereford, attached to the Bishop's Palace. He ruled from 1079 to 1095 and he built this chapel, according to William of Malmesbury, 'imitating the basilica of Aachen'. Now that means the cathedral which was originally the chapel of Charlemagne's palace. Losinga's was also a palace chapel. It does not exist any longer, except for the outlines of two tiers of three arches each against the s wall of the s range of the cloister. In fact the two buildings had only one feature in common: they were *Doppelkapellen*, i.e. two-storeyed, with an opening in the middle to connect the two storeys for eye and ear. At Aachen the opening is wide and octagonal, at Hereford it was small and square. At Aachen an analysis would speak of an octagon with an ambulatory, at Hereford of a square with an opening in the middle supported by four piers. In fact Hereford is much more similar to the palace chapels of Mainz and Goslar, which date from the first third of the C12, i.e. are later than Hereford. However that may be, the chapel was a building of a type unique in England, and it is a great pity that it was pulled down.

14a   Unique also, at least for its date, is the Bishop's Hall, and this also is alas far from complete. It was a hall of the late C12, 55 ft wide and at least 75 ft long, consisting of a nave and aisles, and it was, within the stone walls, built of timber. Two of the enormous piers or posts stand and two of the arcade arches are *in situ*. There may be more hidden in the walls of the palace. What is exposed has recently been made exemplarily accessible.

Herefordshire abounds in timber-built halls, but they are all later. The tradition of the aisled hall did not apparently establish itself, as it did e.g. in Essex, and when we return to domestic building, it will be to consider halls roofed in one span.

So while for domestic architecture there is a gap here,* the same cannot be said of MILITARY ARCHITECTURE. Here the records are uncommonly full for the county, even if rather for earthworks than for stone castles. The need for castles was great in this border country and remained great to the end of the Middle Ages. There is a chain of castles all through the county and on through Monmouthshire and through Shropshire

* One can hardly say that the one Norman doorway which remains at Stretton Court, Stretton Sugwas, of the house of the bishops of Hereford fills that gap.

into Cheshire. What was built immediately after the Conquest was of earth and palisading, the motte and bailey castles of William Fitz Osbern, whom William the Conqueror had made Earl of Hereford, and of one or two Norman friends of Edward the Confessor such as Richard who built Richard's Castle and Ralph the Norman who built Ewyas Harold. Both are mentioned in Domesday, as are Clifford, Eardisley, and Wigmore. The usual arrangement of motte and bailey castles was a roughly circular motte placed in the strategically best corner and a crescent- or oblong-shaped bailey, often with further enclosures beyond the bailey or beyond the motte. It is not always easy to say now whether remains of a motte or an enclosure are medieval or prehistoric.

But, although this book tries to list motte and bailey castles, they are hardly architecture, and when it comes to stone building, the many become few, and the few tell us little. The mid-c12 keep at Goodrich is the only one of the type familiar from so many examples all over England. At Longtown is a circular keep of c.1200, and at Lyonshall scantier remains of another, of perhaps a little later date. Yet scantier are the traces of the keep at Llancillo, and at Hereford not only the keep, but even the whole motte has completely disappeared, though the rampart of the bailey still stands more than 20 ft high above the Castle Pool, i.e. the former moat.* The keep at Kilpeck is polygonal and of the shell type, that at Snodhill Castle, Peterchurch, is an irregular elongated polygon and had a gateway flanked by round towers. The date is probably c.1200. Round towers characterize the work on the curtain walls of the c13, the new type of defence intended to replace the concentration on keeps. Thus at Clifford, early in the c13, they built round towers. The gatehouse stands partly quite high up. Fragments of similar gatehouses can be seen at Longtown and Pembridge. At Pembridge the gatehouse is close to one corner, and that is also the arrangement at Goodrich, the most spectacular and best preserved castle of Herefordshire.

The gatehouse at Goodrich Castle dates, together with hall, solar, kitchen, etc. and the highly interesting semicircular barbican, from c.1280 etc. This was the time when in castles like Harlech a completely symmetrical plan was worked out. It is the asymmetrical position of the gatehouse which distinguishes Goodrich from Harlech. The hall at Goodrich has

* Inside the bailey recent excavations have shown the walls of a former chapel or church, probably Norman.

transomed windows to the outside. The solar lies next to it, the chapel in the bigger of the two gate towers. In an adjoining range three garderobe cubicles survive. Again of *c*.1300 are the gatehouse of the Goodrich kind and the curtain wall with round and polygonal towers of Wilton Castle, Bridstow, and the gatehouse at Brampton Bryan. The C14 remains of Penyard Castle, Weston-under-Penyard, are all but obliterated. Finally, to close this chapter, there is the mighty C14 gateway at Kentchurch, there is Treago Castle, St Weonards, with four round angle towers which may also be of the C14, though the porch is C15 at the earliest, there is Croft Castle, also with round towers, though less regular, and also of the C15 (or C14), and there are
38a with known C15 dates Hampton Court and Bronsil Castle, Eastnor. Licence to crenellate the former dates from 1434, the latter from 1460. Bronsil Castle continues with remarkable stubbornness the C13 type with curtain wall, octagonal towers, and gatehouse. Hampton Court has four ranges round a courtyard, and the finest piece is the chapel with its Perp windows
38b and its beautiful ceiling.

The proximity to Wales called for defences other than castles as well. Some church towers are so massive that it is hard not to believe they were thought of as possible refuges as well. The church at Ewyas Harold has walls over 7 ft thick, and Monnington-on-Wye has battlements with cross-shaped arrowslits. And Hereford, not satisfied with its castle alone, built walls round the town. Much of them survives, including two of the semicircular bastions, but nothing spectacular. We do not know when they were first begun. What exists seems to belong to a campaign which started in 1298.

But this account of military architecture has taken us far too far forward in time. We must now return to the C12. We had left Hereford Cathedral at the time of the consecration, that is before 1150. The building was now complete, and nothing further was undertaken until about 1190, when, it seems, the decision was made to enlarge the E end. This had three parallel apses, like Durham or Ely. Now a retrochoir was added, in the form of a straight double ambulatory to connect the two Norman chancel aisles. At Abbey Dore exactly the same was done at exactly the same time. Abbey Dore, as we have seen, was founded in 1147. But the surviving building is not of that date.
17a It is of *c*.1175–80 to *c*.1210. It is the very reverse of Leominster – the E half, not the W half that was preserved: crossing, transepts, and chancel with aisles, and the retrochoir, which corresponds

to that at Hereford. The history is interesting. Still about 1180 the idea was to have the Cistercian standard plan – i.e. transepts each with two parallel, straight-ended chapels and a projecting straight-ended chancel. Then, however, Bernardian simplicity was abandoned, the inner chapels were opened at their E end, 17b and choir aisles and a retrochoir were built two bays deep, or probably one bay and a row of chapels E of it separated by light partition walls much like at Cîteaux itself in the third building consecrated in 1193 and at Byland, also at the end of the C12, and at Waverley (Surrey) in 1203–14. So this was an internal Cistercian development, and the similarity in plan between Hereford and Dore would tempt one into making the latter the inspiration of the former, if it were not for the fact that the details at Hereford are slightly earlier than those at Dore. After all, at Winchester too a retrochoir had been started and carried quite far before 1204, the date when Bishop de Lucy died.

The E parts of Dore and the retrochoir of Hereford are the principal buildings in the TRANSITIONAL STYLE. What characterizes this moment is that motifs remain Norman for a while, but the spirit has gone E.E., that is Gothic. Arches, where used functionally, turn pointed,* proportions turn more vertical, shafts turn slenderer. Yet zigzag goes on, and similar Norman geometrical motifs tend to become more varied, thicker, and more ruthless. Of details two must be singled out, both types of capitals: the waterleaf capital and the multi-scalloped capital, where each scallop assumes a concave or trumpet shape. The former was specially favoured by the Cistercians and consequently appears at Dore. But it remained rare in Herefordshire,‡ whereas the trumpet capital became a fashion.§ At Dore it can be seen side by side with waterleaf. Other places with trumpet capitals are too numerous to be discussed here.‖ But at Hereford it is at once combined with stiff-leaf, the new Early Gothic motif of decoration. The dividing line cannot be drawn, and yet nobody could miss the change of expression between the beginning and the end at Dore or between the retrochoir and the

---

* Where used functionally is said advisedly; for at Coddington, consecrated as late as 1231, the doorways have round arches.

‡ Clehonger, Garway, King's Pyon.

§ It is even more prominent at Llanthony in Monmouthshire than at Dore.

‖ Acton Beauchamp, Amberley, Blakemere, Bosbury, Bromyard. Burghill, Byford, Colwall, Eastnor, King's Pyon, Kingstone, Ledbury, Preston-on-Wye, Ross, Stanford Bishop, Upton Bishop, Walford-on-Wye, Wellington, Westhide, Weston Beggard, Whitbourne.

18b Lady Chapel at Hereford. The end at Dore may have been just
    about the moment when the Lady Chapel was started at the
    cathedral. Both are works of exuberance as well as nobility,
18a with rich capitals and a multitude of shafts.*
 &
19a   On the less magnificent scale of parish churches the Transi-
    tional makes itself felt as patently if not as grandly. Here are
    some signs. Circular piers are slimmer. The square abacus is
    replaced by the octagonal abacus – with a curious variant at
    All Saints Hereford, Clehonger, Eaton Bishop, and Madley –
    and then by the round abacus. Moulded capitals, at first with
    few, very pronounced mouldings, appear, and of course stiff-leaf
    capitals. Early ones, also at the cathedral and Dore, have the
    stiff-leaf standing upright and leaving the lower part of the bell
    free. Later, i.e. in the mature EARLY ENGLISH, they cover
    the bell in higher relief and the stalks and leaves cross in a more
    agitated movement. Other details, applying generally, and not
    yet registered, are the keeling of shafts and a little later the fillet
    running down a shaft, and also a liking for continuous mouldings
    in doorways and other arches, i.e. no break by a capital between
    jambs and arch. This was a South-West-Country speciality
    already shortly after 1150. In the C13 in Herefordshire it is too
    frequent to be listed here.
       Finally there are detached towers. They are certainly some-
    thing no-one will leave unnoticed. There are not many, but then
    there are not many in England. Nor can one say why they were
    built. The late G. Marshall counted forty in England and Wales
    and gave eight to Cornwall, seven to Herefordshire, three each
    to Bedfordshire, Suffolk, and Norfolk, and so on. In fact Marshall
    refers to nine in Herefordshire, including two which were de-
    tached when they were built. Of these, five are of the first half
37a of the C13 (Kington c.1200, Garway and Holmer early C13,
    Bosbury and Ledbury c.1230–40), Richards Castle is of c.1300,
35a and only Yarpole, Weobley, and Pembridge are of the C14.
 & b   Just as it has been necessary in this case to report on two
    periods in one, so there are other cases where it will be useful
    to do the same. Herefordshire is a county with a very pro-
    nounced character in its architecture. This character is stronger
    than the changing styles, and so the chronological order cus-
    tomary in these introductions to volumes of *The Buildings of*

---

    * The details of the development from the late C12 to c.1220 at Dore and
    c.1240 at Hereford are given on pp. 60 and 157. Incidentally, some capitals
    at Dore were never carved: they remained in the raw, an instructive thing
    for the historian to see. He can also see it at Walford-on-Wye.

England may here for once be broken and some statements made which apply to the GENERAL CHARACTER OF PARISH CHURCHES in Herefordshire. As we were talking TOWERS, one or two more remarks on towers. People do not think of Hereford-shire as a county of spires, yet there are surprisingly many. Among stone spires, the most lasting and monumental, it is easy to list a dozen worth looking for. They are all recessed spires. Weobley comes first. It is the only one with the graceful motif of flying buttresses connecting the spire with the pinnacles on the tower. Then the two medieval parish churches of Hereford, and Peterchurch (alas still waiting for most of it to be rebuilt), and Ross and Goodrich, and Llangarron, Sellack, Stoke Edith, Stretton Grandison, Withington. Where they have lucarnes in the spire, they have only one set, and this starts at the foot of the spire -- quite different e.g. from the Nene Valley customs. Hereford Cathedral used to have a timber and lead spire on its crossing tower, and Fownhope's timber and shingle spire is assigned by the RCHM to the C14.

That Herefordshire is one of the timber-using counties *par excellence* need not be said. The layman thinking of the county thinks of black and white houses. He ought to think also of timber bell-turrets, and although most of them are Victorian, some, with the timber-framing exposed, i.e. black and white, are ancient (Holmer, Vowchurch probably of *c.*1522, and 37a Winforton). And church porches of timber are so many that some may not even have got into the gazetteer. Two particularly good ones of the C14 are Eye and Humber. Their roof timbers 37b deserve study, but they as well as the large roofs of naves, chancels, and aisles must be taken together with domestic roofs (p. 36). However, one kind of internal timber-framing must be noted in the present context: the stout posts and the cross-bracing to support bell-turrets (e.g. Orcop) or indeed the upper timber structure of such detached towers as those of Pembridge 35a and Yarpole. Pembridge with its twice truncated pyramid roof & b is the most impressive of all Herefordshire steeples, externally as well as internally.

The stonework is unbuttressed, and does not reach up high, and both these peculiarities are again typical of the county. So it is the broad, sturdy, squat tower one ought to think of, and, incidentally, not necessarily the W tower; for NW, SW, N, 16b and S towers occur surprisingly often. Crossing towers on the other hand are a great rarity. Apart from the cathedral there are only Mordiford of the late C13 (which anyway does not remain), Bromyard of the C14, and Much Marcle which is Perp.

But we cannot continue so smoothly into the Perp style. We must return to the C13 where we had left off.* On parish churches little needs adding: a fine chancel with lancet windows 16a at Kington, some beautiful work at Madley, including a nobly balanced w tower with variously grouped lancet windows and vaulting-shafts for the chancel and a clerestory of single lancet windows – a motif which recurs at All Saints in Hereford and at Bosbury and Eaton Bishop – and the remarkable addition of a second nave rather than an aisle at Leominster (where it was indeed a parochial nave alongside the monastic one) and at Stretford (where the final effect is made most singular by an early C16 roof covering both parts in one, with the ridge above the arcade wall). At Leominster the new nave is as wide as the old, and indeed the tendency towards spacious aisles which appears in the C13 was to become universal soon, so that in a large number of cases the aisle wall was rebuilt further out and the arcade is older than the fenestration. However, at Leominster of this E.E. work hardly anything remains visible now, except the fine, re-set doorway. No other doorways are here to be noted, though there are not a few. Of piers perhaps a little ought to be added. By far the most usual form is of course the circular pier. With four attached shafts it exists in the chancel chapel of Garway. The quatrefoil pier was used at Holme Lacy, the quatrefoil pier with four slender shafts in the diagonals at first early in the century in the restoration at Dore, then at Byford, where it is still of before 1250, and then between 1250 and 1300 at Lyonshall, Much Cowarne, and St Peter at Hereford, and as late as 1330 at Madley (Chilston Chapel). The only outstanding work of the C13 after the extensions of Hereford and Dore had been completed was again done at Hereford in the cathedral: first the remodelling of the upper parts of the chancel, in style and date following the Lady Chapel immediately, and then the 20 exquisite N transept undertaken by Bishop Aquablanca and so closely connected with his patron and protector's Westminster Abbey that it cannot have been begun before about 1250.

* Only one more general 'undated' note: church dedications. They are perfectly normal in all parts of the county, except one: Archenfield, the district between Hereford and Ross and the Welsh border which had remained settled by the Welsh. Here we find St Dubricius four times (out of six in England – one is Porlock in Somerset) and once each St Deinst, St Dinebo, St Tesilioc, and St Weonard. It is said that in the C17 as much Welsh as English was spoken in Hereford.

Aquablanca was buried in it in 1268, but on the other hand St Thomas Cantelupe's bones were only transferred into it from the Lady Chapel in 1287. So, in all probability, work proceeded beyond 1268. It is characterized by a delight in tensely stretched lines, whether of the superbly tall N and s windows or of the arches with nearly straight sides. It is also characterized by a combination of crispness and richness, and by the use of Purbeck marble shafts, new for Hereford; of the diapering of surfaces (as done at Westminster Abbey), of vaults still quadripartite (that is without ridge-ribs and tiercerons – which was then getting decidedly conservative), and of moulded as well as lush stiff-leaf capitals.* The bishop's monument is the apogee of this 21 character, beautifully erect and slender in its arches and gables, beautifully transparent in its bar tracery, and in its capitals just turning from stiff-leaf to naturalistic foliage. That foliage then dominates on the Cantelupe Shrine, to which we shall have to 19b revert, as it belongs to sculpture as much as to architecture, and also to the late rather than the mid C13.

The YEARS AROUND THIRTEEN HUNDRED are a period which is of special importance for Herefordshire. The parishes had built generously up to about 1200. The C13 was a time of little activity. Around 1300 an enormous amount of renewing, improving, and enlarging was done. In fact, one can say that the typical Herefordshire parish church is one with the windows cusped lancets or pointed-trefoiled lancets, or with Y-tracery, mostly cusped or with pointed trefoils or quatrefoils in the tracery, and in particular with a variant of the current motif of three stepped lancet lights under one super-arch in which the

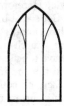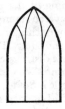

middle light is not strictly a lancet but simply the form which is produced if the mullions between the lights are run straight up until they touch the super-arch. At the cathedral for instance

* The upper floor of the E aisle of this transept is the famous chained library.

the E transepts were built in this style (still with exclusively quadripartite vaults), and the aisles were re-done – all with large, unexciting windows.* What is exciting of that period must be picked: the church at Kingsland, designed by a master of very personal tastes schooled in all probability at Bristol (straight-sided arches or three sides of an octagon instead of an arch), and at Hereford Cathedral the inner N portal with its mass of charming figure sculpture in the voussoirs and the crossing 28a tower. This is an outstanding piece, with its groups of three pinnacles at each corner and its decoration by a veritable studding with ballflower. Ballflower is regarded as the hallmark of the time of Edward II. It is the hallmark of the most ambitious work of his early years in Herefordshire – apart from the crossing tower the W tower at the cathedral (which does not survive), a 25b number of tomb recesses (including that of Bishop Swinefield who died in 1317 and where the back wall has a fine display of naturalistic foliage, and others which look if anything later), and the splendid S aisle at Leominster, closely similar to the Hereford 29 crossing tower,‡ and the equally splendid N chapel at Ledbury which may be a very few years later. Rarely has ballflower been used with so much gusto. The crossing tower at Hereford has in common with the work at Leominster the use of a particular way of cinquefoiling a circle. The same motif (without ballflower) occurs at Marden in the polygonal apse. A polygonal apse is a rare thing in England, though Lichfield Cathedral received one about 1320–30, and in Herefordshire itself Madley 28b a little earlier. The beautifully tall chancel and apse here were under construction in 1318. The E window has reticulated tracery, i.e. is DECORATED.

With the coming of the Dec style, Herefordshire fell back, and it never recovered its impetus. Let social historians explain why there was so much money available about 1300 and so little in the mid C14 and after. The great church building boom of the wool and cloth districts cannot have touched Herefordshire; that much is certain. What can we in the end introduce here to represent the style? Some minor facts of course referring to individual motifs, but they do not add up to much. Piers e.g. are now almost always octagonal. An exception is that at

---

* The documents at Hereford do not allow exact dating, but it should be noted that the chancel at Dilwyn is called newly built in 1305 and has windows with trefoil-pointed lights and large pointed trefoils above.

‡ The sedilia here have ballflower too. So have those of Madley. They are, curiously enough, the only ones of merit in the whole county.

Ledbury the eight sides are concave. Another is the quatrefoil
pier with the lobes made canted or polygonal (with ballflower
at Richards Castle, with added shafts in the diagonals at Kingsland). More significant is of course the ogee arch, but Herefordshire never made much of it. It is emphatically not a county of
flowing tracery. However, nodding ogee arches with their fine
sweep occur in the stalls and the bishop's throne in the cathedral
and in the canopy over the tomb of Johanna de Bohun who died
in 1327. The Chilston Chapel at Madley, begun in 1330, was
provided consistently with reticulated tracery, the porch at
Pembridge with a tierceron-vault, and, again at the cathedral,
there is the entrance to the chapter house, which may be as late 30b
as c.1360, and yet is entirely pre-Perp.*

The coming of the PERPENDICULAR can be fixed relatively
precisely. The monument in the cathedral to Peter de Grandison, 25a
who died in 1352, has a decided emphasis on horizontals instead
of pinnacles and finials, and such an emphasis on the horizontal
is perversely characteristic of the Perpendicular style. At the
same time or a few years earlier or later the chapter house must
have been designed – the contract for its completion within
seven years dates from 1364 – and this had panelled walls
entirely Perp and a fan-vault, another Perp feature. In fact this
may have been the earliest of all major fan-vaults; for of the
Gloucester cloisters which are usually given that honour we
only know that they were started between 1351 and 1377.

There are no Perp buildings of the first order in Herefordshire. In the cathedral the s wall of the s transept was remodelled
about 1400 and given a vast Perp window. Other such large
Perp windows are at All Saints (with two little doorways below,
probably to a former E vestry), in the W front of Leominster
(with two pretty buttresses instead of the principal mullions),
and in the W front of the cathedral (where it was destroyed in
1786). The cloisters at the cathedral were begun, it seems, about
1403–10. They are very even in design and have one of the first
tierceron-vaults of Hereford. The design with a concave-sided
star in the middle repeats in the porch at Ballingham. The
tierceron-vault of the s transept is of c.1430, and several parish

* For no more than chronological reasons the Blackfriars at Hereford
must here be inserted. They began building in 1322, but the one range which
survives is stylistically without interest, and the Preaching Cross, very 40b
interesting as such, must be somewhat later. The FRIARS have not been
included in the survey of monastic foundations and remains in the county:
so it may be said here that the Greyfriars came to Hereford before 1228 and
the Blackfriars before 1248.

churches took up the idea (*see* the tower hall at Linton-by-Ross, the S porch at King's Caple, the chancel chapel in the same church and at Sellack). The extremely ornate and extremely
41b pretty Stanbury Chantry Chapel in the cathedral of about 1480 has a fan-vault instead, and so has the Morton Chapel at Bosbury and the porch to the premises of the Vicars Choral. They exist complete at Hereford with a cloister and a corridor towards the cathedral. They moved to their present site in 1473. The porch however is probably some twenty or twenty-five years later. The two-storeyed Audley Chantry Chapel of before 1502 has an elaborate, cusped star of tiercerons and liernes instead. And liernes, to complete this survey, are also used in
40a the vault of the stately outer N porch built by Bishop Booth and dated 1519.

But any record of work of the C14 and C15 in Herefordshire is incomplete if it does not take in TIMBER. There are no fully timber-framed churches or timber arcades. Timber bell-turrets have been mentioned; so have timber porches. It is the roofs in
36 which we must take an interest now, roofs never as spectacular as those of East Anglia, but roofs of much character and unity of features. They are in fact the same in churches and in houses, and so we must use this opportunity to move on to HOUSES. What characterizes the Herefordshire roof is this: tie-beams may
34b or may not be used, arched braces lead up to collar-beams, and above them there are kingposts or raking struts foiled or later more finely cusped and forming with equally foiled or cusped principals bold trefoils or quatrefoils. The same motif is even
33 more conspicuous in the wind-braces, of which there may be more than one tier. That is the Herefordshire roof, though there are also plenty of simple, single-framed (or trussed-rafter) roofs with or without scissor-bracing, and they are usually considered early. It is doubtful whether this is a dating criterion; for there is e.g. a roof of this kind at Longtown which is dated 1640. Hammerbeam roofs are decidedly rare. The best of them is in the N aisle of All Saints at Hereford. The former Forbury Chapel at Leominster has one, assigned by the RCHM to the C15. The chancel at Holmer has another, and after the Reformation they went on at Rotherwas and Brampton Bryan (1656). In addition the castle hall of Treago Castle, St Weonards, may have had a hammerbeam roof, Little Cobhall, Allensmore, had one (according to the RCHM), and in Booth Hall, Hereford, there is a remarkably big one, where, however, the hammer-beams alternate with tie-beams.

So these are the roofs of houses, undistinguishable from the roofs of churches. In houses also the type with the foiled or cusped wind-braces and the foiling or cusping above tie-beam or collar-beam is the signature tune of the county. Herefordshire has infinitely more timber-framed or, to use the more telling term, black and white houses than can here be recorded. Mr Clifton-Taylor calls the area from Weobley w to Eardisley and N to Dilwyn, Pembridge, and Eardisland in this respect 'un-rivalled in England'. But hardly any of them are dated; few of them are dateable. The RCHM did its best thirty years ago to establish criteria; Sir Cyril Fox and Lord Raglan's work on Monmouthshire houses has added new evidence; Mr J. T. Smith is working on them at present. Yet little has been established. The cruck-truss is still considered the earliest of the trusses. It is a truss consisting simply of two curved, blade-like timbers joined together at the top. In 1949 the Woolhope Club counted 143 buildings with crucks in the county. The RCHM dated many to the C14; Mr Smith is inclined to go later with most of them, which means that we simply do not know what timber roofs of houses were like before. A trussing speciality, more of Cheshire than of Herefordshire, but occurring in Herefordshire too, is the spere-truss, i.e. a truss used where the screen was going to be placed between hall and screens passage. The truss stood on two posts kept sufficiently far away from the walls to have the two doorways into the hall in those spaces and a movable or fixed screen in the middle. Lower Brockhampton House, Wellbrook Manor Peterchurch, and Peg's Farm Wellington Heath are three houses in which the spere-truss and the roof altogether can be well studied.* There are many roofs which show the great visual advantage of foiling and cusping, or would do so if they could be reached at all or without too much discomfort. Halls still open to the roof, as they all were before horizontal dividing began,‡ are at Brinsop Court, at Lower Brockhampton House, at Burton Court Eardisland (and, as we have seen, with hammerbeams, at Booth Hall Hereford). So fond were people of the effect of foiling that Swanstone Court Dilwyn and Wellbrook Manor Peterchurch use a few quatrefoils as wall decoration. They must have been exposed, which is thought-provoking.

* Others are, more or less exposed, Amberley Court, Old Court Bred- 34a wardine, Court Farm Preston Wynne, and Thing Hill Grange Withington.

‡ It began early; for the moulded beams of the ground-floor ceiling at Peg's Farm are clearly of the early C16.

Was timber-framing originally exposed externally? There probably was no rule. Paintings and illuminated manuscripts of the C15 certainly show the black and white effect. Can the framework be dated on internal grounds? There again little progress has been made. It appears now that square framing with heavy timbers comes first, the visually more attractive closely-set uprights later, say some time later in the C15 (e.g. in the gatehouse of Lower Brockhampton House of the late C15 and Rudhall House Brampton Abbotts of the early C16), but square framing later still, in the late C16 and C17.* Lively decorative motifs achieved by means of the braces and struts themselves are definitely later, as we shall see. Before the Reformation there were just the traceried bargeboards or the bargeboards with a vine trail. Other motifs which one can see in East Anglia are absent in Herefordshire.

So users of this volume will find that many timber-framed buildings are listed simply because they look pretty. The difference is this – to illustrate it with two houses of c.1600: The Ley Weobley is black and white but also remarkable because of its symmetrical composition; Upton Court Little Hereford is just exceedingly picturesque. The prettiest places among little towns are Weobley and Pembridge, among villages perhaps Eardisland.

As far as planning is concerned, the C14 and C15 type of the house of some size was a hall in the middle and cross-gabled two-storeyed projecting wings, one for the parlour and solar, the other for kitchen, buttery, etc. Such a plan has been preserved intact at Thing Hill Grange Withington, Amberley Court, and Wellbrook Manor Peterchurch (where incidentally a stone chimneyshaft happens to remain).

But the houses whose appearance and whose roofs and halls we admire are not necessarily timber-framed houses. The larger and more ambitious ones were built of stone. This is true of e.g. Brinsop Court and Burton Court Eardisland. Brinsop Court is the best stone mansion of the C14. It was built round four sides of an oblong courtyard and its hall, apart from the mighty roof, has Dec windows. It lies on the upper floor. The same plan, with four ranges round a courtyard, was adopted at Treago Castle St Weonards in the early C15 or rather earlier, but there the regularity of the square and the circular angle tower form a

_____

* Mr J. T. Smith privately pointed out to me that the fashion for breaking the evenness of the horizontals in square framing by lowered window sills is a sign of a post-medieval date.

connexion back with the Edwardian and the C14 castles rather than with the quadrangular manor house. Croft Castle, also of the C15 or earlier, though not a perfect square, is of the same type and definitely a castle, or at least a fortified mansion. The same is true of the yet less regular Hampton Court, where licence to crenellate was granted in 1434. Hampton Court also has a mighty gatehouse, and of the former hall at least the porch. An impressive deep porch also at Treago and gatehouses at Gillow Manor Hentland, and, much more minor, the Bishop's House at Bosbury. Kentchurch Court and Kinnersley Castle also count as fortified mansions, but their plans are incompletely preserved or known, and there is no more evidence now than a mighty tower and some walls. Both houses were thoroughly remodelled later.

Two appendices to complete secular building of the later Middle Ages. A speciality in the county is the DOVECOTES. Eleven are at present attributed to dates before the Reformation and one of them – an improbable survival – is dated. It is at Garway, and the date is 1326.

In the towns nearly all houses were timber-framed, but Hereford has a number of vaulted stone cellars with four-centred tunnel-vaults or occasionally (2 Eign Street) a rib-vault. Of stone also, though chiefly interesting again for its timber roof, the original hall of the Vicars Choral in Castle Street, of c.1400.

For certain aspects of secular medieval architecture Hereford-shire is, as we have seen, a county of intense interest. For CHURCH FURNISHINGS, to which we must devote a few paragraphs, this can hardly be said, at least if we exclude the work of the Norman school, which has already been dealt with. What else qualifies for this survey? Of FONTS other than those of Castle Frome and Eardisley by far the most exciting is imported – an Italian stoup converted into a font, Cosmati work of the late C12 or early C13. It is at Lea. Otherwise, plenty of Norman fonts remain, as in all counties, but they are mostly plain or have quite inferior decoration.* We may except from this statement the three with figures in arcading at Hereford Cathedral, Orleton, and Burghill. At Burghill the bowl is now the stem, and a C13 bowl sits on top, which is lead and has handsome foliage. The font at Hope-under-Dinmore, also C13,

___
* One font, at Harewood, is of the familiar Purbeck-marble, 'table' type with flat blank arches, but this came to Herefordshire from a church in Dorset.

continues the type with figures in arcading, but they are seated
here. Of the C14 only the font at Weobley needs noting. It belongs
to a type which is quite frequent. It has panels of blank traceried
windows of various early C14 patterns, as if taken from a pattern
book. Perp fonts are frequent but not of interest.

Other items of church furnishing are so discrepant that it
might be worth the attempt at reporting them chronologically.
So the beginning must be the charming NORMAN doorknocker
at Dormington. Norman perhaps also, though a much older age
is claimed, is the so-called St Augustine's Chair at Stanford
Bishop, and a little post-Norman, say early THIRTEENTH
13a CENTURY, the excellent chair, turned throughout, in the
chancel of Hereford Cathedral. Of the same date, also in the
22b cathedral, the wonderful little shrine of St Thomas of Canterbury, not English, but Limoges work. Later C13 (we only know
22a that they are of before 1299) a chalice and paten in the cathedral
treasure. Then, also C13, and again wonderful to look at, the
medallions of stained glass at Madley and in the Lady Chapel
of Hereford Cathedral. That is the C13 at its most refined. At
its most robust it appears in the various 'dug-out' chests which
have been preserved and look venerable enough. The earliest is
probably that at Garway. Others are at Kingstone and Orleton.
They are not the only ones. So to the EARLY FOURTEENTH
CENTURY; for the two finest chests in the county belong to that
date, both with blank tracery on the front surrounded by
rosettes. Both are at Hereford, the more splendid, as it ought
to be, in the cathedral (Lower Library), the other at All Saints.
For early C14 woodwork the *magnum opus* is of course the stalls
with their canopies of nodding ogee arches and the Bishop's
41a Throne in the cathedral. Those at All Saints, excellent too, are
a descendant. No screens of so early a date survive, or at least
none of wood; for Welsh Newton has a stone screen with ballflower decoration. For early C14 stained glass Herefordshire is
24 a most rewarding county. The E window of Eaton Bishop (of
after 1328) is as good as any in England, Dilwyn has two censing
angels which are exquisitely composed, Credenhill two bishops,
Madley part of a Jesse tree, and the cathedral a number of
figures under canopies in two windows (one disastrously
restored).

For the LATE MIDDLE AGES there is of course more, but
enumeration is on the whole enough. Two stone reredoses,
preserved or partly preserved at Hampton Bishop and Leintwardine, also at Leintwardine stalls with misericords, and at

St Peter Hereford (from the Priory of St Guthlac) too, and some misericords at Holme Lacy and Canon Pyon, pulpits at Wigmore (with linenfold panels) and Stretton Grandison, screens at Bosbury, Burghill, and, of superb quality, at Aymestrey and St Margaret's, four good angels in stained glass at Goodrich, 42 and the very large painting of Christ of the Trades at Michaelchurch Escley. In addition, one remark must be added on metalwork. There are three pre-Reformation patens in the county, at Norton Canon (silver-gilt) and at Bacton and Leominster, the latter two preserved with the chalice which they 43a went with. The Leominster chalice is one of the best of the late C15 in the country. Finally a curiosum of metalwork: the two long iron candle-brackets at Rowlstone, sticking out from the side walls of the chancel, each for five candles.

To conclude this synopsis of medieval art in the county, CHURCH MONUMENTS must be recorded. The earliest are coffin-lids, and these are included in the gazetteer only where they are of special artistic merit. That applies to about a dozen decorated in the C13 with foliated crosses.* The earliest effigy may be that of a lady in profile at Woolhope. With the two 23b effigies at Abbey Dore, in the later C13, the series of Knights begins, and with the effigy at Welsh Bicknor the series of Ladies. There are many of both about 1300 and later. No good purpose would be served in enumerating them here. Many are defaced, and few have special points. For sculptural quality the late C13 Lady at Wolferlow, the late C13 and early C14 couple at Edvin 23a Ralph, and the late C13 Priest at Ledbury deserve recording, 27a for architectural quality of the surround several of the monuments in Hereford Cathedral and the tomb recess at Weston Beggard, apart of course from the Aquablanca Monument and the Cantelupe Shrine. Sculpturally the finest work of the late C13 is the *pleureurs* or mourners of the Cantelupe Shrine. They 19b are of *c.*1285–6. They are Templars in varied, lively, well-observed postures. Of the shrine type, i.e. short, with arcading and without effigy or other figures, the two C13 monuments at Bridstow and Goodrich. The priest of *c.*1300 at Clifford must be added because he is of wood, as is the Civilian of about 1360 or 1370 at Much Marcle. To continue for a moment with materials other than stone and techniques other than carving, brasses are very infrequent in Herefordshire. It is true that

* At Brinsop the shaft undulates like a vine. At Aconbury the foliage has turned from stiff-leaf to a naturalistic rendering, at Woolhope from a naturalistic to the nobbly rendering of the C14.

Hereford Cathedral still has many and that in 1717 of indents
of lost brasses alone there were 170. As it is, the Rev. A. J.
Winnington-Ingram counts fourteen only, with effigy, of before
the c16. The earliest is the Bishop Trillack † 1360, a 5 ft figure.
He is one of the best too. Very good also the de la Barr † 1386,
a priest in an ogee cross, the Delamares (he died in 1435), and
the de la Beres (he died in 1514). Outside Hereford there are
the swagger Barres of *c.*1485 at Clehonger, and that is about all.*
Very occasionally one finds indents which seem to have lost
their brasses but have in fact lost a composition of small stones,
a kind of cement, instead. There are two of these in Hereford
Cathedral, of the late c14 and early c15, one of the late c14 at
Allensmore, one of *c.*1400 at Canon Pyon, and one of the early
c15 at Dilwyn. Another substitute for brasses was incised slabs.
They were in use in Herefordshire from the c13 onwards (Sollers
Hope *c.*1225, Avenbury late c13, then Little Hereford and
Edvin Ralph early c14), but seem to have become a fashion
only in the late c15 and early c16 (Stretton Sugwas † 1473,
Hereford Cathedral † 1497, Aymestrey † 1506, Turnastone
† 1522, Westhide † 1524, Hope-under-Dinmore † 1559,
Ledbury † 1596).

But we have not looked at major monuments yet later than
the beginning of the c14. It is easy to pick out half a dozen really
27b outstanding ones of the rest of the c14: the clerical member of
the Swinefield family in Hereford Cathedral, the Sir Richard
Pembrugge of *c.*1340 at Clehonger, full of life, lying slightly on
26 his side, the exquisite Blanche Mortimer at Much Marcle who
died in 1347, with her mantle hanging down over the front of
the tomb-chest, a remarkable trait of illusionism, the Pauncefoot
lady of about 1360 at Ledbury with the same motif repeated,
the mid- and the late-c14 couples at Pembridge (the latter the
earliest alabaster monument in the county), the couple of the
late c14 at Much Marcle, where a puppy pulls at the skirt of the
lady. The series of bishops posthumously recorded at Hereford
Cathedral on the other hand is disappointingly dull.

Of the effigies of the c15 and early c16 many are of alabaster.
Among them there are the excellent Vaughans († 1469) at
Kington and Bishop Stanbury († 1473) at Hereford Cathedral.
The c16 list includes Sir Richard Croft at Croft † 1509, of stone
and perhaps by a member of the workshop providing the
statuary for Henry VII's Chapel at Westminster Abbey, Bishop
Meyew † 1516 in the cathedral, a member of the Cornewall

* Two at Ledbury in addition, and one at Brampton Abbotts.

family of about 1520 at Eye, another of about 1540, and the very good alabaster tomb of William Rudhall and his wife at Ross. He died in 1530.

By 1530 the RENAISSANCE had begun to establish itself in England. But Herefordshire was out of the way, and did not at once take to the fashion. Bishop Parfew's monument in Hereford Cathedral, though he died in 1557, has no Renaissance motifs. The earliest occurrence is on the roof screen at Llandinabo, and this is undated. However, a date after 1530 is unlikely. Then follows the Cornewall monument of c.1540 at Eye, where the Renaissance detail is not at all prominent.* CHURCH PLATE, which was usually early with the Renaissance, does not exist with date records before 1569. Then, incidentally, the same thing happened as in other counties. The Elizabethan Settlement insisted on Holy Communion to the laity 'in both kinds' (Article 30 of the Articles agreed in 1562), and thus there was a new need for a cup and cover in every parish church.‡ Suddenly, therefore, though after a delay of some years, for a few years silversmiths were kept frantically busy. It is in fact a mystery how they could cope with the orders. In Herefordshire there is one dated piece§ of 1569, three of 1570, nineteen of 1571, two of 1572, one of 1573, ten (including five not dated but inscribed) of 1576, and one (inscribed) of 1577. Then the rush was over. For other church furnishings the Elizabethan era was a lean time. There is not a single dated piece to record, though some of the many undated pulpits may well go back to before 1600.

It is different with MONUMENTS, for the pretty obvious reason that monuments, though placed – indeed displayed – in churches, are secular and not religious art. The monuments and the houses tell us of the Elizabethan spirit, and in Herefordshire the monuments more than the churches. Not that there are many of them, and in Hereford Cathedral they (and those of the C17) have moreover been ruthlessly deprived of their architectural settings, but what there is, is of interest, especially two, one at Bosbury and the other at Madley, because they are signed works of a Hereford stone carver, *John Gildon* or *Guldo*. The one at Bosbury is dated 1573, the one at Madley commemorates 44a Richard Willison who died in 1575, and there is a second at

* The Renaissance, or rather Mannerist, panels of the pulpit at Kinnersley 43b (cf. the panels at Ewyas Harold) are Flemish, not English.

‡ I received a welcome letter on this matter from Mr Adams Clarke.

§ For the following table I take a chalice with its paten as one piece, but also count an individual chalice and an individual paten separately.

44b Bosbury dated 1578 and which may or may not be by Guldo. He appears in Hereford documents in 1577-8 and is called variously a freemason, joiner, and carver. Outside the county he signed one of two monuments at Astley in Worcestershire and this is of 1577, and one at Abergavenny with a date of death 1584. There is an outlandish ring in the name Gildon or Guldo, and the Elizabethan style of monumental sculpture was of course closely dependent on the Netherlands. What is curious about these monuments in Herefordshire is that the first of the two at Bosbury is architecturally and sculpturally courtly, relatively speaking, whereas the other is enjoyably but comically rustic, with its two caryatids and its spreading branches everywhere. The Madley piece seems to mediate between the two, but even so, it seems improbable that the two Bosbury monuments can be by the same hand. Apart from this group, only two alabaster monuments need attention: the Scudamores († 1571) at Holme Lacy and the Dentons († 1576) at Hereford Cathedral, and in
45 addition one odd and artless stone monument at Bacton, because in it appears Queen Elizabeth, worshipped, as it were, by Blanche Parry, who had been one of the queen's maids of honour. Here again the sculptural quality is considerably lower than the ornamental.

That applies to DOMESTIC DECORATION as well. Inside the houses there are many chimneypieces and many plaster ceilings. Their style carries on without change beyond the accession of James I and even of Charles I. The chimneypieces usually have flanking pilasters or columns below and, above, either this motif repeated and some large central motif between, or, much more often, caryatids and one tier of short, stumpy blank arches, or two tiers. The inability to carve the caryatids attractively is staggering. In the plaster ceilings there are pretty patterns of ribs, first thin, then broad and flat, with pendants at the principal points and with foliage or individual motifs of fleur-de-lis, pomegranate, rose, a bird, a cherub's head in the panels. Of chimneypieces the one in the Crown Inn at Bosbury is dated 1571 and has the blank arches referred to. Another dated example is in the Talbot Hotel at Ledbury: 1596. The most
49 exuberant is at Canon Frome Court. Of the more restrained type without blank arches and without caryatids one at Stretton Court Stretton Sugwas has a date 1598. For stucco an interestingly early date is for a ceiling at Hellens, Much Marcle, in the same room with a chimneypiece whose decoration with the initials MR indicates a date during Mary Tudor's reign. If the

thin-ribbed ceiling is of the 1550s as well, that would be an exceptionally (but not impossibly) early date. Particularly good is the thin-ribbed ceiling of the 1590s at Kinnersley Castle, [48a] where on the overmantel oak branches spread most splendidly. The motif can be compared with the spreading stucco branches in the porch of Michaelchurch Court Michaelchurch Escley, which is dated 1602.

Michaelchurch Court is a house of moderate size. There is in fact no large Elizabethan or Jacobean mansion in the county. The majority are unassuming, and even symmetrical or nearly symmetrical compositions such as Kingstone Grange, Pontrilas Court, and Fawley Court are rare. Fawley Court, by the way, though as late as c.1630, has arched lights to its mullioned windows, a decidedly conservative motif. The Ley near Weobley, of 1589, is the only symmetrical composition among black and white houses. There is nothing like Pitchford in Shropshire, just as there is nothing in the towns to compare with the rich merchants' houses of Shrewsbury. Ledbury Park at Ledbury comes nearest to them, and Tower Hill House Bromyard of 1630 might also find a place here. It is one of the most ornate timber-framed private houses in the county. Another is the delightful gatehouse of Butthouse King's Pyon, which is dated 1632. The style goes on unchanged for a remarkably long time. Bible House Bromyard with a date 1685 is still Jacobean, as are, in stone, Jackson's Almshouses also at Bromyard which were founded in 1656.

Of stone houses only a few more have to be placed on record: Newhouse Farm outside Goodrich of 1636 because of its plan with the remarkable conceit of three ranges radiating from a centre, Wilton Castle Bridstow and Urishay Castle Peterchurch because they are houses inside medieval castle ruins, and Kinnersley Castle, Rodd Court, Gatley Park Leinthall Earls, and Nun Upton Little Hereford because of the use made of BRICK. There is no question that brick now became fashionable in the county – a hundred years after the brick fashion had started at the court of Henry VIII. At Kinnersley Castle in the 1590s brick gables were placed in front of stone gables, at Rodd Court about 1625 the façade of a stone house was faced with brick, at Nun Upton a Jacobean brick range with big shaped gables was provided to enlarge a timber-framed house, whereas Hellens at Much Marcle (of c.1600) and Gatley Park (of the 1630s) are brick buildings throughout.

By 1630 the situation in the fields of CHURCH BUILDING and

church furnishing had also changed. Between 1630 and the end of the C17 work in connexion with at least five churches can be reported, though no work of any magnitude. Lord Scudamore restored what was left of Abbey Dore, built a wall to cut off the ruinous nave, got *John Abel* – to whom we shall return later – to make a new ceiling, and provided certain furnishings – to which we shall return presently. Of 1656 is the double hammerbeam roof in the church at Brampton Bryan, though the RCHM is probably right in thinking that its more ornate parts were re-used from a roof in Brampton Bryan Castle, which was taken and largely destroyed in 1643.* In 1673 the little church at Foy was given a Perp E window, copied actually from the still existing original Perp E window at Sellack. Monnington-on-Wye, rebuilt in 1679, has, similarly conservatively, all its windows still with arched lights.‡ It gives, with its FURNISHINGS, a very complete picture of a backward-looking village church of the later C17. Lord Scudamore's Abbey Dore, as refurnished in 1633–4, is as complete as Monnington, and of course on a larger scale. The screen in fact is the most ambitious piece of church furnishing of the Laudian years in Herefordshire. But there is also a west gallery (and one on tapering pillars at Sellack) and a pulpit with tester and stained glass. Now for new PULPITS there suddenly came a veritable craze. Of those in the Jacobean style, but often without any doubt post-Jacobean in date, there are about three dozen in the county, not counting those apparently made up later of panels in that style.§ Dates are 1621 (All Saints Hereford), 1632, and 1633. As for the motifs of decoration, twenty-five have the short, heavy blank arches which we have already found as the favoured motif in overmantels. Bedheads of course went in for it too. The dating of beds, chimneypieces, and pieces of church furnishing is in fact not easy. The style went on for a very long time. An example is the breadshelf at All Saints Hereford which is dated 1683 and which one could, without hesitation, call Jacobean on the strength of its style.

It has just been said that Lord Scudamore also presented STAINED GLASS to Abbey Dore church. The E window is a complete and hence interesting piece of 1634. The E window of Sellack, dated 1630, though mixed with medieval fragments, is as

* The roof with tie-beams and queenposts at Vowchurch is dated 1613.
‡ A curious tracery device in a window at Richards Castle can also most probably be explained as dating from the C17.
§ They will often be found in the gazetteer under the term Jacobean even if they are in fact later.

interesting, and the E window of Foy, put in in 1673, is doubly interesting because it is, by the terms of the contract, a copy of the window at Sellack. Of other pieces of furnishing FONTS are the only ones which have a character entirely of their own. Admittedly they continue the octagonal shapes of the Perp time, but bowls are smaller, and the elements of decoration more basic and more isolated. That applies already to Byford of 1638 and Bolstone which the RCHM even calls Jacobean, and even more to Credenhill of 1667, Thruxton of 1677, and the undated Fownhope font. The font at Sutton is quite unconnected with any of the others. The tiny bowl held by an angel is attributed by the RCHM to the years of the Commonwealth.* To return to woodwork, in seating there is a short time about 1665–85 when BENCHES were put in which are just normal domestic forms, with arms, not at all churchy. They have survived at Holme Lacy, where they are probably of before 1671, at Letton, in the chapel of St Giles' Hospital Hereford which was rebuilt in 1682, and at Monnington which was rebuilt in 1679.

It will have been noticed that among dated pieces of church furnishing the years between 1600 and 1620 are blank. The same is true, as it happens, in the case of CHURCH MONUMENTS. Fourteen have here to be recorded for years to 1660, and not one of them is of before 1620. The fourteen can conveniently be divided into typological groups, and some glimpses beyond 1660 will be necessary. Tomb-chests with recumbent effigies do not yet go out of use, but they tend to be of black and white marble now, and the portraits are more accurate, especially in regard to clothes. A Rudhall monument at Ross († 1636) belongs to this group, and the Kyrle monument at Much Marcle († 1650). Then there are the kneeling figures facing one another. They are popular all over England, and in Herefordshire represented by one at Much Dewchurch († 1625), one at Ledbury († 1631), and the sculpturally best of any group, the Smalman monument of 1635 at Kinnersley. Frontal demi-figures usually with a book were a type fashionable for dons and divines. Examples in Herefordshire are at Ledbury († 1629 and † 1631), in Hereford Cathedral (Bishop Field † 1636), at Lugwardine († 1637), once more in Hereford Cathedral (a couple; dated 1659), and at Foy, where the date of death is as

51a

---

* Three later C17 fonts of identical design, with swags on the stem and acanthus on the bowl, are at Holme Lacy, Llanwarne (Christ Church), and How Caple. There is an accomplished little lead bowl of 1689 at Aston Ingham. 53a

late as 1675. Meanwhile, however, the bust had begun to replace
the demi-figure, a more classical, more metropolitan motif. We
find it at Monnington with a date of death 1667 and in a surround
which is definitely post-Jacobean in style. The earliest examples
of the classical setting are in fact a good deal earlier, even in
Herefordshire: a monument with a kneeling effigy at Mordiford
(† 1635) and the Scudamore tablet at Ballingham († 1649).
52 Colonel Rudhall died in 1651, and his monument at Ross is a
statue. That was still something extremely rare in England – the
earliest is the Sir George Holles in Westminster Abbey of 1626
(by Stone), and it was followed in Herefordshire only once
before 1700, in the statue to Colonel Birch at Weobley who died
in 1691.

Concerning smaller, less ambitious, and less costly memorials,
three types are of interest. As in Shropshire, the cast-iron
ledger stone with lettering as its only decoration occurs in
53b Herefordshire in the C17. Examples of 1619 to 1678 are at
Burrington, of 1669 and 1670 at Brilley. Stone or alabaster
tablets on the walls of churches are innumerable. The years from
the fifties to the eighties are recognizable by coarse, exuberant
foliage, putto heads or putti decidedly ugly, sometimes standing
allegorical figures to the l. and r. of the inscription, also coarse
and also ugly, and quite often twisted columns. Twisted columns
were of course a Baroque fashion. Nicholas Stone had made them
large at St Mary Oxford, Bernini larger for the baldacchino in
St Peter's. Thirty or forty years later Herefordshire noticed
them, and so there are more than a dozen tablets using them.
The earliest are at Sutton dated 1654 and at Castle Frome
† 1656. The other dates are Tyberton and Stretton Grandison
† 1668, Hatfield and Dormington † 1669, Pembridge † 1671,
Hatfield † 1673, Sellack † 1678, Wellington † 1683, Turnastone
and Pembridge † 1685, and finally a straggler: Eaton Bishop
† 1714. The twisted columns are also a perennial motif in the
furnishings of Monnington, which was rebuilt in 1679, and at
How Caple the screen of c.1695 has not only twisted columns,
but also *ingénu* twisted arches.

The tablets with allegorical figures run parallel. Among eight
or ten which deserve a record, dates of death are between 1660
51b (Pembridge) and 1673 (Foy) with two stragglers of 1707
(Walford-on-Wye) and 1711 (Fownhope).

These tablets form a direct link between the provincial
Jacobean, a provincial Baroque, and the equally provincial art
of the C18 tombstone in the churchyard. The line of develop-

ment which mattered was that which we have recognized in the
architectural surrounds of more ambitious monuments: from
the strapwork and the details of the Jacobean style to the classical
forms of Inigo Jones and his followers. In Herefordshire
DOMESTIC ARCHITECTURE the turn to the classical style is
less one to Palladian motifs than to placidity. No more gables,
no more bay windows, no more strapwork decoration round
doorways and porches (such as at Rudhall House and Gatley
Park). Instead the 'brick box', i.e. the comfortably proportioned
house of five bays by four or a similar relation, and with a hipped
roof. The type was created well before 1650 (Chevening) and
taken up by some of the leading architects of the generation after
Inigo's, men such as Sir Roger Pratt and *Hugh May*. To May
indeed Mr Colvin has attributed for good reasons Holme Lacy, 54
the only post-Reformation house with which Herefordshire
once again comes forward into the national forefront. The contract for the building dates from 1674. It is large, of brick, with
three perfectly even and symmetrical façades, each with somewhat projecting wings and (up to 1828) hipped roofs. Two of
the three façades have a central pediment. Here is deliberate
understatement: reticence and a sense of never showing off to
the outsider. For inside Holme Lacy has (or had) decoration as
gorgeous as any of those years in any country house or palace
in England and Scotland, overmantels of fruit, flowers, leaves,
birds, carved with the utmost artistry, probably by the great
Grinling Gibbons himself (and now at Kentchurch Court and in 56a
America) and plaster ceilings with naturalistic foliage daringly 56b
detached, wreaths and garlands and swags, and flowers in vases.

Eye Manor of 1680 does exactly the same. The exterior of
five bays with a hipped roof is as noncommittal as a black
double-breasted overcoat. The interior has splendid plaster 57a
ceiling after splendid plaster ceiling. Again the same applies,
though more modestly, to Langstone Court, Llangarron, again
five bays and a hipped roof, and Dingwood Park outside
Ledbury. Such houses now as a rule have sash windows, but
originally their windows were of the mullion-and-transom-cross
type, here and there still preserved entirely or partly. Other
examples of this kind of house are Bernithan Court, Llangarron,
of 1695 and the two office ranges of Treribble, Llangarron.

Hill Court, Walford-on-Wye, of 1698–1700 follows on, but can
just as well serve to start the EIGHTEENTH CENTURY. It is a
little larger, even without considering the enlargement of 1732,
and was of exactly the type of the previously described houses,

even with a hipped roof, except for the pretty doorways with pediments of the open scrolly type. The motif was liked at once, and The Brainge, Putley, used it in 1703 and the Vicarage at Much Marcle in a simplified form in the same year. Both are brick houses of five bays with a hipped roof. So is Putley Court, Putley, of 1712. Another building of the same time and the
55 same type is the school at Lucton founded in 1708 – except that it has seven bays and an arched niche with the statue of the founder in the middle (like the Geffrye Almshouses of 1715 in London, e.g.).

This being a PUBLIC BUILDING so to say, a few remarks on secular architecture other than domestic may follow. One has to go back pretty far of course, to St Katherine's Hospital of c.1330–40 at Ledbury, a dormitory and chapel in one, as it had been the custom of the monastic infirmaries and remained the custom to Chancellor Rollin's hospital at Beaune and after. Next come a number of almshouses at Hereford, but only the Coningsby Hospital founded c.1614 is of any size. It was developed out of the premises of the Hospitallers. Aubrey's Almshouses of 1630 are black and white, with three gables. The most exuberant black and white buildings of the whole county were in fact public buildings, none in the whole of England
47 more fantastical than the Town Hall of Hereford, deprived of its top storey in 1792, and pulled down in 1862. In its absence the Old House, former Butchers' Guildhall, of 1621 must serve,
48b the Market House at Ledbury, and the Market Hall of Leominster, shifted from its original site, but intact. This was built in 1633 and is by *John Abel*, a mysterious character to whom much too much has been attributed. The cold facts are that, according to our oldest source, Blount's collections for a history of Herefordshire, Abel died in 1674, aged 97 (Blount himself died in 1679), that he built the market houses of Brecon (not preserved), Kington (not preserved), and Leominster, constructed a powder mill during the siege of Hereford in 1645, and was given the title of King's Carpenter for this. His tombstone in fact can be seen at Sarnesfield with an inscription starting: 'This craggy stone a covering is for an architect's bed.' The contract for the ceiling of Abbey Dore also exists. Gough in his edition of Camden's *Britannia* of 1806 adds to the list of works the screen at Dore, the roof at Vowchurch, and the Grammar School at Kington. All three works remain; the roof is of 1613, the grammar school of 1625, a stone building architecturally not interesting. But the screen is a splendid piece already referred

to which has the same inscription as the Leominster Market House. The Brecon Town Hall was of 1624 and black and white without anything like the decoration of the Leominster Market House. The attribution of the Hereford Town Hall does not seem to go back further than to Price's *History of Leominster* of 1795.*

This *excursus* has thrown us back into the earlier C17, whereas we had just reached the haven of sedate Queen Anne houses, moderate in size and moderate in decoration. And a moderate century the eighteenth was going to be for Herefordshire. The county was settling down into a retired existence. No vast mansions, no gorgeous interiors. *Robert Adam*'s Moccas Court is small (and was carried out by *Keck*, a local man), *Chambers* built no more than the, admittedly very charming, shooting box called Poston Lodge Vowchurch of c.1780. Canon Frome of 1786, Longworth Lugwardine of c.1788 (by *Keck*), and Sufton Mordiford of before 1790 are all pleasant but not outstanding.‡ *Holland*'s Berrington Hall of 1778–c. 81 is the only large building of the C18. Its interiors are as refined as its exterior, and it 60a would be as remarkable in the Home Counties as it is in Herefordshire. The only comparable Early Georgian interior is the great hall at The Mynde Much Dewchurch. This has as a motif of decoration busts of medieval English kings, an early sign of the turn to a romantic medievalism which was to propel Herefordshire into pioneering again for a generation or two.

For this sudden popularity the county had to thank nature as much as two squires of intellect, sensibility, wealth, and literary ability. Nature of course means the Wye Valley, dis- 1b covered, it is said, by Dr Egerton, future bishop of Durham, when rector of Ross from 1745 to 1771. He had a commodious pleasure boat built to take friends down the river. But even he, though the discoverer of the Wye, cannot be said to have been the first believer in the picturesque in Herefordshire. For John Kyrle, the Man of Ross, built for himself in his tiny garden a Gothick summer house, and the path on which one reached it was crossed by rugged grotto arches. Yet Kyrle died in 1724. So this little garden, still preserved, belongs with Pope's garden at Twickenham to the incunabula of picturesque gardening and

* A propos these various town halls and market halls, the market hall of Ross might find a place here. It is of stone, with the usual open ground floor, and dates from 1660–74.

‡ With these serviceable Georgian houses the General Hospital at Hereford can perhaps be grouped. The initial building of 1779–83 was of brick, nine bays wide, three storeys high, with a five-bay pediment.

has all the artificiality against which a tour down the Wye was a remedy. The tour was made with unforetellable consequences in 1770 by William Gilpin, and Thomas Gray, the poet, travelled in the same year and found 'nameless beauties'. Gilpin, looking rather for 'the principles of picturesque beauty' than for emotion, found especially the view of Goodrich Castle from the river 'correctly picturesque'. Gilpin's *Observations on the River Wye* were finally published in 1782 and started a universal vogue of 'doing' the Wye Valley. In 1799 eight excursion boats were available at Ross. So much for nature unimproved – not the gentle nature that Capability Brown had endeavoured to recreate in his gardens, but a rougher, more dramatic, craggy and shaggy nature. *Richard Payne Knight* was the man to plead for this in improvements and to denounce Capability Brown's gentle undulations. He lived at Downton Castle above the river Teme, and he preserved the savage 60b scenery of the river. His house, moreover, was a castellated building, completely asymmetrical and inspired more by the background of certain paintings by Lorraine than by English medieval castles. He started building about 1772 and finished most of it in 1778. His interiors – of this he made a special point – were not Gothick, but classical, with a spectacular Pantheon room inside the bulkiest tower. Not far from him, at Foxley, Yazor, his friend Sir Uvedale Price lived in a commodious house of 1717, but he planted too, and he published in 1794 the most intelligent and far-seeing analysis of the Picturesque ever undertaken. Also in the same years, at any rate before 1789, at Bollitree Castle, Weston-under-Penyard, extensive outbuildings in the castle style were erected, and the climax of the Age of the Picturesque and the great popularity of the Wye Valley was the building of a new road from the river up to the town of Ross, along the red crags and flanked by sham castle walls and a big round tower. That was in 1837. In the same year the Royal Hotel was built, also Picturesque, but now gabled and bargeboarded in that anglicized chalet style which was to be so popular for Early Victorian villas.

In the field of CHURCH ARCHITECTURE the Gothic Revival 58b appeared early too. Shobdon Church of 1752–6 is a perfect example of the Rococo Gothic. Of other C18 churches in Herefordshire only one can be compared with Shobdon in interest: Norton Canon of 1716 is of brick, but the windows of stone are those of the old church of c.1300, re-used with great care and conscientiousness. Five more churches, not in need of much comment, and that will be all. Byford has a tower of 1717 just like any unbuttressed medieval tower in the country. How Caple is actually of just before 1700. It was built in 1693–5, is small, and has or had arched windows. At Tyberton of 1719–21 the windows have been changed, and Preston Wynne of 1727 is so entirely victorianized as to be useless. Stoke Edith of 1740–2 on the other hand is well preserved externally and internally. Inside, the entrance bay and the altar bay are separated from the rest by giant Tuscan columns, the only attempt at something monumental in a Georgian Herefordshire church.

The FURNISHINGS at Stoke Edith are well preserved too, including the wrought-iron communion rail. At Shobdon they are perfectly preserved, and at Tyberton they include a lectern in the form of a kneeling angel and the reredos etc. designed by 58a *John Wood* of Bath and made in 1728–31. Of the same high quality is the pulpit at Letton, and this is supposed to come from a parish church in Bristol. It is during these same early years that the best MONUMENTS were put up in Herefordshire churches. First a series of noble architectural pieces of reredos type, commemorating men of noble families, but without any figures: a Foley at Stoke Edith († 1699), Viscount Sligo at Holme Lacy († 1716), the second Earl of Oxford at Brampton Bryan († 1724), and of the same type Robert Weever at Aymestrey († 1728). Monuments with reclining, not recumbent, figures, i.e. alive and communicative, not asleep or dead, are the James Scudamore at Holme Lacy of about 1700 and the two 57b (much more provincial) Biddulphs at Ledbury († 1708 and † 1706). Of after 1750 hardly anything needs singling out: an unpretentious signed piece by *Roubiliac* at Canon Pyon († 1753) and a lively bust in Hereford Cathedral attributed to him († 1757), and the two Conyngsbys at Hope-under-Dinmore and 59 their little son of about 1760, two seated figures against a big reredos background. Apart from this small group there are just tablets, tablets by local stonemasons such as *Jennings*, who can be good but are not always recorded in the gazetteer, tablets of slate of any date between c.1720 and c.1820 and often very charming in lettering, tablets by *King* of Bath, tablets by London men.

Of the leading London sculptors *Flaxman* is represented once or twice, *Westmacott* with a beautiful piece at Ledbury († 1825) and some others, e.g. the less familiar elder *Theed*, with an 62a excellent monument at Ross (1817). And so on. But so on now means the NINETEENTH CENTURY, and what qualifies

for this introductory summary? Not much. *Thomas Hardwick*'s
Nelson Column in Castle Green Hereford, still in the C18
61a tradition and not yet Grecian, *Smirke*'s Shire Hall at Hereford
of 1817–19, fanatically Grecian with its hexastyle portico taken
in the details from the Theseum in Athens, the same architect's
Haffield House, Donnington, of 1818, also with Greek Doric
columns though with less correctly proportioned ones, *Day*'s
Catholic Church at Hereford of 1838–9, again Grecian and
taken from the Treasury of the Athenians at Delphi, and
Whitbourne Hall of 1861–2, High Victorian in date and by a
High Victorian gothicist, *Roumieu*, but very purely Grecian and
inspired in the details by the Erechtheum. That is the Greek
contribution; the Gothic or medieval contribution was stronger
and more numerous, but has suffered more from recent demo-
61b lition. The series started with *Smirke*'s Eastnor of 1812–24,
a mighty affair, all symmetrical, all turreted and castellated, but
specially memorable for being Norman and not Gothic. Smirke
was thirty-one when he started at Eastnor, but had already
tried his hand at medievalism on a grand scale some five years
before at Lowther Castle. *Blore* built Goodrich Court in 1828
etc., vast and now gone. Garnestone Castle, also vast, is gone
too. *Nash* in his early years made Kentchurch Court more
medieval than it had been (*c.*1796 etc.), *Wyatville* did the same
to Hampton Court (*c.*1818 etc.). An Islamic Revival was
represented by Hope End, Colwall, where only the stables – also
mildly Islamic – stand.

So to the VICTORIAN AGE and the end; for little remains to
tell. No house of importance before the nineties, the only
interiors of importance those by *Pugin* and by *G. E. Fox* at
Eastnor – they are of the fifties and the seventies – one extremely
62b interesting church by *Seddon*, Hoarwithy, Italian Romanesque
outside, Siculo-Byzantine inside (*c.*1880–5; the internal decoration by *Fox*), three churches by *Bodley*, two early and one late,
and all three at once in certain details or altogether raised from
the common run (Long-Grove 1854–6, Canon Frome 1860,
Hom Green outside Ross 1905–6),* the splendid metal choir
screen of Hereford Cathedral by *Sir G. G. Scott* and *Skidmore* of
Coventry, a masterpiece of High Victorian skill and mentality –
and long may it live – and much stained glass. *Pugin* designed
some windows, as Mrs Stanton has found; others equally good

* The early ones ought to be contrasted with the 'pre-archaeological'
Gothic of Much Birch (1837), St Nicholas Hereford (1842), and St Martin
Hereford (1845).

or better are at Hereford Cathedral (1852, designed by *Cottingham* and made by *Gibbs*; also *c.*1865 by *Hardman*), in *Bodley*'s rose window at Canon Frome (1861, and this one outstanding), in the little village school at Yarkhill (1866, by *Powell*), at Hoarwithy (*c.*1885–90), etc. Some early glass by *Kempe* is also in Herefordshire (1874 at Bridstow, pre-Kempe in style, 1877 at Evesbatch, 1877 etc. at Much Marcle). The s transept window in the cathedral is the largest by Kempe but not the best. It dates from 1895.

But by 1895 the time for Kempe and for the Victorian style was really over. Morris had come and was to go in 1896, and his followers, the men of the Arts and Crafts and the pioneers of the c20, had begun their revolutionary work. In Herefordshire two outstanding works in this new spirit can be seen and admired: *Voysey*'s Perrycroft at Colwall of 1893–4 with later 63 additions, one of his first perfectly mature country houses, easy, effortless, comfortable, unpretentious, and without any of the period trim of the century, and *Lethaby*'s church at Brock- 64 hampton by Ross of 1901–2, perhaps the most thrilling church in any country of the years between historicism and the Modern Movement. With its steep pointed arches inside, its squareness outside, and the contrast between stone and thatch, it heralds the Expressionism of Germany after the First World War – Poelzig, Hoeger, Haering, rather than Gropius. That it is a strong, original, forward-looking work there can be no doubt.

It was not to be followed by others. This story ends in 1902, and it shows no sign, at the time of writing, of recommencing once again. With no industry and little increase in population, there is probably no incitement to new building and certainly none to exciting building. So we must settle down in conclusion to the least exciting task in working out these Introductions: the READING LIST. The principal source is of course the three volumes of the *Royal Commission on Historical Monuments* (RCHM), 1931, 1932, and 1934. The classic on county history and topography is John Duncumb: *Collections towards the History and Antiquities of the County of Hereford*, vols. I–II, 1804–12; vols. III and IV (by W. H. Croke), 1882–92; vols. V and VI, 1887 and 1913. Of more popular guidebooks the most useful are the *Little Guide* by G. W. and J. H. Wade, first published in 1917 (3rd ed. 1930), the *Shell Guide* by David Verey, 1955, and the book in the Robert Hale series by H. L. V. Fletcher, 1948. The archaeological and architectural periodical of the county has a nice old-fashioned name: *Transactions of the*

Woolhope Naturalists' Field Club. On special topics, only the
following need be named: on church plate B. S. Stanhope &
Moffatt, 1903, and on timber-framing J. T. Smith in *Archaeological Journal*, CIX, 1952. Such general and familiar sources
as *Country Life* for country houses, Tristram on wall paintings,
Aymer Vallance for screens in churches, A. Gardner for alabaster
monuments, need not here be specially referred to. That leaves
some books on Hereford in particular. On the history of the
town: W. H. House: *Historic Hereford*, 2nd ed., 1950, and on
the cathedral first Browne Willis in 1742, then Robert Willis's
admirable analysis of 1842, and then A. H. Fisher (*Bell's
Cathedral Series*), 1898 and G. Marshall, 1951.

HEREFORDSHIRE

*

ABBEY DORE

ST MARY, formerly DORE ABBEY. The church is now, at least from outside, a village church in size and prominence, though an odd-looking one. Of the monastic quarters next to nothing is left, and of the church, once some 250 ft long, the whole nave is missing. So what remains is crossing, transepts, and chancel, with a C17 tower in an unusual position. The abbey had been founded for Cistercians from Morimond in 1147, but the first buildings must have been temporary, and style makes it evident that rebuilding of the whole church started about 1175–80 and went on to 1210 or 1220 and beyond. No exact building dates are known. After the Dissolution the building decayed, until Lord Scudamore, about 1633, restored the parts now remaining, closed them to the W, and added the tower. Reconstruction could be celebrated in 1634.

The church as first designed consisted of nave and aisles, a crossing, and a chancel which, it has been convincingly surmised, was to be only two bays long and straight-ended and had closed N and S walls. Beyond these, extending from the transepts, were two one-bay straight-ended E chapels on either side. This is indeed what can be called the standard Cistercian plan of the years of the greatest fervour of the order, the plan remaining at Fontenay, the earliest Burgundian house that survives. Fontenay was built in 1135–9. Then, about 1200 and not later, and still during building, the chancel was lengthened and received aisles into which the inner E chapels of the transepts were merged, and an ambulatory which is taken round the straight end and E of it becomes double. The plan is most similar to that drawn later in Villard de Honnecourt's lodge-book, and similar also to that of Cîteaux itself in its final form. Consecration at Cîteaux was in 1193. In England the nearest relatives of Dore are Byland in Yorkshire of the late C12 and Waverley in Surrey as extended in 1203–31.

EXTERIOR. Red sandstone with grey limestone dressings. 17a

Against the w wall of the present church and in front of it
what remains of nave and aisles, i.e. the SE springer of the
aisle rib-vault, the SE springer of the nave rib-vault, the E
respond with waterleaf capital, the w respond with long,
broad, upright leaves, and the arch mouldings; moreover the
N aisle E respond with early stiff-leaf, the long stalks crossing
one another, the first pier with circular trumpet-scallop
capital, and the NE corbel for the aisle vault, again with
waterleaf. These details are among the earliest in the church,
which shows that, as usual, one build comprised the E parts
and the first bay or bays of the nave. The exterior of the transepts shows the earliest of all features, a round-headed doorway
in the N wall of the N transept and a round-headed window
in the NE chapel. In the N transept there are no N windows,
because the monastic quarters adjoined here. To the w one
tall lancet and a small one above the aisle roof. To the E
one round-headed one and upper lancets. The S transept
is similar except that no window is round-headed and that
there was space for a display to the s. There is a doorway
with one order of shafts, crocket and upright-leaf capitals,
deep mouldings, including a keeled roll, and a hood-mould
with dog-tooth. A second doorway, to the E and higher up,
connected with the dormitory. Above are two very tall shafted
lancets. The capitals have waterleaf and trumpet scallops.
Vesica window above and two small windows, perhaps of the
C17, in the gable. The C17 tower is placed above the inner
chapel or first bay of the ambulatory on the s side. The SE
chapel has lancets again, and the same lancets with chamfered
surrounds now continue all along the ambulatory. They have
a heavy billet frieze connecting them and rising over them as
gables. The windows of the high chancel are of the same type
too. To the E the chancel ends in three stepped lancets and
again two small (later?) ones in the gable. From the ambulatory to the N leads a doorway with deep continuous mouldings
with fillets.

INTERIOR. We must start with transepts and crossing. The
transepts were rib-vaulted, and so were the chapels. The
chapel entries – the w bays of the ambulatory are here called
the inner chapels, because that is what they originally were –
have semi-octagonal responds, differing in section between
N and s. The capitals on the s side are still Norman or near-
Norman, on the N side developing into stiff-leaf. Large hood-
moulds with dog-tooth-like fleurons. The vaulting is by ribs

of paired rolls. The inner N chapel has at the apex of the vault
a small leaf boss, not larger than the crossing of the ribs
themselves. The high vaults of the transepts rest on cinque-
partite supports. The outer shafts carry wall arches, the inner
carried ribs and transverse arches. The capitals high up are
pre-stiff-leaf in the N transept and on the E shafts of the S
transept. In the S chapel fine piscina with pointed-trefoiled
arch on stiff-leaf stops. An aumbry next to it. Also in the
S transept S wall a large aumbry framed by dog-tooth. Above
this, to the E, appears the door of the former night-stair which
led to the dormitory. It has a depressed two-centred arch.

The crossing piers are identical on the N, S, and E, but
different on the W, unless in the C17 some shafts were chiselled
off. The crossing vault rested not on these shafts but on
corbels.

The chancel is of three bays, the first very different from
the others. It has only a very narrow opening of three continuous chamfers and a string course higher than in the other
bays. The irregularity is due to the fact that originally the wall
was closed here between chancel and transept chapels and
that the inner chapels became part of an ambulatory only
when the enlargement of the chancel by such a feature had
been decided upon; which must have been about 1200 or a
little later. The other bays and the three bays of the E wall
belong to this second campaign. Here the piers are low and
very richly shafted, the bases close to the water-holding type,
the arches equally richly moulded, and the E windows, if
not the others, again shafted in superabundance. The E
piers especially, with their fourteen shafts, can only be compared with such south-west English feats as those of Wells.
In the N and S walls of the chancel vaulting-shafts rise to the
former vault but do not take wall arches into consideration.
The capitals have upright leaves, scrolls, and also real crockets.
However, in the arcade piers below the Late Norman types
also all continue. This applies to inside the ambulatory as well.
Ribbed palmettes e.g. can be found, and also, as before,
waterleaf and trumpet-scallops. In the E arcade incidentally
quite a number of capitals were never carved at all.

The arch from the inner chapels into the ambulatory
proper has two continuous chamfers, i.e. belongs to the same
adjustment as the arches from the chapels towards the
chancel. After that the ambulatory goes its splendid, sumptuous way towards the climax of the double walk at the E end 17b

with its four slender piers of eight shafts. Even the irregularity that the shafts for the vaulting of the ambulatory have their capitals lower than those of the arcade between chancel and ambulatory adds life and movement.

Now that the building has been examined, it has become possible to consider details from the point of view of development and chronology. It has already been said that crossing, transepts, chapels E of the transept, and E end of the nave come first.* They have, as we have seen, still Late Norman, that is pre-Gothic, capitals, including waterleaf and trumpet-scallops. Abaci are square or chamfered, bases steepish. The ribs of the s transept chapels are pairs of rolls, and the same applies to the outer N chapel. The ribs of the inner chapel however have a trefoil moulding. In this chapel the ribs are on corbels, not on shafts, i.e. they are an afterthought. That ought to be the same in the inner s chapel, and as there are shafts here, they must be a remodelling, which is borne out by the flat bases of the shafts, a motif that became universal soon. The end of the first campaign is marked by the N chapels, which have stiff-leaf capitals, and the upper parts of both transepts and the old part of the chancel, all of which have stiff-leaf capitals too. This shows clearly that the first campaign on the standard Cistercian plan did not lead to completion. It was interrupted by the second, which included the splendid new retrochoir or double ambulatory. Its very splendour is of course a sin against Bernardian ideals. The bases now are flatter, almost of the water-holding type. The s chancel aisle was built first. Abaci are still square. Ribs have a roll with a fillet. Stiff-leaf capitals are not yet in fashion: they are e.g. not used in the capitals of the arcade responds, and there the N aisle has not got them either. Then the N aisle, the E ambulatory, and the upper parts of the chancel were all built together. They have round abaci, trefoil ribs with fillets, and plenty of stiff-leaf capitals, though not exclusively stiff-leaf capitals. Whether the latter fact means that some of the Late Norman men carried on, or that capitals had been got ready for later use, cannot be said. The openings from the original inner chapels to the chancel and the E which became necessary when the chapels had become part of the chancel aisles have two continuous chamfers, a detail which does not help in dating: it was simply a utilitarian way of connecting

18a

* A parallel to them is a building across the Monmouth border which ought to be seen in conjunction with Dore: Llanthony.

where connexion had become necessary. The other details bear out the completion date of c.1210–20 which has been suggested higher up.

The chancel as well as the transepts have flat ceilings on typically Jacobean corbels. These ceilings are the work of *John Abel*, who in 1633 contracted with Lord Scudamore to make them.

On the nave hardly anything need be added. The pulpitum ran between the second and third bays from the E, the rood screen in the fifth. Part of the wall of the N aisle remains, and the W respond of the N arcade, with angle spurs on the base.

THE MONASTIC QUARTERS have almost entirely disappeared. N of the N transept was the E range, and first a SACRISTY whose tunnel-vault can still be seen indicated in the transept wall. In its W wall was a book cupboard open to the cloister walk. There followed to the N the VESTIBULE to the chapter house, and of this the S respond of the entrance (tripartite with decorated trumpet-scallop capital) and the SE springer of the vault survive. The CHAPTER HOUSE itself was twelve-sided, like that at Margam in Wales, and one drum of the central column is preserved in the S transept. The column had twelve shafts. Above this E range lay the DORMITORY which, as usual, extended further N and ended with the REREDORTER, i.e. the lavatories, set partly above the mill-stream. Slight traces of the wall of the N range. Between the cloister and the W range ran a lane. About 180 ft E of the dormitory stood another building, probably the INFIRMARY. This also runs partly across the mill-stream.

FURNISHINGS. Much is of Lord Scudamore's time, notably the SCREEN, a rather hefty piece with big fancy columns, balusters between, a thick cornice, and coats of arms and obelisks above. – STALLS and BENCHES also have Jacobean-style panelling, and the stalls in addition back panelling. – The PULPIT with tester again belongs to the same style (double blank arches with a little pendant). – COMMUNION RAIL with plain, stout balusters. – WEST GALLERY on columns similar to those of the screen. – POOR BOX dated 1639. – DOOR, N ambulatory. With fine iron hinges, early C13. – SCULPTURE. Many interesting fragments lie about, including big stiff-leaf bosses and a set of beautiful, large figured bosses which must belong to the early C14 (Coronation of the Virgin, Christ in Majesty, a monk kneeling before the abbot, a monk kneeling in front of St Catherine, a monk kneeling in front of the seated Virgin). Where were they originally ? – STAINED GLASS. Late medieval fragments in the SE chapel. – C16 to C17 fragments in the ambulatory E wall, S window. – Also the complete E window with many figures, belonging to Lord Scudamore's work and dated 1634. The dominant colours are yellow, brown, and blue and red. – TILES. Some heraldic tiles of the C13 in the chancel, some undecorated ones by the font. – PLATE. Cup and Cover Paten, 1633; Flagon, 1634, London-made; Paten by *T.P.*, London, 1740. – MONUMENTS. Two late C13 effigies of Knights, ambulatory N and S, both with mail armour, and both cross-legged. – Tomb-chest without effigy of John Hoskins † 1638. – In the SE corner of the churchyard an entrance with an early C18 wrought-iron GATE.

GRANGE FARM, 1¼ m. ENE. Nearly all narrowly-set upright timbers. Early C16 and early C17 plaster ceiling inside on the first floor. Motifs of fleurs-de-lis, little branches, etc.

A portion of the ROMAN ROAD from Kenchester to Abergavenny was exposed in the station yard in 1908. It was 12 ft 9 in. wide and consisted of limestone nodules laid on the natural red marl.

5030

ACONBURY

ST JOHN BAPTIST. The curious evidence of the S wall, where two blocked doorways, several brackets for roof timbers, the springer of an arch towards the W, and windows set high up appear is explained by the fact that this was the church of a nunnery, or rather a house of the Sisters of the Order of St John of Jerusalem, founded before 1237 and soon transferred to Augustinian Canonesses. The church was always as small as it is now. Nave and chancel in one. No aisles or transepts. The style is consistently that of the late C13. W front with three stepped lancets with pointed-trefoiled heads. Framing of a continuous roll. The three are under one arch, and in the spandrels are three trefoils. Single-chamfered W doorway. Clasping buttresses. The timber bell-turret is of course later. In the N wall two two-light windows also with cusped heads and a trefoil over. Chancel with an E window of the Herefordshire type with three stepped lights. In the S wall near the W end high up a small oblong opening to a space in the wall with a quatrefoil window to the outside. This and the springer of the arch mentioned before must have communicated with the W range of the claustral buildings, the upper floor of which

may have been the abbess's or prioress's quarters. The
doorways would have led to the cloister. Deep C14 or C15
porch of timber. Two bays, the tie-beams between supported
by two angels. The side walls open in long wooden window
strips with ogee-headed lights. Inside, on the N side, a tomb
recess with a deeply moulded arch. – WALL PAINTING.
Ashlaring with little flowers and other motifs of the time of
the restoration by *Sir G. G. Scott* (1863). Does it represent
what was there originally? – STAINED GLASS. A few C13
grisaille quarries in a N window. – PLATE. Paten Plate by
Paul Storr, 1796; Chalice, London, 1809. – MONUMENT.
Coffin-lid by the tomb recess with incised foliated cross, with
shields and naturalistic foliage. Inscription in Lombardic
lettering; *c.*1300.

ACONBURY CAMP. An Iron Age hill-fort $\frac{3}{4}$ m. WSW of the
church. The single rampart encloses a sub-rectangular area
of $17\frac{1}{2}$ acres. There are entrances, probably original, at the
SE and SW corners. Trial excavations yielded Iron Age B and
Romano-British pottery.

ACTON BEAUCHAMP   *6050*

ST GILES. Quite on its own. Short W tower with re-set lancet
windows and pyramid roof, nave and chancel. The latter two
rebuilt in 1819, in the Georgian style, with fine large arched
windows. Of the medieval building the Late Norman S doorway was kept. One order of shafts with one capital with
trumpet-scallops, the other with three small heads. Big
roll-moulding in the arch. – FONT. Octagonal, Perp, embattled. – SCULPTURE. Used as the lintel of the S doorway
into the tower, and alas mutilated for the purpose, a very fine
Anglo-Saxon piece of the C9. It is carved with a so-called
inhabited scroll on a scale larger than usual for cross-shafts.
In one scroll a bird, in the other two a fragmentary lion and
a fragmentary goat (?). The style has been compared with
Cropthorne in Worcestershire and with Wroxeter in Shropshire. – PLATE. Cup and Cover Paten, probably late C17. –
MONUMENT. Tablet to Henry Brace † 1773 and members of
his family. Signed by *W. Milton*.

ADFORTON   *4070*

ST ANDREW. By *Seddon*, 1875. Simple and small. Of nave and
apsed chancel. Bellcote on the E gable of the nave. Windows

with pointed-trefoiled lights. One window in the chancel is a cinquefoil with rounded lobes. The fenestration is deliberately irregular: some windows e.g. are shafted internally, others are not. Wagon roofs. – FONT. By *Seddon*.

WIGMORE ABBEY, *see* Wigmore, p. 321.

BRICK HOUSE, NNE of the church, across the road. Inside, flanking a fireplace, two shafts, *c*. 5 ft tall, of the C13, one with a moulded, the other with a leaf capital.

FAIRFIELD, *c*. 250 yds WNW. Inside remains of a bold C14 roof with cusped tie-beam, cusped principals, and cusped raking struts.

PEYTOE HALL, ¾ m. NE, E of Wigmore Abbey. Timber-framed, C16 and C17, and charming to look at. (BARN, partly of ashlar, with worked stones of the C12 and C13, no doubt from Wigmore Abbey.*)

4030   ALLENSMORE

ST ANDREW. Short broad Perp w tower. Late Norman s doorway. Windows mostly late C13 (cusped Y-tracery), but the gabled s window of three lights with its oddly incomplete trefoil shape at the top must be Dec – if it is reliable. The chancel E window is Dec too. It is of four lights and has reticulated tracery. Single-frame roofs. – FONT. High Victorian with stiff-leaf. – PULPIT. Jacobean, with blank arches and strapwork panels above. – STAINED GLASS. In the tracery of the E window original Crucifixus and angels. – PLATE. Beaker-shaped foreign Cup, C17. – MONUMENTS. Large incised slab to Sir Andrew Herl and his wife; late C14. The inlays are of cement. – Richard Grumor (?) † 1702 (?). Tablet with scrolls and cornucopia. – A number of slate tablets of *c*. 1800 with the motif of an open book. – CHURCHYARD CROSS. Steps, base, and part of the shaft.

WOOD STREET FARMHOUSE, 200 yds NE. An early C18 five-bay brick range with hipped roof added to a timber-framed house.

COBHALL, 1 m. w. Timber-framed. The handsome early C17 porch is disintegrating. To its r. an original wooden mullioned and transomed window with a vestigial pediment. In a room inside panelling, a frieze of dolphins, and an overmantel with caryatids and blank arches. All this is also early C17.

* The photographs at the Conway Library, Courtauld Institute of Art, London, show that they are in the style of the so-called Herefordshire School, *see* Shobdon, etc.

(LITTLE COBHALL, 100 yds NNW of the former. The C15
  hall seems to have had a hammerbeam roof. Also carved
  wind-braces. RCHM)
(MAWFIELD FARM, 1 m. NW of the church. Remains of a late
  C15 roof with shaped braces supporting collar-beams and
  shaped wind-braces. RCHM)

ALLT-Y-YNYS see WALTERSTONE

ALMELEY   3050

ST MARY. Short unbuttressed W tower begun c.1200 (see the S
impost of the former tower arch). Late C13 to early C14 aisles
and arcades (four bays, octagonal piers, double-chamfered
arches). Of the late C13 also the chancel, with the splendid
though over-restored Geometrical tracery of its E window.
Chancel arch on busts, and a bust at the apex. Over-restored
cusped and subcusped tomb recess. This however has an
ogee top, and so points into the Dec style. Dec nave clerestory with an alternation of pre-ogee and ogee tracery, and
Dec transepts, or rather chapels extending N and S of the
last aisle bays. They have reticulated tracery. Very pretty
ceilure of the roof above the rood, with painted Tudor roses.
Early C16. – SCREEN. Now under the tower arch. Jacobean,
with vertically symmetrical balusters. – BENCHES. With
Jacobean panels. – STAINED GLASS. Very convincing early
C16 E window made in 1865. Whom by ? – PLATE. Chalice
and Cover Paten, London, 1613; Salver, domestic, by
E. Coker, London, 1771; Flagon, also domestic, London,
1772.
(CASTLE, SW of the churchyard. Circular motte with four-sided
  bailey N of it. The motte has a top diameter of c.36 ft and is
  c.21 ft high above the bottom of the ditch. RCHM)
FRIENDS' MEETING HOUSE, Almeley Wootton. Probably
  of 1672. Modest, one-storeyed black and white house with a
  half-hipped roof, built from the start as a meeting house.
MANOR HOUSE, WNW of the church. Timber-framed with
  brick infilling. Two-storeyed gabled porch. In this and the
  r. gable diagonal bracing. (A room inside with moulded
  beams of c.1500. RCHM)
SUMMER HOUSE, Almeley Wootton, N of the Meeting House.
  Three gables with concave-sided lozenges, the r. one only
  painted on.

(CASTLE FROME, 250 yds S of the church. With cruck-trusses. RCHM)

(OLDCASTLE TWT, c. ⅔ m. NW of the church, on the end of a spur. Circular motte, c.29 ft in diameter at the top and c.18 ft above the bottom of the ditch. Rectangular bailey to the N. RCHM)

5040
AMBERLEY
2 m. ENE of Marden

CHAPEL. Early C14, except for a re-set Late Norman trumpet capital in the E wall inside and the re-set and remodelled porch entrance. Typical simple E window of the special Herefordshire variety of three lancet lights under one arch. More Dec w windows. The other windows with tracery from the Y-type to reticulation motifs (one straight-headed window). Two-light bellcote with cusped straight-headed openings. Inside the E wall also a tall castellated Perp frame rather than recess. Is this re-set too? – PLATE. Cup, Cover, and Paten on foot, 1704.

AMBERLEY COURT. The house is a perfect example of a C14 hall-house with solar wing and buttery wing. The framing is in large squares, and the principal timbers, including the arched braces, are of great thickness. As for the important roofs, the RCHM describes them in detail. At the time of writing no more could be seen than the spere-truss of the hall range. Above the collar-beams are foiled openings. There are also two tiers of trefoiled wind-braces.

34a

6040
ASHPERTON

ST BARTHOLOMEW. E.E. chancel arch, see the water-holding bases of the responds. The rest mostly of the early C14, i.e. nave and chancel and both transepts. Windows ogee-headed lancets, cusped intersected tracery, also the Herefordshire variety of three stepped lancet lights. W tower rebuilt c.1800. – ORGAN CASE on the W gallery, Gothic, and probably early C19. – MONUMENT. To a member of the Wilson family, late C17. Tablet with two short columns and an open segmental pediment. The oval inscription panel framed by a folded ribbon.

THE MOOREND, ½ m. NW. Black and white, early C17. Square framing, the N gable-end also long diagonals and, in the top of the gable, lozenge trellis. Central star-shaped chimney-stack.

COTTAGE, 250 yds NE, i.e. S of Church Lane. With an exposed cruck truss.

(CASTLE, W of the church. Oval island in a moat. Approach by a causeway from the E. Traces of an outer enclosure to the E. It must have embraced the church. Licence to crenellate his house was given to William de Grandison in 1292. RCHM)

ASTON 4070

ST GILES. Surrounded by hills with fir plantations. Norman. Nave and lower chancel. Buff sandstone with some red sandstone dressings. Norman the plain S doorway and the more ornate N doorway. The tympanum of the latter has a lamb with cross in a circle held by the bull of St Luke and the eagle of St John, both with decoratively spread wings. Outer band with animals and leafage surrounding the tympanum. One spray has two birds pecking into it. Imposts with dragons (l.) and foliage (r.). Outer arch surround rich with zigzag. In the N wall one Norman nave, one Norman chancel window. In the S wall windows (lengthened ?) with zigzag and nailhead in the arch. The chancel was rebuilt in the late C13, but the details are renewed: E window of three stepped lancets under one arch. Chancel arch of two continuous chamfered orders. Nave roof with rough tie-beams, queenposts, collar-beams, and wind-braces. According to the RCHM late C14. – PAINTING. Inside the nave red Norman ashlar painting with addorsed flowers on stalks. – SCULPTURE. C12 stone of truncated cone shape, with a dragon, an animal, and foliage.

MOUND, 120 yds NE, probably a castle-mound or tump, c. 24 ft high above the bottom of the ditch. – Another MOUND is ⅕ m. NNE of the church. It is less high.

ASTON INGHAM 6020

ST JOHN BAPTIST. Almost entirely rebuilt by *Nicholson & Son* in 1891, except for the chancel arch and the C16 W tower, which now stands out into the church. – FONT. Of lead. 53a Dated 1689. Cylindrical and not high. Charmingly decorated with bits of foliage, initials, and the date. – PLATE. Elizabethan Cup. – MONUMENTS. To the l. and r. of the altar two c13 effigies under trefoiled heads. One appears behind (or under) a foliated cross, the other is almost totally defaced. – CHURCHYARD CROSS. Steps, base, and shaft are preserved.

6050 AVENBURY

ST MARY. In ruins. Unbuttressed W tower with the pyramid roof going to pieces. The arch towards the nave makes an early C13 date likely. The nave has disappeared. In the chancel Norman windows. – MONUMENT. Incised slab to a Knight, cross-legged, late C13.

HACKLEY FARM, 1¾ m. W. The staircase of c.1600 with a pretty screen of balusters.

6030 AYLTON

CHURCH. Very small, with very small bell-turret. One Norman N window. E window Dec – of two ogee-headed lights. S porch with balusters of 1654. – SCREEN. Wildly assembled. The large tracery forms and their relative purity point to an early date. – PLATE. Small Cup with flowers and foliage, late C17.

4060 AYMESTREY

ST JOHN BAPTIST AND ST ALKMUND. In the chancel two Norman windows in tufa surrounds. The nave arcades of three bays have piers whose profile (quatrefoil set diagonally, with polygonal spurs between) seems late C12. They are either re-used or brought in (from Wigmore Abbey?). The chancel arch also could be C12 in its lower parts. Short broad W tower, the W entrance with continuous triple chamfers. A tunnel-vault inside. The arches of the nave arcades are double-chamfered and may be of any date, but the awkward capitals, as also those of the chancel arch, must be a late medieval alteration. – SCREENS. Early C16. Splendid rood screen, tall, with one-light divisions, linenfold panelling in the dado, a coving with lierne ribs, three foliage friezes in the cornice, and a cresting. The parclose screens have linenfold panels too, but are otherwise appropriately more modest (e.g. one foliage frieze only). – PULPIT. Big, Jacobean, with the usual short blank arches. – PLATE. Set, 1834. – MONUMENTS. Sir John Lingen † 1506 and wife. Incised alabaster slab (chancel N). – Several C18 tablets, especially Robert

Weever † 1728, big, very classical, with fluted Doric pilasters and a metope frieze. No figures. – Dunne Family, 1734–86. Tablet by *Nelson* of Shrewsbury. – CHURCHYARD CROSS, W of the church. High base, slender shaft, knob at the top, the latter probably C17, the rest late medieval.

YATTON COURT, ½ m. NE. A Georgian stone house, ashlar-built, tall, of four by three bays. The shorter sides are the façades. They have tripartite, Venetian, and tripartite-lunette windows. A lower attachment on one side also has some of them. The façades are characterized by an absence of all mouldings.

(CAMP WOOD TUMP, 1¾ m. W of the church. Circular; 41 yds in diameter at the base, 17 ft high. RCHM)

HILL-FORT. A multivallate rampart of roughly triangular plan lies on a ridge 1½ m. NE of the church. The site consists of an inner enclosure of 8¼ acres defended on the S and W by three ramparts and two intermediate ditches and on the N, where the ground slopes more steeply, providing a slight natural defence, by two ramparts. The outer enclosure, S of the principal fortifications, is defended by two ramparts with medial ditch. There are now two entrances to the fort on the W and NE. The former has the ramparts inturned and is almost certainly original; the NE entrance approached by a sunken way may also be a contemporary feature. The site is currently (1962) being excavated and has produced material from Iron Age A times until the Roman occupation, including a number of fine pieces of bronze work.

BACTON

3030

ST FAITH. Short, broad W tower, built after 1573. But the arch towards the nave is of the C13. It has a continuous keeled moulding. Nave and chancel in one. The E wall was rebuilt in 1894. The nave has a single-framed (trussed-rafter) roof, the chancel a wagon roof with bosses. – STALLS. Late medieval. The seats with simple ends, the desks with poppy-heads and simple traceried fronts. – FRONTAL. Beautiful C17 embroidery. Large stylized flowers and small insects, birds, animals between them. – PLATE. Chalice of *c.*1500 with engraved foot; knop with leopards' heads. – Paten of about the same time with the face of Christ in a sexfoiled depression. – MONUMENTS. Blanche Parry, maid of honour of Queen Elizabeth. 45 A very curious monument, curious in that the queen appears

on it as large as Blanche. Blanche kneels in profile, the
queen – very awkwardly – kneels (hardly) or sits or stands
frontally. The idea is really a secular version of the medieval
motif of the worshipper on his monument kneeling before the
Virgin – only it is the Virgin Queen here. Altogether the monument is not a skilled work. Tomb-chest with three shields,
two set in strapwork. Columns l. and r., a shallow coffered
arch between. Top cornice.

Long inscription as follows:

I PARRYE HYS DOUGHTER BLAENCHE OF NEW COURTE BORNE
THAT TRAENYD WAS IN PRYNCYS COURTS WYTHE
GORGIOUS WYGHTS
WHEARE FLEETYNE HONOR SOUNDS WYTHE BLASTE OF HORNE
EACHE OF ACCOUNTE TOO PLACE OF WORLDS DELYGHTS
AM LODGYD HEERE IN THYS STONYE TOOMBE
MY HARPYNGER YS PAEDE I OWGHTE OF DUE
MY FRYNDS OF SPEECHE HEERE IN DOO FYNDE MEE DOOMBE
THE WHICHE IN VAENE THEY DOO SO GREATLYE RHUE
FOR SO MOOCHE AS HYT YS BUT THENDE OF ALL
THYS WORDLYE ROWTE OF STATE WHAT SO THEY BE
THE WHICHE UNTOO THE RESTE HEEREAFTER SHALL
ASSEMBLE THUS EACHE WYGHTE IN HYS DEGREE
ILYVDE ALLWEYS AS HANDMAEDE TOO A QUENE
IN CHAMBER CHIFF MY TYME DYD TOOVERPASSE
UNCAREFULL OF MY WELLTHE THER WAS I SENE
WHYLLSTE I ABODE THE RONNYNGE OF MY GLASSE
NOT DOUBTYNGE WANTE WHYLLSTE THAT MY MYSTRES LYVDE
IN WOMANS STATE WHOSE CRADELL SAW I ROCKTE
HER SERVANNTE THEN AS WHEN SHE HER CROUNE ATTCHEEVED
AND SO REMAENED TYLL DEATHE MY DOORE HAD KNOCKTE
PREFFERRYNGE STYLL THE CAUSYS OF EACHE WYGHTE
AS FARRE AS I DOORSEE MOVE HER GRACE HYS EARE
FOR TOO REWARDE DECERTS BY COURSE OF RYGHTE
AS NEEDS RESSYTTE OF SARVYS DOONNE EACHE WHEARE
SO THAT MY TYME I THUS DYD PASSE AWAYE
A MAEDE IN COURTE AND NEVER NO MANS WYFFE
SWORNE OF QUENE ELLSBETHS HEDD CHAMBER ALLWAYE
WYTHE MAEDEN QUENE A MAEDE DYD ENDE MY LYFFE

– Alexander Stanton † 1620. Tablet with two kneelers facing
one another. Three columns l. and r. and between. Shield at
the top. – Also a pretty slate tablet of 1812, signed by *R. Parry*
of Kilpeck.

(About ¾ m. N is a triangular ENCLOSURE of earth, *c.*⅓ acre in
size. RCHM)

BALLINGHAM   *5030*

ST DUBRICIUS. Over-restored in 1884–5 (*W. E. Martin*). In
the nave one small C13 N lancet. The unbuttressed W tower
seems to belong to the late C13 (the bell-openings have
cusped lancets). It has a parapet and a recessed spire. The
nave is C14, the doorway early, the single-frame roof of any
C14 date. Perp S porch with spandrels carrying shields and
tracery and a vault of diagonal and ridge-ribs forming a
concave-sided star with a flower in the middle (cf. Hereford
cloisters). – PULPIT. Jacobean, with panels with little double
arches and arabesque panels above. – PLATE. Early C18 Cup
and Cover Paten. – SUNDIAL in the churchyard. Handsome
C18 bronze dial by *N. Witham* of London. – MONUMENT.
William Scudamore † 1649 (nave W wall). Black and white
tablet, remarkably classical, with its pediment and neither
figures nor ornament.

BALLINGHAM HALL. Of stone, C17. The windows were
originally mullioned and have hood-moulds. In the gables
blank panels with ovals – a sign usually of a date *c.*1660–70.

BARROW MILL *see* CRADLEY

BARTESTREE   *5040*

ST JAMES. 1888 by *Nicholson & Son*. Nave with bellcote,
chancel and apse. The style of *c.*1300.

CONVENT OF OUR LADY OF CHARITY AND REFUGE,
founded 1863. By *E. Welby Pugin*, with additions of 1881,
1889, 1895 by *Chick*. Red brick. The old parts are Gothic and
asymmetrical with gables and gabled dormers, and they
culminate in a thin tower with the doorway across a corner so
that the corner has to be elaborately corbelled above it.

The CHAPEL OF ST JAMES is of stone and Perp. It was the
chapel of Old Longworth (*see* Lugwardine) and was restored
and re-converted – it had been a barn – in 1860 and re-
erected on the present site in 1869–70. Perp N and E (really
E and S) windows. Roof with collar-beams on arched braces
and cusped wind-braces. – DOOR. C15, with tracery (in the
porch). – MONUMENT. Elizabeth Phillipps † 1852. Brass cross
with two angels in the style of 1300. Set in a marble slab. –
Mary Anne Phillipps † 1858. Standing angel with an inscription scroll in a Gothic niche.

BARTON COURT *see* COLWALL

4030
BELMONT

St Michael's Abbey. Created by Mr F. R. Wegg-Prosser, a very recent convert at the time, and offered to the Benedictines. Foundation stone of the church 1854. Completion *pro tempore* 1856. Start on the monastery 1857. Completion *pro tempore* 1858. Choir lengthened and side chapels built 1860. Crossing tower completed in 1882. All by *Pugin & Pugin*, of course after the death of the greater A. W. N. Pugin. The church became a cathedral provisionally in 1855 and finally in 1916. It ceased to be a cathedral in 1920 and became an abbey. Prominent crossing tower, florid w window, prosperous nave in the style of the early C14. The E parts more modest and clearly earliest. High steep ceiled wooden roof. – In the N transept chapel MONUMENT to the Rev. Thomas Brown † 1880, the first bishop, also by *Pugin & Pugin*. Recumbent effigy in a shrine architecture with big canopy. – MONUMENT to Bishop Hedley † 1915. Recumbent effigy on a white tomb-chest in Renaissance forms.

The other parts of the monastery are in a rather depressingly institutional Gothic, with steep gables and gabled dormers.

To the s ALMSHOUSES with Chapel, also endowed by Mr Wegg-Prosser. 1852 by *Carpenter*.

BELMONT. Tall Victorian mansion with gables; the detail all E.E.

BERNITHAN COURT *see* LLANGARRON

5060
BERRINGTON HALL
1 m. E of Eye

Built for Thomas Harley by *Henry Holland* in 1778–c. 81. Thomas Harley came from an old Herefordshire family (they owned Brampton Bryan Castle), but had gone into the City and become a banker, government contractor, and Lord Mayor. At Berrington *Capability Brown* preceded his son-in-law Holland. He started re-designing the grounds already in 1775. Holland's house has a beautifully simple exterior of greyish-pink sandstone. Seven-bay front with very tall portico of four unfluted Ionic columns. The frieze is decorated only in the middle, a strange irregularity. The motifs are recent, but replace different, original ones. Pediment with segmental tripartite window. The doorway is oddly narrow and elongated. The bays to the l. and r. of the portico have windows under arches on the upper floor. The offices are in the basement. The w front of five bays with a three-bay pediment. The back, i.e. N, faces a courtyard enclosed by three independent ranges of buildings: the laundry and bakery in front, of nine bays with one archway to full height surrounded by pairs of Doric pilasters and pediments, and side ranges of nine bays, having the kitchen etc. and the dairy and servants' hall. The ranges are connected by quadrant links to each other and to the house. The E and W ranges have at their backs, i.e. towards the garden, a central niche, and against their s end, i.e. also towards the garden, a blank feigned niche with coffering in perspective. The entrance side of the house itself is spoiled by a heavy Late Victorian tower, placed asymmetrically to upset the hated poise of the Georgian ensemble.

This ensemble is as perfect inside as it is outside. All rooms on the main floor are of the same date and in the same refined taste. Entrance hall with trophies in roundels above the doors and a ceiling on four shallow segmental arches. They strike one as Soanian, and Soane was indeed in 1778 still connected with Holland's office. Drawing room on the l. The ceiling dainty, with painted medallions and putti between sea-horses. Chimneypiece with two youthful caryatids. Gilt pelmets and drapes. The boudoir, next to the drawing room, has a shallow apse or alcove with a segmental arch on a screen of two blue scagliola columns. The room itself has a segmental tunnel-vault with an oval painting.

In the middle of the house is the splendid staircase. One side of the room has a strip divided off which is covered by a big coffered arch, a Piranesian effect, when seen as one comes in from the entrance hall. On the arch stands the first-floor 60a landing. This is continued as a passage, and there are as well screens of scagliola columns on the s and E sides. The staircase railing is of bronze. Above the staircase a glazed dome. The colours are original and very subtle, with grey, pale blue, biscuit, terracotta, pink, and olive green.

To the E of the staircase hall the dining room. Exquisite chimneypiece. Ceiling with garlands in the form of an octofoil round a circular painting of a Banquet of the Gods. Between the dining room and the entrance hall is the library, in pale green and bistre. Bookcases and wall decorations with pediments. Ceiling with medallions of writers from Chaucer to Addison (and not beyond). Fine chimneypiece with the relief of a Sybil.

LODGE. Of one and a half storeys. The archway goes up to full height. Top balustrade.

ASHTON CAMP, $\frac{5}{8}$ m. NE of Berrington Hall, S of Lower Ashton Farm. Two low mounds. On one the base of a round tower.

BIDNEY FARM see DILWYN

BIRLEY

4050

ST PETER. W tower of c.1200 etc. The lowest windows are entirely Norman, but the tower arch has primitive crocket capitals and fillets down the semicircular responds, two features extremely unlikely before 1200. The arch is pointed and double-chamfered. Tower top with a slightly projecting shingled bell-stage and a pyramid roof. Plain Norman nave S doorway, but lancets on the S and the N sides as well. Chancel C13, see the lancet windows. Only the chancel arch is clearly of the C14. Fine tripartite responds. The S capital with dogs' heads. The shafts of the E face of the arch interrupted by bands with small human heads. Ballflower in the W face of the arch. Perp addition of a S chapel. It is very handsome, with its wide, straight-headed four-light windows. The roof and the timber-framed gable of the chapel are later. Arched braces to collar-beams; cusped wind-braces. – FONT. Norman, with rather disconnected bands of various decoration: saltire crosses, chain, intersected arches, and a kind of incised plait. – PULPIT. 1633. – PLATE. Paten, Dublin, 1725; Chalice, London, 1793.

(MIDDLE HILL, $1\frac{1}{4}$ m. NE. The house still contains one bay of a C14 hall and the C14 E cross-wing. The roof truss of the hall is of the cruck-type with a collar-beam and three foiled openings above it. Exposed square framing on the N side of the cross-wing. RCHM)

6040

BISHOP'S FROME

ST MARY. C14 W tower with diagonal buttresses. The W window and tower arch, i.e. the ground-stage, still of the first half, the rest later. The nave, N aisle, and chancel are all in a terribly pretentious neo-Norman, by *F. R. Kempson* of Hereford. Of 1847 (chancel) and 1861 (nave and aisle). In fact it is not even an archaeologically correct Norman: neo-E.E. elements are casually intermixed. Original Late Norman work the S doorway. The capitals of the two orders of shafts turn into waterleaf forms and even approach stiff-leaf. The chancel arch, which is also original, must be somewhat earlier. Again two orders of shafts. In the arch zigzag at r. angles to the wall surface. This motif recurs in the doorway. – SCREEN. Of one-light divisions; simple, and partially C19. – STAINED GLASS. The small, still pictorial scenes in the E window date no doubt from *c.*1848. – MONUMENTS. In a recess decorated with ballflower stone effigy of a Knight drawing his sword. He wears a mail coif, and his legs are crossed. Late C13. – Margery de la Downes † 1598. Painted. Two kneeling figures facing one another across a prayer-desk. A skeleton below. Many inscriptions, worth reading.

BISHOP'S FROME MANOR, 1⅛ m. NE. Late Georgian, of three bays and two and a half storeys. Low hipped roof. Doorway with broken pediment. Doric pilasters.

CHEYNEY COURT FARM. An outbuilding of stone is said to have been a chapel once. It now has mullioned windows. The prominent chimneyshaft is C19.

LOWER WALTON FARM, ¾ m. SW. Partly stone, partly timber-framed. The W wing has closely-set uprights. The C14 roof with foiled wind-braces is at the time of writing not visible.

(LOWER VINETREE FARM, ¾ m. SSE. The house has a main framework of four cruck-trusses. RCHM)

(WOODCROFT FARM, 2¼ m. SE. Inside a plaster ceiling with a wreath of flowers in high relief. RCHM)

BISHOPSTONE

ST LAWRENCE. One Norman S window blocked and four rather suspicious open ones in the nave W wall. Other nave windows C13 and (W wall) Dec. Late C13 transepts, *see* the typical Herefordshire three-light N and S windows. C14 S porch of timber with cusped bargeboards.* The delightful roof of the chancel with tie-beams and lively strutting looks Jacobean and is called Jacobean by the RCHM, but has been assigned to the restoration of 1842 by G. Marshall. The

---

* This comes from Yazor church.

Victorian bell-turret dates from 1854. – PULPIT. Simple, Jacobean. – WOODWORK. In reredos and stalls some C17 and C18 pieces re-used. – STAINED GLASS. E window by *Warrington*, 1843. – In a chancel s window foreign C16 and C17 panels. – PLATE. Chalice by *W.C.*, silver-gilt, London, 1621; Plate, London, 1811; silver-gilt Flagon and Salver, London, 1839; brass Almsdish with the spies carrying the grapes, in repoussé, Dutch, 1641. – MONUMENTS. John Berinton † 1614 and wife (N transept), two recumbent stone effigies on a plain tomb-chest. – Sarah Freer † 1842. With standing, white, sentimental genius. By *Peter Hollins*.

BISHOPSTONE COURT. Ruinous gateway of *c*.1600. The flanking pilasters can hardly be recognized any longer, and the arch has gone entirely.

ROMAN HOUSE, discovered during the construction of the rectory in the early C19. Wall foundations and a fine mosaic pavement bearing geometrical designs with central octagonal motif and four medallions bearing representations of urns and rayed motifs were uncovered. Small finds included quantities of Samian and coarse wares and a number of coins.

BISHOPSWOOD

5010

ALL SAINTS. 1845, according to GR by *John Plowman Jun*. With a big half-machicolated bellcote facing s down towards the river Wye.

BLACK HALL *see* KINGSLAND

BLAKEMERE

3040

ST LEONARD. Rebuilt in 1877 by *G. Truefitt*, with plenty of old materials. Nave and chancel and bellcote. Chancel s doorway of *c*.1200, with a single chamfer. Fine group of C13 E lancets. Nave s doorway also of *c*.1200. It has continuous mouldings and no decoration. Again of *c*.1200 the pointed chancel arch. The corbels on which it stands are of the trumpet-scallop type. – FONT. Circular, Norman, with a rope moulding at the foot of the bowl. – PULPIT. Made up of Jacobean panels and late C17 turned balusters (of the communion rail?). – MONUMENT. Big, handsome slate tablet of 1815. – CHURCHYARD CROSS. The shaft is preserved.

BLEATHWOOD MANOR FARM *see* LITTLE
HEREFORD

BLEWHENSTONE *see* LLANWARNE

BODCOTT FARM *see* DORSTONE

BODENHAM   *5050*

St Michael. By the winding river Lugg. The position must
have been very poetic before sand-digging started. w tower
begun late in the c13 – *see* e.g. the tall and wide arch towards
the nave with two continuous chamfers. Building continued
into the c14 (bell-openings with Y-tracery) and finished with
the funny but memorable feature of a little pyramid roof set
on top of a never completed recessed spire. The spire has at
the bottom lucarnes with Dec tracery. Dec chancel E window,
re-set when the chancel was rebuilt in 1890. Dec transepts with
big Perp transomed N and S windows. The E windows remain
Dec. Dec also the aisle windows and doorways and the N
(originally S) porch. The doorways have some ballflower
decoration. The two clerestory E windows high up are Dec
also, but must be re-set, as the clerestory cannot be earlier
than the c16. This is part of the work which also included
the heightening of the transepts and the insertion of the big
windows already mentioned and the heightening of the arcade
piers. The four-bay arcades are otherwise of the Dec period
of the aisles. Octagonal piers, double-chamfered arches. –
Font. Octagonal with thin ogee arcading, probably c14 or
c15. – Plate. Cup and small Paten, 1662. – Monuments.
Effigy of a Lady with a child standing by her side. Early c14.
– Nice Georgian tablets with urns, e.g. 1769 by *T. Symonds*,
1799, 1811 by *Preece*.
Village Cross, at the main crossing, N of the church. Only
the steps and a stump of the shaft remain of the original cross.
Moat House, 150 yds NW of the church, on its own. A pretty
black and white house.
Immediately N of the bridge a mid-Georgian brick House of
odd proportions. Recessed centre of three bays with a one-bay
pedimental gable. Projecting wings with their own roofs, just
like turrets.
Broadfield Court, 1½ m. NE. A largish and composite
house, originally probably two separate buildings. The house
proper dates from the first half of the c14, and evidence of it

are a doorway to the N with ballflower decoration on the arch and a window to the S with reticulated tracery. It is not even certain that either is *in situ*. The window, if it is, would be that of the solar.

BOLLINGHAM
3050

2¼ m. N of Eardisley

CHAPEL. Nave and chancel and bellcote. No external feature earlier than Victorian. The roof is original, i.e. C14 or C15, and has tie-beams, kingposts, collar-beams, and pointed-cinque-foiled braces. – Horrid stone FONT and PULPIT. – PLATE. Mid-C17 Cup and Cover Paten.

BOLLITREE CASTLE *see* WESTON-UNDER-PENYARD

BOLSTONE
5030

CHURCH. By *W. E. Martin*, 1877, except for the Norman hood-mould on two long monsters' heads and a pouch-cheeked apex-head (N doorway), the nice group of three small lancets at the E end, and a lancet window in the nave (S). – FONT. Jacobean, octagonal, with two pointed-trefoiled panels on each side. Three of them have a fleur-de-lis, a thistle (hence probably Jacobean), and a flower.

BOSBURY
6040

HOLY TRINITY. A large and consistent church of the transition between Norman and E.E. The W window of the nave and the doorways still have round arches; otherwise lancet windows dominate all round, and there is little of later date except for the spectacular Morton Chapel of the late C15 to early C16 with its large Perp windows and battlements and its plain – a little coarse – fan-vault and panelled arch to the N. The date may be deducible from the initials of Thomas Morton, which appear on the vault. He died in 1511 and, with a brother, took a lease of the bishop's Bosbury house in 1503.* The church has a splendid unbuttressed, detached tower, and this has lancet openings throughout. The entrance is double-chamfered

* On Thomas Morton *see* Hereford Cathedral, p. 160.

in continuous mouldings. That is C13 without doubt. But the S doorway and the impressive six-bay arcades inside still use trumpet-scallop capitals, i.e. capitals of before 1200. The arcades, however, have double-chamfered pointed arches too. Above the arcades lancet clerestory windows. Their heads seem to be interfered with. But the corbel table outside is again typical E.E. and no longer Norman. Again, if one looks at the chancel arch, it has chamfers and a roll with a fillet, yet trumpet capitals. Of later elements the S porch must be added (timber with curved wind-braces) and the single-framed nave roof. – FONT. Of c.1200, i.e. of the time of the church. On five columns, with a moulded top developing from circular to square, like late C12 capitals and abaci. – SCREEN. A large piece with three-light divisions. Big tracery. Ribbed coving. – PULPIT and READER'S DESK. With bits of the C16 or C17. – LECTERN. Jacobean. A turned stem and three volutes supporting it. – STAINED GLASS. In the chancel lancets by *Wailes* (TK), of no value. – MONUMENTS. Coffin-lid with a foliated cross, and two subsidiary crosses and a sword; early C14 (nave S arcade). – John Harford, 1573 by [44a] *John Guldo* of Hereford. Large standing monument of stone. Sarcophagus on two lions. Recumbent effigy under a coffered arch. Tudor roses in the coffers. Pilasters support the arch. Taller Corinthian columns on high bases outside, supporting a pediment. Large leaves and a roundel in the pediment. Vases with branches, shields, and a shell against the back wall above the effigy. Flowers and large leaves in the spandrels above the arch. The whole is quite a metropolitan composition, even if executed with some homely touches. The vases and branches are strongly reminiscent of embroidery. – The monument opposite to Richard Harford and his wife is dated [44b] five years later and has been attributed to the same sculptor. Nothing is more improbable. Here is a home-spun version of what Guldo had done in an elegant way. Many motifs are the same, but the treatment is wholly different. Instead of the column two uncouth caryatids, like Adam and Eve. The piers for the arch filled with branches and leaves. The effigies stiff, and hers a little above his. The back wall again with coarse branches and leaves. In the spandrels the big leaves spout out of the mouths of heads far too big in relation to the rest. Finally the pediment is segmental and again has oversized leaves and is flanked by oversized leaves. The monument may be attractive in its naivety. Nobody can say

that it is great art. – John Brydges † 1742, by *Thomas White*
of Worcester (chancel N). Inscription under opened drapery.
Flanking pilasters. Attic with a segmental top. Tablet without
figures.

Nice black and white houses round the church, notably a
complete C15 hall-house S of the church with the two gabled
cross-wings. To the N OLD COURT FARM, on the site of the
manor of the Bishops of Hereford which was leased by the
Mortons (*see* above). The GATEHOUSE survives, stone, with
a tall archway and a blocked pedestrian entrance. The archway
has a continuous double chamfer. Buttresses l. and r.

To the SW, on the main road, the CROWN INN, and attached to
it the Oak Room, with a big six-light transomed window and
panelling dated 1571. This includes an overmantel with the
characteristic blank arches so popular right into the mid C17,
and shields.

BOSBURY HOUSE, ¾ m. NE. Georgian, with additions of 1873
in the Italian style. Brick and stone dressings. Seven by five
bays with a big balustrade and a porch on pairs of Tuscan
columns.

HILLHOUSE FARM, 1 m. NE. An uncommonly pretty black
and white house on a slight eminence. Mostly of *c.*1600. With
plenty of concave-sided lozenges.

NASHEND FARMHOUSE, just NE of the former. Late Georgian.
Of brick. Three widely spaced bays, two storeys, one-bay
pediment with blank lunette, arched window below.

TEMPLE COURT, ½ m. WSW. Early C18 front of five bays and
two storeys. Brick. Segment-headed windows. Unfortunately
the centre is spoiled. There was a preceptory of the Templars
at Bosbury.

BOTTRELL FARM *see* BREDWARDINE

THE BRAINGE *see* PUTLEY

6020

BRAMPTON ABBOTTS

ST MICHAEL. Norman nave and chancel, see the S doorway
with one order of shafts, scalloped capitals, and a plain
tympanum, the chancel arch also with shafts and scallop
capitals (the arch itself is later), the renewed small single E
window, and the head of a pillar piscina. Timber S porch of
the C14; rebuilt. Timber bell-turret on a renewed, but
impressive substructure inside the church. – FONT. Perp;
octagonal bowl with quatrefoils and fleurons in them. –

PLATE. Cup and Cover Paten, 1572; Salver by *John Bathe*, London, 1711; Chalice and Cover Paten by *Edward Vincent* (?), London, 1734. – MONUMENT. Brass to John Rudhall † 1507 and wife. Only the wife remains. The figure is 13 in. long.

RUDHALL HOUSE, 1½ m. SE. The core of the house is of the C14, as some parts of the original hall-roof and the roof of a cross-wing prove. They have cusped wind-braces. But the house now appears in its most spectacular parts of the early C16. The finest portion is the N side of the W wing, which has narrowly-set uprights, a moulded bressumer on shafts attached to the posts, a deep coving with square panelling, and three bays above. The bays have been altered except for the angle shafts with pinnacles. The window of each of the three is sashed, and there are arched niches l. and r. The gables again with narrowly-set uprights and with finely decorated bargeboards. The other (S) side of this wing now presents a Georgian façade with ashlar facing and sash-windows. However, to the E of it is one original early C16 door with linenfold panelling and some decoration. The main entrance to the house was from the W into the old hall range, not the wing. The entrance is by a Jacobean stone frontispiece, not strictly a porch. Coupled Tuscan columns below and thinner coupled Tuscan columns above. Strapwork at the top. To its r. a Georgian Venetian window. The façade ends in three gables with decorated bargeboards which look early C16. Inside the house, the hall has ceiling beams with pendants. They belong to tie-beams with kingposts and two-way struts inserted early in the C16 below the C14 roof. In one room on the first floor is a chimneypiece of the early C17 with two tiers of the familiar short, stubby blank arches.

BRAMPTON BRYAN

3070

ST BARNABAS. Mostly of 1656, but with parts of the walls of an aisled older church. Also much Victorian alteration, especially of windows. The bellcote is Victorian too. The work of 1656 was done for Sir Robert Harley. His church has a very wide nave and chancel in one, covered by a double-hammerbeam roof which rests on wooden wall-posts. The details are all Jacobean in style, but the constructional system is of course still Perp. It has been suggested that the lower and more ornate timbers were taken from the castle, which was largely destroyed in 1643. – PULPIT. Victorian, but with C17 tarsia panels. – STAINED GLASS. E window and one small N window of the 1880s, according to its style probably by *Powell's*. – PLATE. Chalice, Paten, Flagon, and Almsdish by *Gabriel Sleath*, 1724. – MONUMENTS. Early C14 effigy of a Lady. She is holding her heart in her hands. The recess in which the effigy is set projects externally beyond the chancel S wall. In the recess some C14 and C15 TILES. – Second Earl of Oxford † 1724.* Large, classical wall-monument without effigy. Beautiful architectural frame with garlands along the sides and a flat urn at the top. – Mrs Sarah Harley † 1721, set up in 1724. Smaller tablet, also with the architectural surround.

CASTLE. It passed from the Bramptons to Robert Harley in 1309. Of that period the N part of the deep GATEHOUSE with two orders and a portcullis between. The N arch had ball-flower decoration. Shortly after, the gatehouse was lengthened to the S, another set of two arches with portcullis was built, and this was flanked to the outside, i.e. the S, by two round towers. Here also ballflower ornament occurs. The early C14 hall lay only 30 ft N of the gatehouse, but was separated from it by a ditch. In the Elizabethan period the hall received a two-storeyed porch with a canted front and the entry in the E side. Windows of two and three lights with mullions and transom. The stair tower at the NW end of the gatehouse is Elizabethan too.

HALL. The present Hall is a sizeable Georgian brick house with stone dressings and a hipped roof which lies a little to the W of the castle. The S front is of seven bays with a pedimented three-bay projection. In front of the W wall a porch of two pairs of Roman Doric columns.

Pretty village centre.

BREDENBURY

ST ANDREW. 1877 by *T. H. Wyatt*. In the style of 1300, rock-faced, and roofed with fancy slates. W tower with pyramid roof. Of about the same date the REREDOS (1880) with medallions with the heads of four apostles, and the alabaster PULPIT (1883). STAINED GLASS in the W window by *Charles Gibbs* (date of death 1859) and the chancel N windows by *Mayer & Co.* (1887). – PLATE. Cup, 1650. – Also, from Wacton, Cup, 1601; Cover Paten, inscribed 1615.

BREDENBURY COURT. Big, square Italianate mansion of red,

---

* Robert Harley had become first Earl of Oxford in 1711.

rock-faced sandstone. The earlier part 1873 by *T. H. Wyatt*,
the later partly 1902 (and the balustrade over the older part as
well), partly 1924. The work of 1902 is by *Sir Guy Dawber*.

WICTON FARM, 1¼ m. ESE. Of the early C16, but extended
probably after 1600. Narrowly-set uprights with some
diagonal bracing. The cross-gable with lozenges within
lozenges and cusped concave-sided lozenges.

BREDWARDINE   3040

ST ANDREW.* Unbuttressed NW tower built in 1790. Did it
replace a Norman central tower? Early Norman nave with
herringbone masonry visible on the N side and tufa quoins.
Norman S doorway of tufa except for the capitals of the shafts.
One-scallop capitals with decoration. Enormous lintel with
rosettes and interlocked rosettes even on the underside. The
N doorway is Norman too and has a similar lintel, on which,
however, in the middle, two strange oriental deities seem to
be represented. One has a bird's head, the other a monkey's
(?) head. They stand under arches. Two tufa-framed windows
on the N side as well and one on the S side and, in addition,
one framed in red sandstone also on the S side. Lengthening
of nave and rebuilding of chancel *c*.1300. Fine large three-
light window in the new part of the nave. Cusped intersected
tracery. – FONT. Huge, plain, bowl-shaped, Norman (cf.
Madley and Kilpeck). – MONUMENTS. Chancel N side,
mutilated effigy of a Knight, late C14. – Chancel S side,
alabaster effigy of a Knight, *c*.1450.

CASTLE, SE of the church and extending along the river Wye.
Oblong bailey, and at its S end the former keep, which seems
to have been of 70 by 45 ft. Further S the earthworks continued with traces of two fishponds and a trackway, along
which are two small mounds. For more details *see* RCHM,
vol. III, p. 26.

RED LION INN. Very nice late C17 brick house with hipped
roof. Five bays, two storeys, windows with a wooden cross of
mullion and transom. Steep pedimental gable.

(OLD COURT, 300 yds N. A stone house built in the C14. Two
roof-trusses of the hall remain, one the spere-truss with the
spere-posts, arched braces, a collar-beam, and traceried
spandrels, the other with tie-beam and collar-beam and much
cusping. RCHM)

* Kilvert was rector here from 1877 till he died in 1879.

(BOTTRELL FARM, about 1 m. SW. With a cruck-truss inside.)
NEW WESTON FARM, 1 m. NW. Late Georgian house of brick.
Three widely spaced bays, two and a half storeys, segment-
headed windows. Victorian porch. BARN, originally two,
later joined up to form a structure over 150 ft long. Next to it
a fine TALLAT, also very long.

4030

BREINTON

ST MICHAEL. Nearly all by *F. R. Kempson*, 1866–70, but with a
Norman window in the W gable of the nave and two re-used
heads of small Norman windows above. – STAINED GLASS.
In the N aisle E, NW, and W windows by *Powell*, designed by
H. Burrow, 1874. – PLATE. Cup on baluster stem, London,
1641; Chalice and Paten, London, 1812. – MONUMENT.
Capt. Rudhall Booth † 1685. Painted tablet with inscription
and arms; very rustic.
WARHAM. Picturesque black and white house, with an early
C16 gable with closely-set uprights.
BREINTON CAMP. An Iron Age hill-fort 600 yds SW of the
church, on a spur overlooking the Wye. Low oval mound and
traces of an outer enclosure. A sunk trackway from the W of
the mound led down to a former ford. Evidence of domestic
building in the C12 or C13 has recently been found.

4040

BRIDGE SOLLERS

ST ANDREW. Thin Norman W tower, unbuttressed, with
Norman windows and bell-openings. Unmoulded arch
towards the nave. Norman also the S doorway. Single-stepped
arch. Outer band on broad brackets: a head with two dragons
emanating from the mouth and a dragon in profile. The style
is that of the so-called Herefordshire School (*see* p. 24).
One Norman S window. N arcade of three bays, the two
eastern ones late C12. Circular pier with square abacus.
Unmoulded arch. The third bay of *c.*1300. The arch is pointed
but still unmoulded. The chancel is of *c.*1300 and a little later,
see the window tracery. – STAINED GLASS. E window by
Powell, 1871, excellent. – PLATE. Chalice and Cover Paten,
London, 1678; Salver by *M. Lofthouse*, London, 1713.

BRIDSTOW

ST BRIDGET. Perp W tower. The rest externally all by *T. Nicholson*, 1862. Inside however there are a Norman chancel arch and an E.E. N chapel. The chancel arch has good capitals carved with palmettes etc. and an arch with zigzag, also at r. angles to the wall. The arcade of the N chapel is of two bays and has a circular pier. The capitals are of the crocket type and the arches double-chamfered. – SOUTH DOOR. With large tracery at the top. Dated early C14 by the RCHM. – STAINED GLASS. Annunciation by *Kempe*, 1874, i.e. very early. The glass is indeed in a pre-Kempe style. – PLATE. Cup, 1576; Chalice and Cover Paten by *Edward Pocock*, London, 1733. – MONUMENT. In a recess a small shrine with four by two cusped arches on colonnettes. The lid has a shield and a cross under a gabled canopy and stiff-leaf decoration about. The date probably the late C13 (cf. Goodrich).

WILTON CASTLE, ¼ m. SE. Partly *c.*1300, partly Elizabethan. The castle proper is not easily understood, as the surviving parts are (at the time of writing) much overhung by ivy. The castle is roughly an oblong and had angle towers. In addition there is a tower in the middle of the E curtain. The SW corner is marked by a large apsidal projection, and it can perhaps be assumed that to its S was the gatehouse, i.e. an arrangement corresponding to that at Goodrich. In the apsidal range three openings with double-chamfered depressed two-centred arches remain. The NW tower is polygonal. In its E wall are garderobes. The shouldered lintel of the entry on the lower floor ought to be observed. The curtain wall on the N and W sides retains part of the parapet and wall walk. The E tower seems to have had a machicolated parapet. The Elizabethan house continued the SW ranges of the castle. It has to the N, i.e. the inner bailey, a canted bay window, originally two-storeyed. To the N one window with two transoms.

WILTON BRIDGE, *see* Ross, p. 279.

Close to Wilton Bridge a group of nice houses. The MARIAN SYKES GUESTHOUSE is of dark brick, five bays and two storeys, with stone quoins and slate lintels. Round the corner, to the S, the WHITE LION, dated 1779. Stone, of three bays, with segment-headed windows. The LOCKUP, also of stone, adjoins to the S. A little further S WILTON COURT, late C17, with mullioned windows. In the gable an oval plaque in an oblong panel, typical on the whole of *c*.1660–70. In the front garden base and shaft of a CROSS which was connected with the ford across the river, used before the bridge was built.

(ASSHE FARM, ⅔ m. NNW, has one cruck-truss. RCHM)

BRIERLEY COURT *see* LEOMINSTER,
p. 231

2040   BRILLEY

ST MARY. Thin unbuttressed W tower of 1912 with overhanging pyramid roof. Nave, N transept, chancel, the latter rebuilt in 1890. Most of the windows are re-done, their style being *c*.1300 to Dec. Ogee-headed doorway to the rood-loft stair-case. It is in the vestry. Nave roof with tie-beams, one with cusped raking struts and a cusped collar. Lower ceiled chancel ceiling (cf. Michaelchurch in Radnorshire). – STAINED GLASS. One chancel N window by *Barnett* of Newcastle. – MONUMENTS. Two cast-iron slabs with inscription, 1669–70. The lettering is sans serif.

RHYDSPENCE INN, 1½ m. NE. C16, with closely-set uprights.

(CWMMA FARM, 1½ m. NE. Jacobean with a two-storeyed porch. RCHM)

(FERNHALL, ¼ m. NNE of the former. The house has its original C14 or early C15 truss with cusped braces up to the collar-beam and three foiled openings above it. Also two cruck-trusses at the ends of the hall. RCHM)

(KINTLEY FARM, 1 m. ENE. Trusses of the hall roof of the C14 or early C15. Arched braces forming two central arches below the collar-beams. RCHM)

(LLANHEDRY, 1 m. NE. Remains of one cruck-truss of the hall roof. RCHM)

5060   BRIMFIELD

ST MICHAEL. Unbuttressed C13 W tower with a timber-framed top stage, probably of the C17, and a pyramid roof. Timber-framed N porch. All windows from the restoration. – FONT. C13. Quatrefoil bowl on a quatrefoil stem. – LECTERN. Of iron, in the Arts and Crafts taste. – PLATE. Chalice and Paten, London, 1637.

NUN UPTON, *see* Little Hereford, p. 236.

BRINSOP   4040

ST GEORGE. In the church some of the most characteristic work
of the Herefordshire School of Norman sculptors, dateable
to c.1150–60. Tympanum with St George, a scene more
hieratic than dramatic, with the typical pleated parallel folds.
The composition is, as Dr Zarnecki has found, dependent on
Parthenay-le-Vieux in the west of France. From the west of
France also comes the radial arrangement of the sculpture in
the voussoirs of the arches, the arch belonging to this tympanum, and the inner and outer arches of a N doorway. In the
wedge-shaped panels are human figures with long pleated
skirts standing under arches, animals, a beautifully composed
angel flying down, Sagittarius, knots, etc. They are very
similar to those at Rowlstone. The small church itself dates
from c.1300–50. Nave and N aisle and little Victorian bell-
turret. The arcade is of four bays with circular piers, octagonal
abaci, and double-chamfered arches. E pier and E bay differ
a little and represent a lengthening. S doorway with the
characteristic sunk-quadrant mouldings. Windows with
Y-tracery and the typical Herefordshire arrangement of three
lights with lancets l. and r. and the middle light simply a
taking-up of the mullions to the main arch. – REREDOS.
Alabaster and gold and large figures. Also rood figures,
ceilure, and several STAINED GLASS windows. All by *Comper*,
c.1920–8. – STOUP. Perp, octagonal, with a small frieze of
quatrefoils. – SCREEN. Simple and much restored. – SCULP-
TURE. Two fragments of early sculpture: a Norman fragment
of a frieze of birds in scrolls, four scrolls in two tiers being
preserved; and a small part of an interlace frieze, in the N
chapel at the NE corner, Norman or Saxon. – PAINTING.
Wall painting of the Annunciation and Visitation, c.1300,
much defaced (chancel S), and of the Crucifixion, c.1330–40
(nave, above the S door). – STAINED GLASS. Two beautiful
early C14 panels in the E window, especially a St George. –
Also a very small contemporary seated Christ in the N aisle
NW window. – PLATE. Chalice, London, 1812. – MONU-
MENTS. A coffin-lid of the C13 with an interesting foliated
cross, the shaft undulating like a vine. Symmetrical stiff-
leaves l. and r. in quatrefoils (N chapel). – Another coffin-lid
with a very closely foliated cross is in the vestry. – William
Dansey † 1708. Tablet with two putti.
BRINSOP COURT. A felicitously preserved C14 mansion of

red sandstone with some later timber-framed work. The house originally belonged to the Tirrel family. It is built round an oblong courtyard, and only the E wing is recent work (1913). The N range is of the C14 with original, small, mostly two-light windows, some with the familiar sunk-quadrant mouldings, some with the equally familiar, slightly earlier cusped lights. To the W this range has a large two-light window with transom. Then follows some C16 timber-framing with narrowly-set uprights, and after that timber-framing of c.1700. The S range is the hall range. The windows here are ogee-headed or have reticulation motifs. The court-yard fronts demonstrate the same building periods. The hall range has the same windows and an outer staircase leading to the cusped ogee-headed doorway into the hall, which is on the upper floor. The work of 1913 is all narrowly-set timber-framing. The N range has windows like those to the N, but at its W end also timber-framing. The W range is here Georgian and brick-faced. Of interiors the most impressive is the hall with its splendid original open roof. Cambered tie-beams and kingposts, that is originally a South-East English rather than West Country type, but the foiled four-way struts making pointed trefoiled shapes with the foiled principals are decidedly West Country. Large fireplace with shouldered lintel. Stone window-seats. The stucco ceiling in the adjoining room is a C20 imitation. Jacobean overmantel with caryatids (from Mildmay House, Clerkenwell, London). Stone window-seats also in the NW room on the first floor. This room has a doorway in the NW corner, as has the room below it, proof that there was originally a staircase turret here. The house stands most picturesquely in a wood.

BROADFIELD COURT *see* BODENHAM

BROADWARD HALL *see* LEOMINSTER,
p. 231

3040
BROBURY

ST MARY MAGDALENE. The chancel only remains, and this also is abandoned. The tracery forms are of c.1300. In the S wall a tomb recess with two orders of fleurons; C14.

BROCKBURY *see* COLWALL

BROCKHAMPTON-BY-BROMYARD   6050

NEW CHAPEL. In the grounds of Brockhampton Park. By *George Byfield*, c.1798. In the Gothic style and prettier from outside than inside. Of grey stone, with a small, embraced W tower with tall pinnacles. The windows are Perp, with the simplest tracery, its bars and the mullions having to the outside a circular moulding. Flat buttresses. Battlements, even on the E gable. Thinly ribbed, coved ceiling inside. – REREDOS with mosaic of 1897. – STAINED GLASS. The large Christ from a Transfiguration, now in the SW window, is no doubt of c.1800. – PLATE. Chalice and Cover, London, 1672, a fine piece, really a porringer; Flagon, by *H.P.*, London, 1729. – MONUMENTS. Edmund Higginson † 1798, with a big standing female figure holding a medallion. – Lydia Bulkeley † 1812, with a mourning female figure. Signed by *Bacon Jun.* – John Barneby † 1817. With a standing female figure by a sarcophagus.

BROCKHAMPTON PARK. Mid-C18 house of red brick, sadly altered in its details probably about 1860. The house is of seven bays and has a three-bay pediment. Doorway with pediment on corbels. The window above it with side volutes. Inside some original panelling etc.

    LODGE to the E of the house, on the Worcester road. Temple front of four slim Tuscan columns with a pediment.

OLD CHAPEL. To the W of Lower Brockhampton House. In ruins. Norman. The walls of large tufa blocks. C13 chancel with some lancets. The E window is Early Perp.

LOWER BROCKHAMPTON HOUSE, ¾ m. N, down at the bottom 32b of the little valley, in the woods. Extremely pretty, timber-framed gatehouse of the later C15. Angle posts with moulded capitals. The brackets of the oversailing upper floor stood originally on thin twisted shafts. Narrowly-set uprights, with a few diagonal braces. The bargeboards with vine trails, those towards the house in their original state. DOOR original, studded, and with a very low wicket. The house faces the gatehouse with a late C14 range and the gable of a contemporary cross-wing. The corresponding wing on the l. has disappeared. The remaining wing has all narrowly-set uprights. In the lower range was the original hall. The spere-truss survives, i.e. the timbering into which the screen was fitted. It is characterized by the two speres, vertical posts set wide enough from the wall to allow for the original entrances to go through. The rest of the hall has one cruck-truss and several collar-beams with foiling above them. Also one tier of foiled wind-braces. House and gatehouse are nearly entirely surrounded by a moat.

HOME HOUSE FARM, 1½ m. NE. Stone house of the early C17 with a timber-framed porch. In the gable diagonal trellis strutting.

⁵⁰³⁰   BROCKHAMPTON-BY-ROSS

HOLY TRINITY, S of Brockhampton Court. In ruins and shrouded in ivy. Of the W tower no details at all can be seen. The clearly visible E window is not original. – In the churchyard CROSS with preserved steps, base, and stump of the shaft.

ALL SAINTS. By *W. R. Lethaby*, 1901–2, and one of the most convincing and most impressive churches of its date in any country. Lethaby belonged to the Arts and Crafts, i.e. he was a follower of William Morris in his faith in the spirit of the Middle Ages, his faith in a rational approach to a job, his interest in the materials he used, and his fearless consistency. He wrote a biography of Philip Webb and was one of the founders of the Design and Industries Association. So he used concrete* at All Saints for the vaulting of chancel and transepts, but not for the piers and arches, which are of stone, and he gave the church a medieval character without anywhere imitating the past.

Brockhampton church consists of a nave, short transepts, a crossing tower, a chancel, and in addition a SW porch tower. The crossing tower ends bluntly, but has a stair-turret that rises a little higher. The porch tower has a pyramid roof. The church is thatched otherwise, the reason perhaps for the use of concrete. Windows, where they approach Gothic patterns, are straight-headed and have for the individual lights triangular instead of arched heads. But the big S transept window is just an oblong and has a lattice of concrete bars instead with an ogee shape only in the top lozenge. In the crossing tower also there are windows which are square with a lozenge and 64 two ogee curves set in. The dominant motif inside – to which the porch is the overture – is the steep pointed tunnel-vault with transverse arches. Apart from the porch, it appears in the nave, chancel, and transepts. The crossing arches have the

---

* Not re-inforced concrete.

same extremely steep form and consist of two chamfered orders simply dying into the imposts. This creates an emotionally very powerful impact – Expressionist in the sense in which Central Europe designed churches about 1920. What was Lethaby's source for this motif, or was it conceived entirely originally? His master and friend Norman Shaw had used round arches somewhat similarly at Adcote in Shropshire. Much more similar are the refectories, dormitories, etc. in some South French and Catalan abbeys, notably Poblet, but is Lethaby likely to have known them? So probably the arches at Brockhampton are essentially original. Inside a number of details are entirely original, notably the cylindrical shafts set in the reveals of the nave and chancel windows, in the former two deep. In the s porch, above the s doorway five carved panels, a cross and four birds. They also are noteworthy. The church was built by Alice Madeleine Foster in memory of her parents Eben D. and Julia M. Jordan.

FURNISHINGS. FONT. Designed by *Lethaby*. With two interwoven friezes of vine in shallow relief, very Early Christian. Lethaby had written a detailed, learned book on St Sophia in Constantinople. – SOUTH DOOR. With pretty ironwork. – TAPESTRY. Two angels designed by *Burne-Jones* and made by *Morris & Co.* The design goes back to c.1875 and was originally for stained glass (Salisbury Cathedral). – ALTARPIECES. One Flemish, early C16, with relief scenes in the centre and painted wings. – Another very small, painted, with the Virgin and two Saints, Sienese (?), C15. – Also a late ICON. – STAINED GLASS. E window by *Whall*, six saints and angels. The s transept window by the same is of 1916 and has turned all sentimental. By the same also the w window, also later. – PLATE. Cup on baluster stem, 1637.

LYCHGATE. With massive semicircular supports and a thatched roof. – The PLANTING of creepers against the church deserves special notice.

BROCKHAMPTON COURT HOTEL. The core of the house was of the late C18 rectory. The tower is dated 1893, the older part to the r. 1879. This latter is by *Middleton & Sars*.* The architect of 1893 was *Faulkner Armitage* of Manchester, his clerk of works *Barry Parker*. The whole is a big composition in a neo-Tudor style, decidedly pre-Lethaby. Much sculptural decoration. The LODGE towards Lethaby's church is in a florid imitation-Jacobean black-and-white.

* Information kindly given me by Mr G. Spain.

BROMYARD

ST PETER. The church represents a cruciform Norman church, though the crossing tower in its present form belongs to the C14 – see the four crossing arches inside and the Y-tracery of the bell-openings. The tower receives its specific character from the circular NE stair-turret with its castellated top. Norman are the spectacular S and N doorways, and in addition the masonry of the transepts (see the small N doorway). The main Norman doorways are re-set. They have three orders of shafts with primitively decorated capitals (one face, fingers in mouth, on the S side), arches with lozenge, rosette, and zigzag at r. angles to the wall. The N doorway has an imitation-Norman tympanum: part of the genuine S tympanum has been cut away. Above the S doorway a panel with the figure of St Peter in flat relief. Otherwise the exterior is mostly early C14. In the chancel Y-tracery, in the transept E sides intersected tracery, uncusped and cusped, etc. Only the N transept N window must still be of before 1300, and the nave W window is not C14 Dec but Victorian Dec. The interior is impressive with its high early arcades, but the slender piers were heightened in 1805. There are five bays. The S arcade is a generation or half a generation earlier than the N arcade, but both are later than the doorways. On the S side circular piers, trumpet-scallop capitals, circular abaci, single-step arches; on the N side circular piers, capitals with an odd mixture of vestigial trumpets and leaf crockets, quatrefoil abaci, double-chamfered arches – i.e. S c.1190, N c.1210. The N arcade incidentally ends in a narrower arch and a piece of Norman walling. – FONT. Norman, of tub-shape, with two tiers of decoration, a large flat zigzag below, a tree of life (?) and a running-scroll motif above. – PLATE. Paten on foot, 1677. – MONUMENTS. The church has inside and outside a remarkable number of tomb recesses, all of the C14 (S transept and S aisle external, N transept N, S transept S, N aisle two, S aisle two, all internal). – Nice late C18 tablets. – CURIOSUM. A metal BUSHEL with the inscription 'The Bromyard Bushall by Act of Parl 1670' etc. Bowl on four short feet and with two handles (N aisle W).

CONGREGATIONAL CHAPEL, Sherford Street. Early C19. With a pyramid roof, segment-headed windows, and a doorway with Tuscan columns and a metope frieze. The building is of stone cut to brick size.

PERAMBULATION. Bromyard lies in a dip, and the church does not immediately border on any of the main streets. The perambulation starts s of the church in Church Street. At its w end, at the corner to the Market Place, BIBLE HOUSE, black and white and in no detail demonstrating its late date: 1685. Round the corner in the little MARKET PLACE the HOP POLE HOTEL, which has an early C19 front with a Tuscan porch and two canted bay windows. Behind it in ROWBERRY STREET a timber-framed C16 house with gables l. and r. From the Market Place first s, down SHERFORD STREET with SHERFORD HOUSE halfway down (Georgian, red brick, five bays, two and a half storeys, alas with an incongruous long porch), and then at the bottom BRIDGE HOUSE, black and white with a trellis in the gable and diagonal bracing below it. Then N from the Market Place along BROAD STREET. Mostly honest modest brick, but the FALCON HOTEL timber-framed, with closely-set uprights and some diagonal bracing. Inside the BOOK SHOP opposite a minor Jacobean plaster ceiling with fleurs-de-lis, roses, and birds. Down to the w, at the foot of PUMP STREET, the best house in Bromyard, TOWER HILL HOUSE, built in 1630. To the N narrowly-set uprights and in the gable lozenges within lozenges and cusped concave-sided lozenges. Towards the street two-storeyed gabled porch. The ground floor open with two posts. Back and now along the HIGH STREET. The BAY HORSE INN has closely-set uprights, the KING'S ARMS an added C18 bow window of timber. From the top of the High Street to the E CRUXWELL STREET. At its end the JACKSON ALMSHOUSES, founded in 1656. Of stone, two-storeyed, with doorway and two-light window still entirely pre-classical. Opposite CRUXWELL HOUSE, Georgian, of stone, but whitewashed and with an E front with a humble pediment.

SECONDARY MODERN SCHOOL, ¾ m. SW. 1956–60 by *Robinson & Kay.*

BRONSIL CASTLE *see* EASTNOR

BROXWOOD
3 m. W of Dilwyn

HOLY FAMILY (R.C.). 1863 by *C. F. Hansom.* Dark grey stone. Lancet style. No tower.

INDEPENDENT CHAPEL. 1814 (or 1844?). Stone, with pointed windows.

BROXWOOD COURT. 1891 by *Stokes*. The house has been demolished and replaced.

(BOLTON, ½ m. SW. The house has a cruck-truss in the S wing. RCHM)

BRYNGWYN *see* MUCH DEWCHURCH

6050

BUCKENHILL MANOR
1¼ m. N of Bromyard

S front of *c.*1730, but with gables and finials which are probably Early Victorian. The Georgian work is of brick, two-storeyed, of nine bays with a pedimental gable. Doorway with segmental pediment on two stone columns with Corinthian capitals.

3070

BUCKTON

HILL-FORT. There is an elaborate multivallate Iron Age hill-fort on the W border of the parish, partly in Shropshire. The innermost citadel is of oval plan defended by double ramparts. NE of this enclosure are two further outworks enclosing smaller areas and again defended by double ramparts. The principal entrance appears to be on the W, with elaborate outworks and inturning of the main fortifications.

THE BURCOTT *see* HOLMER

4040

BURGHILL

ST MARY. A biggish church, very much renewed in 1880. The short W tower, probably originally of the C13, was rebuilt in 1812. The history of the church starts with a Norman window in the chancel N wall. Norman also the chancel N doorway with a simple chamfer. The beginning of the N arcade belongs to the same date, see e.g. the trumpet capital of the W respond. The rest of the arcade may be a little later. Circular piers, simply moulded capitals, circular abaci, double-chamfered arches. The W lancet of the aisle must be of the time of the respond. Then the contribution of the early C14, i.e. the S arcade (octagonal piers and double-chamfered arches), the chancel S windows, and the S aisle windows. The head of a bishop in the outer wall looks more C13 than early C14. – FONT. Round stem with small, defaced figures tightly surrounded by arches on colonnettes. The stem is Late Norman. Of the lead bowl the only original part is the rim with its stylized running leaf frieze. This seems to be of *c*.1200. – PULPIT. Simple, Jacobean. – SCREEN. A beautiful tall screen with one-light divisions and fine top tracery. Deep coving with ribs and bosses, so deep that Jacobean posts support it. Two bands of foliage in the cornice and a cresting. – COMMUNION RAIL. Sturdy, turned balusters; late C17. – PLATE. Cup on baluster stem, later C17. – MONUMENTS. Sir John Milbourne and wife, *c*.1440. Alabaster effigies. At the head-end of the tomb-chest three standing angels, at the foot-end two and a figure of the Virgin worshipped by kneeling figures. – Brass to Robert Masters † 1619, a traveller. Stone panel with interlaced quatrefoils. Shield in it. Inscription below and small extra plate with a globe.

BURGHILL HOSPITAL, ¾ m. SE. By *Robert Griffiths* of Stafford, 1868–72, enlarged 1900. Built as the County Asylum. Red and yellow brick. Italianate style with two symmetrically placed towers to the l. and r. of the dining hall. Above the hall is the chapel. Originally the centre parts were three-storeyed, the outlying ones two-storeyed.

BURGHILL COURT, ¼ m. SW. Late Georgian brick house of five bays and two and a half storeys. Three-bay pediment. Porch of two pairs of Greek Doric columns.

BURGHILL GRANGE, 300 yds E. Early Georgian, brick, with recessed centre and, in this, segment-headed windows. Dovecote octagonal with glazed lantern.

THE HERMITAGE, 2 m. NW. Built *c*.1830. With two shallow bow windows and a Tuscan porch.

LYNCHETS, 1 m. ENE of the church and ¾ m. E of the church. The former group of three terraces extends for over 100 yds, and is in good condition. The second group has been almost obliterated by ploughing.

BURNT HENGOED *see* HUNTINGTON

BURRINGTON

4070

A secluded hamlet in the hills.

ST GEORGE. Mostly Victorian, and according to GR the chancel by *Bodley* 1864, the nave by *Pountney Smith* 1855. But can that be so? Nave and chancel seem entirely of one design, and Bodley would hardly have carried on Pountney Smith without any personal contribution. Lancet windows. The upper part of the w tower is timber-framed and carries a spire. – PLATE. Elizabethan Chalice, locally made on the London pattern. – Paten and Flagon by *W.E.*, London, 1712. – MONUMENTS. 53b   E of the E wall six cast-iron slabs dated 1619–78. The lettering is interesting and deserves recording. The slab of 1658 has true sans serif, that of 1645–6 (Richard Knight) more elegant letters with serifs. The slabs are probably connected with the ironworks of the Knight family at Bridgnorth (*see* Downton Castle).

SCHOOL. Picturesque Victorian school opposite the church. In the hamlet a little to the N some pretty black-and-white houses.

BURTON COURT *see* EARDISLAND

BURTON'S FARM *see* WELLINGTON HEATH

BUTTHOUSE *see* KING'S PYON

3040

BYFORD

ST JOHN BAPTIST. In the nave a Norman N window and a simple Late Norman single-chamfered N doorway. With these go the three E bays of the S arcade. Circular piers, trumpet-scallop capitals, but the arches pointed and with two slight chamfers. About the middle of the C13 the building was extended to the W. The nave W wall has two tall lancet windows. Another, less tall, in the N wall. The two W bays of the arcade have wider arches and moulded capitals. The W respond of *c.*1200, however, was re-set. It was placed on a stiff-leaf corbel. Stiff-leaf also in the capitals of the S doorway. Arch with fillet on the roll moulding. Hood-mould on stiff-leaf stops. Again with stiff-leaf, i.e. E.E., the S transept arcade. Two bays, quatrefoil pier with fillets and thin shafts in the diagonals. This takes us to perhaps *c.*1240. There was more stiff-leaf than is *in situ* now, see the two rich fragments in the porch. Chancel of *c.*1300, see the typical Herefordshire three-light E window. Perp S transept window, the E window straight-headed. Finally the W tower, of 1717, and unbuttressed like a medieval Herefordshire tower. – FONT. Dated 1638. Octagonal, finely tooled vertically and horizontally. Small ornamental motifs like badges on four sides. – PAINTING. In the S transept, recently uncovered, St Margaret; C14. Background of stars. – PLATE. Salver, London, 1698; Chalice and Cover Paten by *Nath. Lock*, London, 1711. – MONUMENT. Tablet to the King family, by *J. Jenkins*, 1774.

BYFORD COURT. The main front faces S. It has three gables. The l. and r. ones are the ends of cross-wings of a C16 house and have no original windows. The middle part represents a S extension. It is ashlar-faced and has large mullioned and transomed windows of six lights. Doorway with four-centred head and some decoration above. The E wing on its E side is timber-framed and exhibits narrowly-set uprights.

(FALLSBROOK FARM, SE of the church, has one cruck-truss. MHLG)

BYTON 3060

ST MARY. On a hill, away from the road, and with views to the mountains in the W. 1859–60 by *Bannister* (GR). In the lancet style. Rather a disorderly design, especially in the placing of the clock. Against the S wall a reset Norman TYMPANUM with a lamb and cross in a niche and incised simple big knob ornaments l. and r. – FONT. Norman, of tub-shape, badly preserved. One incised zigzag band. – PLATE. Chalice and Cover Paten, London, 1571.

THE WOODHOUSE, 1 m. SE. C17, but externally mostly Georgian. Brick with Venetian windows and a one-bay pediment. (The staircase is of the late C17 and has twisted balusters. RCHM)

COMBE FARM, 1¾ m. WSW. Timber-framed. The main, that is the tall, block is of *c.*1500 and has narrowly-placed uprights and in the gable narrowly-placed diagonal struts.

MOUND, ¼ m. NNE. Small, and not rising more than 8 ft above the ditch.

CAGEBROOK see EATON BISHOP

CALLOW 4030

ST MARY. 1830 by *L. Johnson*. Nave and chancel with windows altered in 1884, and W tower with corbelled-out battlements. – (FONT. From the old church. Said to be Early Perp.) – PLATE. Elizabethan Cup.

6040

CANON FROME

St James. The church lies immediately s of the house. Unbuttressed w tower of red brick with some black diapering.
The bricks are still laid in English bond, although the tower
was built in 1680. The rest is of 1860, by *Bodley*, who was still
very young then. The exterior is indeed without merit.
Inside, the wide two-bay n chapel deserves notice, because of
its e rose-window. Also, the scissor-braced single-frame roofs
show perhaps some wish to get away from Victorian heavi-
ness. – STAINED GLASS. The glass in the rose-window,
Christ in Majesty and eight angels, is outstanding. Who
could do this about 1860? – PLATE. Cup and Cover Paten,
1670; Salver by *Anthony Nelme*, London, 1710.

CANON FROME COURT (County Secondary School). Built in
1786 (date above the entrance). Red brick, of seven bays and
two storeys, with a three-bay pediment and a crisp little
portico of four one-storeyed attached Tuscan columns with
pediment (cf. Sufton, Mordiford). The n and s sides were
49 identical. Several c20 additions. (Inside, re-set late c16
overmantel with architectural perspectives in blank arches and
allegorical female figures between them. Also two late c18
overmantels with earlier allegorical figures.)

4040

CANON PYON

St Lawrence. The exterior has not much to offer, but the
interior is interesting. Tall tower s of the aisle, c13 to c14
(Dec bell-openings). Early c14 n chapel e and nave w windows.
The other windows unimportant. The interior is memorable
for being so extremely out of plumb. It is also architecturally
rewarding. n arcade of five bays, early c13. Circular piers
and circular abaci. Capitals with stiff-leaf or crockets. Arches
with one chamfer and one filleted roll. The e respond was
shifted one bay e when, early in the c14, the n chapel was
built (*see* above). The s arcade is a little later than the n
arcade: four bays only, circular piers, abaci alternatingly
circular and octagonal. The mouldings of the arches are
unchanged. Three of the piers are propped by heavy flying
buttresses across the aisle. They seem to be as early as the
c14, and certainly not later than the c15. – FONT. Octagonal,
Perp, with a frieze of small quatrefoils. – STALLS. Misericords

with demi-figure of an angel, a pelican, a dog, the fox and geese, etc. – SCREEN. Tall, of one-light divisions. Most of the tracery is C19. – (STALLS. Two poppy-heads, one with two shield-bearers between two animals, the other with two bishops back to back between two monkeys.) – MONUMENTS. Indents of a couple of *c*.1400. They were not for brasses but for a kind of cement composition. – George Sawyer † 1753, signed by *Roubiliac*. Unpretentious, but indeed extremely good. Of immaculate white marble. No effigy. Concave back wall, and in front of it a very classically shaped, draped urn.

GREAT HOUSE, ⅛ m. E. Late Georgian, of brick, with two bow windows and, between them, a heavy Tuscan porch with metope frieze. Fine, though small, wrought-iron garden gates.

CAPLER FARM *see* FOWNHOPE

CASTLE FROME 6040

ST MICHAEL. Nave and chancel and Victorian bell-turret, timber-framed with spire. In the chancel pretty Perp ceilure with panels with diagonal ribs and bosses. Very pretty also the turret and the S porch. These two are both part of the restoration of 1878 by *B. Martin Buckle* of Malvern, and they and the state of the church give one the impression that he was a progressive architect, in the anti-scrape sense as well, i.e. in his respect for the old work. The old work is Early Norman. Its features are the following. W doorway with blank tympanum. Window above it. Flat buttress up the middle of the gable. One nave S and two N windows. One chancel N window. The squared masonry of the nave N side is character-istic of one type of Norman building. S doorway with massive lintel and blank tympanum. Priest's doorway also with massive lintel, so massive that the blank tympanum is part of the same block. Finally the chancel arch, single-stepped on the simplest imposts. All this is Early Norman: the great font is later. – FONT. The font of Castle Frome is one of the masterworks of Romanesque sculpture in England. It would arrest attention in any country. It belongs to the Herefordshire School of carvers, and seems to be its latest surviving work. The sources of the school are manifold (*see* Introduction, p. 24, also Shobdon, p. 288 and Kilpeck, p. 202). The foot of the font of Castle Frome shows that amongst them is Italy. The three tremendous crouching figures, of which only one is sufficiently well preserved, point clearly to Italy. The stem is short and the bowl very large; yet both are made of one block. On the stem loose snaky interlace, along the top of the bowl plaiting. Between them the story and the figures. The story is appropriately the Baptism of Christ. The intensity of feeling and action of St John must be taken in, the naively circular pool in which Christ stands, with its concentric ripples and its two pairs of fishes, and the compositional interplay of the hands of St John, the Hand of God, and the dove of the Holy Ghost. Then – to go clockwise – follow the signs of the four Evangelists: the Angel of St Matthew, the Eagle of St John, the Lion of St Mark, and the Bull of St Luke, the first two addorsed, the next affronted, then again addorsed. Finally, to fill the remaining space, two affronted doves. The long claws of birds and beasts are typical of the school, as is the lion's tail slung between his legs and up again. What is the date of the font? If Shobdon is of c.1140–5 and Kilpeck of c.1140–50, the work at Castle Frome can hardly be earlier than 1170. The development from long, lean to short, sturdy figures and from thin to thick folds was a universal European one during these years. – PULPIT. With plain panels; later C17. – STALLS. Fronts with some Jacobean blank arches. – TILES. Some at the back of the piscina. – SCULPTURE. In the chancel SE window, obviously re-set, a small, very crisply carved bust of a knight in chain-mail holding his heart (or an object) in his hands. What was he? A cusp? – STAINED GLASS. In the top of the nave SE window three figures and fragments of the C15. – PLATE. Cup, 1570; Cover Paten, 1571. – MONUMENT. Tomb-chest with recumbent alabaster effigies of c.1630–40. Both in the same attitude. The children kneel against the tomb-chest. – Francis Unett † 1656. Tablet with twisted columns and segmental pediment.

(CASTLE, ¼ m. E of the church, at Castle Frome. Motte and bailey. The motte is c.60 yds in diameter and c.14 ft high above the bailey. Traces of the bailey to the E and S. Sunken way along the hillside, SW of the motte. RCHM)

THE CEDARS see WALFORD-ON-WYE

CHASE WOOD CAMP see ROSS-ON-WYE

CHOLSTREY COURT see LEOMINSTER,

CINDERS see LAYSTERS

CLEHONGER   4030

ALL SAINTS. Norman stones with zigzag moulding re-used in
the chancel s wall. Also in the w wall of the nave traces of a
Norman window. Late Norman s doorway. The colonnettes
have waterleaf capitals. Keeled roll moulding. Early c13 w
tower, unbuttressed, with an unmoulded arch on the simplest
imposts. Small lancet windows. Then of about the middle of
the c13 the s arcade of four bays. It has circular piers with
octagonal abaci, or rather square ones placed diagonally and
chamfered at the corners (cf. All Saints Hereford, Madley,
and Eaton Bishop). Typically flat bases. Finally of c.1300 the
chancel, the s aisle windows, and the (re-used) N transept
N window. The N transept was built as a chantry chapel by
Sir Richard Pembrugge. He had founded the chantry in 1341.
The E window, straight-headed with three ogee-arched lights,
is probably of that date. So is the double-chamfered arch to
the nave. To the l. of the E window a bracket for an image.
In the chapel the exquisite MONUMENT to Sir Richard. Large,
in armour, the legs not (no longer) crossed, an elegant dog at
his feet. He lies slightly sideways, and his head turns slightly.
His hand lies on his shield.* All these features instil life into the
effigy. – In the same chapel MONUMENT probably to Lady
Pembrugge. A much smaller effigy. Two angels by her pillow.
A big bird pulls her cloak. – Again in the chapel BRASSES to
Sir John Barre † 1483 and wife, both very swagger, he with
his head against his helmet, she turning her bosom towards
him in a swaying gesture. The figures are 36 to 39 in. long. –
Of other MONUMENTS there is the upper half of a coffin-lid
with a handsome foliated cross; c13. – Also Herbert Aubrey
† 1671 and wife. Tablet with an open segmental pediment and
two ugly putti. – STAINED GLASS. In the nave NE window
original fragments. – In the E window glass designed by
A. W. N. Pugin in 1850 for F. R. Wegg-Prosser (cf. Belmont).‡
– PLATE. Dish, 1671; Cup and Cover Paten, late c17.

CLIFFORD   2040

ST MARY. The church and churchyard are in a veritable wood.
Big unbuttressed w tower, mostly of the c18. Nave and

* An interesting detail of his armour is the so-called ailettes behind his
shoulders.
‡ Information kindly provided by Mrs Stanton.

chancel with details of the late C13 to early C14. N aisle
added in 1887–8 (*E. Christian*). Inside the chancel on the N
side near the E wall a curious, large, round-arched recess with
a tufa surround. Can it be something Norman, re-erected? –
PLATE. Cup and Cover Paten, 1710; Salver by *William
Gamble*, London, 1710. – MONUMENTS. Oaken effigy of a
Priest, *c.*1300, very similar to the effigy of Bishop Aquablanca
at Hereford. – Thomas Stallard Penoyre † 1821. By *Reeves* of
Bath. – Francis Rigby Broadbelt Stallard Penoyre † 1827.
Signed by *Bacon*. With two allegorical female figures by an
urn, one standing, the other kneeling.

CALVINISTIC METHODIST CHAPEL, ⅜ m. ENE. Built in
1827. Stone, small, with arched windows and a half-hipped
roof.

CASTLE, ⅔ m. NW of the church, on a cliff above the Wye. The
castle belonged to the Clifford family in the C13, to the
Mortimers later. It is 3½ acres in size. The motte lies on the
W side of the earthworks, the bailey to the E, and a smaller
bailey to the W. The motte rises about 36 ft above the bottom
of the ditch. On the motte a polygonal shell-keep with five
semicircular projections. The two to the E belong to the
gateway. The W projection is the one best preserved. On the
N side of the keep lay the hall range, probably of two storeys.
In the middle of the E bailey traces of a gatehouse with round
turrets to the W and a square tower to the E. All the stone
masonry seems to date from the early C13.

PRIORY FARM, ⅜ m. SSE. On the site of the Cluniac Priory
founded in 1129–30. The farm building is of stone and consists of two parts, a C14 range and an early C18 range of ashlar
with hipped roof. In the basement of the latter a re-set C13
doorway with a continuous filleted roll moulding. In the old
range the roof with cusped wind-braces.

(OLD CASTLETON, 2 m. ENE of the church, by the Wye.
Motte and bailey castle, the motte rising 30 ft on the N but
only 9 ft above the bailey. This is of crescent shape. The whole
area of the castle is 4½ acres. It includes two platforms, E and
W of the bailey, beyond the ditch. They are natural, but were
artificially steepened. RCHM)

(NEWTON TUMP, 2¾ m. ESE of the church. Bailey in the form
of a quarter circle, motte in the NW corner, of oval shape,
*c.*17 ft high. Entrance to the bailey from the S. Another ditch
runs W–E to the S of the bailey. The total area is c.1¾ acres.
RCHM)

CLODOCK

St Clodock. Long Norman nave with two N windows. Latest Norman also the chancel arch. This is remarkably wide and tall. It has one order of shafts with scalloped capitals, but already a pointed double-chamfered arch. Divers other windows, including the chancel E window of three lights and typical Herefordshire design. Unbuttressed late medieval W tower. – PULPIT. Three-decker with tester. To the l. and r. of the back panel handsome openwork foliage carving. The whole is probably of the ending C17. – PEWS. Just panelled, and going with the pulpit. Yet, though one is dated 1701, others are 1660 and 1668. – STALLS. With rustically carved ornamental panels of an earlier style. The date inscribed is 1657. – COMMUNION RAIL. Late C17. One of the relatively rare three-sided ones. – WEST GALLERY with staircase. Of about 1715. – PLATE. Chalice, probably by *Edward Pocock*, London, 1732. – MONUMENTS. Behind the pulpit an extremely interesting slab with a funerary inscription assigned to the C9. It reads (in Mr Ralegh Radford's and Mr Duffy's interpretation) as follows:

> *Hoc tumulum retine(t)*
> *Membra pudic(a) (mu)lie(ris)*
> *Guindda car(ae) coniu(gis)*
> *Quae fuit ipsa (ib)idem*

The last line is obscure. – Several enjoyable slate tablets in the chancel.

WATER MILL. The impressively large wheel was made at Leominster in 1868. The mill machinery inside is also preserved. 2b

(THE MOUND, ⅓ m. N. Motte and bailey. On a spur. Motte *c.*51 yds in diameter and over 30 ft high above the bottom of the ditch. Roughly crescent-shaped bailey to the NE. RCHM)

TY MAWR, ½ m. SSW. The present barn, former hall, has cruck-trusses and wind-braces forming large two-centred arches.

COBHALL *see* ALLENSMORE

CODDINGTON

ALL SAINTS. Early C13 (dedication of three altars 1231) and a W tower of 1865 by *Kempson*. The tower has a broach spire.

The early work has lancet windows, e.g. the two long ones in the E wall, but doorways still with round arches. The chancel arch is on corbels with individual upright stiff-leaves. Double-chamfered arch. Roof with collar-beams on arched braces forming two-centred arches. Is this C13 or C14? – CHURCHYARD CROSS. With steps, base, and shaft.

CODDINGTON COURT. Late Georgian, of brick. Five bays, two and a half storeys, low hipped roof. Three-bay pediment. A blank arch comprises the doorway (with Tuscan columns) and the window above.

COLLINGTON

ST MARY. 1856 by *A. E. Perkins* of Worcester. Nave and chancel; bellcote on the E gable of the nave. – FONT. C13? Octagonal, with pointed arches on colonnettes. – PLATE. Cup and Cover Paten of 1570; specially good.

NETHERWOOD, 1¼ m. NW. The refronted façade faces a weeping cedar-tree and pretty timber-framed outbuildings. The façade is a rebuilding in brick of *c.*1780, of three widely spaced bays with broad segment-headed windows. Two and a half storeys, the top windows lunettes. One-bay pediment. Inside some C16 linenfold panelling brought in from a house in Wales. At the back an early C16 range, originally perhaps independent. It has closely-set uprights. In the garden a circular stone DOVECOTE, perhaps medieval.

COLWALL

ST JAMES. Late Norman S doorway. The colonnettes have trumpet-scallop capitals. E.E. S arcade of five bays with circular piers, circular abaci, and double-chamfered arches. The W respond has a band of heads, the first pier single upright stiff-leaves, the second four sprigs of stiff-leaf and four heads, the others are moulded. Water-holding bases. Lancet E window. The tower stands on the SW. It is C14 below, Perp above. Neo-E.E. chancel of 1865 by *Woodyer*, with an arch emphatically bigger and better than the C13 would have done its E.E. N aisle 1880. Handsome nave roof with collar-beams on arched braces and two tiers of wind-braces, the lower cusped. – PULPIT. Jacobean, with blank arches. Back panel and tester are preserved. – TILES. One with a digging labourer, N aisle N wall. Fragments on the sill of the next window. Probably late C13 and part of the labours of the months. – STAINED GLASS. In the N aisle two windows of 1881 by *Kempe*. – BRASS. Elizabeth Harford † 1590. Oblong panel with standing figures. – John Walweyn, 1587. Stone tablet, heraldic. – CHURCHYARD CROSS. With steps, base, and the stump of the shaft.

PARK FARM, E of the church. Timber-framed with brick-nogging. Narrowly-placed uprights and in the NE gable diagonal bracing.

OLD COLWALL, ½ m. WSW. Early C18, of six bays and two and a half storeys; roughcast. Staircase with twisted balusters, earlier, it seems, than 1700.

HOPE END, 1¼ m. SW. The house was burnt in 1910, but the STABLES with their strange Islamic details remain. The posts with their ogee tops are even more telling than the arched gateway with its pinnacles and cupola.

BARTON COURT, 1 m. S. Georgian, red brick, hipped roof. Six bays with a pediment over the third bay, as if there were five and not six. Lunette window, Venetian window below. Later porch.

BROCKBURY, ½ m. SE. Built in 1698 (or 1738?). Brick, of seven by five bays with a hipped roof.

PERRYCROFT, 1¾ m. ESE, off the road from Upper Wyche to 63 the British camp. By *Voysey*, and one of his earliest houses in the country. Designed in 1893 and completed in 1894. Quite a simple front, long, to enjoy the superb view. The battered buttresses at the angles, the roughcast, the plain massive chimneystacks, the horizontal windows, the pretty oriel on a bracket are all favourite motifs of Voysey. The entrance side has the windows on the upper floor in long bands. It is amazing how un-Victorian this unpretentious, sensible, graceful character is. The interior is uncommonly well preserved – all the woodwork white, the chimneys with Italian marble in white wooden surrounds, two with long, slender, very tapering columns to support the mantelshelf. The door furniture etc. is by Voysey too. There are also original *Morris* wallpapers. – The outbuildings were altered and enlarged later: the stable in 1903, the coachman's cottage in 1907, the lodge in 1914.

HILL-FORT. The Iron Age fort on Hereford Beacon is large 3a and multivallate. It encloses an irregular area of 32 acres. The outer fortifications have the unusual feature of the ditch inside the rampart, the earthwork following the contours of the hill. The innermost defences consist of an oval earthwork with entrances on the NE and S.

ROUND BARROWS. 1¾ m. E of the church are two round barrows, both about 34 ft in diameter and 3 ft high. Both have depressions in their tops, suggesting that they have been opened, although there is no record of the excavation.

7040

CRADLEY

ST JAMES. Largely of 1868–70. The chancel 1868 by *Sir G. G. Scott*, the nave restored and the N aisle added in 1869 by *Perkins*. Quite big, but simple. In the W tower one Norman S window. The tower arch looks as if the scalloped capitals might be Norman, but the slender tripartite filleted responds and the pointing of the single-stepped arch are E.E. Norman S doorway with one order of shafts with scalloped capitals. Zigzag in the arch. Two-light Dec windows in the chancel. – FONT. On a baluster. 1722, and rustic. – CHEST. Extremely long chest (9 ft 3 in.) with iron hinges. – WOODWORK. Parts of the stalls C15. – Near the doorway what seems to be a Jacobean overmantel. – SCULPTURE. On the N wall of the tower outside a length of an Anglo-Saxon frieze with crockets in alternating directions. – Also two little C17 figures, kneeling, no doubt from a monument. – PLATE. A good brass Almsdish of the C18 with the spies carrying the bunch of grapes. – Communion Sets for the sick, 1817 and 1836.

LYCHGATE. Timber-framed; medieval.

PARISH HALL (former school). Timber-framed, C15; an oblong with oversailing upper floor and with moulded bressumers. The windows are all the restorer's work.

RECTORY. Late Georgian, of three bays and two and a half storeys. Doorway with Tuscan demi-columns and a broken pediment. A big robinia in front.

Nice black and white cottages to the S and N of the church.

BARROW MILL, 1¾ m. N. Timber-framed. Jacobean porch with balusters. Staircase with heavy, oblong, pierced balusters.

LOWER NUPEND, 1 m. NW, at Nupend Farm. The exterior Late Georgian, of four wide bays and two and a half storeys, the half-storey having lunette windows. Inside however a room with a Jacobean plaster ceiling. Simple, rustically treated motifs such as series of wavy lines and fleurs-de-lis.

CRASWALL   *2030*

ST MARY. Nave and chancel and bell-turret. The w part of
the church is used as a lobby and vestry. It was cut off by a
wall in the C18. Original Perp chancel windows with ogee-
headed lights and straight tops. The chancel roof has in the
E bays some foliage decoration of the purlins. An outer seat
runs along the E and S sides of the chancel and the E side of
the S porch. The *Shell Guide* suggests Partrishow as a comparison.

To the N of the church a former COCKPIT.

CRASWALL PRIORY lies 1 m. NW of the church, off the new
road to Hay by a gate marked Abbey. The priory belonged
to the rule of Grandmont, which had only three houses in
England. It was founded *c.*1220–5. The ruins are not at all
looked after, and trees and undergrowth are gradually destroy-
ing them. The plan in the volume of the RCHM is certainly
much more telling then the site itself. The church was only
108 ft long and had neither aisles nor transepts. The E end
was apsed. The S wall of the nave and chancel still stands
quite high up, and the apse walls also are easily recognized.
The doorway from the apse to the S into the sacristy is equally
evident. The sacristy was the N apartment of the E range along
the cloister. It was followed as usual by a passage and then
the chapter house. The shafted entrance to this and the
shafted windows l. and r. of it are there, and inside it can be
seen that there were two circular piers dividing the rectangular room into six vaulted bays. Piers, responds, and
doorway shafts have 'water-holding' bases, and shafts are in
several cases provided with fillets.

(The BARN of COURT FARM, ¼ m. N, has cruck-trusses, as has
the former hall of the C15 MIDDLE BLACKHILL FARM,
2¼ m. SSE. RCHM)

CREDENHILL   *4040*

ST MARY. Unbuttressed C14 W tower with concave-sided
pyramid roof. W doorway and tower arch with two continuous
chamfers. Nave and chancel. In the chancel a Late Norman
doorway (re-set ?). The chancel arch is of the early C13, very
prettily flanked by side arches. These are, it is said, Victorian,
but may replace recesses for side altars. The decorated
cusping on the E side representing the style of *c.*1300 is at any

rate considered original. The same little fleurons in the sill of the chancel NW window. Lancet and Geometrical windows in the nave, Dec windows in the chancel, i.e. late C13 to early C14. Nave roof with alternating tie-beams and collar-beams and with arched wind-braces. Tall, sturdy C15 S porch of timber (facing a palm-tree). Cusped bargeboards. – FONT. Dated 1667. Fluted bowl with elementary rosettes, etc. – STAINED GLASS. In a chancel window two beautiful small figures; c.1310.* – In the nave NE window shield with lion, shield with two figures, and other fragments. – In a chancel S window glass by *De Matteis* of Florence; un-English. In the other chancel S window glass by *C. A. Gibbs*. – PLATE. Much defaced Elizabethan Cup.

CREDENHILL COURT, to the NW. Built, according to Duncomb, in 1760. Of five bays and three storeys. Red brick, central Venetian window. Parapet and giant angle pilasters.

IRON AGE HILL-FORT, on the hill-top $\frac{1}{4}$ m. N of the church. The site is of roughly oval plan, defended by a single rampart which follows the contours of the hill. Entrances with inturned banks on the E and SE are probably contemporary. The other gaps in the fortifications appear to be modern. Trial excavations within the ramparts on the SE produced no finds other than a minute fragment of Samian ware from the surface soil.

CROFT

The big castle looms large above the church.

ST MICHAEL. Nave and chancel of c.1300 (Y-tracery). Pretty C17 bell-turret with a balustrade of miniature balusters at the bell-stage and a lead-covered ogee cap. Below, by the NW corner, a doorway of the late C17 with an oval window over. Against the chancel N wall remains of a former chapel which housed the Croft Monument. Inside, the boarded ceiling above the altar ought to be noted which used to have sky, clouds, and stars painted on. – BOX PEWS. – WEST GALLERY. Early C18. Made up of the former family pew. – TILES. Several C14 and C15 tiles, one of them dated 1456. – PLATE. Pair of Chalices and Covers by *Anthony Nelme*, 1720; pair of Patens, London, 1720. – MONUMENT. Sir Richard Croft † 1509 and wife. Tomb-chest with standing angels. On it the

---

* They represent an archbishop and a bishop. The latter is the Thomas of Cantelupe who was canonized in 1320. (Information kindly conveyed to me by Mr Peter Newton.)

effigies, he with an impressive, emaciated face. Above their heads an elaborate canopy, ribbed inside and connected with a w wall which has to the w four figures of saints in two tiers. The male figures are excellent, the female figures rather stocky. Connexion with the workshops busy at the time in Henry VII's Chapel at Westminster Abbey has been suggested, quite convincingly (Mr B. Little).

CROFT CASTLE. A large, irregularly quadrangular castle with four round corner towers. It is of the late C14 or early C15. There is little evidence to arrive at a more precise date. The windows are mostly sashed, and those which remain are of the mullioned or the mullion-and-transom-cross type, i.e. of the late C16 or C17. The entrance, i.e. E side, which seems to have been open originally, received a façade in the new Gothick taste about 1750–60. Two symmetrical canted bay windows, pointed hood-moulds. The porch was added in 1914. The house had belonged to the Croft family in the Middle Ages, and belongs to it again. But in 1746 it passed to Richard Knight, son of the Shropshire ironmaster and uncle of Richard Payne Knight of Downton Castle (see p. 117). His daughter married Thomas Johnes, and their son was Johnes of Hafod. So there was plenty of Gothickry in the family. Inside there is some Jacobean and later C17 panelling and woodwork (especially the chimneypieces in the Oak Room), but the decoration is mostly of c.1750–60. It is partly Rococo (e.g. the ceiling of the Oak Room and the chimneypiece in the Blue and Gold Room), partly Gothick. Delightful Gothick wall decoration of the main staircase, and delightful Gothick chimneypiece in the room s of the entrance hall on the E front. Gothick also the ceiling of the Blue and Gold Room.

Gothick ARCHWAY to the E; as an entrance to the grounds. It tries to appear like a fragment of curtain walling with towers.

CUSOP

ST MARY. Nave and chancel and bellcote. The w front is all of the restoration by *St Aubyn*. Norman the blocked N doorway, with an enormous red-sandstone lintel, remains of a s window, and the chancel arch, single-stepped on the simplest imposts. In the chancel a C13 lancet. – FONT. Norman, tub-shaped. Top frieze of saltire crosses. Below a trellis of lozenges. Evidently re-tooled.

(CUSOP CASTLE, 140 yds SW. Earthwork in a bad state of preservation. RCHM)

(MOUSE CASTLE, ¾ m. NE. Motte and bailey, the motte no longer circular, as it no doubt originally was. Around the motte remains of a broad ditch. Badly preserved. RCHM)

CWARELAU see NEWTON

THE CWM see LLANROTHAL

CWMMA FARM see BRILLEY

DEWSALL

4030

ST MICHAEL. Nave and chancel and bell-turret with shingled broach spire. Mostly of the restoration of 1868. The W doorway single-chamfered, probably C14.* Timber S porch of the C14. The round-arched S doorways are attributed by the RCHM to the C14 too. Why can they not be earlier? – FONT. With some ballflower decoration, i.e. early C14. – PLATE. Cover Paten inscribed 1624; Cup, London, 1799.

DEWSALL COURT, S of the church. H-shaped stone house with hipped roof. Inside an overmantel with unmistakable Jacobean blank arches. Also on another overmantel an English mid-C17 oil painting of the Judgement of Paris, in the style of Lely.

DILWYN

4050

ST MARY. Inside, at the W end, the church makes a strange sight. The W tower has its arch towards the nave only half preserved. The S arcade runs against its apex, and the other half of the arch is blocked. There can be only one explanation. The tower was built to connect with an earlier nave and chancel which have been replaced by the present one. Those former parts, moreover, were in all probability there before the tower; for there can be no more than fifty years between the tower arch, which is triple-chamfered and has inner tripartite responds with fillets, and the S (and also the N) arcade, which are of five bays with circular piers, circular abaci, double-chamfered arches, and also, on three of the four responds, tripartite shafts. The capitals of the piers differ, but all seem no later than c.1300. The exterior confirms these dates up to a point. However, the tower has clasping buttresses

---

* A consecration date of 1340 is recorded.

and Norman windows with double roll mouldings as well as, on the ground stage, little projections with lancets carrying hood-moulds with dog-tooth. That indicates that the tower was Norman and remodelled at the time of the tower arch. Recessed shingled spire. Dog-tooth also still on a bracket against the E pier of the S arcade. The aisle windows, those on the S side larger than the others, have tracery characteristic of the late C13 or c.1300 (quatrefoils in plate and in bar tracery, cusped lights, etc.). The nave has a clerestory as well, though larger Perp windows have probably replaced the original ones of c.1300. These were set above the spandrels, not the apexes of the arches. But the two circular E windows must belong to the heightened clerestory. Are they perhaps re-used material? The chancel was built at the same time as the nave and aisles, see the chancel arch, which, to confirm what has been said before, has details still remarkably near to those even of the tower arch. The E window is of three lights, the middle one cinquecusped, the others with three cusps. Large pointed trefoil at the top. Cusped shoulders to the rere-arch. The priest's doorway has a cinquecusped head. This work can be dated. In a dispute which took place in 1305 between Wormsley Priory and the vicar it was stated that the priory had 'built the chancell new'. The tomb recess in the N wall could still be of before 1305, but is more probably a little later. It has ballflower decoration up a thickly crocketed gable. Buttresses and apex carry finials. The N transept N window is completely Dec: tall, with reticulated tracery. Rere-arch again with cusped shoulders. The rest of the transept windows however go with nave, aisles, and chancel, and so the N window either tells of later completion or is a replacement. Finally, one more curious fact. The tall and splendid S porch is called Perp by the RCHM and indeed has Perp mouldings. The tall shafts with the section of hollows between shafts indicates that vaulting was projected. But along the sides are pairs of large windows of two lights with tracery of the reticulation type, and this is a motif given up when the Dec style was over. The answer is probably the Dec-Perp overlap, which is longer than one usually realizes. Niches l. and r. of the S doorway.

FURNISHINGS. FONT. With very heavy mouldings. – SCREENS. Tall rood-screen with three-light divisions, the mullions rising into the arch. The top parts are reconstruction. – Simpler and lower parclose screens with one-light divisions. – TILES. A number of C14 tiles at the w end of the s aisle. – STAINED GLASS. Elongated quatrefoil panel with two censing angels, an exquisite composition. The framing is beautiful too. This is largely reconstruction work by *Heaton, Butler & Bayne*, of before 1871. The original work is of the early C14 (chancel s). – PLATE. Cup and Cover Paten, 1662; Plate and Flagon by *Whipham & Wright*, London, 1763. – MONUMENTS. Several coffin-lids with foliated crosses at the w end of the s aisle. – In the recess in the chancel effigy of a Knight wearing a mail coif and holding his hand on his sword-hilt. The date is that of the recess, i.e. *c.*1300 or 1310. – Large slab with two indents. The figures were under thick canopies. The recessed work was not filled out in brass but in a kind of composition stone (cf. Canon Pyon). Early C15.

GREAT HOUSE, s of the church on the main road, NW of the big chestnut tree. The house is unattractive, but it has tall gatepiers with a fine wrought-iron gate. Early Georgian.

SWANSTONE COURT, 2 m. ESE. The centre of the house is of the C18. The cross-wing however belongs to the C14 and has several interesting features. Framing in large squares. In the wall between centre, i.e. original hall-range, and wing on the ground floor two decorative quatrefoil panels in the framing measuring inside the quatrefoils 7 ft. In another wall a doorway with ogee head. (The roof has cusped openings above the tiebeams. RCHM)

BIDNEY FARM, 1 m. N. The house has an adorable black and white DOVECOTE of the C17. The square framing is made more interesting by cutting out of the centres of all sides of the square little semicircles, like apses in plan.

(MIDDLETON HOUSE, 1 m. NE. With a cruck-truss and trefoils above it. C14? RCHM)

(YEW TREE COTTAGE, just N of the above. With cruck-trusses and a post which may have belonged to a spere-truss. C14. RCHM)

LUNTLEY COURT, 1½ m. WNW. Timber-framed, Jacobean, but the porch dated 1674. An uncommonly charming house. The Jacobean work has cusped arched braces in the gables, balusters in the porch, in its front as well – for it is entered on the l. and r. – and curved brackets and pendants. Attractive and extensive outbuildings, including a black and white DOVECOTE across the road, and a cowhouse with some cusped concave-sided lozenges.

(MOAT, $\frac{1}{7}$ m. S of the church. Inside the moat a platform c.165 ft in diameter. RCHM)

DINEDOR

5030

ST ANDREW. The W tower is medieval in its masonry. The rest of 1867–8 by *Kempson*. The tower has a pyramid roof. Nave and chancel. – PLATE. Cover Paten by *Richard Bayley*, London, 1716. – Paten on foot, London, 1717. – Chalice, unmarked. – MONUMENT. Francis Brickenden † 1799. By *Davies* of Hereford. Tablet with the usual urn.

ROTHERWAS CHAPEL, 1 m. N. Unbuttressed W tower dated C18 or C19 by the RCHM. It has a weird Victorian spire. Nave and chancel in one with C14 and C16 windows. Roof with tie-beams and two queenposts supporting hammer-beams with pendants. One tie-beam is dated 1589. In the W wall of the nave odd little windows in two tiers arranged to suit the roof. They now go into the tower. Rotherwas House, an eleven-bay mansion, largely of 1732, does not survive. The dining-room panelling and chimneypiece dated 1611 are now at Amherst College, Massachusetts.

IRON AGE HILL-FORT, on Dinedor Hill, $\frac{3}{4}$ m. WSW of the church. The roughly sub-rectangular area of $9\frac{1}{2}$ acres is defended by a high, univallate rampart on the N and E with a lesser bank on the W and S where the ground slopes away steeply from the fort. A single entrance occurs on the E. Trial excavations within the ramparts produced evidence of extensive occupation. From the lowest levels came sherds of Iron Age B pottery, daub, animal bones, and fragments of iron including part of an axe. Above this layer were found sherds of Roman coarse wares.

DINGWOOD PARK *see* LEDBURY

DINMORE

4050

Dinmore was a preceptory of the Knights of St John of Jerusalem. It was founded in 1189. But too little remains of it to form any picture of the establishment. What remains belongs partly to the house, partly to the chapel which lies close to it. Both are far away from any village, up a small, secluded, well-wooded valley.

DINMORE MANOR. The house is a mixture of styles and periods.

What vastly dominates is the W wing, built in 1929–36 by *Ford & Beddington* of Hereford, Gothic, and consisting of a monumental baronial hall done with much gusto, and cloisters behind it, including an octagonal corner piece and a grotto. This part was done on the example of Medmenham Abbey. The W wing is linked by a lower and humbler range of *c.*1700 to the E. block which is, it seems, of *c.*1600, but stands on medieval foundations (see the basement windows and an early C14 doorway to the S). In this block are also some re-set early C14 doorways.

Between the house and the CHAPEL were more medieval buildings, and the N buttresses of the chapel are in fact parts of walls formerly extending towards the house. The building still stood in 1796. The doorway between the buttresses is original and looks, if anything, earlier than 1190. The C12 chapel extended further W than it does now, see the stump of the N wall. Excavations have shown this missing W end to have gone on for *c.*16 ft. The rest of the present chapel, including the W tower, dates from the C14. Well profiled tower arch. The tower carries a recessed spire. S and E windows with reticulated tracery.

DIPPERSMOOR MANOR *see* KILPECK

DOCKLOW

St BARTHOLOMEW. Unbuttressed W tower. Shingled truncated pyramid roof with a small spire. Nave and chancel largely rebuilt by *Thomas Nicholson*. Straight-headed windows. – ORGAN CASE. By *J. C. Bishop*, early C19. Mahogany with brass mountings. – STAINED GLASS. E window by *W. Done* of Done & Davies of Shrewsbury, 1880 (TK). – PLATE Chalice, London, 1666.

Opposite the church a row of three cottages with pretty leaded windows.

UPHAMPTON FARM. Mostly of stone. Three-storeyed and gabled. Probably early C17.

DONNINGTON

St MARY. Nave and chancel ancient but all renewed. The windows of the types of *c.*1300. Victorian wooden bell-turret. N aisle 1862. – PLATE. Chalice, London, 1817. – MONUMENT.

E. H. Webb † 1655. Inscription on drapery. A shako and a military trophy above. By *G. Lew* of Cheltenham.

(DONNINGTON HALL, ½ m. s. Largely of 1909, by an architect supposed to be called *Ogilvy*. A Georgian core is presumed.)

HAFFIELD HOUSE, 1 m. ESE. By *Smirke*, 1818. Seven bays, two storeys, white. Portico of six improbably attenuated Greek Doric columns. Another two and two pillars flank the side entrance. In the house a lush chimneypiece of the mid C18 from Bowood Park.

IRON AGE HILL-FORT, on the hill ¾ m. SSE of the church. The ramparts enclose an irregular area of 8 acres. On the N the site is defended by triple ramparts inturned at the entrance on the NE corner. A single rampart defends the other sides, except on the SE, where the precipitous slope provides a natural defence. There is another small univallate fort of the Iron Age, on an oval plan, covering the hill 1 m. E of the church. A single entrance remains at the NE corner.

DORMINGTON

5040

ST PETER. Nave and chancel and shingled bell-turret with lead-covered spire. The windows all late C13, but all over-restored (1877, *Blashill*). C13 chancel arch. – DOOR KNOCKER. A very fine Norman piece, even if small. The head of a feline animal. – WALL PAINTING. W wall; scarcely recognizable. It represented Christ in Majesty with angels and two scenes l. and r. – PLATE. Salver by *Robert Timbrell*, London, 1715; Chalice and Cover Paten, 1745. – MONUMENTS. Margaret Carpender † 1666. Tablet with two heavily draped standing allegorical figures. Pediment with reclining putti, altered. – John Brydges † 1669. Tablet with twisted columns, an open scrolly pediment, drapery and a garland at the foot, and the following poem:

> Blest soul, whose happy mention is above
> In that quire where they only sing and love
> If Saints view humane actions then shalt see
> A griefe as great as thy loved memory
> Divided thus I'll mourn till Heaven prove just
> And once more match my body to thy dust.

DORMINGTON COURT, E of the church. Brick, yellow-washed. Of odd proportions. Tall, narrow, three-bay centre of two and a half storeys with one-bay pediment and hipped roof, and low, one-storey wings with lean-to roofs. Early C19.

3040

DORSTONE

St Faith. Largely rebuilt in 1889. Good C13 tower arch with one continuous and one dying chamfer. Good chancel E window of *c.*1300, originally no doubt with cusped intersected tracery. On the s side of the chancel one window with Y-tracery and one with Perp tracery. In the s wall, inside, a tomb recess, again of *c.*1300, and a fine double piscina with a bracket inside decorated with half-dog-tooth. – PLATE. Cup and Cover Paten, 1571; pewter Chalice and Paten of the late C13, found in the coffin in the s chancel recess.

Village Cross, sw of the church. Base and part of the shaft.

(Castle, 300 yds sw. Oval motte, 67 by 61 yds at the base and 28 ft above the bottom of the ditch. Kidney-shaped bailey to the NE with a ditch at the s side. The whole area is *c.*2½ acres. MHLG)

Bodcott Farm, 1¾ m. N. Early C16. The porch has closely-set uprights. Two gables l. and r. with diagonal braces. Closely-set uprights below as well.

(Tump at Mynydd-brîth, 2 m. w. Oval mound and enclosure to the sw. The mound is 18 ft high above the bottom of the ditch. RCHM)

3b Arthur's Stone. A chambered tomb on the ridge 1 m. NNE of the church. All traces of the mound covering the chamber have disappeared. The surviving structural remains consist of a series of side slabs of the entrance passage, which bends sharply before entering the chamber proper. The latter is of roughly coffin-shaped plan with vertical side slabs supporting a single enormous capstone over 20 ft long. 11 ft s of the burial chamber are two further stones which may either represent the remains of a second chamber or be vestiges of the retaining wall or kerb which supported the vanished mound.

4070

DOWNTON-ON-THE-ROCK

Old St Giles. In the village. In ruins. The only interesting feature still recognizable is the chancel arch, Norman, un-moulded, on the simplest imposts and as small as a doorway. The other features still mentioned by the RCHM have now mostly disappeared.

Hotel Cottage, sw of the old church. Inside a stone panel

with a very stylized lion passant, called 'medieval' by the RCHM.

NEW ST GILES. 1861 by *S. Pountney Smith*. In the grounds of Downton Castle, at the W end of a long vista from the W side of the house. In the E.E. style, with a SW tower carrying a broach spire. Timber rib-vault inside. – PLATE. Much damaged Chalice and Cover Paten, London, 1571.

DOWNTON CASTLE. Downton Castle was built by *Richard* 6ob *Payne Knight*, virtuoso, archaeologist, anthropologist in his way, prolific writer, and bad poet. He was the grandson of one of the early Shropshire ironmasters, Richard Knight of Madeley (1659–1745), who had bought Downton. There is indeed on the house a rainwater head with the date 1738. Richard Payne Knight was born in 1750 and travelled extensively in Italy in 1767 etc. He started building Downton Castle in 1772 or 1773 and completed most of it in 1778.* The house is one of the earliest contrived castellated castles and one of the earliest asymmetrically composed mansions. In both it is preceded only by the much smaller Vanbrugh Castle and by Strawberry Hill. Robert Adam's Culzean was started a few years after Downton Castle. What the two have in common, and what distinguishes them from Strawberry Hill, is that their interiors are purely classical. Payne Knight in fact argued in his *Analytical Inquiry into the Principles of Taste* in favour of 'uniting the different improvements of different ages in the same building' – an unmistakable hint at the approaching historicism of the Victorian age. The exterior, placed dramatically above the river Teme, is picturesque, irregular, and in its outline and its battlements and machicolations inspired not at all by English castles, but by the semi-fortified houses in the backgrounds of paintings by Claude Lorraine or Gaspard Poussin. Payne Knight was responsible for all of it – he did not employ an architect‡ – except for the E end, one of the round entrance towers at the NW end, the chapel on the N front, the main staircase, the Music Room, and nearly all the windows in their present form. All this is of c.1860–70. Of the same time probably the conversion of the original S entrance (W of the Pantheon tower) into a bay window. The windows were originally of a lancet kind.

* These dates and several other facts are taken from Pauline Beesly: *A brief History of the Knight Family* (mimeographed), 1958.

‡ But Pauline Beesly has found proof that *Thomas Farnolls Pritchard* of Shrewsbury went in 1772 'to fix on a site for the new building'.

The interior of the house is beautifully classical, with the principal room in the biggest of the s towers, built in 1782 in imitation of the Pantheon, i.e. circular with a coffered dome and an 'eye' in its centre. Even the niches in the wall screened by columns derive from the Pantheon. The coffers are painted light blue and gold, the columns dark red and dark green. In the niches statues seemingly of black basalt, but in fact of *Coade* stone, painted. The columns in the drawing-room on the other hand are of genuine antique porphyry. Beautiful peacock-like frieze. Beautiful fireplaces in several rooms too.

Payne Knight was one of the believers in the extreme Picturesque in landscaping. In his *The Landscape* of 1794 he attacked Capability Brown's mild and gentle layouts and pleaded for roughness and an appearance of wild nature. It was easy for him at Downton to comply; for the Teme valley is indeed wild and rugged, and all he had to do was to leave it alone. This he did, and in order to heighten the contrast, he built a terrace along the s façade of the house so as to extend the man-made part of the composition. This was done in opposition to Brown, who liked to lead his undulating lawns right up to the French windows of the houses.* What Payne Knight built of garden furnishings is only this.

CASTLE BRIDGE, to the sw. Three segmental arches; no battlements.

FORGE BRIDGE, to the SE. 1772. Surveyor *Pritchard*.

CAVE, across Castle Bridge and *c.*1200 yds w. The path runs romantically immediately above the river and even through a tunnel. The cave has windows hewn out of the rock.

(ROMAN BATHS, on the N side of the river and close to it, below the cliffs, *c.*1 m. W of the house. With vaulted chambers.)

(DOWNTON CAMP, *c.*½ m. SSE of the old church; N of the river Teme. The area is ½ acre. The entrance is on the N side. The camp is surrounded by a rampart, except on the s side, where there is a scarp and s of it a trackway leading down to a former ford. RCHM)

(MOUND, NW of the church. 22 yds in diameter and 10 ft high. RCHM)

DULAS

ST MICHAEL. Of the old church no more survives than re-assembled fragments of a Norman doorway arranged as a

---

* The VISTA from the w front of the house to the new church is of course Victorian.

garden gate N of Dulas Court. One order of shafts. Defaced capitals. On the l. abacus a small head. Arch with roll moulding. The new church was built in 1865 by *G. C. Haddon* of Hereford. It is really no more than a chapel. The style is that of 1300. – Much C17 WOODWORK, e.g. in the PULPIT (Jacobean panels), the LECTERN (late C17 baluster stem), and a DESK (small foreign panels of Annunciation and Nativity, the rest mostly English). – Also fourteen CHAIRS of the C17. – PLATE. Salver, Dublin, 1725; Chalice, London, 1809.

EARDISLAND   *4050*

ST MARY. Much renewed by *H. Curzon*, 1864. Unbuttressed W tower. Wide early C13 nave, see the small lancet windows, the S doorway with a hood-mould on stiff-leaf stops, the former priest's doorway in the S wall (before the chancel was lengthened), and the simple N doorway. Of the early-C14-looking windows in the S wall, the more ornate is of 1864. The original one has ballflower as well. C14 S porch with solid walls. Of *c.*1300 the sedilia in the chancel and also the doorway into the vestry. In the nave N and S walls, facing each other, two tomb recesses. They are of the early C14, and the latter has a finial of shields. – SCREEN, now under the tower. One-light divisions. Ogee heads with leaf crockets. Top cornice with foliage frieze. – STAINED GLASS. In the E window by *Burlison & Grylls*. – MONUMENT. In the SE corner of the nave incised slab with a foliated cross under an ogee canopy. C15.

(MOUND, N of the church. About 16 ft high above the bottom of the ditch and about 50 yds in diameter at the base. Another MOUND lies ½ m. NNW. This is not high, and only 31 yds at the base. RCHM)

Eardisland is an uncommonly pretty village, both the streets with the black and white houses, and the place by the bridge where the river widens and STAICK HOUSE looks towards it. The old trees make it appear parts of the garden of a private house. Staick House has a projecting E wing of the C17 with lozenge framing in the gable and a recessed hall range of the C14. (The roof of the latter survives almost complete. The N part of the E wing is also of the C14 and also has its roof. RCHM)* Close to the bridge on the S side lies the OLD

* Mr Clifton-Taylor draws attention to the sandstone slates of the roof and their 'swept valleys'.

SCHOOLHOUSE. At its N end the old WHIPPING POST.
Across the road from the Old Schoolhouse is the fine, tall,
four-gabled brick DOVECOTE of the OLD MANOR HOUSE.
It dates from the C17. The Old Manor House itself is C17
too, but timber-framed, though it has a Queen Anne addition
of brick, three bays, two storeys, and a parapet. Big stone
chimneybreast round the corner. Down the main street to
the SW lies KNAPP HOUSE (which has part of its original
hall roof with a cruck-truss of *c.*1400 or later. RCHM and
Arch. J., CIX, 153)

BURTON COURT, 1 m. S, dates from the late C18, but has a
Free Tudor front, an early work by *Clough Williams Ellis*,
dating from 1912, and inside the surprising survival of an
early C14 hall, open to the roof. The roof has arched braces
up to collar-beams. The collars are cusped, and there are two
tiers of cusped wind-braces. To the r. of the hall the dining
room, still Georgian. The wing behind the hall to the l. is also
Georgian. The house was victorianized by *Kempson* in 1865.

EARDISLEY

3040

ST MARY MAGDALENE. The building history of the church is
interesting and can be read more profitably from inside out
than from outside in. The S arcade consists of two parts. So
does the N arcade. The former is evidently earlier. It is also
evidently no more than a cutting through an aisleless nave.
As the arcade piers with their slight chamfers and the leaf
knobs stopping the chamfers top and bottom, and also the
unmoulded round arches, cannot be later than the end of the
C12, the aisleless nave was C12 at the latest. The three bays
of the arcade are followed by a piece of solid wall which must
represent the wall or impost between Norman nave and
chancel. In it a mysterious round-arched recess with an early
C14 moulding. The fourth bay is a little, but not essentially,
different from the first three. The unmoulded arch e.g.
remains. So this must have been an opening of the Norman
chancel wall into a chapel. The N arcade followed in the C13.
Again first three bays. Semicircular responds, octagonal piers,
moulded capitals, double-chamfered arches. Then, in the
early C14, the N side of the chancel was also opened – into
two chapels. The W arch has two sunk quadrant mouldings.
The E arch, probably intended to hold a tomb-chest, has
leaves and a finial on the hood-mould towards the former

chancel as well as the chapel. But here arises a problem. A new chancel E of the former must by then have been begun. The E window of three lights of the typical Herefordshire form can hardly be later than *c*.1300. The S windows go with it, and again the other N aisle windows are all of *c*.1300. The S aisle windows are all renewed (*E. Christian*, 1863), but the narrowness of the aisle shows that its wall at least goes with the S arcade. The tower is placed at the NW corner. It was rebuilt in 1707 and no longer has any earlier features.

FURNISHINGS. FONT. The font of Eardisley is, side by side with the font of Castle Frome, the most exciting piece of the Norman school of Herefordshire, for composition and even more for preservation. The composition admittedly is not harmonious, but it makes up in dynamic and dramatic force what it lacks in balance. The font must be of *c*.1150. It is circular and bowl-shaped. The short stem is decorated with regular knot patterns. The bowl has a plaited band at the top and below a bold frieze of events, figures, and ornament, all intertwined and with no division between motifs or scenes. The chief scenes are two knights fighting and the Harrowing of Hell. They are separated by an unexplained three-quarter figure standing slightly swaying. He has a halo and holds a book. The folds are those typical of the Herefordshire School: ropy and parallel. To his l. the two men are fighting, one with a spear, the other with a sword. The man with the sword gets frighteningly entangled with a long flag of knots and plaits. The two men are brothers of those on one of the shafts of the portal of Kilpeck. The Harrowing of Hell shows Christ energetically pulling a little man out of a limbo of twisted knots like tentacles. For no easily understood reason, the rest of the space is filled by a large lion; a splendid beast, its tail flung up from under its leg to above its head. Its long claws are also a Herefordshire motif. The figure of Christ is shorter and resembles the figures of the chancel arch at Kilpeck rather than those of the portal. The Eardisley font is thus a mixture of the two Kilpeck styles and thus presumably a little later than Kilpeck (though earlier no doubt than the font of Castle Frome). – HELMS (nave E wall). One of the late C15, the other of the late C16. – PLATE. Silver-gilt Chalice and Cover Paten designed by *Bodley*, London, 1889. – GATE. In the S porch entrance. Wrought iron. It looks early C18.

EARDISLEY CASTLE, W of the church. Motte and bailey. A *domus defensabilis* is mentioned in Domesday. Oval enclosure with the motte on the SW. (The motte is $33\frac{1}{2}$ yds in diameter and *c.*14 ft high. RCHM)

CASTLE FARM, W of the church, is a plain, nicely proportioned brick house of the early C18.

EARDISLEY PARK, $\frac{3}{4}$ m. W, is of the same date, with a later top storey. It is of five bays, cemented, and has a contemporary square DOVECOTE, CIDER-HOUSE, and other outbuildings.

The VILLAGE has a proper street, which is not all that frequent in Herefordshire. At the top, by the church, some nice black and white houses, especially that at the SE corner of the road to Almeley. This is of the C15, with traceried bargeboards on the N gable.

UPPER HOUSE FARM lies a little further N, about $\frac{2}{5}$ m. NNW of the church. The N side has some closely-set upright timbering and two projecting mullioned windows, one of them in the staircase projection. (Inside, the former hall has a central roof truss with arched braces up to a collar-beam and the moulded jambs of a doorway in the former screens passage. RCHM)

EARDISLEY WOOTTON, I m. NNW, is dated 'probably C13' by the RCHM, 'more probably C14' by Mr J. T. Smith. It has square framing, and cruck-trusses in the centre, i.e. the former hall, and in a barn close by. The C13 doorway mentioned by the RCHM is partly rotted away, but the two-centred arch remains.

PARTON, $\frac{2}{3}$ m. SE. The older part of the house is Jacobean and has square framing with brick infilling and concave-sided lozenges in the gable.

7030

EASTNOR

ST JOHN. By *Sir G. G. Scott*, 1852, except for the C14 W tower, the Late Norman S doorway with trumpet-scallop capitals, and the N arcade, whose E respond is Norman of the same type and whose piers and arches are E.E. Scott took his cue from the Herefordshire standards and used Geometrical tracery, tracery of *c.*1300, and the ballflower variety of Ledbury. – REREDOS. 1896, with the pretty carved parts from a monument bought at Siena. – STAINED GLASS. E window evidently by *Kempe*. – N chapel E by *Wilmhurst & Oliphant* (TK) *c.*1884. – PLATE. Beaten silver Chalice, 1572; Chalice and Cover Paten designed by *Scott*, 1853. – MONUMENTS. Under the tower Joseph Cocks, designed by *James Stuart* and carved by *Thomas Scheemakers*, 1778. Classical. Brown and white marble sarcophagus with profile in roundel. Two putti on the sarcophagus. – Mary Cocks † 1779, by the same. Big seated woman by an urn. A large putto on the r. Symmetrical drapery behind. – Rev. John Fletcher † 1793. Again by the same. Standing female figure by an urn in front of an obelisk (Somers Chapel). – Tablets, e.g. to John Cocks † 1771. Urn in front of an obelisk. – Also to Edward Charles Cocks † 1782. At the foot books, the square cap of a Westminster boy (he died aged fourteen), and a lamb. – Charles Cocks, Lord Somers, † 1806. By *W. H. Stephens*. – First Earl Somers. Designed by *Sir G. G. Scott*, 1855. Shrine with religious scenes in trefoiled arcading. Big sarcophagus in relief. – Third Earl Somers † 1883. White marble effigy, recumbent. By *Sir J. E. Boehm*. On a grey marble tomb-chest. – In the churchyard SEAT with reliefs by *Lady Henry Somerset* of Eastnor Castle.

RECTORY, WNW of the church. By *Scott*, 1849–50.

SCHOOL, between the entrance gates to Eastnor Castle and the village green. By *Smirke*, 1845 (or *c*.1818 ?).

WELL, on the village green. Erected by Lady Henry Somerset. With a pyramid roof on posts, but inside terracotta reliefs in the Italian Renaissance style.

EASTNOR CASTLE. By *Sir Robert Smirke* for the first Earl 61b Somers. Begun in 1812. An early work of the architect, and an early example of a serious Norman Revival. Smirke had given evidence of medieval partiality already at the age of twenty-four with the design of Lowther Castle (1806–11). Eastnor is a very large symmetrical castle with round, or rather quatrefoil, angle towers and a boldly raised centre. The castle is reached by a low gatehouse with round towers. The chivalric traditions are broken by the *porte-cochère* and the canted bay window in the centre of the two main façades. There is also a discrepancy between Norman and free E.E. windows. The centre of the castle is a great hall 60 ft long and 65 ft high, with only one row of windows high up (with Venetian tracery, curiously enough) and a blank gallery with polished columns below. The wall decoration in the medieval style is said to have been taken from a woven material at Toulouse. At the end of the hall is an octagonal room – again not a medieval conception. It fits into the canted bay and enjoys a view of the lake down below the castellated terrace. Of other rooms the most interesting is the Dining Room (now Drawing Room), designed and furnished by *Pugin*. It has a gently coved ceiling on fan-vaults, a sumptuous fire-place, and a grand Gothic chandelier of two tiers, inspired, it is said, by one that Pugin had seen at Nuremberg. Pugin's was shown at the Great Exhibition of 1851. The Library was designed by *G. E. Fox* in the Italian Renaissance style.* In the adjoining Little Library most of the woodwork comes from the premises of the Accademia degli Intronati at Siena and is datable 1646. The staircase is large but not distinguished.‡ On the upper floor the chapel has some Jacobean panelling with blank arches and excellent stained glass which looks *c.*1875. The gilt-lincrusta coving probably of the same date. To all this may be added the fact that Smirke had his roof-trusses made of iron, which was an extremely progressive thing to do before 1820.

In the grounds to the NE on a hill-top an OBELISK erected in 1812 to the memory of a son of the first earl who fell before Burgos.

BRONSIL CASTLE, 1 m. E of the church. Licence to crenellate was given to Richard Beauchamp in 1460. The castle was rectangular with polygonal angle-towers, intermediate towers, and a gatehouse. All that remains is the moat and a part of one of the two octagonal flanking towers of the gatehouse.

IRON AGE HILL-FORT. There is a bivallate rampart fort on the summits of Midsummer and Hollybush Hills, 1¾ m. E of the church. The entrances on the S and NW corners appear to be original; the former has the ramparts inturned. A number of shallow depressions within the fortifications appear to represent hut sites. Excavations within the fort in 1924 produced sherds of Iron Age B pottery. The ditch was found to have been revetted with dry stone walling.

<small>4030</small>

EATON BISHOP

ST MICHAEL. Norman W tower, unbuttressed and big, with twin bell-openings with a shaft and block capital. Single-step tower arch on simple imposts. The roof-line of the Norman nave is also still visible. No convincing explanation has yet

---

* G. E. Fox also worked at Longleat in the 1870s and at Hoarwithy church (see p. 192) in the 1880s.

‡ On it a wooden portrait medallion of Count Corsini, by *Giuseppe Piamontini*, surrounded by a rich garland. It is dated 1760, though Zani writes that Piamontini died in 1742.

been given of the break in the N and S walls and the set-back
continuation to the E which makes the tower oblong. Later
broach spire of friendly shape. Early C13 arcades of four bays.
Circular piers, octagonal abaci, or rather square abaci set
diagonally and chamfered at the corners (cf. All Saints
Hereford, Madley, and Clehonger). Double-chamfered arches.
The SW respond has a little trefoil-arched decoration. One
S pier has upright stiff-leaves. There were more, but they were
destroyed during the restoration of 1885. There were before
then also more than two head-stops to the hood-moulds.
Similar chancel arch, but the responds with a fillet. The roof-
line of the E.E. chancel appears inside the aisles. The S aisle
windows, N aisle windows, and nave clerestory windows – all
lancets – belong to the same build. Transeptal N window of
c.1300, transeptal S window Dec with an odd large ogee
trefoil in the head. The same motif in the chancel S windows,
whereas the chancel E window is still in the style of 1300: five
stepped lancet lights. The flanking turrets and their dog-tooth
decoration also forbid a later dating. The same five-light
design is repeated (correctly?) in the nave E window above
the chancel arch. – PAINTING. Some little original scroll-
work to the r. of a S aisle window. – STAINED GLASS. Eaton
Bishop has the finest Dec glass in the county, of the unmistakable Dec colour harmony of brown, green, and yellow
with little red and less blue, and of the sophisticated, highly
emotional draughtsmanship, more familiar from illuminated
manuscripts, which belong to the same style. The Eaton
Bishop glass dates probably from c.1330. The date is confirmed by the kneeling figures at the foot referring in their
inscriptions to Adam de Murimonth, Canon of Hereford,
who became Cantor of Exeter in 1328. In one inscription
the word Cantor occurs; so c.1330–5 might be the most
likely date. In the tier above the kneeling figures the Virgin, [24]
three saints including St Michael, and fragments. Above in
the centre the Crucifixion. The tall canopies are typical of
Dec glass. The trellis behind figures or scenes, in white, red,
yellow, is typical of Eaton Bishop. – More glass in the SE
window, including an angel, the Crucifixus, and Christ in
Majesty small at the top. – In the NE window small Crucifixus
at the top. – PLATE. Plate of 1749. – MONUMENT. Richard
Sneade † 1714. Tablet with twisted columns, an open
segmental pediment, and ugly putti.

MARTIN'S CROFT, S of the church. Plain, matter-of-fact brick house of *c.*1700. Three storeys, flat bands between them. Five bays.

LOWER EATON, ¾ m. NNE. Built some time between 1743 and 1796, but sadly remodelled in the High Victorian years to make a Georgian house Gothic without spending too much. The pediments e.g. remained, but were given disfiguring corbels, a loggia was added, the window surrounds were changed, etc.

CAGEBROOK, ⅞ m. S. Of *c.*1700. Brick, seven bays, two and a half storeys. On the l. a later Georgian addition. Yet all – curiously enough – in English bond.

HILL-FORT, probably Iron Age, on a promontory on the S bank of the Wye at its junction with Cage brook. The fort is of triangular plan, the principal defences being a univallate rampart on the W; the other sides are naturally defended by the steep sides of the promontory. A possible entrance exists at the NW corner of the site.

EATON HALL *see* LEOMINSTER, p. 231

EAU WITHINGTON COURT *see* WITHINGTON

ECCLESWELL COURT *see* LINTON-BY-ROSS

EDVIN LOACH

6050

ST MARY. By *Sir George Gilbert Scott.* The date seems un-recorded (1860?). To the E the ruins of the old church. When Sir Gilbert had completed his, the old church still had its roofs on. Now what remains is all overgrown, and of the features mentioned by the RCHM twenty-five years ago only the simple Early Norman S doorway with its mighty blocks of tufa and the herringbone masonry to its E can still be seen. The Victorian church is E.E. and has a polygonal apse and a W tower embraced by the aisles and severely detailed. Its E wall rests inside the church on two fat columns. Fine view to the N. – PLATE. Cup of 1571.

HOPE FARM, ½ m. N. Georgian front, partly of brick, but with a timber-framed gabled C17 porch. The sides of the porch have balusters. The first floor is carried on scrolly brackets.

WEST LODGE to Saltmarshe Castle, castellated and Victorian. The castle itself was pulled down *c.*1955. The EAST LODGE is polygonal and castellated too.

EDVIN RALPH

St Michael. In the chancel one small Norman window with
a slight rope design on the arch. In the nave a Norman s
doorway. Primitive decoration on capitals and abaci. The
arch made pointed in the c13. In the c14 the n doorway was
rebuilt with Norman materials. Unbuttressed c13 w tower
with broad arch towards the nave. Later truncated pyramid
roof and spire. Single-framed roof with one tie-beam, perhaps
for the rood. – PLATE. Chalice, London, 1800. – MONU-
MENTS. In the chancel are two tomb recesses, one with a
slight chamfer, the other with heavier mouldings. Big heads
at the top, perhaps not *in situ*. The recesses belong probably
to the two excellent monuments now disgracefully placed
under the tower. They are to members of the Edefen (Edvin !)
family. The earlier, probably of the late c13, is of husband and
wife, he with a mail coif and crossed legs. The other is of the
early c14 and represents a husband with two wives. He wears
a heavier coif, and his legs are crossed too. In addition a
miniature effigy of a lady, also early c14, and an incised slab
to Maud de Edefen, *c*.1325, with an inscription granting
sixty days of pardon to those saying a paternoster and an ave
for her.

ELTON

St Mary. The small church stands close to the Hall, and the
whole village is beautifully surrounded by hills. Norman, of
nave and chancel. Norman features are the s doorways of nave
and chancel, both simple, and one window in the chancel n
wall. Most windows c13 lancets or in the c13 style. The
bellcote and s porch are Victorian. The church was rebuilt,
except for the walls, by *W. E. Martin* in 1876. – SCREEN.
With c15 and c17 pieces. – PULPIT. Early c17. With the
usual short broad blank arches and, above them, heavy,
simply-shaped strapwork cartouches. – ROYAL ARMS. Of
Queen Elizabeth I. Carved, of wood. – PLATE. Chalice,
London, 1571; Paten (secular), London, 1775; Chalice with
swags of flowers, London, 1781.

Elton Hall. Very pretty c18 brick front of six bays with
hipped roof. The front could be Early Georgian, but the
doorway with its Tuscan pilasters and broken pediment and
the Gothick windows with their broad ogee heads look *c*.1760.

Steep two-bay pedimental gable with circular window. To the l. of the front stables and kitchen wing, C17. Thomas Andrew Knight, Richard Payne Knight's brother (*see* Downton Castle), lived at Elton Hall in the last twenty years of the C18 and up to 1809, when he moved to Downton Castle. He began his experiments in the raising of new varieties of fruit (Elton cherries) at Elton.

ELTON FARM, ⅛ m. SW. C16 to C17. Timber-framed, of H-shape. The framing makes square panels.

EVESBATCH

6040

ST ANDREW. Mostly of 1877. Small; of nave and chancel, with a timber bell-turret. One s window Dec. The s doorway with some re-used stones. – FONT COVER. A modest, very engaging Jacobean piece. – BENCHES. Some with straight-headed C15 or C16 ends. – STAINED GLASS. In the E window, by *Kempe*, an early piece to commemorate the restoration of 1877. – PLATE. Cup and Cover Paten of 1662. – MONUMENTS. Mrs Dobyns † 1658. Frontal demi-figure holding a baby. Standing allegorical figures l. and r. – Catherine Dobyns † 1710. A rustic piece with two putti on the steep slopes of an open pediment and carved roses and other flowers between the pediment and the inscription below.

EWYAS HAROLD

3020

CASTLE. Ewyas Harold Castle was one of the most important castles along the Welsh border. It was built by William FitzOsbern in the late C11. The remains are to be seen on a spur *c.* 300 yds W of the church. The motte is nearly 75 yds in diameter at the base and stands up to 42 ft above the bottom of the ditch. Kidney-shaped bailey to the E. Towards the outside steep scarp and ditch. To the SE probably the area where the small Benedictine priory stood which was founded about 1100.

ST MICHAEL. Broad, impressive C13 W tower with a big, flat clasping SW staircase extension. s doorway with double-chamfered arch. In a window above Geometrical tracery. The bell-openings twin (E) and triple (s and N) with dividing shafts. No openings whatever to the w. The tower was formerly detached from the church. Nave rebuilt in 1868 by *G. C. Haddon* (who kept the old single-frame roof) and chancel of *c*.1300. In the chancel handsomely cusped tomb recess (*see* below). Head stops and head at the apex. – REREDOS. With bits of imported carvings, including two Netherlandish, very Mannerist figures of *c*.1530 (cf. Kinnersley), and two scenes from the Passion, North German, mid-C17. – STALLS. Some have Jacobean panels. – PULPIT. Jacobean. – PLATE. Salver by *L.O.*, London, 1707; Paten on foot, London, 1791; Chalice, London, 1812. – MONUMENT. In the tomb recess, and probably belonging to it, effigy of a Lady holding her heart in her hand. Of *c*.1300.

EYE

4060

ST PETER AND ST PAUL. Of red sandstone. The W tower with its higher stair-turret dates from 1874 (architect *Chick*), but seems not to be a complete rebuilding. The earliest part of the building history appears inside. The arcades of three bays have circular piers with circular abaci and pointed double-chamfered arches. The S side with its concave-sided trumpet-shaped scallops in the capitals must be a little earlier than the N side – say *c*.1190 versus *c*.1210–20. Of the same time the blocked S doorway, round-headed with a roll, the similar blocked chancel N doorway, and the main N doorway. This has one order of colonnettes with upright leaf capitals. Again of the same time the lancet in the chancel S wall which now gives into the vestry. It is shafted inside and has a round rere-arch. Attached to the chancel on the N side is a two-bay chapel with a taller roof than the N aisle. The pier is also round with a round abacus, and the capital has big upright leaves. The arches are double-chamfered and nearly straight-sided. Hood-moulds on stiff-leaf stops. All this looks later in the C13 than the aisles. Yet a little later the chapel E windows of three stepped lancet lights under one arch. This goes with the W arch into the chapel (arch with sunk quadrant moulding on two big heads). The chancel E window seems Late Perp. And what might be the date of the nave clerestory with its quatrefoiled windows in niches? C13 or early C14? The nave roof has tie-beams, and one of them is carved with foliage. The N porch is a good late C14 timber piece with ornately traceried bargeboards. – PULPIT. The usual panels with stubby blank arches are separated by grotesque figures. The style is entirely Jacobean; yet there is a date 1681. –

BENCHES. Some with dolphin panels, dated 1684. – SCULP-
TURE. Standing angel with a shield (chancel s), perhaps from
the tomb-chest of Sir Rowland Cornewall. – PLATE. Chalice,
Cover Paten, and Flagon, London, 1727. – MONUMENTS.
Sir Rowland Cornewall (?), c.1520. Alabaster Knight on a
recent tomb-chest. – Sir Richard Cornewall and wife, c.1540.
Alabaster couple on a fine tomb-chest. Against the w end two
kneeling angels with a shield. Against the s side Annunciation
and kneeling mourners. At the N end an Early Renaissance
pilaster. – Three sons of Lord Cawley † 1914–18. Designed
by *Sir Reginald Blomfield*. In the style of Wren. With two
genii to the l. and r.

EYE MANOR. Built for Ferdinando Gorges, a Barbados trader
in sugar and slaves, known as the King of the Black Market.
He had bought the house in 1673, and there is a date 1680
above the porch. The house is completely unassuming from
outside – brick, five bays, two storeys, dormers with segmental
gables, pitched roof, late c18 windows,* and late c18 porch –
but gorgeously enriched inside by plaster ceilings in nearly
all rooms. They are of the kind with large panels, oblong,
oval, circular, quatrefoil, and of slightly more complex
57a   shapes. In the panels garlands of almost detached fruit,
flowers, and leaves, or leaf trails with little figures (e.g.
cherubs, dogs, lion, cock, greyhound, and also – in the Great
Parlour – Diana, Actaeon?, Hercules, and Hercules as a
child?) or swags. The foliage includes rose, palm, laurel, oak,
poppy. The staircase has twisted balusters, and the landing
pilasters. The floor of the Great Parlour is of Spanish chestnut.

BERRINGTON HALL, *see* p. 72

BERRINGTON HALL, *see* p. 72

4060

EYTON

ALL SAINTS. Nave and chancel in one. In the chancel one
Norman window. The others small lancets with ogee heads;
i.e. C14. – SCREEN. With small one-light divisions. Ogee
arches and quatrefoils in the spandrels. Panelled loft-coving
with bosses and two foliage friezes in the cornice. A good
piece of c.1500. – PLATE. Cup and Cover Paten, 1588;
beautiful covered Porringer with two handles, London,
1697. – MONUMENT. Joseph Coates † 1793. The fine surround
seems of very hard plaster. Urn at the top.

* Two blocked windows on the N side show that originally the windows
had stone mullion and transom crosses.

EYTON COURT, to the SW. The W range of the early C16, with
close-set uprights and oriel windows. On the W side buttress
shafts carrying brackets. Inside, the main ground-floor room
has deeply moulded beams, the room above a panelled ceiling
with many small bosses.

THE MARSH, opposite. Under a corrugated iron roof the
remains of a hall of the late C14. One tie-beam has a big
quatrefoil over. The wind-braces are foiled too.

FAWLEY
5020

ST JOHN. Norman chancel arch, unmoulded, on the plainest
imposts. Late Norman N doorway, single-chamfered. Nothing
architecturally interesting otherwise. – FONT. Of tub-shape,
Norman. The large top scallops look as if they had been
chopped about. – SCREEN. Remains only. The heads show
that there must have been two- or three-light divisions.
Traceried spandrels. – PLATE. Paten on foot, domestic, 1764;
Chalice, London, 1815.

(MUCH FAWLEY, S of the church. With two C14 stone doorways and C14 cruck-trusses. RCHM)

FAWLEY COURT, ¾ m. NW. The back timber-framed, of the
early C16, with narrowly-spaced uprights and diagonals in
the main gable. The front range built of stone c.1630 (fireback
1629, door-knocker 1635). Nearly symmetrical and – a
strangely reactionary choice – with all the lights of all the
windows arched, a Henry VIII rather than a Charles I motif.
On the ground floor a canted bay, a three-light window, a
canted bay, a three-light window, and then the porch. The
windows are transomed. On the upper floor mullioned
windows, evenly spaced, three, three, three, three, two lights.
Inside, the hall with a very large fireplace with four-centred
head and delicately moulded surround and a wooden overmantel, partly of the time of the house but partly mid-C18
(Chippendale style). One room with unusually complete and
even panelling. Staircase with turned balusters.

FELHAMPTON see UPTON BISHOP

FELTON
5040

ST MICHAEL. 1853–4. The spire added in 1891. The church
is in the Dec style and not small. – PLATE. Chalice, London,
1781.

FENHAMPTON see WEOBLEY

FERNHALL see BRILLEY

FLANESFORD PRIORY see GOODRICH

FOLEY COTTAGE see TARRINGTON

5050

FORD

CHAPEL. Built in 1851. Small nave and apse, in the Norman style and perhaps on Norman foundations. – PULPIT. In an elaborate neo-Jacobean, probably carved locally. – PLATE. Chalice and Cover by *W. Gamble* of London, 1689. An uncommon piece in the form of a straight-sided beaker.

FORD ABBEY see PUDLESTON

5030

FOWNHOPE

ST MARY. The church has a Norman central tower with a shingled broach spire called C14 by the RCHM. The W and E arches inside have scalloped capitals and bases with some incised zigzag. The W arch is single-stepped, the E arch a replacement (double-chamfered, pointed). The tower has outside one Norman N window and twin bell-openings with a shaft. To the N a pair of C13 lancets under an arch was inserted below the bell-openings. Of the Norman period also the rere-arch of one nave N window, and of the same period – more precisely, of the mid C12 – the tympanum of a doorway now kept inside and indeed in remarkably good condition. It is dedicated to the Virgin, and she is seated raising one hand in a monumental gesture. The blessing hand of the Child acts as an accompaniment. The draperies have the close parallel folds typical of the Herefordshire School. The legs are not placed with open knees and closed feet, as was more usual, but with feet apart. To the l. and r. big, loose, three-strand trails in wide coils inhabited by a lion and a bird. The long fearsome claws of the lion are again typical of the Herefordshire Romanesque. The C13 is represented at Fownhope by the N doorway (two orders of shafts with shaft-rings, moulded capitals, arch with deep mouldings; much renewed) and the two E arches of the S arcade. They have the flat 'water-holding' bases of the C13, round shafts, round abaci, and double-chamfered arches. The W extension followed about 1300, with an octagonal pier. The windows of the s aisle, and also those along the s side of the central tower, are of c.1300 and the early c14, and so is the s doorway. At the same time the nave N windows were renewed (reticulation motifs), and the chancel was rebuilt. Its windows are rather later c13 than after 1300 (Y- and intersected tracery), and one of the two recesses inside concurs. The other has big ballflowers and is later than 1300. – FONTS. One no doubt of c.1670 (see the typical panels with large elementary fleurs-de-lis), the other a c18 baluster font. – STAINED GLASS. Fragments in the E window; no figures. – PLATE. Chalice and Cover Paten by *R.S.*, London, 1670; Salver by *Richard Bayley*, London, 1716; Flagon by *John Eastt*, London, 1724; Almsdish, London, 1726. – MONUMENTS. Incised slab with wild inscriptions in several directions. – Johanna Lechmere, 1692. Tablet with two putti on the open segmental pediment. – Nicholas Lechmere † 1711. Tablet with allegorical figures l. and r. and open segmental pediment with others. – John Kidley and wife. After 1718. Tablet with garlands l. and r. and cherubs' heads above the inscription. – Capel Lechmere † 1829. Tomb-chest with shields, i.e. medieval revival (chancel s).

NASH FARMHOUSE, $\frac{3}{8}$ m. E. Brick. Three wide bays, two and a half storeys. One-bay pediment. Tripartite windows beneath it. The whole clearly Late Georgian.

(VICARAGE. The BARN has three cruck-trusses. RCHM)

(FOWNHOPE COURT, $\frac{1}{4}$ m. NNW. Jacobean. On the W side the base of a medieval semicircular turret. Re-set in the garden a c13 niche with trefoiled head. RCHM)

(CAPLER FARM, $1\frac{1}{4}$ m. SE. The early part of the BARN has cruck-trusses. RCHM)

FOXLEY *see* YAZOR

FOY

ST MARY. The earliest piece is a small lancet in the chancel. The s porch (see the entrance) is early c14. The W tower with diagonal buttresses is Dec. To the r. of the chancel arch a cusped recess for a lay altar. This also is Dec. The E window is Perp, but in fact a deliberate copy of a Perp window at Sellack by a mason of the 1640s acting under the will of John Abrahall, who, in 1640, had bequeathed lands, goods, and stocks to have made 'a fayer windowe contayning three lights and there place the same after the same manner as such a window is placed in the church of Sellack'. In the gable are the initials of John Abrahall and the date 1673. – FONT. Big, Perp, decagonal, with arcading. – PULPIT. Jacobean, with blank arches. – STALLS. With simple C17 ends. – SCREEN. Except for the mid-C17 door decoration, mostly Victorian restoration. – COMMUNION RAIL. Three-sided, C17, re-used W of the screen. – SOUTH DOOR. C14, two leaves, with iron hinges. – STAINED GLASS. Dated 1675. A copy of the E window of Sellack, like the stone parts of the window. – PLATE. Chalice, London, 1656; Paten on foot by *John Ruslen*(?), London, 1691; Paten by *John Eastt*, London, 1722. – MONUMENTS. Effigy in the chancel, late C13, defaced. The figure is under a trefoiled canopy crowned by a cross and has a rounded object at its feet. – A similar effigy, small, in the nave altar recess. Also trefoiled canopy, also the object at the feet. The effigies are of the C13. – George Abrahall † 1673. With two allegorical figures. – Paul Abrahall † 1675. With frontal demi-figure, wearing a wig and holding a book. – John Abrahall † 1702 and others to 1742. By *Esau Osborn* of Bristol. Architectural tablet.

51b

OLD VICARAGE, to the NW. Of stone, early C18, five bays and two storeys. Round the corner one big bow window of the later C18.

SUSPENSION BRIDGE. Built in 1876, and rebuilt in the 1930s.

DYKE. Just E of Perrystone Court and extending E for some 500 yds are the remains of a massive earthwork, double-ditched at its E end. Its date is uncertain, although Sir Cyril Fox has suggested that it is pre-Offan.

GAINES *see* WHITBOURNE

5010   GANAREW

ST SWITHIN. 1849–50 by *J. Pritchard* of Llandaff. Nave and chancel and small stone bell-turret with spirelet. The style is 'Middle Pointed or Decorated'. – MONUMENT. John Bannerman † 1870. Gothic pinnacle in the churchyard.

LEYS. John Bannerman's house, added to and altered for him by *William Burn* in 1861–2. With Jacobean shaped gables and several turrets with ogee caps, but quoins and a porch with Tuscan columns.

Sellarsbrooke, ⅜ m. NE. Built in 1800. Five bays and two storeys with a three-bay pediment on giant pilasters. Closed porch on coupled pilasters.

Little Doward Camp. An Iron Age hill-fort of roughly oval plan, defended by a univallate rampart enclosing an area of about 26 acres. On the NW is an outwork which is probably modern. The site was considerably damaged in the C19, when paths were cut through the ramparts. At this time too an outwork on the NW of the fort was replaced by a modern straight bank. Within the fort are a number of circular and roughly rectangular MOUNDS of uncertain date. The ramparts are now cut by four entrances, but only excavation can determine which are contemporary with the original structure.

GARNONS see MANSELL GAMAGE

GARWAY

4020

St Michael. Garway is an uncommonly interesting church. It consists now of a four-square, unbuttressed w tower of the early C13 (with lancet windows and a pyramid roof), linked up by a humble C17 corridor* with a late C13 nave whose axis does not coincide with that of the tower at all. In the beginning the tower had been isolated, and the church had consisted of a round nave and a chancel. That will appear less improbable when it is learned that Garway was a preceptory of the Templars. They had founded this house in the later 1180s, and they favoured round churches in memory of the Holy Sepulchre in Jerusalem (cf. e.g. London, Bristol, Dover, Blackby, Temple Bruerne, and the Hospitallers' churches in London – Clerkenwell, Little Maplestead, and St Giles Hereford). Part of the excavated round nave is exposed. To the round nave belonged the still existing chancel arch. Two orders. Capitals still Late Norman (e.g. a head with arms as beaded bands) but also already water-leaf. Arch with various zigzags, including one at r. angles to the wall surface. The innermost moulding, which looks lobed like some French ones made under Oriental influence, is more probably a re-assembly of pieces made for ribs. To the chancel into which this arch led a two-bay chapel was added later in the C13. The pier and responds are circular with four shafts with

---

* In its building Norman tufa blocks were re-used.

shaft-rings. The capitals were left entirely undecorated. The arches are double-chamfered and have an inner roll in addition. The church was rebuilt as a normal oblong building shortly after. Windows partly of that date, partly reset (e.g. the middle window in the chancel E wall, which has plate tracery). Handsome chancel roof with tie-beams, collar-beams, and two tiers of pointed-trefoiled wind-braces. – STALLS. With Jacobean panels. – BENCHES. Very massive and with ends of simple shape; C16 or C17. – PANELLING. Jacobean, fragmentary, in the S chapel. – COMMUNION RAIL. C17. With turned balusters. – SCULPTURE. The small panels outside the church of the Hand of God, a bird, and the Lamb and Cross are clearly not C15, but C17, if not C18. Also curious scratchings, e.g. of chalice and wafer, a fish, and a snake above the piscina in the S chapel, also of emblems of the Passion over the W door of the chapel. These are certainly not medieval either. – PLATE. Cup, 1576.

30a DOVECOTE, S of the church. A circular building with a truncated conical roof outside, flatly domed inside. The dovecote is highly memorable in that it has an inscription referring to the fact that *istud columbarium factum fuit per Ricardum* in 1326.

GATLEY PARK *see* LEINTHALL EARLS

5010
GOODRICH

ST GILES. A large church in a curiously and attractively isolated position. The early building history must be read inside. The N arcade – of six bays, as there is no division of nave and chancel – is clearly of two dates. The centre comes first and must, with its circular piers, belong to the C13. The arches are completely altered. Then, at the end of the same century, the nave was lengthened to the W and the chancel given a two-bay chapel. Octagonal piers and double-chamfered arches. Next come the Dec S porch (see the mouldings of the entrance) and the Dec W tower. The tower is unbuttressed and carries a tall broach spire. The lucarnes at the foot have easily recognizable Dec tracery. Perp chancel E window. Most of the other windows Victorian. – WOODWORK. In the N aisle some foreign C17 panels with religious scenes and some English panels of c.1700 joined together. – STAINED GLASS. In the N aisle E window delightful white and yellow figures of angels holding shields; C15. – Nave E window by

Hardman, c. 1875. – PLATE. Cup on baluster stem, finely
decorated, 1617. Given to the church by Dean Swift, whose
family had come from Goodrich. – Also a cup inscribed 1665.
– MONUMENTS. Shrine, damaged, with curiously cusped
arcading. It must be of the late C13 (cf. Bridstow). – The Rev.
Harry Williams † 1830. With a blindfold Justice at the top.
By *Benjamin Jennings Sen.*

GOODRICH CASTLE. Of red sandstone and looking majestic [15]
from many angles. Of the building called Goodric's Castle
mentioned in 1101–2 nothing remains. Of the period when the
present castle was built, on the other hand, hardly any
documents exist. Architectural evidence must distinguish
between the mid-C12 keep, the curtain walling of the early
C13, of which only masonry on the E side and the foundations
of a SW tower preceding the present one tell us anything, and
the construction of the present castle, to which the gift of
oaks from the Forest of Dean probably refers which is recorded for the years 1280 and 1282.

The castle is approached by an unusually monumental
BARBICAN with a powerful semicircular front. It was entered
on the S side and was of course not roofed. From here the
BRIDGE turned W, or rather a causeway with flat steps carried
on one and a half arches across the moat. The arches have
chamfers dying into the imposts, and this can be considered
the *leitmotif* of the castle. The GATEHOUSE has a mighty semicircular tower on the l. which actually houses the chapel and
a much smaller circular r. tower marking the NE corner of
the castle. The gateway is vaulted and had portcullises at each
end. The porter's room was to the r. in the NE tower. Through
the gatehouse one enters the COURTYARD. Here the arrangement of the various apartments can best be understood. The
castle is roughly square with angle towers in the four corners.
That is the incipient Edwardian scheme which reached its
climax at Harlech. There the gatehouse is exactly in the middle
of one side, here it is still – as at Barnwell in Northamptonshire
about 1260 – close to one corner. Symmetry is thus not fully
appreciated yet.

Of the buildings round the courtyard the oldest is the
KEEP. It is Norman, only 29 ft square, and built of grey, not
of red stone. The flat buttresses are characteristically Norman.
The entry was by an outer staircase to a shafted doorway on
the first floor on the N side. The shafts have scalloped capitals.
The main room was on the top floor. Of its two-light or twin

windows those to N and W are preserved. This main room was however by no means the main room of the C13. The GREAT HALL lies in the W range and is 65 ft long. It has transomed trefoil-headed windows to the outside and, higher up, windows without transoms to the inside. In the W wall is a fireplace with a corbelled hood. Next to the hall stands the SOUTH-WEST TOWER, the biggest of the castle. In its basement part of the foundations of the much smaller early C13 tower have been exposed. On the first floor, which is level with the hall, were the BUTTERY and PANTRY. They communicate with the hall by a doorway and a double hatch. The upper parts of the tower are reached by a staircase to the l. of the buttery door. Behind this tower and the keep was the KITCHEN. Its large fireplace (S) and its tank and sinks (W) can be recognized.

On the other side of the hall were the principal living quarters. First a VESTIBULE, above which was the PRIVATE CHAPEL. It can be identified by the trefoil-headed piscina in the S wall near the E end. The vestibule led into the SOLAR and by a staircase into the room below. The purpose of this room is unknown. It had at its NE end a small doorway, access to the outer bailey (*see* below). The most curious thing about this range is that it has in its centre a very tall and slim octagonal pier which, without any break, ran from the bottom of the lower room to the top of the solar. The solar has to the N two windows with trefoiled heads and transoms. In the C15 an additional building was erected E of the solar.

Finally the E range. Next to the gateway and in the mighty gate tower lies the CHAPEL. This has in the curve of the tower a polygonal apse separated by a chancel arch on brackets from the nave. The sedile is older than the castle and may have come from its predecessor. It has shafts, and a trefoiled head with deep mouldings. That looks mid-C13 rather than late-C13. The room above the chapel has a fireplace with a corbelled hood, and another is in the room above the gateway. Further S is a range of unknown destination. On its outside wall projects a GARDEROBE block, with three separate cubicles and the shoot into the moat preserved.

The MOAT is a most impressive affair, deep and wide, and at its bottom everywhere exposing the underlying shelves of red rock. This empty moat and the towers with their tremendous spurs (cf. Château Gaillard) make an unforgettable picture.

The OUTER BAILEY is fragmentary. It is easily seen, with its two angle towers on the W side. The stables lay between them. It also appears on the N side, where its long wall ends against the barbican. From the barbican a staircase led down into the outer bailey. The bailey was arranged on the two least vulnerable sides. The moat defended the sides where natural defence was lacking.

The view from the castle is superb. Gilpin calls it 'correctly picturesque'.

YE OLDE HOSTELRIE, ⅜ m. NE of the church. A romantic inn in the taste of *c.* 1830, with a tall Gothic chapel window and a diversity of pinnacles. It is said that it was copied from an illustration in a missal. It represents the spirit of GOODRICH COURT, *Blore*'s fantastic and enormous castellated and tower-bedecked house, ½ m. away from the real castle. This was begun in 1828 and has recently been demolished. Wordsworth called it an impertinent structure. Only its E gatehouse on the road to Ross survives, red stone with round towers and machicoulis.

FLANESFORD PRIORY, ½ m. NE. All that stands of this Augustinian priory founded in 1346 is the refectory, a range with two-light windows with a reticulation motif in the head. But it remains strange that the refectory should have been on the upper floor. The cloister lay to the N of the building.

KERN BRIDGE. 1828 by *B. D. Jones*, a fine, long bridge.

ROCKLANDS, ½ m. S. Castellated house with a castellated veranda. Probably of *c.*1820.

HUNTSHAM COURT, 1¼ m. SSW. Of stone. Jacobean or a little later, with mullioned windows and a porch on gross columns.

NEWHOUSE FARM, ⅔ m. WNW. Dated 1636 and built as the parsonage by the Rev. Thomas Smith. An interesting conceit, but carried out a little roughly. Three ranges arranged radially. It could represent the Holy Trinity. There are three storeys. At the end of one arm a canted bay window. The windows are mullioned, up to four lights. It is curious that another New House, built before 1619 and located in Wiltshire, should have the same radial trinitarian arrangement.

GRAFTON

4030

ST PETER. By *F. R. Kempson*, 1880. 'Of C13 character' (*Building News*). Nave and chancel. W tower with thin spire. The bell-openings stick up into it with steep gables. – FONT. Of *c.*1880.

A white marble angel kneeling and holding a shell. – MONU-
MENT. Tablet to John Daubeney. Inscription and naval
appurtenances behind. It all looks later C17, yet he died in
1741.

OLD CHURCH. In the vicarage garden. Ruinous and all covered
with ivy. The RCHM noted *inter alia* indications of two
Norman windows and a blocked Norman N doorway.

To the SE of the new church a pretty black and white HOUSE
with lozenge-trellis bracing in the gable.

GREAT HEATH *see* LAYSTERS

GREAT HOWLE *see* WALFORD-ON-WYE

GREAT PENLAN *see* HUNTINGTON

GREAT TREADDOW *see* HENTLAND

5050

GRENDON BISHOP

ST JOHN BAPTIST. In the fields and not easily accessible.
Built in 1787–8, but completely victorianized. The apse was
added in 1870. Thin W tower. In it, on the S side, a re-set
Norman window. – PLATE. Chalice, London, 1778.

(GRENDON FARM, 300 yds NW, and WESTINGHOUSE COURT,
⅔ m. WNW, have similar Jacobean overmantels with the usual
short blank arches. They are separated by grotesque caryatids.
The overmantel at Grendon Farm has a crude carving of the
Sacrifice of Isaac under the arch. RCHM)

GRENDON COURT *see* PENCOMBE

THE GROVE *see* LLANGARRON

HACKLEY FARM *see* AVENBURY

HAFFIELD HOUSE *see* DONNINGTON

5050

HAMNISH CLIFFORD

ST DUBRICIUS. 1909–10 by *W. J. Weatherley*. In the N window
glass by *Kempe & Tower*, 1924.

HENNOR HOUSE. At the back two stone wings, one with a
date 1679. Later front, added to *c*.1775. To this time belong
the Adamish porch and the fine decoration of two rooms.
Both have excellent fireplaces with reliefs, and one has in
addition a delicate frieze.

HAMPTON BISHOP

5030

St Andrew. Norman one N window in the nave and the S
doorway, which has a very big lintel with scale decoration in
the upper, saltire crosses in the lower half, a blank tympanum,
a zigzag arch, and a hood-mould with billet. Late Norman
the chancel arch, with roll mouldings, one of them keeled.
And Norman too the arch into the N chapel. The E respond
has many scallops. Round arch with two slight chamfers.
However, the RCHM calls this re-set. The N tower is hardly
later. It has Norman windows, though the arches to S and E
are pointed and double-chamfered. The top of the tower is
timber-framed and has a steep pyramid roof. The arcade of
two bays into which the E arch leads belongs to the C13, and
perhaps that arch was only made then. The arcade has a
mighty round pier and double-chamfered arches. Of the
windows, those of the chancel are of *c.*1300 and so are the E
windows of the N chapel. – REREDOS. N chapel. Of stone.
Two tiers of niches; damaged, but yet a memorable survival.
– PULPIT. Jacobean, but apparently made up of re-assembled
panels. – MONUMENTS. James family, *c.*1837. By *J. Biggle-
stone*. With, at the top, a prostrate woman by an urn. – Gothic
tablet to Col. Thomas Weare † 1850, by *Poole*. – CHURCH-
YARD CROSS. With steps, base, and shaft.

Church Farm, S of the church. Timber-framed. Front of the
hall-house type with the two gabled cross-wings. Round the
corner C17 porch with, in the open sides, flat balusters.

The Lawns, 200 yds SSE. Georgian, of brick. Five bays, three
storeys. Doorway with broken pediment on Tuscan columns.

HAMPTON COURT

5050

¾ m. SE of Hope-under-Dinmore

Licence to crenellate was granted to Sir Rowland Lenthall in 38a
1434. The castle was no doubt built then and coincided in
area and layout with the present-day Hampton Court, i.e. had
four ranges round a courtyard. Architecturally much less
remains. The castle, which is of red sandstone, was remodelled by Lord Coningsby about 1700 etc. He died in 1729.
Talman seems to have made plans (according to a letter of
Vanbrugh's), *Colen Campbell* illustrates an embattled front
in *Vitruvius Britannicus* vol. II, 1717, and this may represent
Talman's scheme for a symmetrical medievalizing façade,*

* Mr John Harris's suggestion.

Knyff and Kip painted and illustrated the house in its state
of *c.*1700, and finally *Sir Jeffry Wyatville* was called in by
R. Arkwright, of the cotton spinners' family, to make it more
up-to-dately medieval. Arkwright had bought the estate in
1817.

Of original C15 work the most important is the GATEHOUSE,
though the archways in and out and the big bay window
above the N entry are by *Wyatville*. The cross-slits l. and r.
and the machicolations are original, and also the tall niche in
the S wall. Original moreover the DOOR. Opposite the gatehouse in the courtyard is the former PORCH to the great hall,
with diagonal buttresses and a straight-headed window of
four ogee-headed lights above. The diagonal buttress further
l. belongs to a C15 projection which may have housed the
staircase from the hall to the solar. Original also the CHAPEL,
which is the most rewarding apartment. It projects E at the
NE corner and has large Perp windows – three lights to the N,
five to the E. Excellent ceiling of slight camber, with diagonal
ribs in the panels and many bosses at the intersections. Some
little original STAINED GLASS in the N windows. Otherwise
it is chiefly the walls that are old, including the two N turrets.

Of the period around 1700–15 there remain the fine stone
STAIRCASE to the W of the gatehouse with its restrained iron
balustrade and the grand FIREPLACE in the large room E of
the gatehouse. This is of white and grey marble and has a
segmental opening, two fluted columns l. and r., and two
more, truncated and set on corbels, above it and a coat of arms
at the top.

Wyatville built the corridors all round the courtyard, a
useful and architecturally successful addition. They are all
rib-vaulted, and the red sandstone has behaved so badly that
their exterior looks as old as the C15 work. Wyatville also
altered all windows, converting e.g. the homely Queen Anne
SW projection which had three bays, two storeys, and a
hipped roof into something with two turrets and large Gothic
windows. He also added to the SE corner, and there applied
large straight-ended transomed windows with much panel
tracery.*

* C18 illustrations are a warning that the architectural history of Hampton
Court may have yet further complications. In short the position is that Knyff
and Kip at the beginning of the century show the Queen Anne SW corner
with its hipped Queen Anne roof, but late C18 illustrations and even Neale
in 1826 have a big bow window instead which does not now exist. Also
Neale's N façade is like that in *Vitruvius Britannicus* and not like today's.

HARDWICK 2040

HOLY TRINITY. Built in 1851. The architect is a mystery. He signs himself in the stained glass of a N window as *huius aedificii Architectus*. That is all. – The STAINED GLASS of the E and W windows is by *John Bell* of Bristol. – The architecture of the small church is in the style of the late C13 to early C14.

HAREWOOD 5020
1 m. ESE of Llandinabo

ST DENIS. Disused. Built in 1864. Nave and chancel in one. E.E. front with lancets, Norman E end with blank arcade. Staircase turret on the N side with spirelet. – FONT. Of the Purbeck type, square, with the four usual shallow blank arches on each side. The font came indeed from Chardstock in Dorset. – PLATE. Cup and Cover Paten, 1571.

HAREWOOD PARK. The house has been demolished, but the GATE LODGE remains, pedimented, with a portico of two pairs of Tuscan columns.

HATFIELD 5050

ST LEONARD. Nave with a Norman N doorway. Lintel very big, of three joggled stones. Tympanum with trellis decoration. E of it Early Norman herringbone masonry. Wide unmoulded round chancel arch. Bell turret on four heavy posts. W porch of timber. – STAINED GLASS. E window of c.1870 by *Mayer & Co.*, terrible. – PLATE. Chalice, London, 1571; Cover Paten, inscribed 1614; Salver, London, 1685. – MONUMENTS. Three tablets, of 1641, 1669, and 1673, the former with Ionic columns, the other two with twisted columns.

HATFIELD COURT FARM. This late C16 mansion, still illustrated in the volume of the RCHM, has now all but disappeared.

HAYWOOD 4030

HAYWOOD. Dated 1740. A low farmhouse of stone with no special features except perhaps the gatepiers. The DOVECOTE has been pulled down.

HAYWOOD LODGE. Probably of c.1710. Of brick, seven bays and two storeys with a hipped roof. Doorway with pilasters carrying an open scrolly pediment. To its l. and r. narrow windows. Fine wrought-iron front gates. Nice staircase with some feather inlay on the ends of the steps, carved tread-ends, and oddly shaped turned balusters.

HEATH HOUSE *see* LEINTWARDINE

HELLENS *see* MUCH MARCLE

HELL MOAT *see* SARNESFIELD

HENGOED *see* HUNTINGTON

5020   HENTLAND

St Dubricius. Drastic restoration by *Seddon* in 1853. W tower C14 with bell-openings still Dec but a W window entirely Perp. N aisle of *c.*1300. The windows with trefoiled heads, as also the windows in the chancel. But the E window is of the Herefordshire type of three stepped lancet lights. Four-bay N arcade with octagonal piers and double-chamfered arches. Nave roof single-framed with scissor-bracing. – FONT. Octagonal, Perp. On the bowl two primitive heads, fleurons, and rosettes. – PULPIT. With the blank arches of the Elizabethan and Jacobean type. – WALL PAINTING. The ashlaring and the little flowers seem to belong to the restoration. – STAINED GLASS. Three C15 figures in the E window. – PLATE. Chalice by *William Grundy*, London, 1758. – CHURCHYARD CROSS. With steps, base, stump of the shaft, and defaced head.

Gillow Manor. Of red sandstone. The SW front is of the late C14. It consists of a deep gatehouse with chamfered entry and exit. Four-centred arches. To the l. of the entry a two-light Perp window with transom. The gatehouse is tunnel-vaulted, the section also four-centred. The exit leads into a small courtyard, smaller than it will have been in the C14. In the basement a most curious STATUE of a civilian of *c.*1430. The position of the arms shows that it is not an effigy. Was he one of those apotropaeic figures such as are found on embattled gatehouses in the North of England (Alnwick, Belsay)?

(Great Treaddow, 1½ m. s. On the W front exposed crucks. RCHM)

(Trasech, 2 m. N. In one room a plaster ceiling with four lions passant. RCHM)

HEREFORD

INTRODUCTION

Hereford has no more than 35,000 inhabitants. The centre is small, and there are no industrial suburbs. The cathedral thus dominates unchallenged. Yet, as we shall see, it is not a dominating building, and the town, in a modest way, holds one's interest in its spite.

Hereford became a see in the late C7, the town received its first charter in 1189. By the C15 it had fourteen trade guilds. However, its trade began to decline after the catastrophe of the Civil War, and Defoe describes Hereford as 'lying low'. And even Price's *An Historical Account of the City of Hereford* of 1796, which tends to be seen through rose-coloured spectacles, says that the increase of population between about 1760 and 1790 had not been 'upon that rapid and extensive scale which we see in various other parts of the kingdom'. What would he have said in 1896? Hereford had about 6,000 inhabitants when he wrote, as many as Leominster now.

The area comprised within the medieval walls was about 75 acres. Much survives of the wall, which was, it seems, begun in 1298, and it will be listed below. Hereford, apart from its cathedral, had a mighty castle at that time, five parish churches, and the priory of St Guthlac, which was a merger of a pre-Conquest secular college of St Guthlac in the castle and a secular college of St Peter. The two became a Benedictine priory dependent on Gloucester early in the C12. The Franciscans came before 1228, the Dominicans before 1246. Nothing survives of the former except Friars' Street and Greyfriars Avenue w of St Nicholas. The Dominican establishment lay N of the town, also *extra muros*, and its remains are discussed on p. 183.

THE CATHEDRAL

INTRODUCTION

Hereford Cathedral has been unlucky in a number of ways. Its w front is by *Oldrid Scott* and not one of his best, the nave is more than half *Wyatt*'s (1788 etc.), the crossing and parts of nave and chancel are by *Cottingham* (1842 etc.), and the E view is dominated by *Sir G. G. Scott*'s reconstruction of what Wyatt had replaced (1856–63). Moreover, in distant views of Hereford the cathedral does not dominate the town as do those of Durham and Lincoln or Ely or Wells or Salisbury. Hereford has three church towers, and the two with spires, i.e. those of All Saints and St Peter, are more prominent than the broad crossing tower of the cathedral; for the cathedral has lost its spire and moreover an additional w tower. Its collapse in 1786 started Wyatt on his alterations. And, finally, when one gets near, Hereford Cathedral suffers from the absence of a close proper. King Street and Broad Street run right towards the w front. There are no walls and gates between. The cathedral houses on the N side are part of the town, the Deanery is early C19, the Cathedral School with its busy new buildings faces the E end, the College of the Vicars Choral has a Georgian stone front towards the chancel, and it is only at the corner of the cloisters and the Bishop's Palace that a precinctual feeling can be evoked.

Hereford became a see in the late C7. A new cathedral was built in the first half of the C11 and burnt by the Welsh. There is no evidence that Robert de Losinga, bishop of Hereford from 1079 to 1095 and brother of the bishop of Norwich, began a new cathedral. Reynelm, bishop in 1107–15, is called *fundator ecclesie* in his obit. He will have begun the present church. A consecration took place between 1142 and 1148, and Bishop Robert of Bethune, who died in 1148, was buried in the cathedral, which, as the chronicle says, 'ipse multa impensa et sollicitudine consummavit'. Of this Norman church the E end is not preserved. Excavations have shown that it had three apses. It also has a chancel of three bays with aisles, and scanty but undeniable evidence brought forward by the late Sir Alfred Clapham points

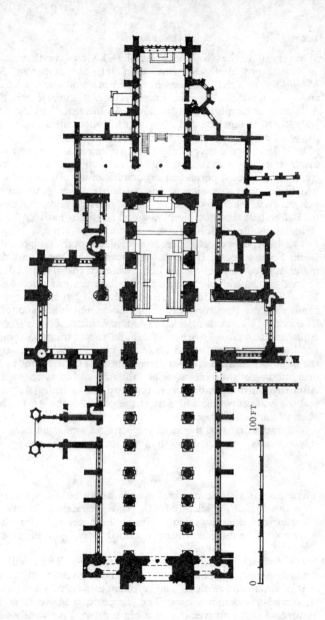

0   100 FT

to towers above the E bays of these aisles – a German rather than
a Norman or Anglo-Norman motif (cf. the destroyed St
Maximinus at Trier, the remains of St Lucius at Werden, etc.,
and also, influenced by the Empire, Ivrea Cathedral and S.
Abbondio at Como in North Italy, and, influenced by North
Italy, S. Nicola at Bari and other South Italian cathedrals). To
the W follow transept and crossing, the latter with a tower (now
of later date), and a nave of eight bays ending in a front with no 5
tower, but turrets to flank the aisles and flank the nave. There
was a single large W portal and any amount of the blank arcading
which was such a passion among English masons. A W tower
was put on in the early C14. Its collapse has already been referred
to. Before that time the Norman E end had been replaced by a
retrochoir widened into E transepts and by a straight-ended
Lady Chapel on a crypt. There is no evidence of the date of this
work. Style suggests c.1190 to c.1230 or 1240. Documents do
not exist to confirm, but it has been suggested that the Interdict
of 1208–14 explains the change of style between retrochoir and
Lady Chapel. Immediately after the Lady Chapel had been
completed, the clerestory of the chancel was rebuilt and vaulted.
The mid C13 seems a reasonable date to assume. Then Bishop
Aquablanca (1240–68) began to rebuild the N transept about
1250 or 1255. Much was done about 1300 and after, namely
the inner N porch, the fenestration of the aisles, the completion
or rebuilding of the E transepts, and the splendid crossing tower.
After that only appendices were provided: two chantry chapels
and the outer N porch. The date of the porch – 1519 – takes us
close to the Reformation.

The cathedral is of the local greyish pink sandstone and, as
it now stands, has a total length of 360 ft and a height of 165.

EXTERIOR

The phases of the architectural history cannot be distinguished
on the outside sufficiently clearly and separately to justify a
chronological arrangement. This will be reserved for the
interior. The outside is here described topographically from
E to W.

We must thus start with the LADY CHAPEL. The E wall is
much renewed by *Scott*, but not without guiding evidence.
It is ornate and restless. The crypt appears only by its small
pointed-trefoiled windows. The composition above is with
turreted angle buttresses and a big E gable. Five widely-set

stepped lancets shafted and with stiff-leaf capitals. Hood-moulds on head-stops of which only few survive. Two tiers of pointed-trefoiled niches l. and r. and between the lancets. Above, blank wall decorated with eight moulded lozenges,* the first and last with dragons on the top, and between the first and second and seventh and eighth an almond shape with dog-tooth. Then a blank gallery with stiff-leaf capitals, hood-moulds with dog-tooth on head-stops. The middle niche is a little higher, and a dog-tooth frieze rises there. Top wheel window with eight columnar spokes, entirely by Scott. L. and r. an arched niche, and at the top an almond shape, all this also by Scott.

The N and S sides are roughly identical. Three pairs of large shafted lancet windows with stiff-leaf capitals. Roundel in the spandrel of each pair. On the N side scenes, e.g. the Crucifixion, in the roundels. Then a frieze of interlaced arches with stiff-leaf capitals. The arches have different patterns, and there are heads in the spandrels. On the N side a porch covers the outer stairway into the crypt. It has a steep gable. Entrance with shafts carrying stiff-leaf capitals. Arch with roll mouldings, one with a fillet, but the inner order a zigzag at r. angles to the wall, i.e. the only Late Norman or Transitional motif in an otherwise E.E. ensemble. It can only be re-used (see the considerations on p. 156 regarding the interior of the retrochoir and Lady Chapel). The porch has a quadripartite rib-vault with a stiff-leaf boss. The ribs stand on corbels with stiff-leaf capitals. The inner doorway has a continuous roll moulding with a fillet. Hood-mould on head-stops.

On the S side the E.E. composition is broken by the AUDLEY CHAPEL, built before Bishop Audley was transferred to Salisbury in 1502. It is on a five-eighths plan with a lowish ground floor and a high, amply glazed upper floor. Panelled buttresses and pinnacles.‡

The architecture of the E transepts and chancel aisles is uniform and has nothing to do with that of the Lady Chapel. Large four-light windows with tracery typical of c.1300, i.e. with three large pointed trefoils in the tracery of two of them and a pointed cinquefoil above. The dating can be verified by comparisons with the windows of the chancel at Dilwyn, which was newly built in 1305 (see p. 111). The

* A motif frequent at Lincoln Cathedral about 1240, etc.

‡ To its W the CHOIR VESTRY, an insignificant C15 addition partly rebuilt c.1860.

uniformity of *c.*1300 is broken by another Perp chantry chapel, that of Bishop Stanbury, erected on the N side after his death in 1473 and apparently some time later, as it is called 'newe bylded' in 1491.

Now the HIGH CHANCEL. The buttresses at the angles are of a different stone and a first hint at the Norman building. The rest is all of *Cottingham*'s doing, i.e. *c.*1842–3. The N and S sides have two-light windows with plate tracery (a quatrefoil) which stylistically precedes Aquablanca's bar tracery of the 1250s. The windows have shafts with shaft-rings and stiff-leaf capitals. Between them runs slender blank arcading. Above this there is on the S side a curious frieze of lozenges and quatrefoiled circles reminiscent of the upper E wall of the Lady Chapel. On the N side there is instead a blank arcade with pointed-trefoiled heads and paterae in the spandrels. The flying buttresses are clearly an afterthought.

One word on the externally visible traces of the Norman towers above the E bays of the chancel aisles. The buttresses on the E wall have already been mentioned. They mask the junction of towers and Norman E wall (above the apse). The E walls of the towers themselves are still in existence above the aisle roofs and now end with a diagonal. Moreover, from the roof of the N chancel aisle one can see the top of a tiny window in what was the S wall of the N tower. It has a stepped rounded top and a primitively carved tympanum. It must have looked down from an upper level of the tower towards the altar. Also the plinth of the S side of the tower exists (inside a new lavatory) and shows that this wall was as thick as the E wall.

The transepts are much more eloquent regarding the Norman building, or at least the SOUTH TRANSEPT. On the E side the upper windows are Norman and shafted. At ground-floor level is the present vestry, consisting of a utilitarian C15 E part and a Norman W part which was used as the Treasury. It looks from outside like a transept E aisle. It has a small, shafted window to the S (and one to the E only visible inside and with difficulty). At clerestory level and hard to see five arches of Norman arcading immediately S of the junction with the chancel. The great S window is of *c.*1400, large, of six lights, and of course Perp. In the W wall are two Perp windows, but between them a fragment of Norman interlace arcading and, below, a blocked Norman window with shafts and zigzag – the first we come across. The N transept is of a different period, and we shall turn to it with enthusiasm in a moment. Of the Norman transept no more is externally visible than one column of the same blind arcade at clerestory level as we have seen (or not seen) on the S side. Maybe the transept was never continued or completed.

So to Peter of Savoy's, i.e. Bishop Aquablanca's, *chef d'œuvre*. The NORTH TRANSEPT was begun by him and sufficiently ready shortly after 1268 to receive his monument,[21] a work as crisp, accomplished, and *dernier cri* as the transept itself. That its source is Westminster Abbey is at once evident from the E clerestory windows, spherical triangles enclosing foiled circles. The same motif occurs at the Abbey in the gallery of the E parts.

Below them are circular windows under round arches on shafts, and below them the aisle windows of three lights with three encircled trefoils in the bar tracery. To the N all is pulled together in an enormous six-light window, 50 ft tall. The E window of the Angel Choir at Lincoln, dating from the same period, is 59 ft in height. The N window of Aquablanca's transept has twice the three circles as before, and above them as a final achievement a large sexfoiled circle, taking up the figure six from the six lights. In the gable three cusped lights – below no cusping of lights occurred yet – and a final group of three quatrefoiled circles. To the W, even more impressive perhaps, two equally tall three-light windows. The transept has buttresses with chamfered angles ending in steep crocketed gables. At the bottom they have strange, steep, much-broken spurs such as castles use, but not churches. The E wall was begun before the rest; for the buttresses here on the set-off above the spurs have bases for shafts which were not continued with. They are to be seen also on the NE buttress facing N, and then stop.

The CROSSING TOWER is the only architectural feature[28a] of the exterior that can compete with the N transept. It must belong to the early C14, as it is studded all over with ball-flower, and it illustrates the change from 1260 to 1310 to perfection, a change from the Greek, i.e. classic, ideal of μηδὲν ἀγάν and the Gothic ideal of *masze*, as Wolfram von Eschenbach glorifies it, to profusion, excesses, and so final exhaustion. The tower has cutwater angle buttresses all the way up and all the way panelled. They end in pinnacles just below the main pinnacles (which date from 1830). There are two tiers of tall two-light windows, but all are blank except two of the lower and two of the upper tier, on each side of which the upper are the bell-openings. The tracery is quatre-foils below, cinquefoils above. A band of cusped lozenges runs between the two stages.

The WEST PARTS need less description. The aisle windows are of the same type and date as those further E, though those of the N aisle have finely subdivided jambs and arch mouldings, where all the others are plainly chamfered. The clerestory windows by *Wyatt* are decent, self-effacing Perp, of two lights. The corbel table carries on from the transepts. On the N side in addition there is the NORTH PORCH, a piece of two dates and equally good in quality of both. The outer part is by Bishop Booth and dated 1519 on a little archway on its E side. It is open in large arches to N, E, and W. The N entrance has traceried spandrels and is flanked by two stair-turrets with oriel-like glazing at the top. Large three-light upper window. Low-pitched gable. The vault inside has diagonal ribs, ridge-ribs, and one set of liernes, making the square space into four squares. Square centre cusped. Lozenge bosses at the four main intersections. The inner part of the porch is earlier – of the time of the aisles. It is two-storeyed, the top storey lit by no more than three small lancets. Below is an elongated quadripartite vault with ridge-ribs and a leaf boss, no longer stiff-leaf, though the ribs stand on corbels still with stiff-leaf. The (former) outer doorway has a glorious surround with three orders of shafts and three orders of little figures and foliage in the arch. The system behind all the little figures will never be found, as there can be none. The middle order may be a Tree of Jesse, but why should, on the outer order, a bagpiper be followed first by a mermaid and then by the symbolic figure of the Synagogue? The inner doorway has five bold large cusps with openwork spandrels. The mouldings are set out with sprigs of stiff-leaf or fleurons. A stair-turret in the SE angle squeezes the adjoining window out of its regularity.*

Of the WEST FRONT little need be said. The Norman front was tall and barren, with much blank arcading, and not much else. A deep, probably impressive, W portal, two thin outer turrets, and two a little more substantial inner turrets – that was all. Rochester has been quoted as the best surviving comparison. A W tower was put on early in the C14, when the crossing tower was built too. It was a little less mighty and a

_____
* Exactly the same occurs E of the N transept, where there is also a stair-turret of c.1300.

little lower, but had a great deal of ballflower too. This is the tower which collapsed in 1786. The W front was taken back one bay, and *Wyatt* erected a noncommittal W front. The one we see today, however, is by *John Oldrid Scott* and was built in 1902–8. He could be so good, so earnest and restrained. What made him choose the fullest-blown Dec to introduce to this cathedral? Moreover, why go so low with the side parts? The line of the aisle roofs is not even in an understandable relation to the line of the nave gable. And all the detail is so vociferous.

INTERIOR

Major churches were usually built from E to W – for the obvious reason that it matters more to house altar and relics than to provide vast spaces for small numbers of monks or worshipping laymen.

At Hereford we do not know what the apses and the E towers were like, but we have the chancel, even if at its E end over-restored by *Cottingham*, and the S transept. Now the embarrassing thing is that the SOUTH TRANSEPT, and 6b especially its E wall, looks decidedly more archaic than the chancel. This is hard to explain, but special conditions connected with the Saxon cathedral and its altar space may have existed. The E wall has a tall blank arcade whose capitals are drastically re-cut, but clearly represent a state of carving not comfortably to be placed later than 1110. Above are three blank arches, the middle one shafted. There follows a triforium in three groups of arches, three, two, three, corresponding to the blank arches below. The triforium columns are very short and have scalloped and volute capitals. At sill level runs a finely decorated string course. Then again blank arcading, quite tall – that is a four-storey impression – and finally the wall passage in front of the clerestory. It has the typically English stepped arrangement of low and very stilted high arches, and these were in a regular rhythm until the transept vault was put on about 1430. The stilted arches are set out with much zigzag, which allows this stage to be dated with some confidence as *c.*1120 at the earliest. The N bay of the E wall differs in that it contains the opening to the S chancel aisle and the S chancel gallery. The details of the responds on the ground floor are all by *Cottingham* (but the arch is original – no zigzag), and the gallery corresponds to that in the chancel (*see* below). The s wall was entirely remodelled about 1400 (*see* below, p. 160). The w wall also is much changed. The s bay belongs to the nave and largely to *Cottingham* (*see* p. 155). The two Perp windows are of course an alteration, but there is one splay and shaft of a Norman window, decorated, as we have seen, externally with zigzag, and in the clerestory one of the low arches of the wall passage. So the zigzag comes in at a lower stage in the w than the e wall, which tells us how building proceeded.

Immediately e of the transept is the former TREASURY, now part of the vestry. It was originally no more than a gangway and is vaulted in two groin-vaults, the oldest in the cathedral. It has – *see* above, p. 150 – one s and one (hidden) e window, both shafted. The doorway to the chancel aisle is tall and completely unmoulded, but there are bits left of a finely ornamented string course.

In the NORTH TRANSEPT nothing Norman remains visible, except of course the arch and gallery arch into the chancel aisle.

The CHANCEL comes next, or so it seems. Three bays of main arcading. Compound piers with (re-cut) decorated capitals: scallops, curly volutes, heads, etc. An outer band of the arches has zigzags arranged to form lozenges. The shafts towards the nave ran up broad and sub-shafted to the ceiling. They were cut off when the new clerestory was built in the c13 (*see* p. 158). Sill course of the gallery also with geometrical decoration, much higher in relief than in the s transept. The gallery has one twin opening to each arch below. The responds are entirely out of keeping with those on the ground stage – halves of fat round piers, a *modus* which is in keeping with the liking for such piers in the West Country, even before 1100, notably at Tewkesbury and Gloucester. At Hereford they meant a change of plan, and the new motif was continued in the nave, as we shall see. Many-scalloped and otherwise ornamented capitals, zigzag in sub- and super-arches, tympana with various geometrical patterns in relief, a motif most closely paralleled at Peterborough, where rebuilding started in 1118. The e wall is opened in one big arch, reaching to the top of the gallery responds. It was entirely re-done by *Cottingham*. Originally it was the arch to the apse. Now the retrochoir appears behind it in the oddest way. This is also due to Cottingham; for when the retrochoir was built (*see* p. 156) the arch was closed by a solid wall into which the N

column of the retrochoir bonded. The wall served no doubt
as a reredos. The capitals of the E arch and the adjoining
N and S capitals are all Cottingham's, but ORIGINAL CAPI- 8a
TALS have been preserved and are displayed in the NE
transept, the main N transept, and the corridor to the Vicars'
College. They are decorated and include little, very primitively
carved scenes such as the Annunciation and Christ in Limbo.
Their style makes Dr Zarnecki's dating *c*.1115 on the whole
convincing, although the *fundatio* under Reynelm, i.e. a
beginning of the whole re-building *c*.1110, suggests 1120–5
rather. Dr Zarnecki's reference to relations back to Anglo-
Saxon traditions is entirely sound. The blank arcading above
the E arch is by *Cottingham*.

Of the Norman CHANCEL AISLES little can be said. The
E side of the N arch from the transept into the aisle indicates
vaulting shafts. The E arches of both aisles (into the E transept)
are original. Above them, on the E face, is a blocked window,
N as well as S. They must have led from the gallery to the
roof above the apses, or rather from the first floor of the E
towers. Of these E towers we have already heard. Evidence
of their existence is scanty inside, but one can see against the
E pier of the N arcade on the N side the chiselled-off remains
of the arch respond which carried the W wall of the N tower.
The evidence is clearer above the aisle vaults, and there exists
for the S as well as the N tower.

Next in order of time came the CROSSING. Cottingham
rebuilt the piers entirely, but of the arches with their version
of zigzag, which is like crenellation with triangular merlons,
much is original. The NAVE must for constructional reasons 5
have been at least started at the same time. There is in fact a
joint clearly visible. The E responds and the first two piers
from the E (though again on the surface all Cottingham's) have
capitals with interlaced trails etc. much like some of the
crossing. Further W all is multi-scalloped capitals. The
arcades have throughout heavy circular piers, a West Country
preference, or at least piers nearly circular; for to the nave
and the aisles they are a little widened by twin shafts. Those
to the aisle were to carry the transverse arches of the aisles,
those to the nave the tie-beams of the ceiling. The diameter
of the piers is about 6 ft 8 in. by 7 ft 2 in. Arches with much
zigzag, also meeting at r. angles. The Norman gallery which
Wyatt removed was relatively low, of two twin openings to
each arcade opening. This Norman nave may have been

completed or not yet completed at the time of the consecration of the 1140s.

Then nothing more happened for about fifty years. After that it was felt, as in so many other major churches, that the E end was too small. So the apses were pulled down, and a retrochoir, two bays deep to serve as an ambulatory too, and a Lady Chapel to its E were started. The dates are again entirely unknown. At Winchester a similar composition was begun by Bishop de Lucy (ruled 1189–1204), and Abbey Dore received its double ambulatory c.1200–20. We can hardly go so late at Hereford; for the style is still Transitional, with some Late Norman motifs kept in an *ensemble* turning decisively Early English. The E transepts, which may have formed part of the scheme, are in their architecture later. What remains is the space E of the E arch of the chancel and the two walls of the vestibule to the Lady Chapel. The RETROCHOIR has two circular shafts with water-holding bases, and octagonal abaci, both perversely on the main axis of the building. Both were rebuilt by *Cottingham*, it is said correctly. One has a capital of upright stiff-leaf, the other of trumpet-shaped scallops. That combination corresponds to the parts of c.1200 at Abbey Dore. The ribs are set out with zigzag combined with chains of lozenges. They are pointed and were also rebuilt by Cottingham. It has already been said that the E arch of the chancel was blocked when the retrochoir was provided. Cottingham opened it, and filled the spandrel which now intrudes itself on our attention as we face the altar with florid E.E. carving of stiff-leaf, the Virgin, angels, and St Ethelbert in a little niche.* The carving was done by *W. Boulton* of Lambeth. The retrochoir is separated from the E transepts by arches not decorated by zigzag, but the W responds still also have trumpet capitals (whereas there is stiff-leaf on the E responds). The windows or openings in the N and S walls of the vestibule to the Lady Chapel are also Late Norman in their details. The openings have keeled shafts, stiff-leaf capitals, and in the arches thick chains of elongated hexagons. The arches are pointed. The vault of the vestibule is quadripartite with an extra rib to run to the middle pier, which interferes so incomprehensibly with the view down the Lady Chapel.

* St Ethelbert had been murdered c.794, and his were the most valuable relics of Hereford. The cathedral is in fact known as St Mary and St Ethelbert.

A Lady Chapel was no doubt planned from the start. The entrance to the vestibule proves that. It was erected on a crypt. The CRYPT fills the space below the Lady Chapel, excluding the vestibule. It is aisled and has five bays with octagonal piers and single-chamfered arches. Against the walls they rest on tripartite corbels, the middle one filleted. That was the final moulding of the ribs at Abbey Dore. In the nave stiff-leaf bosses, the westernmost one a human bust.

The LADY CHAPEL itself is one of the two aesthetically 18b most satisfying interiors in the cathedral. Judging by its style and the profusion of its detail, it must date from c.1220–40. Its proportions give the feeling of a comfortable spreading, and the walls are so richly shafted as to convey luxuriance. In the end, however, the simple quadripartite rib-vaults leave one with a sense of repose. Three bays separated by tripartite vaulting-shafts with stiff-leaf capitals. Ribs and transverse arches all have the same slim mouldings. Stiff-leaf bosses. The E bay has an extra rib to the apex of the E wall. This wall is naturally the richest, and perhaps a little overdone. Shafted windows and detached shafts in front of them. Shaft-rings. Arches with much dog-tooth decoration. The middle arch is moreover seven-cusped. Above, roundels and almond shapes with dog-tooth. The side walls are more even in their richness. There are fewer motifs used. Each bay on either side has two windows. Their shafting of five-nine-five in each bay. The shafts have shaft-rings too. Stiff-leaf capitals, hood-moulds 19a on head-stops, heads at the apexes, in fact a plethora of excellent heads. Also one whole figure of a bishop. In the spandrels roundels with cusped quatrefoils.

Having now discussed retrochoir, vestibule, crypt, and Lady Chapel, this is the moment to point out the small changes of detail which allow relative dating. Many of them have already been referred to, but a summing up may be useful. The bases are steeper in the retrochoir (but not the rebuilt detached piers) than in the crypt and Lady Chapel. The shafts adopt keeling in the retrochoir W responds and the window shafts and ribs of the vestibule, fillets in the crypt, crypt porch, and Lady Chapel ribs and E shafts. As for capitals, trumpet-scallops are confined to the W responds of the retrochoir and the easternmost of the two detached piers. The stiff-leaf capitals, however, show a distinct line of development. They have big, single, upright crockets in the retrochoir w pier, the e responds, and the Lady Chapel vestibule, but go thick, lush, and more confused in the Lady Chapel itself. The abaci are polygonal in the retrochoir, the windows of the vestibule, and the vestibule NE respond, but round in the SE respond. That must have been the last touch before work proceeded to the E; for in the crypt and the Lady Chapel all abaci are round. These details ought to be compared with those at Abbey Dore.

They can at Hereford also be watched in the upper parts of the CHANCEL, whose remodelling must have taken place before or just after the Lady Chapel was finished. The Norman clerestory was cut down or drastically remodelled. The vaulting-shafts were cut off and finished with twin gables with leaf motifs. Above them filleted tripartite vaulting-shafts with thick, 'disturbed' stiff-leaf capitals support a quadripartite rib-vault, also with stiff-leaf bosses. The clerestory carries on with the Norman motif of stepped arcading in front of a wall-passage. There are however two tall arches flanked by two low arches to each bay now. The tall arches have a kind of Y-tracery with stiff-leaf capitals. The windows corresponding to the paired tall arches have, it will be remembered, plate tracery.

With the NORTH TRANSEPT we are once again on the highest level of architectural art. It was no doubt planned by Bishop Aquablanca, who died in 1268 and is buried in it, and the motifs so evidently derived from Westminster Abbey make a start before c.1250 or 1255 all but impossible. As for the completion, it must be remembered that Bishop Cantelupe's shrine was only set up in 1287.* Until then the holy bishop had been buried (and worshipped) in the Lady Chapel. The E arcade is of two bays with the astringent, almost straight-sided arches already discussed. Compound piers with stone shafts and also Purbeck shafts – again an import from Westminster Abbey. The Purbeck shafts have shaft-rings. Thick, rich stiff-leaf capital on the pier (which the Abbey has not), moulded capitals on the responds. Handsome little stiff-leaf sprigs on the bases. One big entirely under-cut dog-tooth moulding in the arch. Hood-moulds on head-stops. Vaulting-shafts on deliberately thin corbels. Blank gallery of two triple openings to each bay below. Thinly cusped, again almost straight-sided arches – all structural elements in this

* Money *ad fabricam* (which may of course refer to any part of the building) is mentioned in 1256, 1262, and 1283.

transept are thin. Three encircled quatrefoils in bar tracery
above. The arches of course again nearly straight-sided. The
diapering above, direct from Westminster Abbey, has been
re-cut in the C19. The famous Westminster clerestory
windows of spherical-triangle form have very deep, stepped
sills to the inside.* Quadripartite vaults with fillets on the ribs
and bosses. The E aisle has windows shafted in Purbeck
marble and with stiff-leaf capitals. Above the E aisle was the
Muniment Room. It is now the CHAINED LIBRARY. That is 39
why the gallery has always been blank. The only openings
are small and paired and have shouldered lintels, typical of
the later C13. The arch to the chancel aisle below which
Aquablanca's monument was set is essentially triple-
chamfered and may be a later adjustment. The adjoining W
bay of the N chancel aisle was re-vaulted at the same time, and
it has at its E end a double-chamfered arch dying into the
imposts. The marvellous W window and N window are much
shafted and much ringed.

The EAST TRANSEPTS pose a problem. There is evidence
that they were begun at the time of the Lady Chapel campaign.
A respond on the W wall of the N side has been chiselled off
later, and on the E side there are two bases with attached bases
for flat columns which were later not used. They correspond
to the remains of a S doorway out of the SE transept preceding
the present one. The bases of shafts are all flat. As it finally
turned out, the transepts were built about 1300 – see their
windows. They have each a central octagonal pier with a foliage
capital already nobbly. The octagonal piers continue above it,
and the ribs of the vault die against this vertical piece. The
vault has leaf bosses. The RCHM dates the NE transept with its
vault to the early, the SE transept to the late C14. They can
only have been guided by the vault; for the SE windows are
exactly the same as those of the NE.

In the early C14, or indeed about 1300, several other
adjustments were made. They are the vaulting or re-vaulting
of the chancel aisles (minus the NW bay – see above) and of
both nave aisles. The ribs and bosses on the S side, at least
the first five bays from the E, are original. The bosses have
naturalistic foliage.

Later additions and alterations can be taken as one goes

* No wonder that Aquablanca should have followed Henry III's favourite
building so closely. He was a close follower of Henry III himself – to the
detriment of his relations with Hereford.

from E to W. Off the Lady Chapel to the S is the AUDLEY CHAPEL, built, as we have seen, before 1502. It presents to the Lady Chapel a panelled wall with a low doorway and a small four-light window spared out of the panelling. The arch is also panelled. The chapel is two-storeyed. The lower floor has a star-vault, hemmed in by the stair-turret. The upper floor has a lierne star-vault with cusped panels connected with the wall by fans. Off the N chancel aisle another chantry chapel had been added a little earlier, Bishop STANBURY'S CHAPEL. This has a fan-vault throughout. It was erected about 1480, and Mr Marshall has found that Thomas Morton, Archdeacon of Salop and later of Hereford, an executor of the bishop, a brother of the Archbishop of Canterbury, and with another brother a lessee of the bishop's house at Bosbury, can be connected with the fan-vault here as well as at Bosbury (see p. 78) and the porch of the Vicars' College (see p. 171). The chapel is small and highly decorated. All walls have stone panelling with many shields displayed in the panels. The S wall has it too, except that the doorway cuts into it. In the same wall by the side of the chapel the bishop's tomb (see Furnishings, p. 164). Wide shafts with foliage stops. Instead of capitals two angels, mermaids, and monsters.

When the CROSSING TOWER was rebuilt early in the C14, the interior stage visible inside received a strange palisade of completely undecorated, chamfered stone piers very closely set and with one transom. The whole may be a device to reduce the weight of the wall. The SOUTH TRANSEPT received a new S wall about 1400. The date is supported by the fact that Bishop Trevenant (1389–1404) has his monument clearly as part of the new architecture of the wall. The monument with its three canopies is below the great Perp window. L. and r. of this there is panelling, and more and closer panelling above it. The vault has the arms of Bishop Spoffard (1421–43) and is of the tierceron type, with one by two pairs of tiercerons and square bosses, the earliest tierceron-vault in the cathedral, an unbelievable conservatism. Also in the C15 the VESTRY was enlarged to the E by a two-storeyed piece. The ground floor has a plain quadripartite rib-vault with single-chamfered ribs.

Wyatt's work has been unjustly maligned. The decision to reduce the length of the nave by one bay was taken by dean and chapter in 1786, i.e. two years before he appeared on the stage, and although he could have saved the Norman gallery and inadequately continued it, his E.E. gallery with the simplest Y-tracery is not in the least offensive, and he repeated the Perp windows in an equally innocuous way. His vault is of timber, but that one cannot see, and the ribbing is again self-effacing: one by one pair of tiercerons in each bay. The vaulting corbels, of which one cannot quite say that, are by *Cottingham*.

FURNISHINGS

They are described as follows: Lady Chapel – Audley Chapel – Crypt – Vestibule – E Transepts N and S – Chancel Aisles N and S – Chancel – Crossing – Transepts N and S – Nave – N Aisle – N Porch – S Aisle. For every part monuments are placed at the end.

Hereford has many monuments, but only two or three of the first class, and it is unfortunate that those of the C17 and C18 have been all but wiped out.

LADY CHAPEL. ALTARPIECE. By *W. H. R. Blacking*, c.1950. Mixed Comper and Feibusch ingredients, and not a convincing mixture. – PAINTING. Painted figures under canopies, c.1500, against the screen of the Audley Chapel. Too dim to be judged. – STAINED GLASS. In the W bay on the S side the most beautiful glass in the cathedral. One light is patterns only, in the other, above Christ in Majesty, and below three quatrefoils. Of the late C13. – E window by *C. A. Gibbs*, 1852, and quite good; in the style of the C13. The design, it is said, was *Cottingham*'s. Mosaic-like effect of very small pieces of clean colours. – SE and all N windows also by *Gibbs*, 1867. Influenced by the C13 glass. – MONUMENTS. Johanna de Bohun, Countess of Hereford, † 1327. She is praying and wears a wimple. Over her head a nodding ogee canopy on two head-stops. Fleurons and little heads on the border. Arch on two head-stops. The top just ogee. – Peter de Grandison † 1352, brother of Bishop Grandison of Exeter. Tomb-chest with panelling. The legs of the effigy no longer crossed. Rib-vaulted recess with straight top. Above an open screen with four figures of saints and the Coronation 25a of the Virgin under arches. The top again straight, with a cresting. All simple, large forms. An early case of a decidedly Perp feeling – Perp in that it stresses the horizontals so much. – Brass to Richard de la Barr † 1386. The canon is represented (a 26 in. figure) inside a handsome ogee-cusped cross-head.

AUDLEY CHAPEL. DOORS. Three original doors, that into the chapel specially attractive. – RELIEF. Tuscan, C15, Virgin and Child, in an original frame. – STAINED GLASS. In the upper chapel shields and some small fragments.

CRYPT. ALTAR by *William Goscombe John*, 1920. – MONUMENT. Incised slab to Andrew Jones † 1497 and wife. Large figures under a massive double canopy.

27b   VESTIBULE. MONUMENT. A member of the Swinefield family; early C14. Beautiful long, slender figure with short beard. The hems of the gown fall nearly symmetrically and very melodiously. Arch with two hollow chamfers and one sunk quadrant. In the hollow chamfers many swine. At the foot also a few ballflowers. No ogee arches yet. Remains of PAINTING against the back wall. The recognizable head of one figure shows that this also was of high quality.

NORTH EAST TRANSEPT. SCULPTURE. The Norman capitals have already been discussed (p. 155). – PAINTING. Effaced wall-paintings on the s wall, high up. – STAINED GLASS. In the SE window four early C14 figures under tall canopies, nearly entirely, however, by *Warrington*, 1864. – The first window from the W on the N side is by *Heaton, Butler & Bayne*, 1877. – MONUMENTS. Coffin-lid of the C13, uncommonly densely foliated. – Parts of several others. – Recess with two orders of big ballflower. In it Civilian, badly defaced; late C13. – Indents, not for brass, but for a composition or cement infilling: one Priest late C14, one Knight early C15. – Dean Dawes, by *Matthew Noble*, 1869. Alabaster tomb-chest designed by *Scott*. White marble effigy on veined black marble slab. – Bishop Parfew † 1557, the effigy no more than a shapeless lump. Tomb-chest still entirely in the Gothic tradition. Four shields in quatrefoils. – Bishop Swinefield † 1317. Big recess. No effigy left. Arch with fine mouldings. Small ballflowers, also on the gable mouldings. The gable stands on two heads. In the gable an openwork pointed trefoil. Against the back wall a chiselled-off Crucifixion and a per-
25b   fectly remaining all-over pattern of trailing vine, still treated quite naturalistically. – Four unnamed stone effigies on the floor; all of the early C14 and all in their state of preservation past enjoying. – Brasses against the W wall. Bits of canopies, also a Priest, early C16, 13 in. long, and a late C15 Knight, of 2 ft 3 in.

SOUTH EAST TRANSEPT. WOODWORK. On the E wall frieze of ogee arches from a screen (cf. S chancel aisle). –

SCULPTURE. Statue of St John Baptist, about 4 ft tall; C15.
– STAINED GLASS. In the NE window, by *Warrington*, 1863.
In Warrington's glass it can be observed that only the shapes
of the medallions are inspired by the C13, but the groups are
still three-dimensional and realistic in the Renaissance
sense. – MONUMENTS. On the W wall brass to Richard
Rudhall † 1476, 4 ft 2 in. long, with parts of the buttress
strips l. and r., on which figures of saints. – On the S wall
brasses to a Priest † 1434 (2 ft), to Edmund Ryall † 1428
(headless; now 20½ in.), to a bearded Civilian † 1394 (19½ in.).
– Dean Harvey † 1500 (?). Tomb-chest with three shields in
quatrefoils. Alabaster effigy, defaced. – Brasses to Dean
Chaundler † 1490 (fragment, 23 in. long) and to John Stockton,
Mayor of Hereford, † 1480 (25 in.). – Bishop Lindsell † 1634.
Recumbent effigy. – Brass to William Porter † 1524. Only
parts are preserved. Large Annunciation from a canopy, and
eight small saints separately. – James Thomas † 1757. White
marble bust attributed by Mrs Esdaile to *Roubiliac*. – Bishop
Coke † 1646. Recumbent effigy. The architectural setting
destroyed by *Wyatt*. When was the group made which crowns
it now? – Bishop Charlton † 1369. Recumbent effigy, the
head chiselled off. Tomb-chest with shields in cusped foiled
fields. – On the floor Sir Richard de la Bere † 1514 and two
wives; 19 in. figures. – Also two ledger-stones, dates of death
1669 and 1691. Two clasped hands tie the two together, and
the inscription: In vita conjuncti, in morte non divisi.

NORTH CHANCEL AISLE. DOOR to the Stanbury Chapel;
original. – STAINED GLASS. NE window by *Warrington*, 1862.
Comment as above. – To its W Hunt Memorial Window by
Clayton & Bell. It must be a very early work. Charmingly
humble busts in medallions. – MAPPA MUNDI. Here is not
the place to discuss this. It is sufficient to recapitulate that it
is the work of *Richard de Bello*, treasurer of Lincoln Cathedral,
and that it was made shortly after 1280.* It is on vellum and
the Orbis terrarum itself is 4 ft 4 in. in diameter. From the
point of view of the history of art the most interesting facts
are these. The geography is based more on Greek (Pliny),
Roman (the Antonine Itinerary, the Physiologus), and Early
Christian literature than on travels, the population on

* On the one hand he signs himself Richard of Haldingham and Lafford,
and he held this prebend only till 1283; on the other hand Conway and
Caernarvon appear on his map, and Edward I began the great castles there
only in 1283.

bestiaries, and the books on the Marvels of the East. The purpose is part-informative, part-religious. At the bottom l. Caesar with a papal tiara orders the world to be surveyed. Here also Richard is found kneeling. Geography includes the pillars of Hercules (two columns), the wall built by Alexander the Great to enclose the giants, the Colossus of Rhodes, the Garden of Eden, the Labyrinth of Minos, Mount Olympus, but also Abraham at Ur, Lot's wife as a pillar of salt, the pyramid as Joseph's granary (a medieval barn), and a Norwegian on skis. True zoology is represented by elephant, lion, tiger, leopard, camel, crocodile, rhinoceros, bear, bull, ostrich, and parrot. They mix freely with manticora, pelican, yale, sphinx, phoenix, and the like, and human monstrosities abound (the cynocephales, the blemyae, the gangines and monocoli). – METAL GATES to the transept. By *Scott*, 1864, and made by *Skidmore*. – MONUMENTS. So-called Reynelm. This is the first of a distressingly uniform series of posthumous effigies of bishops made in the early C14 and placed under distressingly uniform arches. If one has 26 fleurons on the inner arch moulding and 25 on the hood-mould and another 22 and 31, that is all that can be said. Only the little heads at the foot and apex of the hood-moulds are rewarding. Most of the effigies are ponderous stuff too. – Bishop Stanbury † 1473. Alabaster monument, not in his chantry chapel but between aisle and altar, a place of honour. Tomb-chest with statuettes, still enjoyable. The effigy is quite powerful. – So-called Clive; *see* above under Reynelm. – So-called Mapenor. Again the same gesture, but shallow relief, the plinth tipped, not straight, better, and perhaps a little earlier than the others. – Bishop Bennett † 1617. Only the alabaster effigy. The setting included two columns and a coffered arch. – So-called Broase, same gesture as Reynelm, but no arch, and one hand holds a tower. This is usually a symbol of prominent building activity. So perhaps he was meant to be Reynelm. – Bishop Aquablanca, *see* N transept, below.

SOUTH CHANCEL AISLE. WOODWORK. Frieze of six plus six little blank ogee arches on colonnettes with shaft-ring. Probably from a C14 screen. – STAINED GLASS. Four excellent early C14 figures under big canopies. Also much grisaille. – METAL GATES. Like their N aisle companion by *Scott* and *Skidmore*, 1864. – MONUMENTS. In the s wall four more of the tedious recesses with posthumous effigies of bishops. The so-called Vere seems the earliest, a little lower in relief and with a little naturalistic foliage on the crozier. All recesses with ballflower. – Bishop Meyew † 1516. On a tall tomb-chest with eight saints. Recumbent effigy. The bold canopy, with crocketed ogee gables over pendant arches, the middle one canted forward, rib-vaulting inside, and pierced panelling above and behind the gables, is terribly re-cut. Stone screen towards the chancel. – So-called Losinga. Again the too familiar type. But he also holds a token-church. Low, almost straight-sided arch with big ballflowers to S and N.

CHANCEL. REREDOS. By *Cottingham*, 1852, executed by *W. Boulton* of Lambeth. – STALLS. Early C14, and of considerable interest, both historical and aesthetic. There are sixteen on the N side, fifteen plus the triple-throne of the bishop on the S side. The fronts are imitation, imitated from the original panelled front of the Bishop's Throne, but the back parts are fully original. They have nodding ogee canopies on detached shafts, with panelling going forward and backward above the canopies and a straight cornice or top-rail. The back panels have simple tracery. The ends are again panelled and have pairs of nodding ogee arches with pinnacles to finish them. The set of MISERICORDS is one of the best of its date in England, an early date, it must be remembered. They represent a variety of subjects, all secular, including woodwoses, a mermaid, a fox and geese, a stag and hound, a hunter and a boar, a lion and lioness, a griffin, a goat playing the lute, divers monsters, divers human heads, a domestic scene of husband and wife by a cauldron, etc. – The BISHOP'S THRONE is three-seated. The side-seats have nodding ogee arches like the stalls, but tall crowning crocketed pinnacles. The Bishop's Throne proper has a three-sided canopy with ogee arches instead, and above a thicket of thin shafts rising to the full height of the arcade. – CHAIR. Of the early C13; 13a i.e. something extremely rare. Armchair, with all members turned. The front below the seat had little arches. Two are preserved. – SCULPTURE. Statue of St Ethelbert. Stone, and to be assigned to the C14. – STAINED GLASS. The E window high up was designed by *Pugin* – so Mrs Stanton has discovered – and made by *Hardman* in 1851. – The window over the organ is of 1889, by *Burlison & Grylls*. – TILE PAVEMENT. By *William Godwin* of Lugwardine, the design by *Scott*. – MONUMENT. Brass to Bishop Trillack † 1360. A 5 ft figure under a cusped and sub-cusped arch with an ogee gable. Above, round arch and straight top – the turn from Dec to Perp.

CROSSING. SCREEN. Designed by *Scott* and made by *Skidmore* of Coventry in 1862. The *Illustrated London News* calls it 'a beautiful specimen of art manufacture', enumerates what is iron, what copper, and what brass, and mentions that about 300 cut and polished stones are made use of. The passion flower, naturalistically treated, appears often and prominently. The screen was shown at the International Exhibition of 1862. It is indeed a High Victorian monument of the first order. It is not imitative, but shows an original handling of Gothic motifs, fully representative of its own date, in self-confidence, robustness, and zest in ornamentation. Remarkable sense of what wrought metal can do. Many of the fine openwork scrolls are doubled in depth.

NORTH TRANSEPT. SCULPTURE. More Norman capitals (*see* p. 155). – STAINED GLASS. The N window is a Victorian piece to be proud of. It is by *Hardman*, of 1864. Two very large medallions going through three lights each, and twenty smaller medallions. – In the W windows C15 figure fragments said to come from the nave W window. – The circular clerestory windows are by *Clayton & Bell*, *c*.1875–90. – Also by *Clayton & Bell* the transept aisle N, *c*.1870. – By Wailes, *c*. 1865–70, the N and S windows in the E wall. – MONUMENTS. The N transept holds the only two monuments at Hereford which are outstanding among any of their time in England: Bishop Aquablanca's and St Thomas of Cantelupe's. Bishop Aquablanca † 1268. Between the chancel aisle and the transept which he created. The architecture is more important now than the sculpture; for the effigy is defaced, and though the little heads on the border separated by slender blank two-light windows are charming, well preserved on the N side, and even exhibit some of their original colour, this cannot compete with the spare, incisive architecture of the canopy with its steeply erect gables. The head of the bishop lies on a diagonally placed pillow which in its turn lies on a cusped arch. The canopy stands on the most delicate Purbeck shafts or groups of them. It has exquisitely moulded arches with a quatrefoiled circle in each. In the gables a circle without foiling. All these details are in bar tracery, i.e. entirely transparent. Between the gables quatrefoil shafts rise and end in spires. The crockets and the small foliage at the top otherwise is all stiff-leaf, but of the bosses inside the little three-bay vault the E and W ones are naturalistic. Such foliage had been introduced at Westminster Abbey between 1245

and c.1250, but did not as a rule become much accepted outside until later in the century. In fact, the Crucifixus on the
central finial on the s side hangs from a cross that is all stiff-
leaf. – Bishop Cantelupe's Shrine. Erected probably for the
transfer of the body to this place in 1287. The tomb-chest is 19b
of six bays. Knights (probably Templars, as Cantelupe was
Provincial Grand Master of the order) in a diversity of nimble
attitudes, extremely well observed, stand under cinquefoiled
pointed arches. The arches rest on short colonnettes with
leaf capitals. Naturalistic, yet skilfully composed foliage in the
spandrels. The effigy is missing. It was covered by an upper
structure with open, pointed-trefoiled arches on shafts with
moulded capitals but again naturalistically foliated spandrels.
The top was no doubt to carry the *feretrum*, or shrine proper.
– Defaced effigy of a Priest, early C14. – Brass to Dean
Frowsetoure † 1529. The figure 4 ft 3 in.; side strips with
saints. – Brasses to Richard Delamare † 1435 and wife.
Excellent large figures (5 ft 6 in.) under two ogee-sided
gables. – Bishop Field † 1636, alabaster demi-figure, a type
usual for dons and divines. – Bishop Charlton † 1343. Effigy
with his head on a pillow stuffed into an ample canopy whose
top projects as a semicircle. Cusped and sub-cusped arch.
On two of the cusps censing angels, on the others large leaves.
Crocketed gable with finial. No ogees. – Bishop Westphaling
† 1601, an Elizabethan mandarin. The effigy is again deprived
of its setting. – Bishop Atlay † 1894. Free-standing tomb-chest
of white and red marble. Recumbent effigy by *Forsyth*.*

SOUTH TRANSEPT. ALTARPIECE. A South German
triptych, the centre a relief of about 1520–30, the painted
wings mid-C16 and of quite a different school. – Five STALLS
from the choir, *see* above, p. 165. They are built up of original
parts in the canopies and some original bits below (the figures
on the end arm-rests e.g.). – STAINED GLASS. The great s
window by *Kempe*, 1895. It is curious how parochial, i.e.
un-cathedral, his glass is. – MONUMENTS. Bishop Trevenant
† 1404. The effigy is deprived of its face, a special trick of the
Hereford vandals. Fine triple canopy with a rib-vault inside
represented almost in plan, i.e. almost vertically. Ogee gables,
crocketed, and finials. Very well tied into the architecture of
the whole wall. – Alexander Denton † 1576 and wife. Alabaster
effigies, a baby lying by her leg. Pilasters on the tomb-chest.

* On the gallery of the N transept William Evans and wife, dated 1659.
Two frontal demi-figures, his hand on a book, hers on a skull.

NAVE. PULPITS. One oblong, of plain boards with a pierced quatrefoil, perhaps not made for the purpose, yet traditionally said to be in use in the Civil War. The other of the mid C17, with big panels separated by pairs of columns. Strapwork cartouches against the underside of the pulpit. C18 tester, Gothick. – FONT. Norman, tub-shaped. Figures in an arcade. Greek key above, a motif rare in England. Against the foot four demi-figures of lions (of marble?). – MONUMENT. Sir Richard Pembridge † 1375. Alabaster Knight, his head on his helmet. Tomb-chest with shields in quatrefoils.

NORTH AISLE. STAINED GLASS. Above the Booth monument. By *Warrington*, 1862. – First window from E by *Heaton, Butler & Bayne*, 1888. – MONUMENT. Bishop Booth † 1535. Recumbent effigy. Ogee arch with five cusps. Crockets and finial. In front iron railing.

NORTH PORCH. DOORS. Small original door to the stair-turret. – Large N door by *Potter* of London, c.1854.

SOUTH AISLE. STAINED GLASS. In one window a jumble of old fragments. – MONUMENTS. Two of c.1330–40, one under a septfoiled arch and with a good small head at the apex, the other faceless under an arch similar to that of Bishop Charlton in the N transept.

PLATE. Chalice and Paten from the grave of Chancellor Swinefield, i.e. of before 1299. Dated by Oman one late C12 to late C13, the other C13. The paten has the *manus dei*. – Bishop's Mace, probably mid-C17. – Dean's Mace, c.1660–80. – Tall, silver-gilt Candlesticks, London, 1719. – Bishop's Mace, 1746. – Two Chalices, two Flagons, and Almsdish, silver-gilt, London, 1772. – Bishop's Mace, c.1830. – Tray and Straining Spoon, silver-gilt, London, 1831. – Chalice, neo-medieval, Birmingham, 1866. – Also, belonging to St John Baptist, the parish church in the cathedral: two Chalices, London, 1762. – Paten and two Plates, Sheffield, 1819. – Finally (exhibited in the Chained Library) the Shrine of St Thomas of Canterbury, early C13, with Limoges enamel, 7 by 3½ in. On the front the martyrdom of St Thomas, on the front of the roof his funeral. On the ends saints under arches.

THE PRECINCT

As has been pointed out, Hereford has no precinct proper. Only to the S of the cathedral are there traces of a consistent group of sustained interest. To the W, N, and E the cathedral, except for the lawn, might be in a Continental town.

BISHOP'S CLOISTER. This is the normal cathedral cloister, although not normal in never having had a N walk, and unfortunate in having been deprived of half its w walk. The cloister was built in the C15. A *clericus novi claustri* is referred to in 1412–13, and the name of a man is inscribed in the vault of the E walk who became a canon in 1406. However, the E wall of the E walk is substantially earlier, see a Norman buttress. Also the chapter-house entrance is part of it, and this, as we shall see, dates from the 1360s. The C15 arcading towards the garth is, with one exception, the same all the way through. Four lights with an irregularly sexfoiled circle in an odd place in each light. Four-centred arches. The exception is the bay where the entry to the chapter house is placed. Here there is a taller opening with a two-centred arch, and an upper storey, known as the Lady's Arbour. The inside of this is very light, as the walls are generously glazed: five lights w, four N, four s. Stair-turret at the SE corner. The cloister is entered from the s aisle by a doorway of *c*.1300 (two orders of shafts with nobbly-leaf capitals, arch depressed – two-centred on vertical pieces). The vaults of the E range are partly of plaster, probably Georgian, and partly original. The original part begins in the bay with the entrance to the chapter house. The vaults – all except the SE corner – are tierceron stars, each cell arched towards the apex so that the main boss forms a concave-sided octagon. The bosses are figured, but of a comparatively elementary quality. The same design continues in the s walk, but this is now separated as the LOWER LIBRARY.* The w range has nothing but two openings to the garth. The rest was rebuilt as a LIBRARY by *Sir Arthur Blomfield* in 1897. In the centre of the garth, in former times, stood a preaching cross. – MONUMENTS. In the E walk Col. John Matthews † 1826. Of stone, local workmanship. An angel comforts a seated mourning woman. – Several pretty tablets. – In the Lower Library Richard James Powell † 1834. Inscription held by a seraph. Very Gothic surround.

CHAPTER HOUSE. The chapter house was disgracefully pulled down in 1769, after the lead of the roof had been stripped off in the Civil War. The building has recently been recognized as of uncommon architectural interest, in so far as, according to old illustrations, it was fan-vaulted, and its fan-vault is

---

* In the Library an extremely fine CHEST of about 1300. Big rosettes on the broad side-uprights. Arches with close intersected tracery between. The design is both rich and elegant.

one of the earliest if not the earliest of which we know. The cloisters of Gloucester are always given this honour, but we know of them only that they were begun by an abbot who ruled from 1351 till 1377. Now for Hereford we have the contract of 1364 binding Thomas de Cantebrugge of Hereford to continue and finish ('continuaverit et perfecerit') the work of the new chapter house in the course of the next seven years. What remains today is as follows. First the entrance from the cloister. Two orders of shafts and a *trumeau* in the middle. Nobbly capitals and arch mouldings with fillets. The two openings have shapely trefoiled heads. A pierced pointed quatrefoil over with a slight ogee curve at the foot. Gable with trefoil. All this is entirely Dec and has not a touch of Perp. Through this entrance one reaches a vestibule, which was rib-vaulted. The springers of the filleted ribs remain, and a fragment of the s jamb of the portal to the chapter house proper. The chapter house was decagonal. Three sides on the s stand up to a certain height and show their tall panelling with cusped blank arches and scanty remains of scenes in the spandrels. In the middle lies what seems the defaced central springing stone of the fan-vault. It need not be added that the panelling of walls as well as fan-vaulting are Perp motifs.

COLLEGE OF VICARS CHORAL. The vicars choral were a body of men in orders or minor orders who acted for absent prebendaries. The college was founded at Hereford in 1396. It was to have twenty-six vicars and a custos. Its original hall is partly preserved behind No. 29 Castle Street (*see* p. 189). They were given the present site in 1473 and built here four ranges round a not quite regular quadrangle as their living quarters, with hall and chapel, both since completely altered. The arrangement was much like that of e.g. the fellows of Eton College. The quadrangle was connected by a corridor with the s transept of the cathedral, and had in addition a separate entrance with porch on the s side into which the corridor also runs. The premises are more complete than any of such an institution other than Wells and Windsor. The CORRIDOR is reached from the church by a small doorway with a four-centred head, set in a rectangular frame. The corridor has simple two-light windows to the E only and a handsome tie-beam roof with cambered, traceried tie-beams and decorated principals. Kingposts with figures carved against them. Moulded purlins and rafters. Close to the doorway from the church parts of the CHOIR SCREEN of the

30b

cathedral have been assembled into a door. The dado had
uncommonly fine six-light blank arcading in intersected
arches – a Perp version of a motif of 1300. In the corridor yet
more of the original Norman capitals are put together.* By a
turn to the E one gets to the PORCH, a pretty, fan-vaulted room
open to the corridor and the N. To the N a portal with two-
centred arch and tracery in the spandrels. The porch has an
upper storey which is too weathered to be recognizable in its
carved details. Original DOOR. Oddly enough the porch doors
connect with the cloister only by a dog-legged corridor. The
cloister has extremely simple two-light openings with very
flat arches. The upper storey projects to above the walks and
has only one-light windows. To the N, i.e. the close, the whole
college was opened out in the C18 by giving it large sash
windows on both storeys. The HALL lies in the centre of the
S wing. It projects beyond the S range and is also entirely
georgianized. Large windows, that to the S arched. Plain
panelling on the walls. The CHAPEL is in the E range projecting E. The projecting part is stone, the inner walls timber-
framed. To the cloister walk the chapel originally opened in
a screen. Its Jacobean balusters are *in situ*. The thin roof-
timbers are C17 too. In addition, on the first floor in the SE
corner is the LIBRARY (now Dean's private study). This was
made Gothic in 1830. The date is in the STAINED GLASS of
the added canted bay window. The room has a coved ceiling,
Gothic doors, and a Gothic small-patterned wallpaper.

BISHOP'S PALACE. The bishop's palace lies to the SW of the
cathedral. It is entered by a Perp GATEHOUSE with four-
centred arches, double-chamfered and triple-chamfered, to
the entry and exit. Timber-framed gable to the outside above.
The range to its E is all timber-framed to the N, brick-faced
to the S. The forecourt of the palace proper which this brick
front overlooks from the N has a large plane tree in the middle
and the STABLES on the w. Stone, symmetrical, with gables,
probably of the 1840s. The palace proper does not make a
show. Its façade consists of various parts, first one of brick,
gabled and apparently Victorian, then a neo-Norman porch,
probably of the Cottingham time, then five bays of two-
storeyed, sashed Georgian brick, and then a projecting recent
wing. To the E the impression is not more unified. Georgian
centre, stone-faced with sash windows on one and two
floors, and a later gabled bay on the r. On the l. and round the

* They should all be collected in one place and adequately displayed.

corner to the s, i.e. the garden sloping down to the river, it is
Victorian brick, with gables. The Georgian work is attributed
to Bishop Bisse (1712–21) but may be later. The neo-Tudor
part has rainwater heads with the date 1841. The palace is
entered by the porch. The porch is the first hint at what gives
the palace national and even international importance: the
fact that its main range, indifferent as it looks, encases the
14a BISHOPS' GREAT HALL, a structure of the late C12; of its
monumental timber arcading, dividing a nave from two aisles,
surprisingly much is preserved and now made exemplarily
easy of access. The hall is about 55 ft wide and was at least
75 ft long. We have evidence of three bays, but there may
have been four. The nave spanned 29 ft, each aisle 13 ft.
Encased in the pilasters of the entrance hall are the mighty
arcade posts, square, 16 by 16 in., with sturdy shafts, four of
them, or rather two posts and two responds, and a third in
the s wall of a room adjoining to the s. The timbers used for
the posts must, as the shafts are not separate and jointed on,
have been of a $4\frac{1}{2}$ by $4\frac{1}{2}$ ft scantling. One post ascends into
the roof, and so one is able to see in addition two scalloped
capitals and one full arch connecting them, i.e. an arcade arch.
It has a moulding of a half-roll and two quadrant hollows and
a nailed-on hood-mould with nail-head decoration. The use
of nails is most surprising. A second arch, in two pieces, lies
at the time of writing in the gatehouse. These arcade arches
are of course really longitudinal arched braces supporting the
wall-plate. However, Messrs Jones and Smith have recently
proved that this wall-plate was only a sub-plate and that the
real wall-plate, i.e. the eaves line of the roof, sat higher up.
How the original roof was built is not certain. No transverse
arches across nave or aisles are preserved. The structure is
one of the oldest secular timber structures in England.*
Of later interiors it is enough to mention the PANELLING
now in the chapel but formerly in the drawing room. This is
grandly done, with tall Corinthian pilasters, and has been
convincingly ascribed to Bisse. When it was still the DRAWING
ROOM, this room had right in the middle an exposed Norman
pier. The wife of a C20 bishop, so it is said, had it cut off.
The ENTRANCE HALL is an odd tripartite room, the centre

* Priority may have to go to the roof of the great hall of Leicester Castle,
if Professor W. Horn is right in his dating. Messrs S. R. Jones and J. T. Smith,
whose paper appeared in *Mediaeval Archaeology*, IV, 1960, consider the
former existence of a clerestory at Hereford possible. It would be a unique
feature.

with giant pilasters, the ends with lower pilasters to support apses. The idea of the apse was no doubt developed from the Norman arcade arches which run or ran immediately above the place where the apses meet the higher part. The conception of the room may be Bisse's, the more recent remodelling is of the last third of the C19.

Only one more fragment must now be discussed, but one which, side by side with the bishop's hall, is the most ancient of Hereford: the scanty remains of the BISHOP'S CHAPEL or Chapel of St Katherine and Mary Magdalene. This was built by Bishop Losinga, i.e. before 1095. William of Malmesbury says that Losinga built *ecclesiam in tereti scemate Aquensem basilicam pro modo imitatus suo*. 'Pro modo suo' has to be taken with more than one pinch of salt; for the chapel is similar to Charlemagne's palace only in so far as it was what the Germans call a *Doppelkapelle*. It is, however, much more similar to those of Mainz and Goslar, but earlier than they, and indeed the earliest of all surviving examples of its type, a type described erroneously by Dr Schürer, the German specialist on *Doppelkapellen*, as 'an autochthonous invention of German architecture and its exclusive property'. The type is characterized by square shape, and a horizontal division into a lower and an upper church. This latter feature was the usual thing in oblong palace chapels as well – cf. e.g. the Sainte Chapelle in Paris and the Chapel of St Stephen at Westminster Palace. However, in both these cases the two are entirely separated, whereas they were vertically united here, and that also was a customary thing which still applies to the chapel at Versailles, i.e. to about 1700, and even the Asams' private chapel at Munich of about 1740. At Hereford (and also at Mainz and Goslar) the connexion was made in the following way. The building which still stood in 1737, when Stukeley illustrated it, had four middle piers. Between them there was the opening linking the lower with the upper chapel. At Aachen of course the opening is much larger and octagonal and the upper chapel is essentially (as at Versailles and the Asam church) a gallery round the opening. The Bishop's Chapel at Hereford had a deeply splayed W entrance, almost like a niche – which does connect it with Aachen – and a short oblong E chancel. All that survives is the wall against the S range of the cloister. On the ground floor one sees three low, plain, unmoulded arches. Set under the W and E arches a small window, under the middle arch probably a third, at some later stage converted into a doorway. The upper floor has segmental arches on lowish imposts, all now blocked. Much tufa, no doubt from the chapel, is used in the blocking. – In the r. window on the lower floor some PAINTING of scrolls in red, probably C13.

OTHER CHURCHES

Before the Civil War Hereford had five parish churches. St Martin and St Owen were destroyed in the siege of 1645. St Martin was rebuilt in 1845, St Nicholas in 1842. So there are only two medieval parish churches left. Both, however, are substantial buildings.

ALL SAINTS, High Street. The steeple faces down Broad Street towards the area in front of the cathedral. The church is large and essentially of the period when Herefordshire was most active in parochial architecture, the late C13 to early C14. But there is older evidence preserved, though it must be looked for. In the pier separating the N aisle arcade from the N chancel chapel arcade, parts have been exposed of a compound pier of the earlier C13 of which the long s shaft with a fillet was part of the respond of the chancel arch, the group of shafts to the W the E respond of the aisle arcade, and the group to the N the s respond of the arch between aisle and former chapel. The capitals of the latter are moulded, of the former two decorated with stiff-leaf. Excavations have proved that the aisle was narrower than the present aisle. The corbel table of the chapel, which exists and can be seen from inside the present chapel, shows that it was also lower. On the s side evidence of the same development exists in the E responds of the s chapel arch, again of respond and arch, and again with stiff-leaf. The rebuilding of the late C13 to early C14 was sweeping. It began at the E end of the s arcade, where the respond is a corbel still with stiff-leaf. It is true that this respond is not *in situ*, but that does not alter the case. It was shifted W and the E bay of the arcade made narrower when the stair-turret to the rood-loft was inserted in the C15. The arcade is of five bays, and the piers to the widened aisle are circular with octagonal abaci, or rather square abaci set diagonally and chamfered at the corners (cf. Clehonger, Eaton Bishop, Madley). The arches are triple-chamfered. The arch to the widened s chapel is of two continuous chamfers. The N arcade starts E of the tower which occupies the NW corner. It is a grand tower and seems to have been begun a

little before the N arcade. It has a very tall W lancet and a
quadruple-chamfered arch towards the arcade, but no opening
to the nave. The bell-openings are, on each side, three
beautifully tall stepped lancet lights under one arch; i.e. even
that stage was reached before 1300. The spire rises behind
battlements, and has big lucarnes at its foot. They are gabled
and Dec. The N arcade differs from the S arcade only in having
round abaci. The N chapel opens to the chancel in a single arch,
but one wider than that opposite. The windows confirm the
stylistic evidence of the arcade. Those of the clerestory are
single lancets (entirely renewed). The W window is of five
stepped lancet lights (much renewed). The windows of the N
aisle of three stepped lancet lights with the peculiar Herefordshire details.* The transition to the Dec style is evident in the
chancel N and S windows and the piscina decorated with
ballflower. The sedilia are too badly damaged to be considered.
Dec also the straight-headed S aisle windows with the reticulation units. Finally Perp the large five-light E window, to the
l. and r. of which small doorways must have led into an E
vestry (cf. East Anglia), and the ornate, shallow little porch
which has been shifted from the aisle S doorway to the chancel
S doorway. It has a cusped and subcusped arch, tracery in the
spandrels, and battlements. The nave roof has tie-beams on
arched braces, kingposts, and much tracery to their l. and r.
The chancel roof is of the wagon type with bosses at the
intersections. The roof of the N aisle has hammerbeams and
is of such a size as to have made it necessary to do away with
the N clerestory windows of the nave.

FURNISHINGS. PULPIT. Dated 1621. An unusually ornate
piece, with the familiar short blank arches all studded and the
space below them filled with decoration. Also panels above
of a type more usual after 1630 than before. – STALLS.
Excellent C14 set with panelled backs and canopies. Panels 41a
as well as canopies with richly cusped ogee arches, the latter
three-dimensional or nodding. Much delicate tracery above.
The seats have MISERICORDS of foliage, bearded faces (one
a king), an angel, two mermaids, a whole creeping human
figure, two birds, two mice, two bears (?) addorsed, a lion,
etc. – REREDOS in the S chapel. Of c.1700. To the l. and r. a
niche flanked by fluted Corinthian pilasters, the centre a little
lower and perhaps not in its original shape. – CHEST. Excellent
C14 chest with chip-carved interlaced arches and tracery and

* The chapel E window is C19.

l. and r. and above rosettes etc. – BREADSHELF (N aisle w).
Dated 1683, yet still with strapwork and little obelisks at the
top. – TILES. Some of the C15; N aisle, E end, s pier. – PAINT-
ING. On the E wall, s of the window, defaced C15 painting of
a large kneeling female figure. – STAINED GLASS. E window
by *M. E. Aldrich Rope*, 1933. – HOUR GLASS with wooden
stand, C17 or C18 (vestry). – PLATE. Chalice and Cover Paten
by *H.S.*, 1571; Chalice and Cover Paten, 1634; Paten on foot,
1707; pair of Patens by *John Eastt*, 1724; Flagon, 1731; all
made in London. – CURIOSUM. Chained books in the s
chapel, given by one who died in 1715.

ST FRANCIS XAVIER (R.C.), Broad Street. 1838–9 by *Charles
Day*. The front, hemmed in by houses, is bewildering, and
would have driven Pugin frantic had he known it. It is an
imitation of the Treasury of the Athenians at Delphi, only
taller and narrower in the proportions. Two giant Greek
Doric columns *in antis* and a pediment – all stuccoed. Short
towers had been planned. Inside coved ceiling. Of the three
square centre panels the easternmost is replaced by a dome
on pendentives glazed along its sides. The altar is framed by
unfluted Ionic columns.

ST JAMES, Green Street. 1869 by *Thomas Nicholson*. The
interior burnt out in 1901 and rebuilt in 1902–3 to the
design of *Nicholson & Hartree*. In the Geometrical style; no
tower.

ST MARTIN, Ross Road. This was in the Middle Ages the
mother church to which All Saints belonged as a chapel.
1845 by *R. W. Jearrad*; the chancel remodelled as usual. This
is by *Nicholson & Sons*, 1894. The church in the lancet style
with a thin w tower and a spire on squashed broaches. Much
buttressing. Roof with heavy hammerbeams, but ceiled. –
PLATE. Flagon, London, 1741.

ST NICHOLAS, Friars Street. 1842 by *Thomas Duckham*. Of
stone, in the lancet style, with a w tower. Wide, barren
interior. – PLATE. Chalice, 1778; Paten, 1780; fine Flagon by
Edward Pocock, 1782; all London-made.

ST PAUL, Church Road, Tupsley. 1865 by *F. R. Kempson*. A
prosperous church. Plate and bar tracery. SW tower with
broach spire. Ornate foliate capitals on piers of blue stone.

ST PETER, St Peter Street. Restoration by *Nicholson*, 1880–5.
Externally very overdone; the nave, s aisle, and s porch
actually rebuilt. The powerful tower is at the SE end. It dates
from the late C13 and has big angle buttresses connected by a

diagonal. Small single-chamfered doorway to the w, once leading to the outside, not into the aisle. To the chancel a C13 and a larger C14 arch. The bell-openings are pairs of trefoil-headed lancets. C19 pinnacles. Recessed spire with heavily gabled lucarnes at the foot. About 1300 most of the building was erected in its present form. The arcades of four bays have slim and tall quatrefoil piers with thin shafts in the diagonals and almost straight-sided double-chamfered arches. The S arcade actually is a complete rebuilding of the 1880s. The chancel arch, the chancel windows, the aisle and chapel windows all belong to c.1300. There is no ogee arch anywhere. The best roof is that of the S chapel, which has a low pitch and kingposts and some tracery on the tie-beams. – STALLS. C15. Originally provided for the priory of St Guthlac. With panelled backs and a top frieze of little pendant arches and a quatrefoil frieze. Panelled fronts as well. MISERICORDS with roses. – ORGAN CASE. Made up with panels of c.1700, including two with musical still lifes. – ROYAL ARMS of William III, carved (N aisle). – GABLE CROSS. C13, a fine simple stone piece, probably from St Guthlac's Priory. – PLATE. Chalice and Cover Paten, Flagon, and Salver by *H.O.*, 1713; two Plates by *John Eastt*, 1720; silver-gilt Chalice by *Edward Vincent* (?), 1729; Flagon, the largest in Herefordshire, 1729, also by *Vincent*; Chalice and Cover Paten, 1749; all London-made.

HOLY TRINITY. 1883 by *F. R. Kempson*; chancel 1907 by *Nicholson & Hartree*. In the E.E. style, large, prosperous, and uniform, as yet without a tower. The late H. S. Goodhart-Rendel called it 'the dullest design I have ever seen – not worth describing'.

BAPTIST CHURCH, Commercial Road. 1880. Italianate and bare. Yellow brick and stone. The windows with Venetian tracery; a pedimental gable right across the façade.

EIGNBROOK CONGREGATIONAL CHURCH, Eign Street. A perverse little Gothic job, with a NW tower (i.e. ritually NW) doing the oddest things, and a bevelled SW corner. It was called in a contemporary newspaper 'piquant looking'. So this quality was felt at the time. They also refer to the iron pillars (by the Coalbrookdale Company) with foliated caps, and the polygonal apse. 1872–3 by *Haddon Bros*.

FRIENDS MEETING HOUSE, No. 21 King Street. Built in a backyard in 1822. Red brick, quite plain, and with a three-bay house nearly attached to it.

PUBLIC BUILDINGS

61a SHIRE HALL, St Peter Street. 1817–19 by *Sir Robert Smirke*. Greek Doric portico of six columns with two return columns and a pediment. The order is taken from the so-called Theseion in Athens. Plain, square flanking bays l. and r. The hall at the back is of 1862; Venetian tracery in the windows. – The STATUE in the forecourt represents Sir George Cornewall Lewis and is by *Baron Marochetti*, 1864.

TOWN HALL, St Owen Street. 1902–4 by *H. A. Cheers*. Very typical of its date. All brown terracotta. All very gay and busy. Symmetrical with two domed polygonal angle towers, a steep gable in the middle, and a wooden lantern with detached columns. Arched doorway under a deep arched canopy. – REGALIA. Principal Sword, 1677. – Second Sword, hilt and pommel probably C15, blade Elizabethan. – Porter's Badges presented in 1583. – Silver Bailiff's Seal, C14. – Silver Seal, late C17. – Four Maces said to have been presented in 1676. – Covered Cup presented in 1675. – Two Candlesticks dated 1667–70.

POLICE STATION, Gaol Street. 1842 by *Trehern & Duckham*. Built as the city gaol. Two-storeyed, rock-faced. The r. wing demolished when Delany Street was cut through. The centre is of three bays, pedimented, with a heavily rusticated doorway. The remaining wing has four bays. The arched upper windows are barred.

GENERAL POST OFFICE, Broad Street. At the back, in Church Street, a re-erected C15 doorway. It comes from a house in Broad Street (RCHM, Mon. No. 34).

WATERWORKS, Broomy Hill. The very prominent Italianate tower (in the national waterworks style) is of yellow and red brick and dates from 1880–2. It is 101 ft high.

PUBLIC LIBRARY AND MUSEUM, Broad Street. 1872–4 by *F. R. Kempson*. Very Gothic, and too tall for its place in the street so close to the cathedral. Much ornamental carving, and three bristly dormers above the quatrefoil frieze at the top.

HEREFORDSHIRE TECHNICAL COLLEGE, Folly Lane. By *A. W. Usher* (County Architect) with *E. Blight*. First part begun in 1954, second part in 1957.

HEREFORDSHIRE COLLEGE OF ART, Castle Green, see p. 190.

HEREFORD TRAINING COLLEGE, Venns Lane. 1881 by *Kempson*. Gothic and institutional. The tower has the unusual feature of four steep stepped gables.

CATHEDRAL SCHOOL, immediately E of the cathedral. In 1796 the school went into a brick building taking the place of the W range of the cloister. This had been built in 1779 and does not exist any longer. The present premises are of 1875 with additions of 1911 and after. Among the additions are a number of existing houses adapted for school use, e.g. the Deanery and No. 1 Castle Street.

BLUECOAT SCHOOL, Widemarsh Street. Former Girls' High School. Built in 1914–15. Architect *G. H. Jack*, the county surveyor. Red brick and brown stone. Symmetrical, with large middle windows and middle lantern. Typical the shallow curves over the two entrances.

HIGH SCHOOL FOR BOYS, Widemarsh Street. 1910–12 by *G. H. Jack*. Also symmetrical, and also typical, e.g. in the fancy turret and the semicircular gables and doorhood.

HIGH SCHOOL FOR GIRLS, Folly Lane. Begun in 1954. By *A. W. Usher*, the County Architect (with *M. F. Brake*).

GENERAL HOSPITAL, Nelson Street. The oldest part is of 1779–83 and ascribed to *William Parker*. It is of brick, nine bays wide and three storeys high with a five-bay pediment, and it overlooks the river Wye. The *Hereford Guide* of 1796 calls it 'commodious and elegant'. Additions 1833, 1887, etc.

MARKET HALL (former), *see* p. 181.

STATION. 1855 by *Johnson* of Birkenhead. Tudor.

WYE BRIDGE. Essentially of 1490, though often repaired, and in 1826 widened. Six arches and cutwaters. Four of the arches are original. They are four-centred and double-chamfered. One arch was rebuilt segmental after the siege of 1645, and the southernmost arch is of the C18 and supports a second, probably C17, arch.

FOOTBRIDGE, S of Castle Green. A suspension bridge built in 1898.

PERAMBULATIONS

INNER HEREFORD

Inner Hereford is here meant to comprise the following area: The river forms the s boundary. The boundary then runs N along Victoria Street and Edgar Street, then E to the railway station, s along the railway, and s w by Ledbury Road, St James Road, and Nelson Street back to the river.

As in several cathedral cities, the urban artery, i.e. High Street, High Town, etc., runs N of the cathedral and parallel with it. Since this is an urban perambulation, it is where the start must be made.

The centre of Hereford was different from what it is now, as long as HIGH TOWN was not the wide, market-place-like open space it has become. It had on an island some of the most important buildings of the town, including the High Cross, the Town Hall, and the Tolsey. The OLD TOWN 47 HALL in particular was a sight to thrill any visitor from England or abroad. It was the most fantastic black and white building imaginable, three-storeyed, with gables and the richest, most curious decoration. It was built about 1600 and has without sufficient reason been attributed to *John Abel*. Its upper floor was taken down in 1792 and the rest was demolished in 1862 – a memorable piece of municipal vandalism (and stupidity). In its absence the OLD HOUSE, really the Butchers' Hall, can take its place. This stands free now like a town hall and is certainly lively enough too in its black and white. It was built in 1621 (see the overmantel with three caryatids on the upper floor) and has all narrowly-set uprights. The windows project on brackets, the bargeboards are carved, and there are angle pendants to the gabled top storey. On the s side the timbering beneath the gables has concave-sided lozenge-bracing, and in the middle this is cusped. There is also on that side a porch with thoroughly decorated posts, lintel, brackets, and bargeboards. Inside, one ground-floor room has a plaster ceiling with small motifs including cherubs' heads.

Taking the Old House as our hub, we first move to the w along HIGH TOWN. On the s side ALBAN HOUSE, c.1865, but still with giant pilasters, pedimented first-floor windows, and a top balustrade. (Then No. 20, which has a tunnel-vaulted cellar with a four-centred section, probably of c.1500, and, on the N side of the street, Nos 14–15 with exposed timber-framing at the back and an upper room with original panelling. RCHM) Opposite the former MARKET HALL, 1861 by *John Clayton*, only one bay, i.e. not detached, and in a kind of free English Wren–Gibbs style, handled without much respect.

High Town is continued in HIGH STREET, where No. 3 is one of the few ornate black and white houses left. Only one gable in width, but concave-sided lozenges and decorated barge-boards; c.1600. Nos 6–8 is memorable for the grimness of Victorian Gothic. Flat, and of yellow brick with red and black brick accents. Immediately w of All Saints, No. 2 EIGN STREET has a cellar with a rib-vault. There are two bays left, and there may have been more. Heavy, chamfered ribs and a number of chamfered recesses, pointed and round-arched.

From High Street and High Town the rest of the centre can easily be explored without covering long distances. The s expedition is very different from the others, as it leads to the cathedral. But first the other directions. To the w little is to be seen except that a first acquaintance can be made with the medieval WALLS. Down Victoria Street a few steps from the w end of Eign Street and turning back E into WEST STREET, one sees them along a passage which would lead back to Eign Street, and one can see more, including a small semi-circular bastion, in the yard of No. 19 VICTORIA STREET. There the wall stands up nearly as high as the first-floor ceilings of the houses. There also, better visible from behind the houses in Berrington Street (*see* below), flat buttresses remain which indicate a C12 date. For the continuation S *see* below (St Nicholas Street).

From Eign Street NE one can follow the WALLS. The street is called WALL STREET, and the walls need not be pointed out. But a look up N from Eign Street, i.e. a look up EDGAR STREET, is also interesting, though for a different reason. Here Hereford spread beyond the walls about 1820–40. Clarence Terrace is dated 1837, Elizabeth Place in PORTLAND STREET is undated but very similar, and then follow, lying back from Edgar Street, MOORFIELD TERRACE dated 1823 (?) and with a pediment, and three pairs of houses, the first with Greek Doric porches. All these are, needless to say, of brick.

Now N from the meeting place of High Street and High Town, i.e. along WIDEMARSH STREET. No. 3 has two tunnel-vaulted cellars set at r. angles to one another. In one of these vaults two panels with shields and one cusped one which was an air vent. (Nos 5–7 has an early C17 back building with a ceiling with fleurs-de-lis, lion, leaf, and rose enrichments. The BLACK SWAN also has on the first floor a room with birds etc. on the ceiling. RCHM) Then Nos 25–29, the MANSION HOUSE, of *c.*1700, handsome, but ruined by the shopfronts. Five bays, two storeys, hipped roof on carved modillions, five dormers of which one, three, and five are pedimented. (Inside a ceiling with roses, oak-leaves, etc; RCHM. Inside Nos 35–37 also two plaster ceilings, one with vine, the other with fleurs-de-lis; RCHM.) Opposite, Nos 36–40 are of the early C18 and have a handsome cast-iron balcony on the first floor. No. 42 is the end here. It is an ambitious timber-framed house of the early C17, the ground floor stone-faced in the C18. Former doorway with thickly carved Jacobean brackets. The second floor projects and the bressumer has pendants here. The back has similar gables. After that one passes the former Gate and can see the WALLS to the W in Wall Street (*see* above), to the E in BLUESCHOOL STREET S of an arched passage. It stands here about 12 ft high. In Blueschool Street also the former premises of the BLUE COAT GIRLS SCHOOL. C18 front of two bays with pediment and attached wings of one blank bay.

Extra muros, Widemarsh Street runs on to the CONINGSBY HOSPITAL. This was founded by Sir Thomas Coningsby *c.*1614, and he made use of what was left on the site of a house of the Order of St John of Jerusalem. These remains are of the C13 to C14. The hospital is of four ranges round a court-yard. The hall and chapel fill the N range, and it is this range which has features antedating the time of Sir Thomas. The chapel has three stepped lancets, renewed but probably accurate, and the hall has a simple Early Perp W window. The single-chamfered doorways may be of any time. The hospital windows are of single lights trefoiled. The only more ornate piece is – or was – the gateway at the SW end, and this, with its flanking columns, is so weathered that nothing is recognizable any longer. Also, though attached to the hospital, it did not lead into it, but to Sir Thomas's house behind, see below. – PULPIT. Made up of C17 panels. – FAMILY PEW. Simple panels with little decoration. – SHIELD. A stone shield with the Coningsby arms and the date 1597. – STAINED GLASS. A heraldic pane with the same arms and the date 1614. – PLATE. Cover Paten, 1675.

Immediately behind the house of the Knights of St John was the house of the Friars Preachers, or Dominicans, or BLACK-FRIARS. It was begun, after endless quarrels with the cathedral chapter, in 1322. All that remains is the range W of the cloister and the preaching cross.* After the Dissolution the premises went to the Scudamores and then to the Coningsbys. Sir Thomas Coningsby (see above) lived here, and most of the features of the W range, e.g. the cross windows, the fireplaces, and the stair-turret, belong to his time. The original work is characterized by the fact that the W walk of the cloister was recessed into the ground floor of the W range. Two of the three-light openings survive, though concealed in ivy at the time of writing. The PREACHING CROSS is of the C14 and the only surviving example in England of a friars' preaching cross. It stood in the cemetery of the friars. It is hexagonal and stands on high steps. The parapet is of openwork panels. A solid hexagonal core with shafts supporting ribs, a stone roof, and the tall cross-shaft and cross does not give the preacher much space to stand and move about.

From here one can return to High Town by Coningsby Street, Commercial Road, and Commercial Street. In COMMERCIAL ROAD the pretty ARCH erected to commemorate the Rev. John Venn † 1890 looks an ancient piece; so badly has the red sandstone weathered. Opposite the Bus Station and in its centre the remains of *John Nash*'s COUNTY GAOL, built in

---

* The nave lay to the S of this range. Recent excavations have revealed the N wall of the church and the S walk of the cloister.

1792–7 and demolished in 1929. What remains was the governor's house. The three-bay front has arched doorway and windows, heavily rusticated. Behind them are lavatories now. Behind the Bus Station to the E, in UNION ROAD, the former WORKHOUSE, now part of the County Hospital. It is of red brick and was built in 1839. Across the S end of Commercial Road the KERRY ARMS, rendered, symmetrical, and in Early Tudor style. In COMMERCIAL STREET first the KERRY ALMSHOUSES, built in 1821, two low ranges of brick with pointed windows (then Nos 51–54 with a cellar with C13 stone fragments, No. 61, also with a medieval cellar, and No. 55, with a timber-framed addition at the back and an upper ceiling with fleur-de-lis decoration. RCHM).

From the S end of Commercial Street one can turn SE immediately and start out in that direction, past the Old House (*see* p. 180 above), past a recently exposed corner of a timber-framed house, just W of the corner of Offa Street,* and down ST OWEN STREET, the most consistent Georgian brick street in Hereford. Nos 19–21 are an early C18 pair. Opposite, No. 12 is Late Georgian grandly, seven bays and two and a half storeys, with a five-bay pediment and one-and-a-half-storey single-bay wings. Doorway with broken pediment on Tuscan columns. No. 14 next door has on the first floor wall paintings of the Nine Muses, or rather six of them, named and numbered 3, 4, 5, 6, 7, 8. They are demi-figures, alas so sharply redrawn that they look too Botticelli to be true. Even so, they can't have been rustic work, and they seem to belong to the mid C16. No. 22 is of *c.*1700. It is of five or six or seven bays, however one counts. The house stands free on the l., and the roof is hipped there. Three pedimental dormers. The doorway is flanked by two narrow windows characteristic of 1700. The end, i.e. the place where the city gates are, is marked by No. 44 of the late C17. Three storeys, plain, except for a moulded string course and the wooden doorcase with fluted Corinthian pilasters and an open curly pediment. By turning for a moment N and for a moment S, one can see a little more of the WALLS. They are visible at the back of a car park in BATH STREET, only a few feet high, and W of MILL STREET somewhat higher. S of this they joined up with the castle defences. In St Owen Street, beyond the gate,

---

* Is this the house which, according to the RCHM, has inside three decorated brackets of the former overhang, several moulded beams, and a chimneybreast on C14 columns, not *in situ*?

once more *extra muros*, two hospitals or almshouses. The
WILLIAMS ALMSHOUSES are of 1893 but have their old
plaque of 1675. At the r. end, re-set, the joined capital of a
double column with a figure between two animals; Norman.
Dr Zarnecki considers it a representation of the Good
Shepherd. Then ST GILES HOSPITAL. The present building
is of 1770, single-storeyed, with a pediment. But the foundation goes back to the C12, and when the chapel, rebuilt in
1682, was rebuilt again in 1927, foundations were found of one
of the rare circular chapels. This form was usual for churches
of the Templars and Hospitallers (in commemoration of the
Holy Sepulchre), and St Giles's was, if not a house of the
Hospitallers, a hospital administered by the Hospitallers of
Dinmore. The circle was the nave, and it was followed by an
apse, just as e.g. in the Temple Church in London and Holy
Sepulchre Northampton. In the w wall of the hospital, re-set,
a Norman TYMPANUM of the old chapel, with Christ blessing,
in an almond-shaped glory supported by angels. One can see
that the quality must have been very high, but the surface has
nearly everywhere perished. The representation is all but a
copy of that at Shobdon. – In the new chapel PULPIT. Late
C17, with tester, simple. – COMMUNION RAIL. Same date,
thin turned balusters, also simple. – BENCHES. Of the same
date; plain domestic benches, not like church benches.

The exploration of the small area s of the High-Street–High-
Town area is a more intricate affair, and steps will have to be
retraced. First there is a mews-like narrow street immediately
s of the axis: West Street and EAST STREET. The latter has
two memorable buildings. The CONSTITUTIONAL CLUB,
unpromising externally, has inside a good plaster ceiling,
work of *c.*1670, divided into panels which are subdivided
geometrically and have foliage in vases as their decoration.
Also wood panelling and an overmantel with panels with
open pediments on triple columns. The two reliefs of Ver
and Hiems seem to be re-used. The BOOTH HALL HOTEL
uses as its dining room a first-floor hall of *c.*1400 with a
(much restored) timber roof. In all probability it was the hall
of the Merchants' Guild. The roof has attenuated tie-beams
and hammerbeams, an East Anglian, not a West Country, type.
The hammerbeams end in carved figures. Above the tie-
beams are king-posts and much tracery. There are also, and
this is West Country style, three tiers of wind-braces, and they
form pointed trefoils top and bottom and quatrefoils between.

Also a good chimneypiece with big tapering pilasters, and above Ionic pilasters l. and r. of panels with blank arches filled by shields.

Now, to move southward, it is advisable to start from w and move E. s of West Street first BERRINGTON STREET, with AUBREY'S ALMSHOUSES, founded in 1630. They are timber-framed, low, and have three broad gables. Below the gable windows some concave-sided lozenges. On the other side of the street ST VINCENT'S, with a C17 plaster ceiling on the first floor which has fleur-de-lis, pomegranates, etc. (No. 42 also has a plaster ceiling, C17, with swans, birds, etc. RCHM) From the s end of Berrington Street w into ST NICHOLAS STREET. No. 2 was built in 1745. It is of four bays and three storeys and has a hipped roof. Doorway with fluted Corinthian pilasters. Hood on brackets. Inside, a staircase essentially Jacobean, also in its modest stucco-work. On the other side Nos 19–23 are a tall late C17 terrace, completely plain. They have two and a half storeys above a high basement. Stairs lead up to the doorways. Next to them, in the garden of No. 25, a last stretch of the WALLS is exposed, including a (recently rebuilt) semicircular bastion.

From the s end of Berrington Street s BRIDGE STREET runs to the bridge. At the N end on the w side a group of c.1700, especially No. 44, with quoins and hipped roof (four bays, three storeys). Then Nos 42–43 (with a C17 plaster ceiling; RCHM). Opposite, Nos 6–7 are a Later Georgian four-bay pair with joint doorways under a segmental pediment. More plain brick houses. Then No. 33, with a sumptuous overmantel dated 1632. Three blank arches and caryatids. Plants under the arches. Also a dolphin frieze. Next door the BLACK LION, which has on the first floor a very complete C17 room, i.e. a ceiling with simple stucco reliefs, an overmantel with four blank arches and caryatids, and rustic wall paintings of some of the Ten Commandments.

Across the bridge in ST MARTIN STREET minor Georgian houses, including the nice terrace Nos 25–27, two-storeyed with a pediment. At the s end, projecting a little, DRYBRIDGE HOUSE of c.1700. Five bays, two storeys, pedimental gable with a lunette window. Doorway with semicircular hood.*

---

* On the r. bank of the Wye, 300 yds SE of the bridge, is ROW DITCH, a damaged earthwork which probably formed part of the defences of the medieval city in Norman times.

Now E from the junction of Berrington Street and Bridge Street,
i.e. down KING STREET to the cathedral. Nothing on the
N side. On the s side Nos 4–5 have bargeboarded gables, and
the l. pair of bargeboards have tracery, the r. a vine trail.
Both gables are of pre-Reformation date. No. 3 has some
simple C17 plasterwork on the ground floor, now inside a
shop. No. 2 is the SPREAD EAGLE. In its cellar the octagonal
pier of a former vault. No. 1, facing the cathedral, is so
terribly restored and looks so *triste* now that it would be better
for the setting of the cathedral if it were not there.

Up BROAD STREET, to get back to our axis. The Public Library
is the one building in the street which is high beyond its
station, No. 39 is the other. But whereas the Library is
pretentious in its architecture too, No. 39 is amazingly blunt –
a warehouse, it seems, much like those of Bristol. It was built
in the 1860s and, apart from the two Norman columns on the
ground floor, has no period details. Chunks of beige stone
and some red stone. Four storeys. Between these two, as
surprisingly humble as they are insistent, the former CORN
EXCHANGE, then Kemble Theatre, 1857 by *William Stanton*.
It has an attached portico and a pediment. Then, opposite,
No. 39, a nine-bay building, rendered and no doubt Early
Victorian. Its l. third is the DISTRICT BANK, which reaches
across the pavement with a florid Victorian canopy of cast
iron. The neighbour of this is the NATIONAL PROVINCIAL
BANK of 1863,* three-storeyed, i.e. taller than the previous
buildings, in the palazzo style, with pedimented first-floor
windows and a top balustrade. After that, again on the w side,
the GREEN DRAGON HOTEL, a surprisingly large building
of 1857. White, of thirteen bays, punctuated by giant pilasters,
plus a six-bay addition on the r. Inside, however, *in situ*, a
Jacobean room on the first floor with thin-ribbed star patterns
in plaster focused on short pendants and a dolphin frieze of
wood. Also, re-set, a C15 frieze of interlaced arches with little
pointed trefoils and flowers, a very pretty design. A little
further N, on the E side, the CITY ARMS HOTEL, built as the
Duke of Norfolk's town house in 1790. Three plus three bays,
but a composition as if another three bays had been intended
on the l. The three bays forming the l. end, as it is, are pedimented. Stuccoed ground floor, exposed brick above. The
first-floor windows arched. (At the back a range assigned by
the RCHM to the C15.) Opposite the CHINESE RESTAURANT

* By *Elmslie, Franey & Haddon*; so Mr. G. Spain tells me.

with, on the first as well as the second floor, modest plaster
ceilings with vine, pomegranate, fleur-de-lis, etc. Yet a little
further N, No. 53 has a cellar with a four-centred, probably
medieval, tunnel-vault (RCHM), No. 54 at the back a C17 wing
with a ground-floor loggia on tapering pillars. Behind, earlier
arched braces on shafts with moulded capitals. In addition a
fine pre-Reformation roof has more recently been discovered.
It may have belonged to a guildhall; for the room was 24 ft
by 22 ft in size. Four trusses, one with a tie-beam. Above
cusped patterns. Also wind-braces with cusped tracery.

So we are back at East Street, where we started. We must now
look up and down the streets connecting it with the cathedral
and first CHURCH STREET. (Here, on the W side, near the S
end, a house with C15 cellars. One of them is tunnel-vaulted.
There are also two doorways and remains of a third. Re-set
mid-C17 staircase. Good Jacobean plaster ceiling on the first
floor. The collar-beams and braces are also plastered and
decorated. RCHM) S of this a C14 stone doorway from No. 35
Broad Street has been re-set. (The house opposite has a C15
roof with tie-beams, arched braces, kingposts, and fourway
struts. RCHM)

Parallel with Church Street ST JOHN STREET also leads to the
cathedral. Close to its S end a house with two early C16
windows, one of four, the other of three lights. (The roof of
another part of the house has simple hammerbeams. RCHM)

The range of houses facing the cathedral, where Church Street
and St John Street emerge, is called CATHEDRAL CLOSE.
It is really part of the Close, but not determined as such by any
enclosure. The first house is the Prudential Insurance, anyway, mercifully not too prudential, and the second is the
Telephone Exchange, anyway, discreetly Neo-Georgian.
Then a five-bay brick house of two and a half storeys which
had only three bays in the C18. The l. bays and the unmistakable details were added in the Early Victorian decades.
The middle bay is flanked by rusticated pillars of brick. The
next house is more convincingly Georgian. Also five bays, also
two and a half storeys, but a doorway with fluted Doric
pilasters. Nice curved brick walls l. and r. The NE corner of
the close is a building with a stone ground floor and a timber-
framed upper floor with brick infilling, like a barn.

Across St John's Street and at the entry to the little cul-de-sac
HARLEY COURT an oddly monumental house of 1739, two-
and-a-half storeyed, all of stone and with blank end walls of

stone. The stone is re-used. It came from the chapter house, when this was pulled down. The house is of five bays with a one-bay pediment. (Nos 4–5 Harley Court have a C14 roof with tie-beams and collar-beams. RCHM)

From the E end of the cathedral CASTLE STREET goes in an easterly direction, a secluded street of very attractive character. It starts by the Grammar School (*see* Public Buildings, p. 179). No. 1 Castle Street is white, of six bays and two-and-a-half storeys, and Early Victorian, like a club. Porch on four pillars. All first-floor windows with pediments. Opposite nice red-brick houses. Nos 28–29 look like the others – an Early Georgian pair of five bays with segment-headed windows and a pretty Gothick eaves cornice. But (No. 28 has inside, above a fireplace, a richly carved early C16 frieze of running foliage – *see* RCHM – and) No. 29 has a much greater surprise, the original HALL OF THE VICARS CHORAL, probably built at the end of the C14. Stone walls with traces of large windows and a roof with collar-beams and cusped raking queenposts. Also exceptionally daintily cusped wind-braces, originally with fleurons as the cusps. More nice red houses on the other side, especially No. 9 and the recessed pair Nos 10–11, all three with Late Georgian cast-iron balconies on the first floor. Opposite ST ETHELBERT'S HOSPITAL of 1805. One-storeyed, of red sandstone with pointed windows with wooden Y-tracery. Above the exit to the garden two re-set spandrels from the destroyed chapter house, both with figures, but both much defaced. Above them a capital with nobbly foliage. Across the E end of Castle Street the CASTLE POOL HOTEL, built as a pair of Late Georgian houses and later altered. White, with a two-bay pediment on giant pilasters.

Castle Pool Hotel is so called after the Castle Pool, N of the Castle Green. The Green is on part of the site of the castle, the pool is part of the moat. The CASTLE was first built by Norman Ralph, nephew of Edward the Confessor, c.1048, and destroyed by the Welsh in 1055. It was rebuilt by William FitzOsbern, Earl of Hereford, and consisted of motte and bailey. The present CASTLE GREEN is the bailey. Its ramparts are between 20 and nearly 30 ft high, and the promenade inside was made as early as 1746.* The NELSON COLUMN is by *Thomas Hardwick* and dates from 1806–9. It is really still

* Excavations have recently been undertaken in Castle Green. Their result so far is the exposure of the foundations of a small C12 church in the bailey, consisting of nave and chancel. It lay S of the Nelson Column.

pre-Grecian, i.e. of moderate height and girth, Tuscan, with swags below the capital and an urn on the top. Of the keep nothing at all remains, and even the motte has been levelled completely. It lay to the W of the green. The only medieval building in the bailey is CASTLE CLIFFE, now the SCHOOL OF ART AND CRAFTS, and even this appears early C19, white and with Doric pilasters. However, in the W part of the building the stone crops out, and there are two or three C14 doorways. N of Castle Cliffe is THE FOSSE, a Jacobean villa of c.1825 with the glazing bars set in as octagons. Between the two a lane runs to Quay Street and thus back to the cathedral. In the lane the scanty remains of ST ETHELBERT'S WELL, nothing but a defaced bishop's head above a small modern wall fountain, and a good view of two square brick SUMMER HOUSES of the C17 behind No. 29 Castle Street (*see* p. 170).

(*see* p. 170)

OUTER HEREFORD

Several sallies are recommended. None of them will produce great booty. The best is to the NW from Eign Street along Whitecross Street and WHITECROSS ROAD. One can watch how plain Georgian brick housing (Nos 1–8) gives way to the various Victorian styles mostly with gables. The date 1864 occurs. No. 181 deserves notice for its fancy ironwork. Of special buildings two need attention. First PRICE'S ALMS-HOUSES, of 1665, brick on a stone base and with blank stone-faced gable-ends to the l. and r. Small central gable with a little lantern. The chapel inconspicuous, accessible from the r. angle. Then LINGEN'S HOSPITAL, one-storeyed of 1609 with a more prosperous Tudor addition of 1849. Further out the WHITE CROSS, erected by Bishop Charlton (1361–70), much restored in 1864. Steps, base, and shields in panels. Shaft and head of 1864. Then to the N along THREE ELMS ROAD, and there, just off, at the end of Moor Park Lane, THE MOOR, a farmhouse, now in the town area. Timber-framed with brick infilling. The bricks seem to be the original ones. They are C17 bricks anyway. Porch with pierced flat balusters. Star chimneyshafts. Further N in Three Elms Road the new BAKERY of Mother's Pride Bread, 1958–9 by *A. W. Whalley*.

The second sally goes to the N and NE. There is little to pick up here. Just N of the railway station in LINK ROAD is an estate which started before 1909 as the BARR'S COURT GARDEN CITY. The cottages are in pairs and groups of more, with a brick ground floor and roughcast upper floor and gables painted green or other colours. The style comes clearly from Parker & Unwin, i.e. Letchworth. At the start of Link Road AYLE-STONE ROAD also starts. It runs NE and is a main road out of Hereford. So here again one can observe some architectural history. AYLESTONE HOUSE is still pre-Victorian. Five bays, two and a half storeys, red brick, with a porch with Greek Doric columns. Opposite three three-bay villas. One of them also has a Greek Doric porch. Immediately NE of Aylestone House yet another three-bay villa, this one still with the Georgian motif of two little curved walls l. and r., a vestigial survival of Palladian quadrants. Then the THREE COUNTIES HOTEL, built as a private house c.1850 by the founder of the *Hereford Times*. The style is turning debased and Italianate. White, with giant pilasters, their capitals without historical authority. Opposite, across Folly Lane, an Early-Victorian-Tudor villa.

The only other worthwhile exploration is to the s, from the roundabout at the s end of St Martin's Street. Facing the roundabout and just a little down BELMONT ROAD two farmhouses survive – i.e. Hereford was at an end here: CAUSEWAY FARM and POOL FARM, both black and white, the former of the C17, the latter of the C15 with a porch dated 1624. (The C15 roof-truss of the original hall has shafts attached to the wall-posts and arched braces. RCHM) Turning SE from the roundabout and following HINTON ROAD one reaches yet another farmhouse: PUTSON MANOR HOUSE (No. 147). It lies close to the river and was built early in the C16. It is timber-framed, L-shaped, and has closely-set uprights. Further on to the N and s of the road to Holme Lacy a Roman Catholic colony: the CONVENT OF THE POOR CLARES, 1887 by *Kempson*, red brick and of course Gothic, on the s side, and on the N side ST ELIZABETH'S HOUSE, now CONVENT OF THE MARIAN FATHERS, 1860(?), with a chapel of 1905 and former schools to the E, also Gothic and also of brick. A little to its E ST CHARLES'S HOME, by *Pugin & Pugin*, 1887, small, of red brick, picturesque.*

HERGEST COURT *see* KINGTON

HIGHLAND *see* RODD

* The dates and details of this group of Catholic buildings need further elucidation.

HIGH LANE *see* TEDSTONE WAFRE

HILL COURT *see* WALFORD-ON-WYE

HILLHOUSE FARM *see* BOSBURY

5020

HOARWITHY

St Catherine. Called in 1885 'still far from complete' but under construction 'for several years'. By *J. P. Seddon*. The job was one of encasing and embellishing a church of 1843 which was called at the time 'a neat modern brick building'. So one can picture what it was like. Seddon did his job in the most dramatic way. He chose the South Italian Romanesque and semi-Byzantine style and acted as follows. The church is approached up steps from the E. Here stands the campanile, and to its r. a trefoiled E end, or rather an E apse and two half-apses to N and S. The ground floor of the tower is open, and through it one enjoys the most unexpected and enchanting vista of arch behind arch, belonging to a cloister walk which
62b   runs along the S side of the church. Its W bay is a porch. On the N side there is a corresponding porch, and they are connected by a low atrium inside. The nave is the old one, except for the three large Romanesque N windows, the row of small ones on the S side above the cloister, and the display of windows in the W gable. But the climax of the church is the E end – purely Byzantine. Four monolithic columns of grey Devonshire marble carry large Byzantine capitals. The columns support an inner cupola. There are tunnel-vaults to N and S, and there is an apse to the E with the correct gold mosaic of the Pantokrator. The 'complete scheme of decoration' was said in 1885 to be in the hands of *George Fox*, no doubt the G. E. Fox of Eastnor and Longleat. Mosaic pavements, even in the cloister, and an immense variety of neo-Romanesque capitals. – AMBO with Cosmati work. – STAINED GLASS. Excellent and quite out of the ordinary. W side ten saints; apse a different style; N one two-light window, the best of all. The artists do not seem to be recorded.

Blewhenstone, *see* Llanwarne, p. 241.

5030

HOLME LACY

St Cuthbert. The interior is most curious. Nave and S aisle, chancel and S chapel, without structural division, and both

(a) *Scenery:* Wormbridge

(b) *Scenery:* The Wye, Symond's Yat

I

(a) *Town Building:* Weobley, Broad Street

(b) *Rural Building:* Clodock, water mill

(a) Colwall, Hereford Beacon, Iron Age hill-fort

(b) Dorstone, Arthur's Stone, Neolithic

3

(a) Kenchester, Roman mosaic pavement (now Hereford Museum)

(b) Peterchurch church, Norman

Hereford Cathedral, the Norman nave as it was before 1786

5

(a) Leominster Priory, begun soon after 1123

(b) Hereford Cathedral, south transept, c.1110–20

Kilpeck church, begun c.1135

(a) Hereford Cathedral, capital from the chancel, *c*.1115

(b) Leominster Priory, capitals of the west portal, *c*.1150

(a) Shobdon church, former chancel arch (plaster cast), *c.*1130

(b) Kilpeck church, shaft of south
doorway, *c.*1140-5

(c) Kilpeck church, shaft of chancel
arch, *c.*1145

9

Stretton Sugwas church, tympanum, Norman

(b) Rowlstone church, chancel arch, Norman

(a) Eardisley church, font, c.1150

Castle Frome church, font, c.1170

(a) Hereford Cathedral, chair, early thirteenth century

(b) Lea church, font, Italian, c.1200

13

(b) Longtown Castle, keep, c.1200

(a) Hereford, Bishop's Palace, great hall, late twelfth century

14

Goodrich Castle, mid twelfth–late thirteenth centuries

(b) Kinnersley church, north-west tower, early fourteenth century

(a) Madley church, west tower, early thirteenth century

16

(b) Abbey Dore, ambulatory, c.1200

(a) Abbey Dore, begun c.1175–80

17

(a) Abbey Dore, capital in the ambulatory, *c.*1210–20

(b) Hereford Cathedral, Lady Chapel, *c.*1220–40

18

(a) Hereford Cathedral, capitals in the Lady Chapel, *c.*1240

(b) Hereford Cathedral, Bishop Cantelupe's Shrine, *c.*1285

Hereford Cathedral, north transept, begun *c.* 1250–5

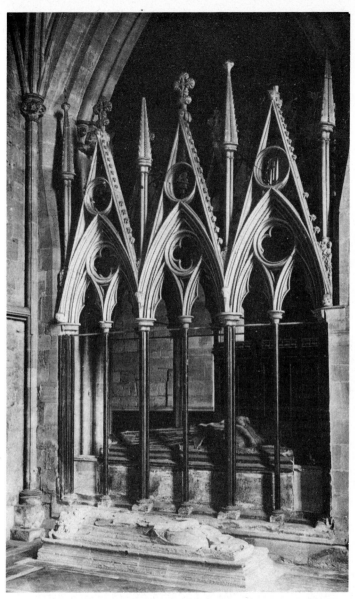

Hereford Cathedral, monument to Bishop Aquablanca †1268

(b) Hereford Cathedral, Shrine of St Thomas of Canterbury, early thirteenth century

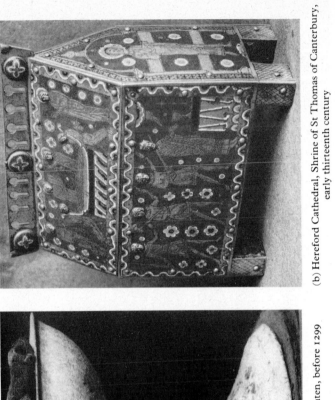

(a) Hereford Cathedral, Chalice and Paten, before 1299

22

(a) *Above*: Wolferlow church, effigy of a Lady, late thirteenth century

(b) *Right*: Woolhope church, coffin-lid, thirteenth century(?)

23

Eaton Bishop church, stained glass, *c.*1330

(a) Hereford Cathedral, monument to Peter de Grandison †1352

(b) Hereford Cathedral, monument to Bishop Swinefield †1317, detail

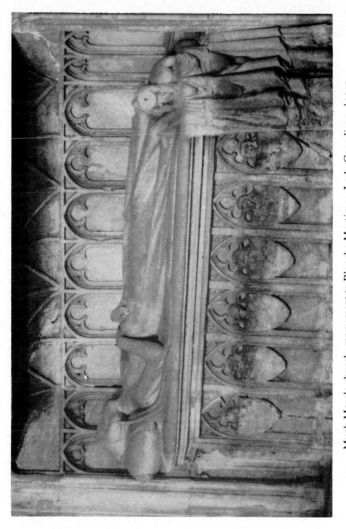

Much Marcle church, monument to Blanche Mortimer, Lady Grandison, †1347

(a) Ledbury church, monument to a Priest, late thirteenth century

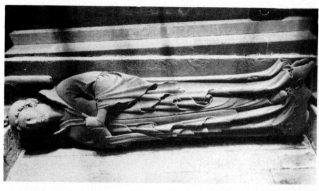

(b) Hereford Cathedral, monument to a member of the Swinefield family, early fourteenth century

27

(a) Hereford Cathedral, crossing tower and north transept, early fourteenth century

(b) Madley church, early fourteenth century

28

Ledbury church, north chapel, mid fourteenth century

(b) Hereford Cathedral, doorway to the chapter house, c.1360

(a) Garway, dovecote, 1326

Weobley, a black and white house in Broad Street

(a) Preston Wynne, Court Farm, fourteenth and seventeenth centuries

(b) Brockhampton-by-Bromyard, Lower Brockhampton House,
late fourteenth and late fifteenth centuries

32

Lingen, Chapel Farm, hall roof, early fifteenth century

(b) Colwall church, nave roof

(a) Amberley Court, hall roof, fourteenth century

(b) **Pembridge** church, bell-house, later fourteenth century

(a) **Pembridge** church, bell-house, later fourteenth century, roof

35

Wellington church, north aisle roof, Perpendicular(?)

(a) Holmer church, tower, c.1200, timber-framing sixteenth century

(b) Eye church, timber north porch, late fourteenth century

37

(a) Hampton Court, begun *c*.1434

(b) Hampton Court, chapel roof, fifteenth century

38

Hereford Cathedral, chained library

(b) Hereford, Blackfriars' preaching cross, fourteenth century

(a) Hereford Cathedral, north porch, 1519

(a) Hereford, All Saints, stalls, fourteenth century

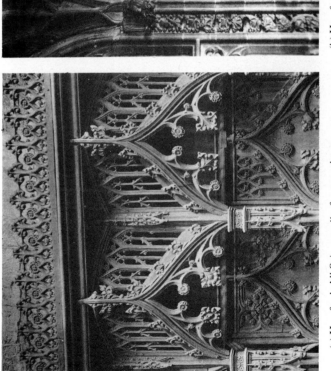

(b) Hereford Cathedral, Bishop Stanbury's Chapel, *c*.1480

41

St Margaret's church, rood screen, c.1520

42

(b) Kinnersley church, panel of the pulpit,
Flemish, c.1530

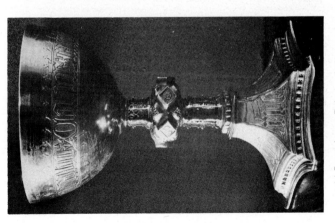

(a) Leominster Priory, chalice,
late fifteenth century

43

(a) Bosbury church, monument to John Harford, by John Guldo, 1573

(b) Bosbury church, monument to Richard Harford and his wife, 1578

44

Bacton church, monument to Blanche Parry, Elizabethan

(a) Richards Castle church, north transept window, seventeenth century(?)

(b) Monnington-on-Wye church, 1679

Hereford, former town hall (demolished), possibly by John Abel, c.1600

47

(a) Kinnersley Castle, drawing room, plaster ceiling and fireplace, 1590s

(b) Leominster, old town hall, by John Abel, 1633

Canon Frome Court, overmantel, late sixteenth century

Abbey Dore, screen, *c*.1633

(a) Kinnersley church, monument to
Francis Smalman, 1635

(b) Foy church, monument to
George Abrahall †1673

51

Ross-on-Wye church, monument to
Colonel William Rudhall †1651

(a) Aston Ingham church, lead font, 1689

(b) Burrington church, cast-iron slab to
Maria Hare †1674

53

Holme Lacy House, by Hugh May, c.1675, south front

Lucton School, founded 1708

(b) Holme Lacy House, plaster ceiling in the saloon, c.1680-90

(a) Kentchurch Court, wood-work from Holme Lacy, by Grinling Gibbons, c.1680-90

(b) Holme Lacy church, monument to James Scudamore, early eighteenth century

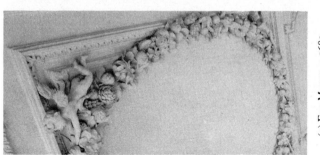

(a) Eye Manor, c.1680, plaster ceiling

57

(a) Tyberton church, panelling in the apse, by John Wood, 1728-31

(b) Shobdon church, 1752-6

Hope-under-Dinmore church, monument to Earl and Countess Conyngsby
and their son, *c.*1760, detail

(a) Berrington Hall, by Henry Holland, 1778–c.81, staircase landing

(b) Downton-on-the-Rock, Downton Castle, by Richard Payne Knight, c.1772–8

(a) Hereford, Shire Hall, by Sir Robert Smirke, 1817–19

(b) Eastnor Castle, by Sir Robert Smirke, begun 1812

(a) Ross-on-Wye church, monument to Thomas Westfaling, by William Theed Sen., 1817, detail

(b) Hoarwithy church, by J. P. Seddon, 1880s

Colwall, Perrycroft, by C. F. A. Voysey, 1893-4

Brockhampton-by-Ross, All Saints, by W. R. Lethaby, 1901-2

of about the same width. Moreover both with plaster tunnel-vaults running right through from w to e. They go back to
c.1660–70. The arcade separating them is curious too. Six
bays of massive piers and arches with single continuous
chamfers and an inner chamfer dying into the piers. The last
of them is a recent adjustment. The forms are unusual and
not easily dated. The RCHM suggests the first half of the C14,
which would go with most of the external features, i.e. the
windows, and the mouldings of s doorway and s porch entrance. But to the e this arcade is continued by two bays
clearly of the late C13. Steeper double-chamfered arches,
quatrefoil pier, e respond on a tripartite corbel. The chapel e
window fits the date (cusped lights, pointed trefoil). w tower
started in the early C14 (arch of three continuous chamfers)
and completed Perp. The arch into the n transept and the
chancel e window also Perp. – FONT. Late C17. Stone with
swags, bowl with acanthus and cherubs' heads (cf. Llanwarne
and How Caple). – LECTERN. A gilt wooden eagle. – STALLS.
Perp, with MISERICORDS (lion, bird, angel, human face,
monster face). – BENCHES. Two fronts with Jacobean panels,
but most benches plain, domestic, quite unchurchy pieces.
They are probably part of the work done by Viscount Scudamore, who died in 1671. – STAINED GLASS. In one n window
many fragments. – PLATE. Cup inscribed 1576 and Cover
Paten; pair of Plates, London, 1798. – HELM, probably C16
(chancel s).

MONUMENTS. Mostly to the Scudamores. In the s chapel:
John Scudamore † 1571 and wife. Alabaster effigies of very
good quality. Tomb-chest with shields and flat Renaissance
balusters. Against the head end fine group of two kneeling
angels holding a shield. – Mary Scudamore Stanhope † 1859.
By *Matthew Noble*, 1861. Large white figure of Faith. –
Viscount Sligo † 1716. Marble, with noble fluted Ionic
pilasters and an open segmental pediment. Sarcophagus on a
base with two wreathed skulls. On the sarcophagus two putti.
Obelisk and drapes l. and r. of it. – In the chancel: Jane
Scudamore † 1699. At the bottom drapery and five beautiful
cherubs' heads. Above oddly detailed base with obelisk and
coupled pilasters l. and r. The obelisk is garlanded, and putti
are placed l. and r. of it. – James Scudamore † 1668, but 57b
clearly of the early C18. Elegantly semi-reclining gentleman;
telling gesture. He lies on a sarcophagus. To the l. and r.
pilasters with fluted capitals and outside them big volutes.

Urn and shield at the top. – N transept: Chandos Scudamore
Stanhope † 1871. By *Noble*. Naval still-life and a rising angel
in relief behind. – s aisle: Tablet to the twelfth Earl of
Chesterfield † 1935. Excellently restrained, with just the coat
of arms and good lettering. By *Mrs Scudamore Stanhope*. –
Very different from the tenth Earl, who died in 1933. In the
churchyard. Bronze soldier by *Gilbert Bayes*. – The C18
wrought-iron churchyard gate comes no doubt from the
house.

HOLME LACY HOUSE. Built by the second Viscount Scudamore after he got married in 1672. The contract with the
builder *Anthony Deane* is dated 1674, and in it *Hugh May* is
mentioned in case of a need for arbitration. So he probably
designed the house. The glorious interior decoration looks
*c.*1680–90. The house is easily the largest in the county. It has
three main façades and had four. The fourth, to the w, was
the entrance side. But the outbuildings flanking the entrance
which were there were swept away when Sir Robert Lucas-
Tooth bought the house about 1910 and decided that it was
not large enough and added the ballroom, where a courtyard
had been, the main staircase, and extensive service quarters.
The features of the late C17 are uncommonly reticent and
54   also very much like each other. Between the s and the E façade
there is really only the difference that the wings of one project
one bay, of the other four, and that the windows are differently
spaced. Both façades (and the other two) are of red sandstone
ashlar and two-storeyed. The only decoration is a pediment
over one window of the ground floor of the projecting wings
and a three-bay pediment over the centre. In addition the
three middle windows of the E façade are arched. The N front
is again very similar, though much longer – a total of seventeen
bays (as against thirteen). The porch was added in 1828–31,
as were the architraves of the windows and the balustrade
along all fronts, which involved a change of the roofs. Formerly
(*see* an illustration of 1786 in the Hereford Library) they had
been hipped. The architect of the alteration of 1828–31 was
William Atkinson.

After the façades the interior is a thrilling surprise, even
now that it is stripped of all original furniture and all its best
56b   woodwork. The plaster ceilings of nine rooms (one on the
upper floor, two now in one) are amongst the finest of their
date in England. The artist is not known. The artist of the
56a   equally accomplished wooden garlands and trophies of the

overmantels is supposed to be *Grinling Gibbons*. They are certainly worthy of him, but they have left the house for Kentchurch Court and the Metropolitan Museum in New York. The plasterwork is organized in circular, oval, octagonal, oblong panels with accompanying panels of various shapes. The garlands, friezes, branches, sprigs are nearly entirely detached from the ceiling. They are as different from the more compact work of 1630–60 as from the equally detached work in the Palladian houses of the C18.

ORANGERY, to the SW. Not large; of brick. Fine arched windows to the S. Parapet.

HOLMER   5040

ST BARTHOLOMEW. Of a late C12 church the only testimony is the round-arched priest's doorway. The nave S doorway with its steep arch looks early C13. With it goes the fenestration of the chancel. Two single lancets in the E wall (and a third higher up and perhaps a little later) and two lancets in the N wall. The S windows are late C13. So perhaps the late C12 and the early C13 elements are in fact of one build. Early C13 also the stone parts of the detached tower. E doorway with a 37a continuous chamfer. The very attractive timber-framed upper parts are assigned to the C16. Pyramid roof. Perp W window in the nave above the C19 W vestry. Fine roofs. That in the nave single-framed with scissor-bracing. In the chancel however there are hammerbeams and collar-beams and tracery above both – an ambitious type unusual in Herefordshire. Assigned to *c.*1500. – ORGAN CASE. A Victorian showpiece, as though it had been made for an international exhibition. With bulbous columns and caryatids. Said to come from a private house. – CHURCHYARD CROSS. Ballflower at the corners of the base.

HOLMER HOUSE, N of the church. Built in 1739. Five bays and three storeys with a hipped roof. Apparently much recast. It seems to have been of only three bays originally with a low annexe.

THE BURCOTT, 1½ m. ESE. Early C19, white, of five bays and two storeys. With a one-storey porch of coupled Greek Doric columns. A tripartite window above.

FACTORY (Henry Wiggins & Co.). New buildings by *W. S. Atkins & Partners* of London.

HOM GREEN *see* ROSS-ON-WYE

HOMME HOUSE *see* MUCH MARCLE

HOPE END *see* COLWALL

6010
HOPE MANSELL

St Michael. Nave and chancel and a Victorian bellcote replacing a former w tower. Plain Norman n doorway, altered
later. The chancel windows are early c14. In the nave several
windows of the c18. A s arcade was evidently ripped out at
some stage. Perhaps this is what the c18 did. Single-frame
roofs with scissor-bracing in nave and chancel. – pulpit.
Of wrought iron, Victorian, probably of the time of the
restoration (1889). – plate. Cup, London, 1792.

Parkfields. Late Georgian house of red sandstone. Five by
two bays. The two bays of the short side have one-storeyed
bows. A Victorian bay window disfigures the front.

5050
HOPE-UNDER-DINMORE

St Mary. Up the green slope of Dinmore Hill. Essentially the
church built by *F. R. Kempson* of Hereford in 1879 and
1896. – font. Mid- or later c13. Circular, with small seated
figures of Christ, the Evangelists and St John Baptist, St
Peter and St Paul. They are placed under cinquefoiled arches.
Stiff-leaf in the spandrels. The posture or the arrangement of
the legs is still in the c12 and early c13 tradition. – plate.
Chalice and Paten, London, 1833–4. – monuments. Incised
slab to Humfry Conynsby † 1559 and wife, the slab later. –
59   Earl and Countess Conyngsby and their infant son choked
by a cherry. The untimely accident happened in 1708, but
the monument is clearly of about 1760. The parents are seen,
white and seated, in front of a noble classical reredos background of coupled Corinthian pilasters with an open segmental pediment. Lady Conyngsby is holding the child, and
the child is holding the cherry. The centre of the background
is a large baldacchino drape, meant no doubt for the inscription. The sculptor is unrecorded.

Winsley House, 1¾ m. w. The main front is rustic Georgian,
of five bays with a five-bay pediment. But at the back is a
timber-framed Jacobean porch with a half-effaced inscription
on the bargeboards, and inside is a part of a c14 roof with
cusped wind-braces.

MIDDLE HILL, see Birley, p. 74.
HAMPTON COURT, see p. 141.

HOW CAPLE

ST ANDREW AND ST MARY. W tower, nave, and S transept all
of 1693–5. They are ashlar-faced, but with no original windows
left. Only the chancel is medieval (see the C14 windows),
complete with its roof, of low pitch, ceiled and with bosses,
and, in addition, a re-set Dec window in the nave (w). –
FONT. Octagonal, Late Norman, with haphazard vegetable
and geometrical motifs. – In the churchyard is a second
FONT, round with some acanthus decoration and the date
1698 (cf. Holme Lacy, Llanwarne). – PULPIT. Jacobean.
With tall blank arches. The tester is a copy of that in Oxford
Cathedral. – ALTARPIECE. Two wings of a South German
early C16 altar, painted on both sides. – ROYAL ARMS. Of
William III, splendidly carved and supported by a crazy
SCREEN, no doubt also of the 1690s, with twisted columns
and – is this unique? – twisted arches, i.e. a twisted roll
instead of an arch. – STAINED GLASS. Three N windows,
designed by *L. B. Lee* and made by *A. J. Davies*, c.1920.
With much black, and rather like book illustrations. – By the
same the E window. – PLATE. Cup and Cover Paten, 1641. –
Flagon by *John Eastt*, London, 1720. – MONUMENTS.
William Gregory † 1765. With a relief of a mourning putto
by an urn. – Several other Gregory tablets. The Gregorys did
the rebuilding work in the late C17.

HUMBER

ST MARY. Slender, unbuttressed W tower with shingled broach
spire. Chancel of c.1200; see the small lancet windows.
Chancel roof perhaps of the C14. Heavy timbers. Tie-beams,
kingposts, and cusped two-way struts. The S porch also of
heavy timbers and also probably C14. Traceried bargeboards.
The church was heavily restored in 1876–8 by *T. H. Wyatt*. –
FONT. Norman, but ill-handled. The rope moulding is
original. – PLATE. Chalice and Cover Paten, inscribed 1669.
RISBURY CAMP is a multivallate Iron Age hill-fort of roughly
oval plan with a medial ditch, on a knoll $\frac{3}{4}$ m. SSE of the church.
There are entrances on the E and W sides.

4040
HUNTINGTON
2 m. NW of Hereford Cathedral

ST MARY MAGDALENE. 1850 by *B. Cranstoun*. Neo-Norman.
Nave, chancel, and apse. The apse has a single-framed roof
to fit in with nave and chancel.

HUNTINGTON COURT. Late Georgian, white, of four bays
and two storeys. Hipped roof. Pretty, curly cast-iron porch.
The house stands close to the Yazor Brook.

2050
HUNTINGTON
4 m. SW of Kington

ST THOMAS OF CANTERBURY. Nave and chancel in one.
Timber bell-turret on posts ascribed to the C17. The windows
of *c.*1300 and a little later. – BENCHES. Very primitive;
massive, roughly trefoiled ends; C16 or C17. – PLATE.
Elizabethan Cup and Cover Paten; Elizabethan Cup and
Cover Paten, the latter inscribed 1576. – MONUMENTS.
Several pretty slate tablets of the early C19, signed by their
makers (*R. Davies, R. Burgoyne*).

CONGREGATIONAL CHAPEL and GOFF'S ENDOWED DAY
SCHOOL, Hengoed. The school is a simple three-bay stone
house of two storeys, and a plaque gives the name and the
date 1791. The chapel is tiny and has no features. According
to Kelly it was built in 1804.

CASTLE, ¼ m. N of the church. Motte about 40 yds in diameter
and 30 ft high, with oval inner bailey to the NE and crescent-
shaped outer bailey further to the NE. The inner bailey has
remains of a C13 wall standing on the W side, in one place
20 ft high. The wall climbed up the motte. Remains of a N
tower.

TURRET CASTLE, ⅝ m. E of the church. Circular motte with
bailey to the E. The motte is *c.*50 yds in diameter and *c.*30 ft
high above the bottom of the ditch. No remains of walling.

HUNTINGTON PARK. Later Georgian, of red brick. Five bays,
two storeys, with Victorian additions. Derelict at the time of
writing.

(The RCHM records cruck-trusses at an outbuilding at BURNT
HENGOED, 1¼ m. SE, at LITTLE PENLAN, 1000 yds ESE of
the former, at GREAT PENLAN, 350 yds NNE of Little
Penlan, and at PENLAN, ⅖ m. SSE of the church.)

HUNTSHAM COURT see GOODRICH

IVINGTON see LEOMINSTER, p. 231

KENDERCHURCH

4020

ST MARY. Small and alone on a hill by the main Abergavenny road. Nave and chancel and a Victorian bellcote. Of ancient features the restoration of 1871 has left hardly anything. The exception is the chancel roof, a wagon roof with small bosses at the junction. – FONT. Of chalice shape. Norman. The top of the rim with incised zigzag. – PULPIT. Jacobean, with blank arches and smaller panels over. – SCREEN. The top rail with its band of running vine trails is Perp.

KENCHESTER

4040

Kenchester is chiefly famous for the excavation of the Roman station and town of MAGNA. The site of the Roman town is now represented by a hexagonal bank enclosing an area of 22 acres. Sporadic excavations conducted in the area of the town have produced a considerable quantity of information regarding the layout of the site, although its date is still uncertain. The whole area was defended by a stone wall 7 ft thick, possibly backed by an earthen bank, as in a number of Romano-British townships. Traces of this wall can be seen on the NW sector of the site. No traces of the original gateways survive above ground, although four are shown on an C18 plan. From the E gate ran the principal street, 22 ft wide and consisting of successive layers of cobbles, sand, and gravel. A central drainage channel ran down the length of the street, with stone-lined drains along its edges. Samian ware of the C1 A.D. was found in the bedding of one of these lateral drains. Near the centre of the town a second street crossed the main street at r. angles. Buildings appear to have lined the length of the latter street, three having mosaic floors bearing non-representational patterns. Fragments of decorated wall plaster were also recovered from a number of rooms.

Isolated burials, both cremated and unburnt, have been found within the walls, although no regular cemetery has so far been located. Small finds from the town include quantities of Samian and coarse wares, coins, and a small bronze ox head, probably of native manufacture. The site appears to have been occupied shortly after the subjugation of Wales in the latter half of the C1 A.D. and to have remained a Roman settlement until the end of the C 4.

St Michael. Two Norman chancel windows and a Late Norman S doorway. Bellcote of the C13, with two openings placed below the nave gable, and above a considerable thickening of the wall. Late C13 chancel E window of the typical Herefordshire form of three stepped lights under one arch. Charming Jacobean chancel roof with much decoration above the collar-beams and with pendants. The N post is a re-used part of the Perp SCREEN. It has a running vine frieze. – FONT. Circular, early, of a very unusual shape. The RCHM suggests that it may be a re-used and re-modelled Roman piece. – PLATE. Paten by *Ebenezer Coker*, London, 1769.

Methodist Chapel, ⅜ m. SE. 1830. Called Lady Southampton's Chapel. It was built for the Countess of Huntingdon's Connexion. Red brick with arched windows. The manse is under the same pyramid roof.

New Weir, ¾ m. S. Built in 1784. Plain cemented front, but with a handsome semicircular timber porch.

4020   KENTCHURCH

St Mary. Built in 1859. Nave and chancel in the Dec style. Short W tower with truncated pyramid roof, low cusped bell-openings, and a spire. – MONUMENT. John Scudamore † 1616. Only the figures remain: the architectural setting has disappeared. Two semi-reclining effigies, lying on their sides, head propped up by hand and elbow. Ten children, one in a cradle.

Kentchurch Court is or was a C14 castle. But it was largely rebuilt by *Nash* – an early job, obtained perhaps through the friendship between the then Scudamore and Uvedale Price of Foxley. The exact date is not known. Illustrations prove that the work was not yet done in 1795. In 1807 it is called new. The remaining medieval parts, not counting masonry without special features, are confined to a GATEWAY SE of the house, the mighty NW tower, heightened however by Nash, and the range projecting E at the N end. This was once independent, it seems. The hall of the house lay on the E front, N of Nash's porch. This can be recognized in the background of an early Flemish painting belonging to the house, and also from the original two-light windows in the basement of that part of the house, facing N. The staircase in the tower runs up in the thickness of the walls. There is also a projecting garderobe on the N side. Nash faced the hall part with ashlar, gave Georgian-type windows hood-moulds (or inserted the windows), and put his porch to the S of the existing porch, for that purpose cutting off one bay of a pretty three-bay part of the house which must have been of about 1700, but was a remodelling job, as the masonry is medieval. In the C19, between Nash's ashlar-faced part and the medieval, eastward projecting range at the N end, a neo-Norman piece was put in, rather painfully. Nash's oddest addition is the so-called chapel window on the N side immediately E of the tower. One expects a prominent room behind it. What happens instead is that from the porch a corridor leads into the house, turns at r. angles N, at its end reaches a flight of about twelve steps towards the chapel window, and there comes to naught. The staircase continues on the smallest scale. There must here be a change of plan, a reduction of the original scheme. Of fitments the most interesting are STAINED GLASS arranged in the chapel window, notably a Swiss series dated 1521, and some exquisite WOODWORK transferred from Holme Lacy. 56a This is attributed to *Grinling Gibbons* and certainly up to his standard. Garlands with birds, fruit, vegetables, etc., from overmantels, and also an external pediment.

PONTRILAS COURT, *see* p. 272.

(TUMP, 1 m. NNE. Oval, and 50 by 43 yds in size. The height is 12 ft above the bottom of the ditch. RCHM)

KILPECK   4030

ST MARY AND ST DAVID. One of the most perfect Norman village churches in England, small but extremely generously decorated, and also uncommonly well preserved. The red sandstone must have been selected with great acumen to have stood up so well to eight hundred years of wear and tear, and *Cottingham*'s restoration of 1848 seems to have been a competent and disciplined job. A comparison between G. R. Lewis's lithographs of 1842 and the building as it is now shows that not much has been lost over the last four or five generations. If the church is so sumptuous, the reason was the presence of a Benedictine PRIORY, founded in 1134 as a cell of Gloucester, and of the castle – on which *see* below. The church may well have been begun immediately after 1134.

The sculpture of its S doorway is so close to Shobdon, which must be of *c*.1140–5, that the date makes sense.

The church is designed on the simple plan of nave, chancel, apse, in decreasing width and height. The exterior is articulated by means of flat buttresses and clasping corner buttresses. A corbel table runs all round, decorated with flat zigzag, rope, etc., and the corbels are the best preparation for the profusion of decorative sculpture and fantasy throughout the church. Of motifs there are the Lamb and Cross, a dog and a rabbit, two wrestlers, a sheila-na-gig (all these apse), another Lamb and Cross (chancel), and many heads. The corbels are clearly not all by the same hand – the best have an irresistible comic-strip character – and not by the hand of the brilliant master of the S doorway.

The S doorway is sumptuously decorated but not sumptuous. One order of decorated shafts and decorated jambs, decorated voussoirs in two orders, tympanum. In the tympanum simply a Tree of Life, beaded and with thick grapes. Vertical zigzag on the lintel. The outer order of the arch has linked medallions inhabited by dragons, birds, etc. In the inner order are beakheads – a motif which reached Herefordshire probably by way of Leominster, as it is a Reading motif – and also heads and a flying angel, all radially arranged. The shafts are decorated very much like those of Shobdon, one with symmetrical trails and palmettes, the other with two splendid long wiry figures, one on top of the other, and both enmeshed in wild, thin trails. The tight clothes with close parallel folds like ribs are unmistakable. On the jambs hideous fat and long dragons, one snaking up, the other down, and in the abaci a head with beaded trails coming out of the mouth, and a pair of affronted dragons. The sources of this sculpture are varied, as Dr Zarnecki has shown. The fat snake-like dragons are purely Viking, of the so-called Ringerike style. The style is equally clearly reflected in the dragon heads at the corners, projecting at corbel-level like wooden ships' figure-heads. The figures on one shaft are very different, nimble, lively, and ready to jump. For them no source has yet been found for although the founder of Shobdon Priory had visited Santiago de Compostela and although on the Puerta de las Platerias figures also stand on top of each other, the style is entirely different.

Moreover, to complicate matters further, the chancel arch at Kilpeck again has figures on top of each other, and they differ in style as much from those of the s doorway as from Santiago. They are stockier, shorter, not at all nimble, and wear clothes with folds sparser, heavier, and differently arranged. If their placing one on top of the other needs foreign precedent, one would be drawn more to Ferrara (1135) than to Santiago. The chancel arch is different from the doorway in its voussoirs as well. The motifs are all conventionally English, zigzags and their combinations, and also zigzag at r. angles to the wall, an early appearance (but cf. Shobdon). The apse is rib-vaulted, and the ribs are again decorated by zigzag. So are the arches of the nook-shafted apse windows. The shafts on which the ribs rest have small scalloped capitals. There is no boss, or indeed proper keystone, in the rib-vault. Could the church have been begun c.1135 in this style, and the Shobdon workshop then have moved to Kilpeck when work at Shobdon was completed, c.1145?

Of further details few need attention. The w window is nook-shafted, and the shafts are strikingly similar to those of the Shobdon doorways (beaded bands of interlace). The bellcote dates from 1864, the chancel windows and deeply moulded doorway from c.1300. The NE quoins of the nave ought to be observed, as they continue the Saxon long-and-short tradition.

STOUP. This has a very primitive base with four animal heads and on the bowl two hands gripping two heads. – FONT. Of breccia, enormous and plain, on five feet. (The bowl has its original stopper for the double drain-hole. G. Marshall) – WEST GALLERY. Jacobean. – STAINED GLASS. In the apse by *Pugin*, 1849.*

CASTLE, W of the church. Motte and bailey. The motte is nearly 54 yds in diameter at its base and rises to c. 27 ft. above the bottom of the ditch. Remains of a polygonal shell-keep, especially two large fragments of masonry, probably of the C12. On the N side was a fireplace. Kidney-shaped bailey to the E. The entrance to this was on the SW. There were here also three outer enclosures. To the NE the rectangular enclosure of the village, including the church. The size of this enclosure is c. 200 by 300 yds.

(DIPPERSMOOR MANOR. Partly C15 and incorporating two crucks, one of them exposed. RCHM and information from Mr J. T. Smith.)

* Information kindly conveyed to me by Mrs Stanton.

KIMBOLTON

5060

ST JAMES. In the chancel two Norman windows, that in the
E wall perhaps re-set. Unbuttressed short C13 W tower.
Bell-openings with plate tracery. Tall shingled broach spire.
C13 also the S side of the nave, including the doorway. The N
windows (pointed-trefoiled heads) of the late C13. Of the
same date the S transept – see the two E lancets and the bar
tracery of the upper S window. – STALL BACKS. Early C16,
with linenfold panels.

STOCKTON BURY, ¾ m. SW. C18 brick house of four bays with
a two-bay pediment and a hipped roof. (DOVECOTE. Circular,
of stone, with conical roof, perhaps medieval. RCHM)

HILL-FORT. A small Iron Age hill-fort of oval plan lies on a
ridge 1½ m. SE of the church, enclosing an area of 6 acres. The
univallate defences are cut by entrances on the E and W, the E
entrance having the ramparts slightly inturned.

KING'S CAPLE

5020

ST JOHN BAPTIST. Quite a large church. In the nave S wall
one late C13 window with Geometrical tracery and a tomb
recess inside beneath it. Unbuttressed W tower Dec, *see* the
string course with ballflower. Perp bell-openings. Recessed
spire. Perp N chapel (Aramstone Chapel) – *see* the N window
of four lights and the rib-vault with diagonal and ridge-ribs,
a very unusual thing for a chapel (but cf. Sellack, near by).
The same design of ribs in the S porch. Entrance with traceried
spandrels. – PULPIT. Tall, Jacobean, with tester. – SEATING.
In the nave, very rough, C17? – STALLS. Front with Jacobean
panels. – Of the same date two BOX PEWS in the N chapel. –
WEST GALLERY. Probably early C18. – STAINED GLASS. C15
fragments in the N chapel. – PLATE. Chalice and Flagon by
John Edwards, 1728; two Patens by *William Fleming*, 1729;
all London-made. – MONUMENTS. Mrs Holcombe Ferguson
† 1814. By *Flaxman*. With a charming relief of the young
widow teaching her little boy. – Eliza Woodhouse † 1833.
With a kneeling, mourning woman by an urn. By *Westmacott*.
– Big sarcophagus in the churchyard to Edmund Jones † 1828.

ARAMSTONE HOUSE has been pulled down.

KINGSLAND

4060

ST MICHAEL. A sizeable church, all of a piece, built in the late
C13 to early C14, and by a master with pronounced tastes,

familiar, it seems, with the workshops of Bristol. His liking
for triangles and three sides of polygons instead of arches
points in that direction. Big W tower with angle buttresses,
decorated with some panelling. The top Perp. The stairs run
up in the NW angle and corbel out a little, supported by two
small heads in trefoil arches. N doorway with a cusped head.
Below the bell-stage round windows with barbed quatrefoils
(i.e. inserted triangles). Nave and aisles, pseudo-transepts and
chancel. The aisles with circular W and E windows. The W
ones are cinquefoiled, but the E ones are barbed trefoils. The
other aisle windows and those of the transepts and chancel are
of the same style, i.e. with unencircled trefoils or quatrefoils
or pointed cinquefoils or arches upon arches (chancel E) in the
tracery.* To the chancel a vestry is added, and this was
heightened by an upper storey in the C16. Clerestory of sexfoiled circular windows. Sanctus-bell-turret on the nave E
gable. The S porch is C15, of timber with bargeboards. But
the most surprising and fanciful feature is the N porch with
the attached Volka Chapel.‡ The porch has again a foiled
window, and its inner doorway a cusped and sub-cusped head
of three sides of an octagon. Some of the cusping is triangular.
Off the porch to the E is the chapel, with a small E window of
four lights with tracery of the Y-type, and a N wall opening in
a low straight-headed window of six lights, i.e. with five plain
mullions. Below it, inside, three octofoils. Towards the S,
i.e. the N aisle, tomb recess, again with barbed cusping and a
plain, straight-headed four-light window to the aisle in its
back wall. The coffin of the burial is still there and now open.
  Inside the church, five bays of tall arcading. The piers have
slender polygonal projections and hollows in the diagonals.
Double-chamfered arches. The clerestory windows are above
the spandrels, not the apexes, of the arches. There is a pair
of them facing E in addition. The tower arch is double-
chamfered too and rests on two heads. The chancel arch
seems to be interfered with. In the chancel doorway to the
vestry with three-sided, cusped head. Nave roof perhaps
original, with tie-beams, kingposts, and four-way struts.
Chancel roof ceiled and very prettily painted (restoration

---

  * But in the transept E walls close to the chancel arch are two nearly
hidden small lancet windows which seem to be survivors of an earlier C13
aisle E wall.
  ‡ The name cannot be traced back beyond the later C17 or early C18, and
is there Vaukel.

under *Bodley*, 1866–8). – STAINED GLASS. Good small figures in the chancel windows, e.g. Coronation of the Virgin and Christ in Glory in the E window, also Tobias and the Angel, Annunciation, St Michael, a saintly Archbishop, and other saints.

CASTLE, W of the church. Motte and bailey. The motte has a diameter of *c*.60 yds and is *c*.17 ft high. Two baileys, to N and E and to E and SE, separated by a ditch.

MONUMENT to the Battle of Mortimer's Cross of 1461, 2 m. SE. Put up in 1799. A base with an inscription.

Several enjoyable black and white houses are in the village street, the most notable ANGEL HOUSE on the N side, N of the church. From the cross-roads S to the rectory. On the way, on the E, a nice modest early C18 brick house of three bays. One-bay pediment and pedimented doorway. Quoins. The former RECTORY (now Kingsland House) lies in its grounds. It is also of the early C18, but much statelier. Five bays, two storeys, hipped roof. The porch seems a later addition, taken over from another, slightly earlier house. Very tapering pilasters, bulgy frieze.

MUST MILL, 1 m. W, S of the lane to Shobdon. Of *c*.1500 and with close-set vertical timbers.

BLACK HALL, 1¼ m. NE. At the back an interesting C14 survival: two heavy diagonal braces and between them, blocked, a window of four lights with pointed trefoiled heads.

KING'S PYON

4050

ST MARY. Norman N aisle windows. Late Norman S and N doorways. The S doorway has one order of shafts with trumpet capitals. In the arch a keeled roll moulding. Late Norman chancel arch with tripartite keeled responds and trumpet as well as typical late C12 leaf capitals. Late C13 to early C14 (dedication of two altars 1329) the S transept (the N transept is of 1872) with its beautifully openwork cusped and subcusped tomb recess and its two-bay arcade (circular pier, octagonal abacus, double-chamfered arches, but the responds tripartite with a fillet) and also its decidedly Dec E window, straight-headed with reticulation units. The chancel, much renewed, seems of the same period – *see* the charming priest's doorway with its cinquefoiled head. Unbuttressed C14 W tower. Excellent nave roof with tie-beams, cusped raking struts, collar-beams on cusped arched braces, and two tiers of big pointed-trefoiled wind-braces. – PLATE. Chalice by *John Eastt*, London, 1726; Paten by *John Gamon*, London, 1732; Chalice by *Ed. Pocock*, London, 1736. – MONUMENTS. In the tomb recess in the S transept alabaster effigy of a Knight and stone effigy of a Lady, both of the later C14, i.e. too late for the recess.

BROOK HOUSE, N of the church. The house is rather forbidding. Its façade seems to be of the mid C19. But close to it is a charming DOVECOTE, black and white, with a glazed lantern.

(BLACKHALL, ⅛ m. SW, has a BARN with medieval cruck-trusses. RCHM)

BUTTHOUSE, 1 m. S. Early C17. Timber-framed with brick infilling. Narrowly-placed uprights almost exclusively. To the E two gables and below them two lower gabled bays. The part between is Victorian. To the N of the house stands a delightful black and white GATEHOUSE, dated 1632. It has an oversailing upper storey. Twisted angle shafts carrying brackets. The bressumer is carved with dragons and scrolls. So are the bargeboards. The upper S window has a moulded sill, and below it are two of the familiar blank arches. The N side is a little simpler.

THE HILL, 700 yds N. Mostly with narrow uprights, but one gable with close diagonal bracing. C16 and C17, according to the RCHM.

KINGSTONE

4030

ST MICHAEL. An interesting church. It starts as an aisleless Norman building of which the simple S doorway (unmoulded arch, plain imposts) is evidence. To this a N aisle was added shortly after 1200. This had three bays, though its E respond is missing. Circular piers with spurs, trumpet-scalloped capitals, circular abaci, and double-chamfered pointed arches. A little later the chancel was rebuilt and the N chapel built. The details are similar, but the capitals now have upright stiff-leaves. There is some confusion around the chancel arch. It rests on the S side on a corbel below which is a second corbel. Was this meant for the N side, and was then the solution accepted of simply running the two arcade arches and the chancel arch down on a normal pier like all the others? The pier has a human bust facing W. So have the next E.E. pier and the corbel below the E respond. Between c.1300 and c.1330 the N aisle was widened – *see* the windows, from lancets and Geometrical tracery to reticulation motifs. Concurrently a tower was built W of the widened aisle (lancets below and a triple-chamfered arch to the nave, Dec bell-openings, ballflower frieze).* Then the nave was lengthened to end flush with it. This W bay is ashlar-faced and has Dec tracery in the windows. The flowing tracery of the W window, if correctly restored, is an exception in Herefordshire. – FONT. An impressive, completely unadorned, blackish bowl, said to be of breccia (cf. Kilpeck). – REREDOS. With Jacobean panels. – CHEST. A 'dug-out', 8½ ft long. – PLATE. Chalice and Cover Paten by *Edward Holeday*, London, Early Georgian. – Salver by *John Eastt*, London, 1722.

BRIDGE COURT, ½ m. NNE. Late Georgian, of brick. Two-storeyed with a three-storeyed one-bay centre. The lower parts half-hipped, the centre with pyramid roof. Broad segment-headed windows. At the top a lunette window. Two doorways, l. and r. of the centre.

ARKSTONE COURT, ½ m. NE. Late C18, of brick. Two canted bay windows, and in the recessed centre an arched doorway and at the top a lunette window.

KINGSTONE GRANGE, ¾ m. S. Timber-framed, of *c*.1600, with a symmetrical gabled S front. Three gables, two in the projecting cross wings, one over the centre of the recessed centre. Below this a gabled porch. The gables unfortunately are slate-hung.

WHITFIELD. Georgian, of brick, two storeys on a high basement. With two big bows. Stable range with arches and pediment.

KINGTON

ST MARY. Outside the town, on a hill. Large and of grey stone. The S tower stands outside the S aisle and not exactly in axis with the church. It is unbuttressed and has a batter at the base. It was built *c*.1200. The outer staircase is of course Victorian. The two truncated pyramids and the broach spire were rebuilt in 1794. The arch from the tower to the N into the aisle is round with a continuous roll moulding, which fits the suggested date. Next in the history of the church comes the noble chancel with its group of three stepped widely spaced lancet windows to the E and six evenly spaced

---

* The N doorway is Perp, and the battlements and tall pinnacles are of 1852.

smaller lancers to the N. The chancel must be of the early C13. Only to the s one of the windows is late C13 (Y-tracery). The chancel arch with its sunk chamfers also looks late rather than early C13. Shortly after, say about 1300, the nave was rebuilt and given aisles. The w wall has a window of four stepped lancet lights under one arch, and the arcades of five bays have octagonal piers and double-chamfered arches. The capitals differ a little. The s chancel chapel is fully Dec – *see* e.g. the E window with reticulated tracery and the half-arch towards the w with a sunk quadrant moulding. The two-bay arcade, however, is given a Perp date by the RCHM. One of the s windows is indeed Perp. Many other windows of the church are Victorian. The most sweeping Victorian alteration was the addition of an outer N aisle, at the same time widening the old N aisle into what amounts to a N nave. This was done in 1874.

FURNISHINGS. FONT. Norman, circular, with a rope moulding near the foot of the bowl and incised zigzag at the top.* – STAINED GLASS. In the chancel N and s windows and the outer N aisle NE window good imitation-C13 glass. – PLATE. Elizabethan Chalice and Cover Paten with the date 1576 inscribed; Chalice and Cover Paten, London, 1633; Salver by *Seth Lofthouse*, London, 1702; Flagon by *William Parker*, London, 1731. – MONUMENTS. Thomas Vaughan † 1469 and wife. Alabaster effigies on a tomb-chest with ten by four alabaster angels (front and foot-end), upright and holding shields. Much restored. – William Mathews † 1688 (s aisle w). Big tablet with two columns and, at the top, two standing putti. – CHURCHYARD CROSS, s of the church. With a stump of the shaft preserved.

(CASTLE, N of the church. Not much more than an irregular knoll and traces of a rampart. RCHM)

PERAMBULATION (including PUBLIC BUILDINGS). The main streets of Kington, a cross, longer w–e than s–N, lie away from the church and castle, as if they were two different settlements. The only connexion is CHURCH ROAD, the continuation of Church Street. In this, sw of the church, the LADY MARGARET HAWKINS GRAMMAR SCHOOL, designed in 1625 by *John Abel*, but not timber-framed.‡ The building is much altered and changed about, but the original division into schoolroom on the E and headmaster's house on

* To its s an IMMERSION PIT of uncertain date.
‡ Contract of 1625 for the sum of £240.

the w can still be seen, and also a five-light mullioned and transomed window to the N. From here to the centre of the town little of interest except for the widening of Church Street called COMMON CLOSE, where THE TERRACE is an early C19 composition of seven bays and two and a half storeys with a pretty central doorway (Tuscan columns and broken pediment). Further s the main junction of the town marked by the ugly MARKET HALL of 1885 (by *Kempson*, replacing one of 1654 by *John Abel*). This is of red brick and received a Jubilee tower in 1897. In front of it a signpost, former PUMP, of cast iron and very Victorian, with an urn at the top. Now first down MILL STREET to sample BURTON HOUSE HOTEL, red brick, of 1851, with two porches across the pavement and an added Assembly Room of 1856, still curiously Georgian in simplicity. In the HIGH STREET Nos 51–53, formerly the CHAINED SWAN INN, C18 with a humble pediment, a little feature displayed by other houses as well. Then, facing down Bridge Street, the former TOWN HALL, by *Benjamin Wishlade*. Wishlade was, as a history of the town says, 'a celebrated builder and respectable man'. The town hall was built in 1845. Five-bay centre with lower wings, all with giant pilasters and all with a cornice decorated with pretty wreaths. The centre has coupled Corinthian pilasters. Opposite, in BRIDGE STREET, the ALBION HOUSE HOTEL, modest Georgian, of three bays, with another little pediment and a thinly decorated doorway. At the end of Bridge Street, lying back, the CORN MILL, with the miller's house, the former of four storeys, stone and brick and weatherboarding, the latter with a big lunette window in the broken pediment.

The direct continuation of High Street is Duke Street, and this is continued in VICTORIA ROAD. At the very end of this, lying back on the N side, a Laundry which was built in 1820 as a FOUNDRY (MHLG).

KINGSWOOD HOUSE (formerly Workhouse), ½ m. SSE. By *Wishlade*, 1857. Stone, of the usual radial plan, and decidedly not yet Victorian.

HERGEST COURT, 1¼ m. SW. L-shaped. In its fragmentary form gaunt but impressive. Much closely-set timbering, probably of the C15. In the angle between this and the other range (which is of stone) a doorway with a two-centred head, probably yet earlier.

(The RCHM mentions MAHOLLAM COTTAGES, 2 m. SW, for

cruck-trusses, and for the same reason APOSTLES FARM, 2¾ m. S, POUND FARM, 1½ m. S, LILWALL FARM, 1¾ m. SSE, and OLD HOUSE, 1½ m. NE.)

OFFA'S DYKE. A good stretch of the dyke occurs on Rushock Hill and in Kennel Wood, in the NE part of the parish. This portion is structurally interesting, as the dyke on Rushock Hill has a S ditch and that part in Kennel Wood a N ditch. This variation suggests that two different gangs were employed in the construction of these portions of the earthwork.

KINNERSLEY   3040

ST JAMES. Immediately W of the castle. The oldest pieces are the blocked Norman W doorway, the string course with rope moulding above, and the string course of the N wall now inside the N aisle. The tall window above is Perp. Most of the church, however, is of c.1300: the chancel with its large three-light E window, the N aisle with its E window of three stepped and cusped lancet lights, the S doorway, and the N arcade of four bays with octagonal piers and double-chamfered arches. Tomb recess in the chancel N wall. But the most impressive feature of the church, the mighty NW tower with its sheer out- 16b line and its saddleback roof, is a little later still, though it looks decidedly elementary. The windows are ogee-headed. Perp S arcade with thin piers of the typical four-shafts-and-four-hollows section and arches corresponding to it. The timber S porch is more likely to be C14 than C15. It has traceried bargeboards. Victorian chancel arch of 1868. The nave and chancel decoration was designed by *Bodley* and carried out by the Rector, the *Rev. Frederick Andrews*. It is exceedingly pretty. – The ORGAN CASE is also *Bodley*'s design, but less attractive. – REREDOS. With Jacobean panels. – PULPIT. Also of divers pieces. They include four very fine and very 43b Mannerist allegorical figures. Flemish, c.1530, and similar to the free-standing figurines of King's College Chapel Cambridge. – STALLS in the chancel, with Jacobean panels. – SCREEN. Only the base, with a small frieze of openwork quatrefoils. – STAINED GLASS. In the chancel, of c.1850. – MONUMENTS. William Leviot, rector, † 1421. Brass bust and inscription (chancel N). – Above this Francis Smalman, 1635. 51a Alabaster and marble. A very fine piece. Two kneeling figures facing one another below a baldacchino held by two trumpet-blowing cherubs. In the 'predella' more kneeling figures,

kneeling in both directions – all very lively and not at all stiff.
– Lady Morgan † 1764. By *Nicholas Read*. An angel with big
decorative wings, in a rather artificial attitude, points to the
medallion bust of the deceased – a bust of classical nudity. –
John Parkinson † 1804. The monument has a very fine roundel
with a mourning female figure at the foot. The lettering is
good and restrained too.

KINNERSLEY CASTLE. The house appears towering, commanding, and forbidding behind the church. It is Elizabethan
– built by Roger Vaughan* between *c.*1585 and 1601 – and
appears so in most features, but it must be a remodelling of a
true castle, as e.g. the existence of the five-storeyed embattled
tower proves. The tower stands in the angle between two
ranges running from it S and E. It is likely that castle as well
as house were larger. In any case vaulted brick cellars extend
beyond the E end. The most enjoyable Elizabethan features
are the following: the N doorway, the original N door and
surround, now in the Victorian porch,‡ and the mullioned
windows with two transoms on ground floor and first floor,
with one transom on the second. The stepped brick gables
on a stone house and a veneer in front of actual stone gables
are specially interesting, as they were no doubt at the moment
fashionable, though quite unusual in Herefordshire. Finally
48a a splendid plaster ceiling and frieze in the upper SW room.
This has panels with thin-ribbed frames and in them and
around them cornucopias, sea serpents, etc. Noble chimneypiece with two big, vaguely Ionic columns, the Vaughan arms,
and a wonderful oak-branch spreading over the whole overmantel. Other overmantels are Elizabethan or Jacobean too.
One is dated 1618. The NW room on the ground floor was
remodelled early in the C18 and received a new fireplace
*c.*1740. On the second floor in two rooms more modest friezes
similar to that of the room with the plaster ceiling.

3060   KINSHAM

ALL SAINTS. Of *c.*1300; nave and chancel in one. The windows,
all renewed, have pointed-trefoiled lights. The E window is of
two lights with a quatrefoil in bar tracery. – WOODWORK.
Simple; early C18. – STAINED GLASS. Original bits assembled

* As Mr H. Garratt Adams has worked out.
‡ A Victorian owner also added two windows and some other features.

in the E window. – MONUMENT. Tablet to Thomas Harley
† 1738. With simple architectural surround.

LOWER COURT, ⅓ m. SSW. Partly C14 to C15, with an ogee-
headed doorway and heavy timber-framing in the gable. The
upper storey projects. The rest of the house C17.

KINTLEY FARM see BRILLEY

KNILL   2060

ST MICHAEL. Surrounded by trees, close to the ruin of the
burnt Knill Court and below afforested hills. Nave and
chancel (one Norman chancel window) and broad, very short
W tower. – FONT. Octagonal, with framed panels with knots,
St Andrew's crosses, a raw palmette, etc.; probably c.1200. –
PLATE. Chalice and Cover Paten, London, 1696. – CHURCH-
YARD CROSS. With short, tapering shaft and square tabernacle
head.

KNOAKE'S COURT see LEOMINSTER,
p. 231

LANGSTONE COURT see LLANGARRON

LAYSTERS   5060

ST ANDREW. A small church below a big cedar-tree. Wonderfully poetic in its peaceful, remote setting. Short unbuttressed
W tower with pyramid roof, probably of the early C13. In the
nave one blocked Norman N window. The S doorway also
Norman. It is of an odd shape, with a shouldered lintel with
a roll moulding and above it a tympanum. Good C14 roof
with arched braces up to the collar-beams and foiled wind-
braces, forming two and a half tiers of lozenges. – PLATE.
Flagon by *David Willaume* of 'Pell Mell', 1724.

CINDERS, 1½ m. NE. Stone house of the C14 with a doorway
with two-centred arch and a window with a trefoiled head.
One chimneybreast at the back is contemporary. It has a
brick star-stack of c.1600. The main stack is of brick with
lively rustication; probably early C18.

(GREAT HEATH, 1 m. WSW, has a CIDER HOUSE with a press
dated 1771. Another cider press, probably of the C17, is at
WHITEHOUSE, ½ m. further SW. RCHM)

LEA

ST JOHN BAPTIST. Small W tower with recessed spire; Dec.
The rest mostly restoration of 1854. Original Perp work the
N arcade of three bays. Octagonal piers, capitals with small
heads, four-centred arches. The chancel E window is original
too, and may be connected with a reconstruction of 1418. –
FONT. The most surprising font in Herefordshire, an Italian
13b stoup of the late C12 or C13. The bowl stands on a shaft
carried by an elephant. The elephant is a motif familiar from
the bishop's throne at Canossa of the 1080s and the window
of the apse of Bari Cathedral. The shaft has a knot round its
waist, and this motif compares e.g. with a column at Gropina
in Tuscany. The elephant's saddle is decorated by two small
figures of saints and some Cosmati work. Cosmati work also
on the rim of the shallow bowl. Below it an exquisite frieze of
foliage scrolls with small human figures and animals. The
font was bought from a dealer and given to the church in
1907. – SCREEN. In the N aisle some re-used parts. – CHEST.
Very mighty and bulky C13 'dug-out'. – PLATE. Late C17
Cup.

CASTLE END, ½ m. NW. Seven bays and two storeys with a
hipped roof. The date of the front probably early C18. Close
by the DOVECOTE, C17, octagonal.

¼ m. E, nearly opposite the Crown Inn, a HOUSE of the early C18
which is of brick, five bays and two storeys, with an arched
hood above the doorway.

LEDBURY

ST MICHAEL. The premier (or première) parish church of
Herefordshire and a church exceptionally rich in monuments.
Moreover it has an unusual variety of fine elements, including
the detached tower and the splendid N chapel. The history of
the building begins with two Norman phases, the earlier being
represented by the circular bases of the four W piers of the N
arcade. They have a diameter of about five feet and must
belong to an arcade of Hereford or Tewkesbury type. It is
possible that to the same building belonged the existing
chancel windows, one N, one S, and traces of two to the E, the
clasping chancel buttresses, and the chancel chapels; for they
have flat, square, many-scalloped capitals and single-stepped

arches.* Above them are circular clerestory windows, and above these outside (but now inside) the roof corbels. Of the same style the remaining s jamb of the arch which formerly led E from the N aisle. This also has scalloped capitals. The evidence in this place is, however, disturbed. What e.g. was the C14 corbel-head to support? A new building campaign began c.1200. The old arcades were replaced by new ones, but of these also there are only a few indications left – namely the E responds and NW respond. The NE respond is doubtful and may still belong to the earlier work, but the SE and NW responds have tripartite shafts, keeled or with fillets. In addition the SE respond has turned from scalloped to trumpet-scalloped capitals. Moreover, the double-chamfered pointed arches now carried by later piers (*see* below) are probably part of this work, which may thus well have extended to 1210. Trumpet capitals, keeled shafts, and a double-chamfered pointed arch also in the chancel aisle. The W portal is in an in-between position. The arch is round, the zigzags meeting at r. angles are extremely Late Norman, and so are the capitals of the three orders of shafts, e.g. the two with faces whose mouths are biting into the shafts. Yet the shafts are keeled. Turrets with clustered shafts and steep pyramid roofs flank the nave W wall.

This W façade could be developed because the tower was built away to the N. The reason why this was done remains obscure. The first Norman church perhaps had a crossing tower. The present tower is of the early C13. It has lancet windows throughout and a double-chamfered doorway. The upper parts, clearly of different masonry, and the recessed spire were built in 1727–34 by *Nathaniel Wilkinson* of Worcester. The spire replaces a shingled timber spire.

As so often in Herefordshire, much remodelling took place in the late C13 and early C14. Evidence of that is so prominent on the exterior that the church seems to belong to that period predominantly. The E window of the N chapel and the W window of the N aisle have very good Geometrical tracery with three quatrefoils in circles. In the W window the bars are slender rolls. The s aisle W window is not medieval. The s side of s aisle and s chapel are buttressed consistently, and the windows have cusped intersected and cusped Y-tracery,

* On the s side it can be seen that the arcades were formerly closed by a screen wall. In the SE bay the remains of a doorway through the screen wall survive.

or belong to the Herefordshire type of three stepped lancet lights. There is also the many-moulded arch of the s chapel doorway and the chapel E window, which has intersected tracery without cusping. The N doorway and the inner part of the N porch are equally elegant. Nearly straight-sided depressed arch on short vertical pieces, which comes of course from Aquablanca's Hereford Cathedral. Shafts inside the church as well as outside. Many fine mouldings. Shafted also the little twin W window. The outer parts of the porch, the upper storey, and the E extension are attributed by the RCHM to the mid C14. N aisle windows of the Herefordshire type of the three stepped lancet lights. And so to the outer N chapel, which is a *tour de force* by the same group of masons who worked at Leominster. Large four-light windows to E, N, and W, studded with ballflower. The tracery is of the stage immediately before the ogee curve came in, though perhaps a few years older than that of Leominster. Trefoil-headed lights, and above elongated pointed quatrefoils of three sizes, small, medium, and large. The two latter have big leaf cusps. It is a successful conceit, already Dec in spirit, though not in forms. Perp mainly the chancel E window. Inside the church the late Middle Ages have made less impact and a less fortunate impact. The Late Norman arcades were replaced by arcades of octagonal piers, on the s side in the Dec style, with concave sides, on the N side in ill-defined, yet later shapes. The arches however were at least partly re-used. They are double-chamfered. At the E responds the junction has caused much confusion, and two large and beautiful corbels of the early C14 got involved in that. One has a lion in combat with a dragon, the other a human-headed monster. Good aisle roofs with arched braces to collar-beams and curved wind-braces.

FURNISHINGS. REREDOS. 1824. Copy by *T. Ballard* after Leonardo's Last Supper. Corinthian columns l. and r. – STALLS. Heavy, probably C16. – (SCREEN. Parts loose on the upper floor of the N porch. RCHM) – STAINED GLASS. E window by *Kempe*, 1895, incorporating some small C15 figures, probably *in situ*. – Also by *Kempe* chancel s and most of s chapel and s aisle; 1895–1904. – In the outer N chapel W window a jumble of old bits, including two C13 medallions. Old glass also in a panel in the N aisle W window. – Also shields of c.1500 in the N chapel NE window. – Of c.1820 the copies of *Reynolds*'s New College windows with Faith, Hope, and Charity (N aisle). – PLATE. Tall Cup, 1571;

Cover Paten, probably C17; Paten on foot, probably late C17; two Flagons by *John Bodington*, 1698; two Chalices, London, 1819. – SWORD. In the outer N chapel. C17, with a Solingen blade.

MONUMENTS. Chancel N: Thomas Thornton, Master of St Katherine's Hospital, † 1629. Demi-figure preaching. Columns l. and r. and a semicircular pediment. – Chancel s: John Hoskins, rector, † 1631. The same type, but below a baldacchino. – Edward Skynner † 1631. Large kneeling couple facing one another, but instead of a prayer desk, between them on the floor their dead little girl, lying on her side. Three columns in front. The children kneeling in the 'predella'. Mrs Skynner's hat ought to be noted. – John Hamilton † 1851. A little boy of white marble, asleep. Against the wall behind two angels in relief. By *Mrs Thornycroft* and her husband *Thomas Thornycroft*. The monument was in the 1851 exhibition. – At the E end of the s arcade brasses to William Calwe, a priest, early C15, kneeling, 12 in. long, and to Thomas Capel † 1490, 27 in. long. Also brass plate to John Hayward † 1614. – s chapel: incised slab to Edward Cooper † 1596. – Daniel Ellis Saunders † 1825. By *Westmacott*, and very fine, with the relief of the 'repose of a poor family'. – s aisle: William Miles † 1803. By *Flaxman*. Reading woman on the ground in front of an obelisk. Rather frigid.* – Capt. Samuel Skynner † 1725. By *Thomas White*. The very reverse: jolly, if anything. Bust in front of a naval trophy. Rich foliage and scrolls below, l. and r. of the inscription. – Robert Myddelton Biddulph † 1814. Again by *Westmacott*. Mourning woman by an urn. Against the pillars of the low pedimented back delicate reliefs of his three children. – s aisle w: Anthony Biddulph † 1718 and his wife † 1706. Both semi-reclining, but placed so that their feet point at each other. The big back-plate reaches up into the w window. With contemporary railings. – Michael Biddulph † 1800. By *Charles Regnart*. Draped female figure on the ground by an urn and under a weeping tree. – N chapel: A sister of Grymbald Pauncefoot, *c.*1360. The lady lies on a tomb-chest, and the train of her skirt hangs down over its edge – a fascinating proof of the growing desire for naturalism in Chaucer's age (cf. Much Marcle). The effigy is unfortunately not in a good state, and the top parts of the monument have disappeared. Against the

* The composition is the same as on the Brathwaite Monument († 1800) on Barbados.

tomb-chest and the back wall and sides a total of eighteen shields, proof of the universal sin of genealogical pride. – Edward Moulton Barrett † 1857. By *J. G. Lough*. Small, white. He lies on a couch. A woman mourns at his feet. Behind, an angel opens a door and figures appear inside in the shallowest relief. – Outer N chapel: Perhaps the finest monument in the church. A priest of the late C13, his face full of feeling, as he prays. The canopy is cusped, the pillow placed diagonally.

27a

PUBLIC BUILDINGS

MARKET HOUSE. Begun after 1617, completed after 1655. The attribution to *John Abel* has no documentary foundation. Six by two bays. Open ground floor with stop-chamfered posts. On the upper floor special emphasis on the S side, i.e. down the High Street, by means of herringbone bracing. Roof with tie-beams, collar-beams, and diagonal struts.

BARRETT BROWNING MEMORIAL INSTITUTE and CLOCK TOWER. 1892–6 by *Brightwen Binyon*. Really terrible. It leaves one baffled as to how the black-and-white tradition could have been used and yet used, it seems, only to defeat the original black-and-white work of Ledbury.

BELL ORCHARD HOUSE (former Workhouse). Of brick, 1836. The usual cruciform plan. The style is still Late Classical, though there is a pedimental gable instead of a pediment.

RAILWAY VIADUCT. Very impressive. 1859–61. Designed by *Thomas Brassey* (or *Stephen Ballard*?).

PERAMBULATION

The town builds itself up nicely against the hill, like a second Malvern or some resort on the Continent.

Our perambulation had better start with the *clou* of Ledbury straightaway, CHURCH LANE, connecting the churchyard with the Market House. It is a narrow lane, cobbled and straight, and with some of the best black and white work l. and r. At the start, at the NW end the COUNCIL OFFICES, built in the C15, with oversailing upper floor on a moulded bressumer. At the end the OLD GRAMMAR SCHOOL on the N, dating from *c.*1500, CHURCH HOUSE on the S side, of *c.*1600. The latter has a porch on brackets, and inside a room with some minor plasterwork, lozenge-shaped panels with lion, bird, etc.

The HIGH STREET runs S from the Market House, a wide street,

the sides not strictly parallel. On the W side is first, facing
the Market House, ST KATHERINE'S HOSPITAL. The
present hospital premises are not ancient, the l. part by *Smirke*
1822, the r. part 1866. To the s at r. angles the old range,
chapel and hospital in one, built early in the C14 of red stone.
Three windows in the E wall, the upper with reticulated
tracery. The side windows of one or two lights. The chapel
was divided from the parts where the beds stood at r. angles
to the walls by a timber truss with a tie-beam on arched
braces and a collar-beam on arched braces. The roof has in
addition two tiers of curved wind-braces. In the E window
some original STAINED GLASS. Also some C14 or C15 TILES.
The former MASTER'S HOUSE lies back. It has no architectural features of interest outside (but inside, now hidden,
the roof of the house as it was in the C15, including the spere-
truss with the spere-posts; RCHM). After the Hospital the
FEATHERS HOTEL, a prominent black and white house of
*c.*1560–70 with a top floor and a N addition of the C17. The
house has closely-set uprights, occasionally crossed by horizontals. The l. part has five equal little gables, the r. side a
straight top cornice. The windows are sashed. The main posts
of the l. part carry vases with tall flowers, on the second floor
Ionic pilasters on high bases. The r. part has only foliated
brackets. Inside, wall paintings were discovered some ten
years ago. Intricate pattern of interlaced ogee arches. Opposite
modest houses. A characteristic pair, now united, is No. 17.
Early C19 front with giant pilasters and a black and white
front with closely-set uprights. Behind No. 14 a house has
been re-erected that belonged to Butchers' Row, a little
street in the centre of the High Street, pulled down in the
early C19. No. 9 has gables with ornamented bargeboards at
the back.

At the main crossing of Ledbury, where far too much traffic
passes, i.e. at the corner of Southend and Worcester Road,
lies LEDBURY PARK, built by the Biddulph family about
1600. It is the grandest black and white house in the county
and the only one to vie with the houses of Shrewsbury. Front
of five gables. The windows below have on two floors windows
with projecting sills placed between stop-chamfered posts.
The timbering otherwise is all of closely-set verticals. Along
Worcester Road an extension of 1820 with pedimented cross-
windows. Behind, extensive brick stables and outbuildings,
also a garden whose wall follows all along Southend – a rare

fusion of town and country house. In SOUTHEND little else
of note. No. 10 has a brick front with a recessed centre and
three pediments, the l. and r. ones lower and in front of an
attic: an odd composition, probably Late Georgian. It is said
to have been an inn. Then the COOKERY SCHOOL, black and
white of 1910, but with the internal fitments of the Southend
Charity School re-arranged as they were when it was founded
in 1706. Especially noteworthy the master's high chair with
segmental pediment on corbels. No. 24 is of brick and lies
back from the road. It looks c.1700, with its cross-windows.
Three widely-spaced bays.

However, at the corner of Southend and NEW STREET stands
one of the most prominent timber-framed houses in Ledbury,
the one whose front is projected on posts across the pavement
and leans forwards picturesquely and precariously. The posts
are stop-chamfered. A little to the w the TALBOT HOTEL,
low and picturesque. Inside, a room dated 1596, with panelling and an overmantel with the usual blank arches. On the
other side THE STEPPES, also picturesque, with closely-
spaced uprights, but partly a reconstruction.

N of the Market House, in HOMEND, first No. 13, a Late
Georgian five-bay brick house of three storeys with a parapet.
This is on the E side. Then, on the w side, a nice Georgian
double shop-front. On the same side No. 36, the best later
house in the town, of c.1700, with a fine shell-hood and two
dormers. No. 42 a black and white house with a projecting
porch, and opposite it, also black and white, and also originally
with a porch, ABBEY HOUSE, the most prominent house in
the street. It seems to be of c.1600. To its N, No. 67 has three
bays and four giant pilasters. Finally, at the very N end, close
to the station, No. 235, with exposed crucks.

A transition between town and rural surroundings are LOWER
HALL and UPPER HALL, N of the church, in gardens. Upper
Hall has been swamped by the Grammar School, Lower Hall
has a Georgian front of five bays with a pediment with lunette
windows, a pedimented doorway, and segment-headed
windows. The front is visible from the churchyard. The two
houses were formerly the houses of the Lay Vicars of Ledbury
Church.

UNDERDOWN, ½ m. SSE, is Late Georgian, grey, of two and a
half storeys with two bow windows.

DINGWOOD PARK, 1¾ m. SSE, is of c.1700. It is of brick, five
bays wide and two storeys high, with a hipped roof. The

windows originally had stone crosses (*see* the back and side).
The centre window above the (later) doorway is narrower
than the others – a Queen Anne motif. Inside two rooms with
good stucco, especially the one which displays roses, vine,
thorn, oak, etc., in oblong panels.

LEDICOT *see* SHOBDON

LEINTHALL EARLS
2 m. NE of Aymestrey

4060

ST ANDREW. A humble chapel. Nave and chancel in one.
Octagonal timber bellcote with conical roof. In the chancel
two Norman windows. The E window probably of *c.*1800. In
the nave simple Norman W doorway. Timber-framed W
gable. Tie-beam roof with queenposts. – PULPIT. Jacobean,
with two tiers of the usual stumpy blank arches. – PLATE.
Paten, London, 1774 and Chalice, London, 1799, both originally domestic.

GATLEY PARK. In a beautifully sheltered position above a
tiny wooded valley. Square centre of the 1630s* with additions
of 1894 and after. Brick, of two storeys and gabled. The only
original addition to the square is the porch with a (C19)
strapwork parapet. Mullioned and transomed windows.
(Staircase with heavy turned balusters and two decorated
overmantels. RCHM)

LEINTHALL STARKES

4060

ST MARY MAGDALENE. Away from the village and, with it
and the neighbouring villages, surrounded by hills. Four old
yew trees stand close to the church, two W, two E. Nave and
lower chancel. Norman – *see* the one small chancel E window,
one chancel N window, one nave N window, the plain,
curiously wide S doorway, and one W window high up, because
of a former W annexe. Traces of the W doorway to this
(RCHM) and of the corbels and string course of its (lean-to ?)
roof remain. The other windows of the church simple, C13,
and renewed. Bellcote of two round arches perhaps C17.
Nave roof with braces joining to form segmental arches across.
Cusped wind-braces. – SCREEN. Simple, one-light divisions
with thin tracery. – PLATE. Paten, 1571; Chalice, probably
London-made and Elizabethan.

* Firebacks dated 1634 and 1639; cistern dated 1637.

COTTAGE, ⅓ m. w. On the N side of the main road. To the w one cruck-truss is exposed. (Others inside.)

OLD FARM, off the s side of the road, further w. The house lies behind a farm, and its principal feature, the pretty NW gable with a little cusped diagonal and horizontal bracing, is visible from the road.

LEINTWARDINE

4070

ST MARY MAGDALENE. A large church, of buff sandstone with pale pink sandstone trim. The oldest piece is the w doorway, not now in the centre of the w wall. This is Transitional, with a round arch and one order of colonnettes with leaf capitals. Next follows the tall chancel, severely over-restored and with a steep-pitched roof. Original only the priest's doorway with a shouldered round arch. All windows C19. Of the later C13 the s arcade and s doorway. The doorway has beautiful deep mouldings, some with fillets. The s arcade of five bays is tall (heightened in the early C14?) and has round piers and round abaci. The arches have one step and one chamfer. The w lancet could well be contemporary, but is more likely to be of the early C14, as are the s windows. The s aisle is embattled and has below the battlements big gargoyles. The N arcade is early C14, but the N aisle w window is identical with the s aisle w window. The arcade has octagonal piers and double-chamfered arches. The N aisle windows are C15, but the jambs etc. may be early C14. Of the same date also the transeptal N chapel and the tall and broad sw porch tower. It has a semi-circular staircase projection to the w. The s entrance is of three continuous chamfers. Again of the same date the N chapel and its windows and its arcade to the chancel (three bays, short octagonal piers, double-chamfered arches). The w arch from the N transept is double-chamfered and dies into the imposts. Perp clerestory and roof. The roof is of low pitch, boarded and panelled, with many bosses. – REREDOS. Of stone, C15 or early C16. Closely panelled. All that remains is the parts N and s of the Victorian E window. – STALLS. Perhaps from Wigmore Abbey. Tall back wall with one-light divisions, panel tracery, and canopies. Heads on the arm-rests. Misericords preserved on the s side, a good set: for instance Resurrection, Annunciation, two wrestlers. On the ends of the front desks figures instead of poppy-heads. On the fronts of the desks tracery with spandrels carved with foliage and monsters. – WOODWORK. In various places tracery panels, partly from the stalls, partly perhaps from a screen. Also, in the N chapel, standing angels from a roof. – MONUMENT. Sir Banastre Tarlaton. By *Rouw*, 1835. Big, with a military still life.

HEATH HOUSE, 2 m. NW. Probably of *c*.1650–60. Brick, English bond, with two projecting wings to the N. Hipped roof with dormers. The S side is flat, of eight bays and two storeys. Doorway (re-set?) in the third bay, with tapering pilasters, beaded up the edges. What remains of original windows is of the wooden cross type. The staircase with turned balusters is either imported or re-used, i.e. original in its parts but not in their assembly. On the first floor a room with fine, strong mid-C17 panelling.

The ROMAN SETTLEMENT of BRAVINIUM is represented by a roughly rectangular area of 10 acres enclosed by banks which have been largely obliterated, except on the NW corner, by the modern village. Finds made in the C19 include Samian and coarse wares, roof tiles, part of a rotary quern, and a bronze ring and coins.

WATLING STREET, which runs through the settlement, is now overlain by a modern road (High Street) for ½ m. to the N of the site and 2 m. to the S.

LEOMINSTER

4050

Leominster is two things, a town of *c*.6,500 inhabitants, and what remains of the priory, and – visually – the two never meet.

PRIORY OF ST PETER AND ST PAUL

The prehistory of the Benedictine priory of Leominster is a nunnery which existed in the C9 at the latest and was dissolved in 1046. The manor was given by Henry I to his newly founded Reading Abbey in 1123, and building must have started soon after and proceeded quickly; for an altar in the E bay of the nave was consecrated in 1130. The parts E of this, which were probably erected between 1123 and 1130, are only known from excavations. They consisted of transepts, each with one E chapel, a chancel with apse, and an ambulatory with three radiating chapels, i.e. the scheme of Reading and before that of St Augustine Canterbury and Battle Abbey in England and many more in France. The E chapel was later (C14?) replaced by a long, straight-ended Lady Chapel. These

E parts were demolished after the Dissolution, and what
survives is, apart from one fragment of the s transept s wall,
the nave and N aisle plus a bold later enlargement of the s side.
The cloister lay on the N and has disappeared, and of the
monastic buildings also little remains.

The church today stands, pale red on juicy green, in a
curious isolation surrounded on three sides by lawn (and the
churchyard), and these lawns and open spaces stretch quite a
distance to the s. The building thus looks neither like a priory
church nor like a parish church. One is almost reminded of a
model.

The Norman building can be reconstructed externally by
one N aisle window and the clerestory windows. They have
plain, single-stepped reveals. The sides were evidently very
simple. All the more distinguished was the w front, which,
from the style of its sculpture, seems to be of c.1150. This
has a grand w portal with a slightly pointed arch (which is
remarkable), and three orders of sturdy columns carrying
highly fancifully decorated capitals and an arch of stepped
orders which are left unadorned, except for one, and this has
zigzag at r. angles to the wall surfaces – a motif usually
considered Late Norman, but appearing at Peterborough
and also c.1140–5 at Shobdon. The capitals have affronted
lions, affronted birds, two affronted men bending down
(and tending trees ?), a trail of two symmetrical snakes, a
trail of horizontally placed elementary three-part palmettes,
and also heavily ribbed upright leaves in three overlapping
tiers. Above is a billet frieze and then one large window, also
strongly shafted and with capitals in the same style. One of
them has two pairs of affronted birds, one standing on top of
the other. More than this we cannot say. The s aisle has
disappeared, for reasons which we shall see later. The N aisle
has in its w wall one Norman circular window. The window
below, of three stepped lancet lights, is of the later C13, as is
also one of five stepped lancet lights in the aisle N wall. The
other N windows with their gables and wooden mullions may
belong to the C18. Above the centre of the w front rises a C15
tower. The parapet, battlements, and pinnacles are Victorian.
It is to be assumed that one Norman w tower was planned or
built, not a pair. The strength of the substructure favours the
assumption, and the N aisle w bay is oblong and has no
strengthening of its N wall.

Inside, this bay is roughly groin-vaulted, again a strength-

8b

ening of the centre of the w end. The system of the nave 6a
deserves some closer description. The E bay, i.e. the bay
originally w of the crossing, and the second bay from the w,
or rather from the tower bay, have stronger walls than the
parts between, and instead of a normal arcade opening solid
chunks of walls only opened in a tall, narrow, single-stepped
arch. The RCHM suggests that another such bay existed in the
middle, and that there the original rhythm of the nave was
the unusual one of (from the E) narrow–wide–narrow–wide–
narrow–wide, and then the tower bay.* The RCHM also
suggests that during building this design was given up, and
instead – probably after some pulling down – the centre of
the arcade was made into three normal arches on normal
piers. These piers are circular with circular multi-scalloped
capitals (cf. Hereford Cathedral) and single-stepped arches.
Some have a little zigzag or billet in the abacus. The responds
are partly of the same kind, partly with stepped capitals, as if
they had been intended for tripartite, not semicircular responds. To this ought to be added a further small irregularity:
the bay E of the tower bay has on both sides a change of level,
so that the w responds lie lower than the E responds and the
arches have to descend on to the former. Above the arcade
runs a false triforium, now blocked, but originally open into
the aisles, and this has a rhythm completely independent of
the arcade below, and indeed of the clerestory above. It is a
long row of twin arches with a dividing square pier under one
round relieving arch. The clerestory windows are set in a
system of continuous arcading, always two blank and then one
window.

The w or tower bay is different. Here there is a gallery
with as wide an opening as that of the arcade arch below. But
this bay was much changed about when the tower was built:
a broad arch was set in between it and the nave and received
decorative panelling. In the upper storeys arches were also
drawn in or strengthened. The w portal has decoration inside
as well as outside. The style is the same, but the motifs are
different: capitals with interlace, trails emanating from a
mouth, intersected circles. In the abacus above the latter
capital is a small representation of Samson and the Lion
copied from, rather than the pattern for, the tympanum of

* Dr Zarnecki and Professor Bony connect this unusual system with
Périgueux, and are inclined to assume that the original plan foresaw vaulting
by domes – a bold assumption to make.

Stretton Sugwas. Here lies the only connexion between the Leominster decoration and the so-called Herefordshire School of Norman Sculpture. The school may have developed out of the Leominster workshop, which in its turn may have depended on Reading, but there is no early Leominster sculpture left to prove this, and by the time the w portal was built, inspiration seems to have gone the other way.

In the C13 the Norman s aisle was replaced by a new aisle, or rather parochial nave to get rid of parish duties in the priory church. Of this no more remains than some masonry of the w wall and the sw buttress. The 45-ft-high w window is of course Perp. It is of eight lights, the two middle ones surprisingly but convincingly flanked by slim buttresses instead of mullions. The E.E. enlargement was consecrated by Bishop Ralph of Maidstone, who ruled from 1234 to 1240. But there is another, extremely fine piece of architecture whose style proves that it belongs to the same years, though it must be re-set: the spacious s porch. The entrance as well as the inner doorway with their orders of tall, slender columns and their upright stiff-leaf capitals and their many deep and filleted mouldings are clearly E.E. The porch was re-erected and the three outer niches added, with their ballflower decoration, and this motif fixes the re-erection to the years when the parochial nave was given a wide s aisle. They must be the years about 1310, as the motifs – ballflower, and tracery forms yet entirely without ogee arches – prove. The aisle is a showpiece indeed. It has a w window and four s windows, all identical, all tall and wide, of four lights, with the same tracery, and absolutely studded with ballflowers. The tracery has cusped cinquefoils, cusped daggers, pointed trefoils and the like, i.e. forms of c.1300, possible still no doubt c.1310. Panelled top parapet.

Inside, the parochial nave is separated from the s aisle by slender quatrefoil piers put in in 1872–9 by *Sir G. G. Scott* to replace the Tuscan pillars which had replaced the original piers in 1699. In the s aisle is a C13 piscina, re-set (pointed trefoiled, with a hood-mould on two heads and a third head at the apex) and early C14 sedilia with pointed trefoiled heads and gables with much ballflower. The windows also have ballflower inside.

FURNISHINGS. Relatively little has survived the fire of 1699. ORGAN CASE. A fine piece of 1739. Its front was originally placed to face the chancel. – TILES. Some, probably of the c14, in the w recess in the s nave. – PAINTING. On the N wall of the nave large Wheel of Life, c.1275. Large circle enclosing two smaller circles formerly with figure subjects. To the w a big seated figure. – STAINED GLASS. In the s nave w window by *Mayer & Co.* of Munich, 1878. – In the s aisle SE and second window by *Kempe*, 1898 and 1903, i.e. without and with Kempe's trademark, the wheatsheaf. – In the Lady Chapel window by *Martin Travers* and after his death in 1948 by *Lawrence Lee*. – PLATE. Late c15 Chalice, one of 43ᵃ the best surviving in England. It has a concave-sided hexagonal base inscribed IHC and XPC, a finely detailed hexagonal stem, a knop with lozenge-projections, and a semiglobular bowl with inscription on the outside. – Cover Paten belonging to the former and with the face of Christ in a sunk sexfoil. – Cup and Cover Paten by *I.P.*, London, 1576. – Dutch c17 Almsdish with Adam and Eve in *repoussé*. – Salver Paten by *Hugh Roberts* of London, 1698. – Flagon by *John Eastt* of London, 1720. – Plate, London, 1741. – CURIOSUM. Ducking stool, preserved in the N aisle. – CHURCHYARD GATES. Very good, of cast iron, 1788, made at Stourport. – (The entrance from the Grange has wrought-iron gates of 1791.)

MONASTIC QUARTERS. All that survives is this: an early c14 doorway with ballflower from the N aisle to the former cloister, now half-buried, and the so-called PRIORY HOUSE, a range running W–E and now at the N end of the Old People's Home, formerly the workhouse. This may have been the infirmary, or more probably the reredorter or lavatories. Under it indeed runs a brook. It consists of a w part, rebuilt, it seems, after the Dissolution, and a c15 E part with some small original windows and a good large doorway on the first floor.

OTHER CHURCHES

FORBURY CHAPEL, *see* Perambulation, p. 230.
ST ETHELBERT (R.C.), Bargates. By *P. P. Pugin*, 1897–8.
BAPTIST CHAPEL, Etnam Street. 1771. Brick, with a façade of three bays. Doorway with a broad surround of Tuscan demi-columns and a broken pediment. Arched windows l. and r. The chapel is set back from the street, and to the l. and r. of the forecourt are the manse and dwellings for poor persons.

PUBLIC BUILDINGS

TOWN HALL, High Street. 1855 by *James Cranston* of Birmingham. Modest. 'In a mixed Italian style' (Kelly).*

48b OLD TOWN HALL (Grange Court). Built by *John Abel*, King's Carpenter, in 1633. The town hall originally stood at the junction of High Street and Broad Street. It is timber-framed, two-storeyed, of five by two bays, and quite prodigiously decorated. The ground floor was open. Short, fancy-Ionic columns on tall plinths. Spandrels with shields, monsters, lions. Above them an inscription which reads as follows: 'Vive deo gratus, Toti mundo tumulatus, Crimine mundatus, Semper transire paratus. Where Justice rule, there vertu flow. Vive ut post vivas. Sat cito si sat bene. Like columnes do upprop the fabrik of abuilding, so noble gentri dos support the honor of a Kingdom. In memoria aeterna erit justus.' Oversailing upper floor on brackets, including diagonal angle-brackets. They have busts of men and of bare-bosomed women. The upper windows project in the usual fashion. The sills are carried on brackets or (N and S) grotesque caryatids. The bracing is done by diagonals and cusped concave-sided lozenges, and in the gables by ogee arches with little fleurs-de-lis set in. The bressumers of the gables rest on small decorative carved arches.

PERAMBULATION

Leominster was a wool-town. It is described as such by Leland and Camden and by Dryden in his *Polyolbion* ('her wool whose staple doth excel').

The pivot of the town is the junction of High Street, West Street, South Street, and Corn Street. CORN SQUARE lies a little off to the E. In it the former CORN EXCHANGE, 1858–9 by *Cranston*, quite prettily Gothic, an unusual choice for Corn Exchanges. Lower wings curving back. On the S side at the angle of School Lane a timber-framed house with a plain angle-bracket and cusped bargeboards in the gable. To its r. a house of *c.*1400 (with one original roof-truss inside which has cusped principals with diagonal bracing. RCHM).

First to the S along SOUTH STREET. On the E side the ROYAL OAK HOTEL, Georgian, of five bays with a three-bay pediment. Then to the E ETNAM STREET, mostly Georgian

* REGALIA. Two Maces presented in 1692.

brick, but interspersed with some black and white. Opposite
the hotel DUTTON HOUSE, Gothic, of c.1850, with gables.*
Then among the Georgian houses No. 20 with a nice doorway,
and No. 40 with two canted bays. Black and white the
CHEQUERS INN, No. 61, of c.1600, with two gables of which
one has decorated bargeboards. Nos 89–91 look externally
all Early Victorian Tudor, but have inside a fine roof of
c.1400 with kingposts, collars, and trefoils above them
(RCHM). At the E end, a little projecting, the WHITE LION,
early C16, with square framing. SOUTH STREET, further S,
is essentially Georgian. Nice doorways, e.g. Nos 26, 28, 38,
40, and, on the other side, BRYAN HOUSE.

Now to the W, along WEST STREET. The TALBOT HOTEL
consists of three houses, the first Georgian with two canted
bays and between – a most curious motif – three blank arches
in three tiers one above the other. Then a three-bay Early
Georgian house with segment-headed windows and aprons
below them, and a timber-framed house. Then N along
Rainbow Street and W along GREEN LANE to TOWNSEND
HOUSE, which does not at first look promising outside, but
has a hall of the early C16 and, to the N, a Jacobean five-light
mullioned and transomed window and a porch with Ionic
pilasters. Other mullioned and transomed windows too.
(Inside a date 1604 in stucco. RCHM)

The HIGH STREET runs N from our starting point. In it No. 41
is black and white, narrow, with one gable and diagonal as
well as cusped concave-sided-lozenge bracing. No. 20 has
two gables and the same decoration. Opposite is No. 21 with
a Roman Doric shopfront. No. 8 has three gables on four
brackets with faces. From the top of the High Street DRAPERS
LANE, a pedestrian street, runs back to Corn Square. Nos 9–11
have a projecting top storey with moulded bressumer and
two gables. The uprights are closely set, and there is inside
a recent but credible date 1575. Nos 20–22 have an angle
bracket and a doorway in the passage. The date is early
Tudor.

Again from the top of the High Street, BURGESS STREET runs
W. On its S side GRAFTON HOUSE, which may go back to the
late C14. The front has foiled diagonal braces. In the back
one window with an ogee head. (Inside, roof with collar-
beams on arched braces and foiled wind-braces. RCHM)

Once more from the top of the High Street and now E, down

* But structurally and in some details late C16.

CHURCH STREET. Here on the l. first the former chapel of St Thomas Becket or FORBURY CHAPEL, a plain oblong of the late C13. E window of three stepped lancet lights under one arch, s and N windows with pointed-trefoiled cusping. The roof seems late C15. Hammerbeams with coarse pendants. The hammers stand on faces. Opposite and around the best Georgian houses in Leominster: opposite Nos 12–16, to the E THE FORBURY, brick, of five bays and two and a half storeys with a five-bay pediment. Doorway with fluted Doric pilasters, a metope frieze, and a segmental pediment. Back with a three-bay pedimented projection. Along PINSLEY ROAD the precinct wall of the priory appears and is continued to the E further s.

Finally to the N. In BROAD STREET a mixture of black and white and of red brick. No. 18 is black and white, of c.1600. It has four storeys. The third and fourth project on brackets. (Staircase with flat pierced balusters. RCHM) No. 15 opposite is the LION WORKS, Regency probably, with tripartite windows, a top frieze with wreath, and a recumbent lion at the top. The ground floor is heavily victorianized. (Opposite, No. 24 has some plaster decoration inside. RCHM) No. 34 has a Georgian doorway. PINSLEY HOUSE, at the corner of Vicarage Street, is Georgian too. Three bays, Venetian windows with pretty Gothick glazing details.

Then BRIDGE STREET, starting on the E side with No. 2, a stately late C17 house with a big hipped roof. It is of five by six bays. Entrance with arched hood on carved brackets. (Staircase with twisted balusters. RCHM) The street has mostly brick houses. Nos 9–11 is of chequered brick. No. 29 is timber-framed with traceried bargeboards and heavy cusped diagonal braces – probably c.1400. Opposite is MARSH HOUSE, No. 34, also timber-framed, but with a pediment with dentils. Door-hood with pediment on scrolly iron brackets. Nos 55 etc. more black and white.*

Then E into MILL STREET with No. 61 (POPLANDS), timber-framed, early C16, one gable only, bressumer with little intersected arches and leaf decoration. Bargeboards decorated with a foliage trail. Back and yet further N, in OLD LUDLOW ROAD, No. 97 with much gay diagonal bracing. Doorway with a pediment on brackets, i.e. a Restoration or later type, yet still covered in carving of Jacobean character.

* But some of it is only painted on.

OUTER LEOMINSTER

The buildings to be referred to are all w or s of Leominster.

St John, Ivington, 2¼ m. sw. 1842. Nave and chancel in one. Lancet style.

Ivington Bury. The Jacobean gatehouse is of stone below, timber-framed above, both probably pre-Reformation. The timbers are partly closely-set verticals, partly diagonal.

Cholstrey Court, 2 m. w. The house has a BARN of cruck construction.

(Stogbatch, 2½ m. wsw. In the N wing a c14 cruck-truss with remains of foiling. Medieval barn of cruck construction. RCHM)

Knoake's Court, 1¼ m. sw of Ivington. Brick, of the early c18, see the typical narrow windows l. and r. of the doorway and the middle window above it. Pitched roof.

Brierley Court, 2 m. s. c18. Of red sandstone. Three bays, two storeys, hipped roof. Fine gatepiers with vases to the front garden.

Broadward Hall, 1½ m. s. Stately Georgian brick house of five bays and two storeys. Three-bay pediment. Nicely detailed Venetian window below. Doorway with Tuscan pilasters and a pediment. Garden wall with Chippendale wooden fencing. (DOVECOTE, square, with the date 1652. RCHM)

Eaton Hall, 1 m. se. Mostly of the mid c14, though the exterior betrays nothing of it. Hall roof with collar-beams on arched braces and trefoils above them. The posts of the spere-truss which formerly separated the hall from the screens passage survive but are not now visible. se of the house a BRIDGE across the Lugg, two spans, c17 or earlier.

Wharton Court, 2½ m. sse. A somewhat forbidding, tall, oblong stone house with a porch added in 1659. The house itself is probably Jacobean. Three and a half storeys in height by only three bays in width. Renewed mullioned and transomed windows. The porch is two-storeyed and ends in a balcony. It has three round-arched openings on the ground floor, the front one with fancy columns, the side ones with pilasters. Pilasters also flank the front window on the upper floor. The sides here have blank upright ovals, and such ovals were also made in the adjoining wall of the house itself. The hipped roof and the four chimneys which crown the house symmetrically close to the four corners could be of *c.*1659, but not earlier. They may well be later. The chimneys connect with the fireplaces in the four rooms below, all placed – most unusually – across the outer corners. Handsome staircase through all three floors. Tall finials, pineapple pendants.

IRON AGE HILL-FORT, on the SW end of the ridge, 3 m. S of Leominster. This large, multivallate rampart fort is one of the most spectacular monuments in the county, with ramparts following the contours of the ridge. The entrance on the SE is extremely elaborate, with inturned ramparts and additional complex outworks. A second, probably original, entrance on the NE is less complex, with the ends of the inner ramparts inturned.

3070

LETTON
1½ m. SE of Brampton Bryan

In the GATEPIERS of the garden of the first house coming from Brampton Bryan or Walford are a number of C12 and C13 stones probably from Wigmore Abbey. They include Norman lozenge friezes of different kinds and one especially fine stiff-leaf capital of *c.*1230–40. Also pieces of various shafts.

(LODGE FARM, 1 m. SE, in the parish of Wigmore. Timber-framed. Early C16 to C17. With close-set framing. RCHM)

3040

LETTON
1½ m. SE of Willersley

ST JOHN BAPTIST. Norman the S doorway. With zigzag up the jambs. Lintel of red sandstone with one big rosette and several smaller ones. Undecorated tympanum over. Norman also the nave W doorway with a tufa tympanum and a tufa frieze and some herringbone masonry on the N side. Unbuttressed C14 W tower, the top stage later and weatherboarded. Low arch with one continuous slight chamfer to the nave. Chancel of *c.*1300, *see* the windows, particularly the E window of the special Herefordshire three-light type, and the tomb recess inside which has pierced cusps and subcusps. Early C14 S transept, *see* the tomb recess with ballflower decoration in the E wall. Two more, almost entirely dismantled tomb recesses in the S wall. In the W wall a curious small doorway coming out close to the nave S doorway. The arch from transept to nave is obviously much interfered with.

– PULPIT. Splendid early C18 piece with tester, said to come from a Bristol church. – READER'S DESK. Probably part of the pulpit composition. – BENCHES. In the chancel, C17 – just plain, homely benches, not a bit churchy. – DOOR. The s door is an outstandingly good piece of the C12. Large hinges forming a daring, spiky, not entirely logical pattern.

A pretty black and white house with a gabled porch just W of the churchyard.

THE LEY *see* WEOBLEY

LEYS *see* GANAREW

LIMEBROOK
1 m. SE of Lingen

3060

PRIORY. Founded *c*.1189 for Augustinian Canonesses. All that remains is the ruin of one building with some roughly recognizable windows and a doorway on the s side. The suggested date is the C13.

LIMEBROOK COTTAGE, NNW of the priory ruin. Inside, some moulded beams and a length of re-used bargeboarding with a running vine-trail.

(UPPER LIMEBROOK FARM, in Wigmore Parish, ⅜ m. N of the priory ruin. With three cruck-trusses. RCHM)

LINGEN
3060

Under the hills, which come close to the village on the E side.

ST MICHAEL. C16 (?) W tower with C19 timber bell-stage and shingled spire. The rest of 1891 by *H. Curzon* (GR). Nave and lower chancel. The windows with pointed-trefoiled lights, i.e. in the style of *c*.1300, on the model of the original piscina in the chancel. – BENCHES. Plain, straight-topped, probably early C16. – PLATE. Chalice and Cover Paten, 1571. – MONUMENT. John Downes † 1687. Small tablet with pretty, curly foliage surround.

CASTLE, N of the church. Of motte-and-bailey type. (The motte is about 22 ft high above the bottom of the ditch. Square bailey with remains of an inner rampart. RCHM)

(CHAPEL FARM, 2 m. NE, in the parish of Wigmore. With an early C15 hall, later horizontally divided. The original roof exists, with tie-beams on cusped brackets instead of arched braces and with three tiers of cusped wind-braces. Also traces of original four-light windows on the N side, and an original doorway on the W side. RCHM)

(THE CHURCHYARD, ⅔ m. NNE. A mound, rising c.12 ft above the ditch, and c. 40 yds in diameter at the top. RCHM)

LYNCHETS. There are six undated terraces ⅓ m. SW of the church, running for over 100 yds.

6020 LINTON-BY-ROSS

ST MARY. The exposed fragment of a Norman S doorway with a fat roll moulding prepares for the N arcade inside, which is also Norman and consists of two unmoulded arches connecting the responds with a circular pier much too fat for them. It has a scalloped capital. To the W of the arcade is a substantial piece of solid wall. The building must be explained as follows. This wall belonged to a Norman W tower. Proof is the N wall, with an outer string course decorated with zigzag, and also, in an indirect way, the S arcade, which is of the C13 except for the W bay. The arcade has circular piers with circular abaci and double-chamfered arches. The W bay is evidently later. To build it, the S wall of the old tower had to come down. So this is the time when the present W tower was built, which is indeed Perp. Diagonal buttresses, recessed spire, and inside the ambitious conceit of a rib-vault. The ribs form a tierceron star with a big centre hole for the bell-ropes. Leaf bosses at the junction and little figures on the wall corbels. So far the chancel has not been mentioned. The arch with continuous chamfers and the S lancet allocate it to the C13. The E window with reticulated tracery is a Dec replacement. – PLATE. Chalice and Cover Paten by *E.G.*, probably London, c.1675. – Flagon by *C. Wright* (?), London, 1768. – MONUMENTS. One coffin-lid of the C13 with a very ornate foliated cross. – John Elmehurst † 1662. Funny tablet with, l. and r. of the inscription, two draped female figures and in addition two ugly cherubs and two ugly cherubs' heads. – Rev. Peter Senhouse † 1760. Tall, quite elegant tablet. – Two nice local tablets by *Vick* of Hereford († 1799) and by *Jennings* of Hereford († 1810). – Plenty of enjoyable headstones in the churchyard.

(PRIEST'S HOUSE, N of the church. With original cruck-trusses. RCHM)

BURTON COURT. Brick-faced stone house. Five bays, two

storeys, with steep three-bay pediment with lunette windows. Segment-headed windows. The façade looks early c18.

(ECCLESWELL CASTLE, at Ecceswell Court, 1¼ m. SSW of the church. Earthworks in bad preservation. Above the entrance to the dovecote a c14 label-stop of a man wearing a bascinet. RCHM)

EARTHWORK. A ditch and bank 130 yds long, of unknown date, lie ¼ m. NW of the church.

Many flint cores, scrapers, and other tools have been found in the area, suggesting the existence of an OCCUPATION SITE or working floor of the Neolithic or Early Bronze Age periods.

LITTLE BIRCH   *5030*

ST MARY. 1869 by *W. Chick*. In the Geometrical style, with a bellcote and a polygonal apse. – FONT. Norman, cup-shaped, with a rope moulding at the foot of the bowl. – SCREEN. Tall, of wrought iron, i.e. of *c*.1870. – PLATE. Elizabethan Cup; Cover Paten inscribed 1576. The underside of the latter shows traces of having been a pre-Reformation plate.

PRIMITIVE METHODIST CHAPEL, 1 m. NW. 1858, i.e. still with the arched windows of the early c19, but already with bargeboards.

LITTLE BRAMPTON *see* RODD

LITTLE COWARNE   *6050*

CHURCH. Mostly Victorian (by *F. R. Kempson*, 1870). W tower with saddleback roof and S gable. In the chancel one re-set Norman window, in the nave one c13 lancet. – PLATE. Chalice and Cover Paten inscribed 1829.

LITTLE DEWCHURCH   *5030*

ST DAVID. 1869–71 by *F. Preedy*, except for the c14 W tower. (In this the bell-chamber has a pointed tunnel-vault running N–S and with transverse chamfered arches. RCHM) Of old materials some c13 and c14 windows were used. – PLATE. Paten, originally domestic, London, 1763. – CHURCHYARD CROSS. With steps, base, and part of the shaft.

(COURT FARMHOUSE, ENE of the church. The ceilings mentioned by the RCHM do not exist any longer. MHLG)

SCHOOL. Gothic, 1867, with a recent little cubic addition of glass and wood.

LITTLE HEREFORD

ST MARY MAGDALENE. Broad, unbuttressed C13 W tower
with pyramid roof. The W doorway has the same details as
the nave S doorway. The nave indeed has a lancet window W
of the doorway. However, the nave itself must be at least
partially Norman, *see* the one remaining N window. The other
nave and the chancel windows are late C13 to early C14.
Inside, the remarkable features are the tower arch, as stately
as a chancel arch (simple moulded capitals, arch mouldings
with fillets), and the chancel arch, as narrow as a tower arch.
The latter has a chamfered W and a chamfered E arch, and
between the two is the entrance to the rood stair, which rises
in the wall S of the arch – a very unusual solution. Above the
chancel arch a big arched niche with a shelf; probably for the
rood and the lights beneath it. – STAINED GLASS. E window
with the monogram of *W. Wailes* and the date 1851. – PLATE.
Set by *Humphrey Payne*: Chalice and Cover Paten, 1726,
Flagon, 1735, Paten on feet, 1738. All in the original leather
cases. – MONUMENTS. Three fine tomb recesses, early C14,
one in the nave with a cusped and subcusped arch, ballflower
on the gable, and side-buttresses, the other two as a pair in
the chancel, with ogee gables with crockets. In the easternmost of them effigy of a Lady, incised in stone. It could well
belong to the recess. – Joseph Bailey † 1850. By *J. Evan
Thomas*. With a big white mourning woman below a cross.

EARTHWORKS, around and to the SE of the churchyard.

BLEATHWOOD MANOR FARM, 1⅛ m. NNE. Brick, laid in
Flemish bond; of the late C17. Irregular, with straight and
semicircular gables, relieving arches to the windows, and
dentil friezes and corbel friezes. (Staircase with flat pierced
balusters. RCHM)

NUN UPTON (actually in Brimfield Park), 1¼ m. SW. An
exceptionally fine house. The centre black and white with
gabled porch. Close-set uprights. Additions in brick on both
sides. These are probably Jacobean or a little later. The brickwork is in English bond. Big shaped gables. Moulded straight
hoods over the windows. Bits of dentil friezes. Porch with
semicircular gable. One chimneystack is star-shaped, the
other, with brick rustication, must be of *c.*1700.

UPTON COURT, 1¼ m. S. Timber-framed. A long façade with
two gables and a gabled porch, all with diagonal bracing. Brick
star chimneys. Simple brick back. A specially lively ensemble.

(BRIDGE over the Teme. Dated 1761. Of five round arches, with some decoration.)

LITTLE MARCLE

6030

ST MICHAEL. By *J. W. Hugall*, 1870. Nave and chancel and a polygonal bell-turret with spire. It stands on a shaft which stands on a buttress. Everything must be varied and unexpected. The skyline is made lively not only by the bell-turret but also by the chimney of the vestry and by crosses on nave, chancel, and porch. Hugall was evidently one of the naughtier High Victorians. – PLATE. Cup, 1570; Cover Paten, 1571; Salver by *Richard Bayley* of London, 1718.

LITTLE PENLAN *see* HUNTINGTON

LITTLE SARNESFIELD *see* WEOBLEY

LIVERS OCLE *see* OCLE PYCHARD

LLANCILLO

3020

ST PETER. Difficult to reach. By Llancillo Court, approached from the main Abergavenny road. Nave and chancel. The chancel has tufa quoins and one altered Norman N window. – PULPIT. Dated 1632. With arabesque panels, on each side two vertical panels and one above horizontal. No blank arches. – CHEST. Very elementary C13 'dug-out'. – PLATE. Chalice by *John Emes*, London, 1802; Cup, 1836.

(MOUND, just E of the church. On the top traces of a round keep of 50 ft diameter, probably a shell keep.

LLANDINABO

3020

ST DINABO. A dedication unique in England. 1881 by *A. Lloyd Oswell* of Shrewsbury. Nave and chancel and timber-framed bell-turret. – PULPIT. Two Jacobean sides, with the usual blank arches. – SCREEN. An extremely pretty piece of hardly later date than 1525 or 1530. One-light divisions. The mullions decorated with lozenges, elongated hexagons, and other motifs. In the cornice a band of dolphins, and above the entry a little ornament which also shows the coming of the Renaissance. – STAINED GLASS. In the E window by *Kempe*, 1893. – PLATE. Chalice, inscribed 1728; Paten, London, 1789. – MONUMENT. Brass to Thomas Tompkins † 1629.

A plate 7½ in. high with the frontal demi-figure of a boy standing in a pool and praying. The child was in fact drowned.

LLANDINABO FARMHOUSE, to the NW. Stone, of five bays and two storeys, with a hipped roof and three dormers, i.e. a type of the late C17. (The house contains a late C17 staircase. RCHM)

LLANGARRON

ST DEINST. There is only one other dedication to this Celtic saint. It is at Itton, Monmouthshire. C14 W tower with diagonal buttresses with many set-offs. Parapet and good recessed spire. C14 also the chancel, *see* the scissor-braced single-frame roof. Most of the rest C19, especially the N arcade. Of original windows, the Dec window re-set in a C19 dormer and the big Perp S aisle window further E may be mentioned. Below the latter a cusped tomb recess of about 1300. – FONT. Substantial, octagonal, Perp. On the bowl quatrefoils, on the stem tracery and fleurons. – PULPIT. Jacobean, with the familiar blank arches, here specially tall. – COMMUNION RAIL. Nice late C17 work, re-used. – SCULPTURE. In the SE buttress a stone with some Norman interlace. – PLATE. Cup and Cover Paten and a fine Flagon, all 1683. – MONUMENTS. In the nave (s) small effigy placed upright. Big head on a five-sided pillow. Small body, crossed hands. Is it C13? – Rowland Scudamore † 1697 (nave S). Nice tablet with scrolly surround. – Another nice tablet, with a scrolly top, outside the nave (S side): to Johan Philpott de Sonke † 1689. – William Gwyllym † 1698 (chancel E). Uncommonly large tablet with foliage, putti, good big putto heads, and a skull at the foot. – Mrs Audley née Gwyllym † 1715. Smaller, but with the same kind of scrolly, flowery surround.

LANGSTONE COURT, ½ m. NNE. The best house of its date and size in the county. The date is the late C17, the size five bays and two storeys. The house is of brick, has quoins, and had wooden (or stone) cross-windows. It also has the indispensable hipped roof with gabled dormers and two symmetrically placed blank-arched chimneystacks. The doorway has a bolection moulding, as have the fireplaces inside, and the steep pediment on corbels is the only unsatisfactory feature. It seems too highly placed. Behind is an older range, as the inside rather than the outside shows. There are in that part some Jacobean plasterwork, especially one low ceiling with broad bands of strapwork, and a staircase with openwork slatted balusters. The interior decoration of the front range is of a higher order, although it is decidedly conservative. This comes out very illuminatingly in the two stucco ceilings, which combine the thick fruit and leaf wreaths of the late C17 – not as daring as at Holme Lacy or Hill Court – with such motifs as fleurs-de-lis or friezes of dolphins, in the Jacobean tradition. The staircase also has dumb-bell balusters, rather 1675- than 1695-looking. In addition some of the panelling appears to be of about the same date. To the s, in 1825, an ample bow window was added. It belongs to a large new room which has a screen of two columns between room and bow. The front garden has an outbuilding on the N side and was probably meant to have another to be its counterpart (cf. Trerible, below). Nice gatepiers and C18 iron gates.

BERNITHAN COURT, ¾ m. ENE. Of the same time and style as Langstone – in fact with a date 1695 on a barn. Also five bays, also two storeys, also hipped roof, also wooden cross-windows (but they are preserved here), and also two symmetrical chimneystacks. Finally also gatepiers with vases and iron gates, also a staircase with dumb-bell balusters, and – the most surprising similarity – also the doorway pediment raised unexplainedly high. (Plasterwork in one room with fleurs-de-lis, pomegranates, and grapes. RCHM)

RUXTON COURT, 1¼ m. SE. Stone on the r., with mullioned windows. The rest timber-framed, with a porch. The roof timbers inside are said to have been altered recently.

TRERIBBLE, 1¼ m. NW. Five-bay house of c.1700 with three storeys, rendered. Doorway with later pedimental hood. To the l. and r. of the front garden two brick ranges of three bays and two storeys with quoins, cross-windows, and hipped roofs. The front garden is entered by a gate with gatepiers with vases.

(THE GROVE, 1 m. s. One room has a plaster ceiling with thin ribs forming lozenges, angular quatrefoils, etc. Also small fleurs-de-lis and the date 1594. RCHM)

LLANGROVE see LONG-GROVE

LLANHEDRY see BRILLEY

LLANROTHAL

4010

ST JOHN BAPTIST. Only the E end is in use. Norman nave, see one N and one W window. On the s side windows and

doorway of c.1300. The chancel E window is contemporary
or a little earlier. Two cusped lights, but a circle in plate
tracery above it. The chancel arch would go with this as well
as the nave s windows. Finally on the s side one large four-
light Perp window, obviously mutilated at the top. – PULPIT.
With modest Jacobean panels. – CHANDELIER. Brass, with a
figure of the Virgin. Probably partly C15, partly mid C19,
from Thrumpton Hall, Nottinghamshire.* – CROSS and
CANDLESTICKS, wood, silvered, probably C17 and Italian.
The crucifixus does not belong to the cross.

LLANROTHAL COURT, NW of the church. The centre of the
house is a stone-built early C14 hall. Simple, single-chamfered
doorway. In addition, two windows have recently been
discovered. They are of two cusped lights.

THE CWM, 1¼ m. SE. Built in 1830. Spacious and not regular.
With a Greek Doric porch. The predecessor of the house,
soon after 1600, was made the headquarters of the Jesuit
mission in South Wales, and in 1622 became the residence of
a new Jesuit province. In 1678 the secret came out and the
Bishop of Hereford raided and ransacked the house.

(TREGATE CASTLE, 1 m. SSE. Motte of c.60 yds diameter,
rising to 12 ft above the bailey. RCHM)

₃₀₃₀

LLANVEYNOE

ST PETER. Beautifully situated in the hills, with views across
the Olchon valley towards the noble range of mountains
beyond which lies Llanthony. However, of scarcely any
architectural interest. Nave and chancel and bellcote. Mostly
C19 and C20. – SCULPTURE. Panel of a Crucifixus, over 4 ft
high, very elementarily carved, the head like a child's drawing,
the feet in profile, both in the same direction. An C11 date
has been suggested. – Also a smaller panel, just with an incised
cross and some inscriptions. XRC once, IHS twice, A Ω
once, and also HAEFDUR FECIT CRUCEM. This is also assigned
to the C11.

Many old farmhouses in the parish, but none need recording.

₅₀₂₀

LLANWARNE

ST JOHN BAPTIST. Ruinous and picturesquely placed against
trees. Late medieval W tower. Dec s aisle, see the reticulated

* The dating was suggested by Mr. Michael Taylor.

tracery of the windows and the four-bay arcade with circular piers and double-chamfered arches. Early Perp chancel E window. One S window Georgian. The N chapel of one bay has a C13 entrance arch. – MONUMENT. Of 1608–9. With four shields in strapwork surrounds, framed by two Ionic columns. – LYCHGATE. Late medieval; of timber.

CHRIST CHURCH, a little further W. 1864 by Messrs *Elmslie* (GR). In the Geometrical style, with a N porch tower ending in a wilful octagonal open bell-stage with tracery and a spire. Also transepts and a polygonal apse. – FONT. Late C17. Bowl with acanthus, stem with swags. Cf. Holme Lacy and How Caple. – STAINED GLASS. Many Netherlandish medallions of the C16 and C17. – PLATE. Chalice and Cover Paten, London, 1717.

(BLEWHENSTONE, 2 m. NE. Inside the house cruck-trusses. *See Trans. Woolh. N.F.C.*, XXXIII, 89.)

LONG-GROVE   *5010*

CHRIST CHURCH. 1854–6 by *Bodley*, one of his earliest churches. Nave and chancel and bellcote. The style of *c.*1300. Is the future Bodley recognizable in any features ? Not in the exterior. Inside, however, there are the piers of the S arcade, just oblong with chamfers and no capitals, there are the purposely simple trussed-rafter roof of the nave and open wagon roof of the chancel, and there may be the careful detailing of the sizes of the stones of the walls.

LONGTOWN   *3020*

ST PETER. Nave and chancel and bellcote. Mostly of 1868; by *T. Nicholson*. But the chancel E window is Dec, and the chancel roof is pre-Victorian too. It has a date 1640, and is of single-frame construction with collar-beams. – No furnishings of interest.

CASTLE. On the S end of a spur, overlooking the river Monnow. Rectangular enclosure of *c.* 3 acres. The motte rises in the NW angle. On it a circular keep. The W half of the enclosure is divided by a wall with gateway into a N half, the inner bailey, and a S half, the outer bailey. Outworks to the N of the enclosure. The structure of the keep and bailey seems to date from the late C12 to early C13. The keep has three semi-circular projections. In one of them was a spiral staircase. The   14b windows in their present form probably C14. On the ground floor they are straight-topped with segmental relieving arches. On the first floor, in the NW projection, outlet of a garderobe. The wall between the two baileys stands up to a height of *c*. 11 ft. The gateway has a round-arched head and is flanked by semicircular turrets. Further traces of walling SE of the gateway.

OLD COURT FARM, 1¼ m. NE of the castle. The centre of the house is of the early C14. It has at the back a tall transomed two-light window with trefoiled lights, and inside a doorway with a two-centred arch. Much of the roof, which has cruck-trusses, survives too.

The RCHM lists over forty HOUSES of before 1714 in the parish.

(THE MOUND, Ponthendre, N of Clodock church, on a spur of the foothills of the Black Mountains. The motte is 51 yds in diameter and 30–40 ft tall. Crescent-shaped bailey to the NE, protected mostly by a scarp only. RCHM)

LONGWORTH see LUGWARDINE

LOWER BROCKHAMPTON
see BROCKHAMPTON-BY-BROMYARD

LOWER EATON see EATON BISHOP

LOWER NUPEND see CRADLEY

LOWER VINETREE FARM
see BISHOP'S FROME

LOWER WALTON FARM
see BISHOP'S FROME

4060

LUCTON

ST PETER. 1850 by *Cranston* (GR). With lancet windows and a bell-turret with spire. – PLATE. Chalice, Cover Paten, Paten Plate, and Flagon, London, 1716. – MONUMENT. Tablet to John Pierrepont † 1711. With scrolly surround and two mourning putti on the concave slopes below the top urn.

LUCTON SCHOOL. Founded by John Pierrepont in 1708. The N range is his building, the rest is recent additions. Pierrepont's range is of brick, seven bays long and two storeys high, and has a hipped roof and a bell-turret. The doorway has an apsed hood, and above in an arched niche stands the excellent,

animated STATUE of the founder, of wood, painted white.
The range is eight bays deep on one side, five on the other.

LUCTON COURT, 100 yds S of the church. Timber-framed,
C16–17, pretty.

NEW HOUSE FARM, to the W of Lucton Court. C17, of stone,
tall, with two projecting wings and a hipped roof.

LUGWARDINE   *5040*

ST PETER. A very puzzling church, puzzling primarily because
of the Norman window in the S aisle facing W. The masonry
looks convincing and the quoin stones big. Was this a Norman
transept then; for the width is not that of an aisle? Yet the
RCHM calls the wall 'modern' and the window re-set. What
confuses in trying to understand the church is that the aisles
on both sides are of transeptal width and consist of two parts,
either of them possible as a former transept. The RCHM calls
the E half of the aisles C13 transepts. Inside, the C19 (*F. R.
Kempson*, 1871–2) has increased the confusion by building a
two-bay arcade from W to E in front of the W half of these
transeptal projections, a two-bay arcade running S–N to
separate the W from the E half, and a wide third bay E of the
others to separate the nave from the E half. Original late C13
chancel with lancets with pointed-trefoiled heads. Original
Perp W tower, big, with diagonal buttresses. – PLATE. Cup,
inscribed 1673; Cover Paten, 1709; Salver, London, 1709;
Flagon, London, 1737. – MONUMENTS. Mrs Best † 1622.
Brass plate in a wooden surround with columns. – William
Reed † 1634. Semi-reclining effigy, propped up on an elbow.
Columns l. and r., straight top. The children kneel against the
tomb-chest. – John Best † 1637. Frontal demi-figure preach-
ing. The background has disappeared.

LUGG BRIDGE. Medieval, of three arches, the W arch probably
C14, the middle arch with C14 materials, the E arch C15.
Cutwaters.

COTTAGE, NE of the church. Once the office of Godwin's
brickworks. Oblong, of two storeys, completely covered with
blank arcading, the upper floor syncopated. Probably later
C19.

LONGWORTH, 1¼ m. SE. Built *c.*1788 by *Anthony Keck*. Six
bays and two storeys plus spacious bows l. and r. on front and
back. Monumental LODGES on the A-road to the E. Stone.
Hipped roofs, quoins, doorways with Gibbs surrounds, and

pediments. Windows with Tuscan columns and pediments. They look c 20 classical. On the w side, facing the entrance to New Court, another, smaller, and more convincing LODGE. Polygonal, thatched, with raised pilaster strips up the edges. To the N of the house under a tree MONUMENT with an urn to commemorate a race-horse.

NEW COURT. Georgian house, gothicized in 1809–10 by *H. H. Seward*. Five bays with recessed centre, porch, and two turrets. All castellated. But in the entrance hall fine coved Rococo plaster ceiling of *c.*1750.

NEW INN, in the village. Very Gothic in the High Victorian sense, more Suburban-Hereford than Lugwardine-Village.

LUNTLEY COURT *see* DILWYN

4060

LUSTON
1½ m. SE of Yarpole

TUDOR HOUSE, opposite the Methodist Chapel. Jacobean; timber-framed. With pretty cusped concave-sided lozenges below the gable.

(A house next to the chapel has a cruck-truss inside. RCHM)

BURY FARM, by the fork with the Eyton Road. Handsome timber-framed house of the C17.

3030

LYONSHALL

ST MICHAEL. The earliest feature is the tall Norman window in the nave w wall. It was the w wall of a former tower; for the w bay of the s arcade was only opened at the time of *Bodley*'s restoration of 1872. Until then it had been solid. The s arcade is Dec (octagonal piers, double-chamfered arches), but the N arcade dates from *c.*1250, except for the slightly simplified w bay, which came soon after, and would prove the beginning of a removal of the former tower, probably because the new one was then begun or decided upon. Piers quatrefoil with slim shafts in the diagonals. Moulded capitals (except for two with a little stiff-leaf), double-chamfered arches. The w tower is unbuttressed. Most of the windows of the church are typical of *c.*1300, including those of the transepts. Ornate timber porch, probably of 1872. – FONT. On a C19 stem of eight shafts with tall stiff-leaf capitals of the C13. The bowl of the same shape; plain. – PLATE. Cup and Cover Paten, 1571. – MONUMENT. Headless stone effigy of a civilian; C13.

Castle, immediately NE of the church. In a rectangular enclosure representing the outer bailey (with a subsidiary bailey further N) stands the circular inner bailey, surrounded by a moat. The inner bailey has a wall standing partly high up on the E side. A polygonal projection on the N side holds the circular keep. The masonry altogether may be of the C13. The castle belonged to the Careys and then the Devereuxs.

(The Wharf, s of the church. In the E wing remains of two cruck-trusses. RCHM)

Offa's Dyke. There is a fine stretch of the dyke $\frac{1}{4}$ m. SW of the church, running E–W for approximately $1\frac{3}{4}$ m. At this point the bank is prominent and the flat-bottomed ditch some 12 to 13 ft broad.

MADLEY   4030

Nativity of the Virgin.* The most interesting are not always the most beautiful churches. It is lucky if the two coincide. Madley has both a pure, noble, and generous[28b] interior and a fascinating building history. It starts with the mysterious Norman W and E windows in the mysteriously spacious N porch. The mystery is not too hard for the expert to solve. This must have been the transept of a cruciform Norman church. There is more evidence to corroborate the assumption. Above the doorway into the porch is the blocked arch of a Norman window. The W wall of the later outer s chapel is in line with the W wall of the N porch and has the outline of another such window blocked. Moreover, the N and s arcades have in their upper walls a straight joint where the E walls of the transepts would have met an aisleless Norman chancel. The joints of the W walls have been obliterated. But outside, on the N as well as the s side, even the roof-line of the transept can still be seen.

Early in the C13 a complete remodelling of this Norman church began. It started, no doubt outside the nave, with the W tower. The tower is embraced by the aisles, or rather by separate W bays of the aisles. The arches into these have semicircular responds with octagonal abaci and double-chamfered pointed arches. The E piers, i.e. the tower arch proper, are strong, compound affairs, thin shafts with broad fillets, and their capitals are still of a vestigial many-scalloped

---

* I am grateful to the Rev. W. L. Paterson for contributions to this entry.

type, the only Norman survival in an otherwise pure E.E. job. The E shaft, i.e. the actual respond for the arcades, is the only one which is moulded and has no scallops. So the arcades were started. They are of six bays, but clearly divided into three plus three by a small stretch of wall converting the third pier into two responds. The wall is too thin for a chancel arch to have been there, though the link must correspond to the Norman chancel arch.* The arcade piers are round and have a variety of octagonal abaci or really square abaci set diagonally and chamfered at the corners (cf. Clehonger, Eaton Bishop, Hereford All Saints). All arches are double-chamfered, and all capitals are moulded, except for one on the s side, the w respond of the E half, which has early upright stiff-leaves. Another one on the same side incidentally has tiny sprigs of stiff-leaf on the underside of the abacus. The aisles are largely still as they were built, relatively narrow and with single lancet windows. The clerestory also has single lancets, a little out of order only where the transept wall caused confusion. E of the sixth bay a new chancel was begun too. It is flanked by square shafted turrets, one of them containing a staircase. The chancel arch survives and, to its E, in the corners the bases of shafts built to carry a rib-vault. The masonry above shows traces of where the vault sprang. The chancel arch has tripartite responds with fillets. Tripartite by the way are also the responds of the arches from the aisle w (i.e. tower) bay to the other bays.

16a   Meanwhile the tower went up. It is a beautiful piece, stately and trustworthy, neither slender nor massive. It has a w doorway with one order of colonnettes carrying fillets and a continuous inner roll moulding. Above is a group of three large, stepped, generously shafted lancets. Their capitals are long and a little barren. Above that a pair of twin lancets under one arch (only one to the other sides), and then the three large, even bell-openings, with continuous chamfers. The battlements are Victorian. At the sw corner a square stair-turret rises higher, embattled also, as if it were the turret of a keep.

Of other external features the N and s doorways deserve notice, that on the s side similar to the w doorway, that on the N side round-arched with a continuous filleted roll moulding. The N entrance broken into the N wall of the Norman N transept to convert it into a porch has continuous mouldings.

* The intriguing marks on the wall come from two former stovepipes.

It seems a little later than the rest. The upper window is of the late c13.

The church was now ready, spacious and even in character. But about 1310 a new campaign was started and did not come to an end till about 1340 or later. First, the chancel was considered inadequate, and a splendid new chancel was begun. It was under construction in 1318, when offerings were made *ad fabricam novi cancelli*. It ends in a polygonal apse, a usually successful motif, rare in England, though it was adopted at Wells and Lichfield Cathedrals (the former of *c.*1300–20, the latter of *c.*1320–30) and in Herefordshire at Marden. The chancel is tall and spacious with an E window with reticulated tracery, flanked by two windows with Latest Geometrical tracery. The others are simple and less interesting: a large pointed trefoil above two cusped lights. A frieze of ballflower runs immediately below the eaves. The chancel was felt to need greater width than the E.E. one, and so the W bay was slightly canted outward. That caused some trouble in the outer walls (visible at the E ends of the aisles), and some corbelling had to be done to achieve a straight roof-line above. Between the chancel and apse windows are buttresses carrying little turrets as finials. Fine sedilia inside with filleted shafts and ballflower decoration.

Below the apse the falling ground allowed for a crypt. This has a central octagonal pier and, starting from it, painfully without any capital or abacus, ten ribs of an unusual wavy outline. There are ten and not eight because the W wall is straight, and additional ribs run into the corners. The ribs start against the outer walls on tripartite corbels. The crypt is accessible from the E ends of the aisles by a narrow passage.

The chancel may still have been building or may just have been completed when the Chilston Chapel was founded in 1330. It is an outer S chapel five bays long, divided from the inner aisle by quatrefoil piers with subsidiary shafts in the diagonals, polygonal abaci decorated with ballflower, and arches with the typical sunk quadrant mouldings. The chapel has all along even, tall three-light windows with reticulated tracery. When the authorities had seen them, they decided also to open just such windows on the N side, E of the porch-transept; altogether four of them. All this Dec work makes the church now appear wonderfully light. Stained glass (*see* below) originally forbade that impression.

FURNISHINGS. FONT. Enormously large, and undecorated. – SCREEN. Parclose screen in the N aisle. C17, but with some C15 parts. – STALLS, with MISERICORDS. Only the supporting side pieces have some foliage decoration. – WOODWORK. At the E end of the s aisle late C17 pieces re-assembled: panels with acanthus decoration and four twisted 'Salomonic' columns, decorated with vine. Bought in Spain or Portugal. – WEST DOOR. With long C13 ornamental hinges. – C13 ironwork also, though minor, in the DOOR to the staircase tower. – PAINTING. Traces above the chancel arch. – STAINED GLASS. In the E window a number of very beautiful C13 roundels, and also figures of the early C14 belonging to a Jesse window. – In the NE and SE windows many fragments of the C13 to C15. – PLATE. Two Chalices, a Paten, and a Flagon by *Aug. Courtauld* of London, 1727; Paten by *Edward Pocock*, London, 1736. – MONUMENTS. Richard Willison † 1575 and wife. Recumbent stone effigies on a tomb-chest, his face sliced off and his legs also missing. Against the tomb-chest blank arches with shields; also two rather grotesque kneeling figures. Ionic piers separate them. The monument is signed by *John* (IHON) *Gildo*, and the two segmental arches (cf. Abergavenny) as well as the large leaves in the spandrels and the flower vases on the pilasters are characteristic of him (cf. Bosbury). – Peter Garnons and family, *c.*1626. Small tablet (chancel N side) with kneeling figures. – CHURCHYARD CROSS. The head is preserved, though badly. On one side the Crucifixus is still recognizable.

VILLAGE CROSS. With a long original shaft.

TOWN HOUSE, to its SE. Probably a C16 house. Timber-framed. On the H-plan, the roof eaves of the centre projecting so as to give an even line with the wings.

ROUND BARROWS, 1½ m. WNW of the church. The group consists of a bell barrow 33 ft in diameter and a disc barrow 64 ft in diameter; near by are three small round barrows encircled by a slight bank and ditch.

MAINSTONE COURT *see* MUNSLEY

MANSELL GAMAGE

ST GILES. On the edge of the grounds of Garnons. Simple s doorway of *c.*1200. Several windows of *c.*1300, including the s transept s window. C14 or C15 timber porch with quatrefoils above the tie-beams and cusped and traceried bargeboards. w tower of 1824. The interior, the N transept, and the

E window all of 1877 (*L. Powell*). Complicated thin timbers over the crossing. – PLATE. Chalice and Cover Paten, unmarked. – MONUMENTS. Huge coffin-lid of the C13 with foliated cross. – Frances Isabella Evans † 1813. With a mourning young man by an urn on a tall pedestal. By *J. Smith* of London.

GARNONS. The house as it is at present consists of an ashlar-faced castellated range of one plus six bays on the l., and then a loggia and a three-bay conservatory, also in a medieval taste. The architect of the main range is unrecorded. It was built *c.*1860 as an addition to a house designed by *William Atkinson* and begun in 1815. This was composed of a tall broad tower whose ground floor front part is the present loggia, and a three-bay range to its r. whose ground floor is now the conservatory. To the l. of this, in Atkinson's time, stood a gabled Elizabethan or Jacobean house. This was replaced by the range of *c.*1860. Before Atkinson, in 1791, *Repton* had made plans for the landscaping of the grounds. They were indeed landscaped by him. In connexion with this he proposed a castellated mansion to be built by Wyatt. This came to nothing, nor did a project by Tatham shown at the Royal Academy in 1802. The range of *c.*1860 was georgianized internally about 1907 by *Sir Reginald Blomfield*. He introduced quite a number of excellent original later C18 chimneypieces. The siting of Garnons is superb, and the grounds do the highest credit to Repton.

MANSELL LACY

ST MICHAEL. Norman nave, *see* the blocked N doorway. C13 the S aisle (three low bays, octagonal piers with odd spurs on the bases, double-chamfered arches, and, E of the arcade, doorway with shouldered lintel and a bust over), the chancel arch, and the nave W wall. Unbuttressed, with pyramid roof. Early C14 windows in various places, e.g. the chancel E window, with ballflower enrichment. – MONUMENTS. Two tablets in the chancel, both characteristic of their dates: 1676 and 1691.

HOUSE, 200 yds SW, off the road. Probably early C16. Narrowly-placed uprights in the gabled wing.

MARDEN

ST MARY. By the river Lugg. The church has one memorable feature: a chancel continued in a polygonal apse. This feature is of the early C14, as is the polygonal apse of Madley, and the tracery of the two-light windows with encircled cinquefoils prettily cusped is almost identical with that of the s aisle at Leominster. Nave and aisles were rebuilt in 1858 by *T. Nicholson*, but, inside, the arches are original and older than the chancel and apse. Both arcades (four bays) are E.E., the N arcade a little earlier. It has circular piers with moulded capitals, circular abaci, and double-chamfered arches. The s arcade has octagonal abaci instead, but both E responds are identical and, though in their present shape Victorian, in style corresponding to the N rather than the s arcade. The s doorway has beautiful E.E. mouldings (much restored). The NW tower borders on the N aisle and is internally not connected with it. It is ashlar-faced, with a parapet, square pinnacles, and a recessed stone spire. – FONT. Dodecagonal, with blank trefoiled arches. Of *c.*1300? – PLATE. Cup, unmarked; Cover Paten, Paten on foot, and Flagon, London, 1706–7. The flagon is by *David Willaume*.

LAYSTONE BRIDGE. C17, except for the heightened middle arch, which is Georgian.

WISTESTON COURT, 1 m. NNE. At the time of writing derelict.

VAULD FARM, 2 m. NE. Early C16. Black and white. With a centre and two cross-gables, the l. one with a moulded bressumer.

3050

MARSTON

ST MATTHEW. 1855 by *T. Nicholson*. Nave and chancel and steeply gabled bellcote.

(YEW TREE FARMHOUSE. Black and white house of the C16, with a C17 wing. Staircase with flat, pierced balusters. RCHM)

MARSTON STANNETT *see* PENCOMBE

7040

MATHON

ST JOHN BAPTIST. The nave Early Norman, at least as far E as the herringbone masonry on both sides goes. Head of a Norman window close to the w end on the s side. Both doorways with plain tympana, except for a rope-moulding along the foot. The N tympanum is mutilated. It is said that an apse was found below the present chancel which is Later Norman and has in its E wall two long arched windows and a round one over. Also, in the s wall, a single-chamfered priest's doorway. Good later medieval timber s porch, and good nave roof with two tie-beams and more collar-beams. Two tiers of wind-braces, the lower one cusped. Good C14 w tower. – PULPIT. Jacobean, with the usual short blank arches. – PAINTING. A French C17 Flight into Egypt in landscape setting; very good. – MONUMENT. Jane Walweyn † 1617. Tomb-chest. On it square panel with two figures kneeling and facing one another. Superstructure. The whole makes an odd shape.

MICHAELCHURCH 5020

St Michael. Very small, of nave and chancel with a timber bell-turret. Said to have been founded in 1056 by Bishop Herwald of Llandaff. Nothing so early remains, but there are a few Norman windows, especially the pair in the E wall, and there is something left of the Norman N doorway: a fragment of the tympanum with a lattice pattern. – FONT. The font is Norman too. Of tub shape, with characteristically un-disciplined motifs, e.g. a knot frieze which suddenly for a bit changes to zigzag. Above this frieze saltire crosses, and above them interlaced arches. – SCREEN. Only the framing is old. – SCULPTURE. In the nave N wall. A Roman altar, partly cut back to form a rough capital. It bears the inscription *Deo Tri-(vii) Beccicus donavit ara(m)*. – PAINTING. Much C13 wall decoration of feigned ashlaring, with a flower in the centre of each block. Also chequerwork and two encircled crosses. – PLATE. Salver by *Seth Lofthouse*, London, 1705; Chalice, inscribed 1725.

MICHAELCHURCH ESCLEY 3030

St Michael. Solid w tower of 1897, unbuttressed, with pyramid roof. Nave and chancel in one. No special features. Open wagon roof inside with small bosses. – PAINTING. On the N wall very large Christ of the Trades, i.e. three-quarter figure of Christ surrounded by tools: scissors, shears, axe, L-square, plough, flail, etc. The subject is rare, but occurs several times in Cornwall and also at Ampney St Mary Gloucestershire, West Chiltington Sussex, and Hessall Suffolk. – PLATE. Cup of 1628.

MICHAELCHURCH COURT, ½ m. WNW. L-shaped, the l. wing

of *c.*1870 and the major part of the r. wing of the C17, timber-
framed on a stone ground floor. Three gables with narrow
uprights and many concave-sided lozenges. In the porch
delightful plaster decoration of long branches or trails with
leaves and berry or grape-like fruit. There is also the date
1602.

(The BARN of QUAKER'S FARM, 2 m. NW, has cruck-trusses.
So has the BARN of LOWER HOUSE FARM, ¼ m. NW of the
former, and that of UPPER PEN-Y-PARK, ¾ m. NW of
Urishay Chapel in Peterchurch parish. RCHM)

(THE CAMP, 1½ m. NW. An oval enclosure of earth; its purpose
is unknown. RCHM)

MIDDLE BLACKHILL FARM *see* CRASWALL

MIDDLE HILL *see* BIRLEY

MIDDLETON HOUSE *see* DILWYN

MIDDLETON-ON-THE-HILL

ST MARY. Norman nave and chancel, *see* the shallow buttresses,
three nave windows, one chancel window, the priest's doorway, and the two nave doorways with zigzag in the arches.
The N doorway seems tampered with. The pairs of little
heads l. and r. cannot be *in situ*. Are they from the former
corbel-table? The S doorway has its zigzag at r. angles to the
wall, the N doorway has a hood-mould with pellets. Broad,
unbuttressed early C13 tower. Slender lancet windows. Arch
to the nave single-chamfered on the simplest imposts. Close
to the NE end of the tower, outside, a little of the Norman nave
NW quoin has been exposed. Only the chancel E window is
later. It must be of *c.*1300 and is not *in situ*. It came from
Pudleston church. Inside, the chancel arch has imposts with
some saltire-cross decoration and a single-stepped arch.
Above it a Norman opening, perhaps into the former chancel
roof. – FONT. Norman, with zigzag band. Inside each triangle
a kind of raised drop. – PLATE. Chalice and Cover Paten,
London, 1721.

MIDDLETON FARM, N of the church and forming a charming
picture with it. Brick, of four bays and two storeys, with red
sandstone quoins and a hipped roof. On a quoin the date
1692. To the SE of the house a square brick GAZEBO.

MOCCAS

ST MICHAEL. Moccas, if it were not for the bellcote and some
tall Dec windows which help to let light into the interior,
would be the perfect example of a Norman village church.*
Nave, lower chancel, yet lower apse. All tufa. The apse has
its three original windows and a simply moulded string course
below them. One Norman window in the N wall, one high up
in the W wall. Two Norman doorways of red sandstone. The
tympana are effaced. That on the S side contained a tree of
life flanked by human figures and beasts. On the N side were
a beast and scrolls. The scrolls appear in frantic disorder.
The doorways have one order of shafts with decorated capitals.
The Dec windows are of c.1300 in the chancel (cusped
spherical triangle above two cusped lights), later in the nave
(two-light and reticulation unit). Dec also the timber S porch,
though it is much renewed. The bargeboards are cusped and
have an ogee top. The side pieces are trefoiled with ogee tops.
Inside there is a beautiful sequence of tall noble chancel arch
and lower apse arch. The latter has the simplest imposts and
zigzag, the former small saltire crosses, stars, etc. in the abaci
and zigzag at r. angles to the wall surface. – STAINED GLASS.
In the Dec windows splendid early C14 canopies, containing
two tiny figures each. It is curious that the artist was permitted
to repeat them from window to window. On the S side only
shields are preserved. – MONUMENT. Stone effigy of a Knight
on a tomb-chest, depressingly cleaned-up. The tomb-chest
has shields in quatrefoils. The Knight's legs are crossed.
Early C14.

MOCCAS COURT. Built in 1775–81 to *Robert Adam*'s designs,
but executed by a local man, *Anthony Keck*. A simple red-
brick house overlooking the river Wye. Seven by five bays.
Two and a half storeys. The only embellishments are a one-
storeyed bow on the entrance side containing the doorway
and a fine Venetian window above. The bow looks an afterthought. On the river side is a wider bow. Inside there is a
fine sequence of rooms across the middle axis. Entrance hall
into which, in the bow, two little arms of the staircase rise,
curving round an urn on a pedestal. Restrained but very
refined stucco decoration. Staircase hall oval in a transverse

* According to Mr Ferriday's card index the church was repaired by
Westmacott in 1803 and then restored by *G. G. Scott Jun.* in 1870, including
the new ceiling 'chastely carved' (*Building News*, 1871).

direction with a glazed oval dome and a flying staircase with
the most reticent iron handrail. Circular room in the bow
towards the river – undoubtedly the climax of the house. The
walls are papered and panelled with exquisite 'grottesche' or
Etruscan, i.e. Pompeian, decoration. Fine fireplaces in several
rooms, including one with a frieze decorated with alternate
medallions with the heads of Bacchus and Ceres. This comes
from the dining room. – The grounds were landscaped by
Capability Brown. His plan is dated 1778. Gardens were
usually begun before the house. But *Humphry Repton* also
worked at Moccas, as he says in his *Observations* etc. of 1803
(p. 10). The LODGES are by *John Nash*, or rather by *G. S.
Repton*, who was working at the time in Nash's office.

ROUND HOUSE, ¾ m. SE, on the main road. Evidently the stump
of a brick tower-mill.

(MOCCAS CASTLE, ¾ m. SW. Very small motte and bailey, the
whole enclosure roughly oval and c. 2¼ acres in extent.
RCHM)

MONKLAND

ALL SAINTS. A cell of the Benedictine abbey of Conches in
Normandy was founded here in the late C11. The church,
rebuilt in 1866 by *Street*, still has two Norman s and N win-
dows in original tufa surrounds. On the N side E of them a late
C13 window, on the s side windows of the same time. The s
doorway goes with them. Late C13 also the wide tower arch.
The tower has a shingled spire with big broaches. – STAINED
GLASS. In the E windows by *Hardman* to Street's design.

By *Street* also the LYCHGATE.

MONNINGTON-ON-WYE

ST MARY. Unbuttressed Perp w tower with very large battlements pierced by cruciform arrow-slits. The rest of the
46b church dates from 1679, and is uncommonly complete, in
structure and furnishings. It was built for Uvedall Tomkyns.
The plan is entirely the medieval one of nave and chancel.
The windows are mullioned and transomed with round arches
to the lights at the top and below the transom. Porch with
round-arched entrance. Inside, plain white ceiling segmentally
vaulted in plaster. – SCREEN, COMMUNION RAIL, two-valve
GATE in the tower arch, all with thin twisted columns of very

elongated twists. – PULPIT. With panels typical of the third quarter of the C17. It was originally a two-decker. At the angles again twisted balusters. – PANELLING. In the chancel, including the REREDOS. – BENCHES. Quite domestic benches with arms. – ROYAL ARMS. Of Charles II. Finely carved, once more between twisted columns. – FONT. Dated 1680. Octagonal, simple. Small bowl. – MONUMENTS. Black ledger-stone of Uvedall Tomkyns (chancel). – Robert Perrott † 1667. Frontal bust. Long hair and an emaciated face.

MONNINGTON COURT. By the church. Doorway with a shaped head with two monsters. This leads into the former screens passage. Of the sumptuous screen the upper part is preserved. It is dated 1656. Or is it an assembly of parts? The hall ceiling is also preserved. It dates from *c*.1600. Panels of eight-pointed stars and quatrefoils. In addition fleurs-de-lis and other small motifs.

MORDIFORD   *5030*

HOLY ROOD. Norman S doorway. One order of colonnettes with scallop capitals. Arch with zigzag at r. angles to the wall. In the vestry a re-set single-chamfered doorway of *c*.1200. The architectural interest of the church is the evidence of a central tower which existed until *c*.1811, when the present SW tower was built. The shape of its lancet windows is indeed rather 1800 than 1200. The tower has a pyramid roof. The former central tower is now only recognizable by its W and E arches of three continuous chamfers. That makes a late C13 date probable. The windows of the church all belong to the Victorian restoration, but the inner appearance of the NE lancet in the chancel is trustworthy. That also points to the C13. Very Victorian N arcade with foliage capitals (by *Kempson*). – PAINTING. Alas no longer in existence. Till 1811, on the outside of the tower, a large green dragon could be seen, 12 ft long, with a red mouth and tongue. Professor Tristram calls it C14. – PLATE. Cover Paten, 1576; Salver, London, 1709. – MONUMENTS. Small C13 coffin-lid with foliated cross and foliate etc. decoration all over. – Mary Vaughan † 1635. Kneeling in profile in a surround no longer Jacobean. Niche with volutes. Top with pedimental segmental curve. The inscription says that she 'died at her prayers in the forme as you see her portrature'. – Francis Woodhouse

† 1710. With ugly putti on an open segmental pediment. – Several nice tablets, e.g. Francis Woodhouse † 1726 and James Hereford † 1823 (the latter by *Hollins* of Birmingham).

Very handsome group of church, rectory, and bridge.* The BRIDGE is probably of the C14 (the pointed w arch) and the C16 (the round E arch). C16 perhaps also the flood arches further w. – The RECTORY is a very fine Early Georgian brick house with brick quoins. Five bays and two and a half storeys with a one-bay projection. In this the windows are segment-headed. The principal windows all have heads as keystones.

SUFTON, ½ m. NE. Built before 1790. Of Bath stone. Five bays, two and a half storeys, with a one-bay pediment, a Venetian window beneath it, and a porch of four attached unfluted Ionic columns with a pediment (cf. Canon Frome).‡ Nice fireplaces.

OLD SUFTON, ¾ m. NE. (In a chimneystack a C13 coffin-lid with an incised cross. RCHM) Nice circular C18 brick DOVECOTE with lantern.

6040   MORETON JEFFRIES

CHURCH. Small; nave and chancel in one. Timber bell-turret. Over-restored. Plain C14 s doorway. Chancel roof with tie-beams and raking struts. – PULPIT. A stately piece, square, with sounding-board. Jacobean or a little later. – PLATE. Cup, 1629.

5040   MORETON-ON-LUGG

ST ANDREW. 1867 by *W. H. Knight*. In the Geometrical style, with a sw tower with stone spire. In the s wall of the chancel remains of a Norman window. Perp s arcade, low, with octagonal piers and low, four-centred, double-chamfered arches. Single-framed nave roof with collar-beams. – SCREEN. Very nice. With one-light divisions, one band of running vine in the cornice, and a cresting. – REREDOS, etc. All *Salviati* mosaic of 1887. The mosaic angels in the nave are of 1899. – PLATE. Cup and Cover Paten, the latter inscribed 1680.

MORETON BRIDGE. Probably C16. Placed where a side-stream

---

* Painted incidentally about 1790 by *Girtin*.

‡ In a drawing of March 1790 (Hereford Library) this porch is not there, and a Gothick doorway appears instead.

joins the Lugg, so that the bridge on one side spans one stream, on the other two. The bridge has three spans.

MOUSE CASTLE *see* CUSOP

MUCH BIRCH   *5030*

St Mary and St Thomas of Canterbury. 1837 by *Thomas Foster*. Nave, short chancel, and w tower. All eaves on corbels, and the w tower, a typical feature of the date, with battlements on corbels. Equally typical the steeply gabled tower buttresses not going up to the full height, the light interior, and the thin timbers of the ceiling. The windows are lancets, and the whole is characteristically pre-archaeological. – The PAINTING on the vaulted chancel ceiling is of cherubs' heads in the sky peeping over little clouds. – The STAINED GLASS in the E window however is High Victorian, probably of the sixties. – PLATE. Chalice and Paten, London, 1836.

MUCH COWARNE   *6040*

St Mary. w tower Norman to E.E. The bell-openings are twin openings under one arch. The arches are all pointed. Of the separating piers, one has a waterleaf capital. But the tower arch is double-chamfered and pointed on simple Norman imposts. The church originally had two aisles. The N aisle was demolished, but the arcade can still be seen from the outside. It has round piers with round abaci and double-chamfered arches. That makes it early C13. The s arcade came a generation later. The piers are now quatrefoil with another four thin shafts in the diagonals. Moulded capitals, those of the thin shafts having their capitals smaller and their abaci lower. Also double-chamfered arches. The s aisle was widened about *c.*1300 – *see* the doorway with two sunk quadrant mouldings and the windows with cusped Y-tracery. But the circular w window goes better with *c.*1250 than with *c.*1300. Dec chancel with Early Perp E window. – PLATE. Cup and Cover Paten, 1572. – MONUMENTS. In the s aisle defaced and fragmentary late C13 stone effigy of a Knight. He wears a mail coif and has his legs crossed. – Also in the s aisle Edmund Fox † 1617 and wife. Recumbent stone effigies on a tomb-chest. Against this ten kneeling figures and (at the head end) three babes in a cradle. – Sybil Reed † 1624.

Recumbent stone effigy in the chancel. Back slab with four kneeling figures. Semicircular top gable.

SCHOOL. Of 1858, very Gothic.

(At COWARNE COURT, ½ m. SSW, is a circular DOVECOTE which may be medieval. RCHM)

(PARSONAGE FARM, ¼ m. N, has a two-storeyed timber-framed porch with balusters in the side walls. RCHM)

MUCH DEWCHURCH

4030

ST DAVID. Plain Norman S doorway with an uncarved tympanum, Norman S window above the porch, Norman chancel window now into the vestry, and plain Norman chancel arch with a single-step arch on the simplest imposts. But in the porch pieces of Norman interlace. The short, broad, unbuttressed W tower is clearly of the C13 (*see* the lancet openings), except for the Victorian pyramid roof with dormers. The arch towards the nave has three continuous chamfers. A number of windows of the late C13 or *c.*1300. Of the same time the plain tomb recess inside the nave. C14 S porch of timber with pointed-trefoiled wind-braces. Only the chancel E window is Perp. – FONT. Cylindrical, Norman, with defaced arcading. Against the foot small heads and (re-cut) flowers. – PULPIT. Jacobean, with tall blank arches and fluted panels above them. – PLATE. Almsdish, 1686; Chalice, London, 1806. – MONUMENTS. A shelf N of the altar is part of a foliated C13 coffin-lid. – John and Walter Pye, *c.*1570. Two recumbent effigies, praying. The older man has his long pointed beard between his finger tips. – Walter Pye † 1625 and wife. Large hanging monument with two kneeling figures facing one another across a prayer desk. They kneel under a shallow coffered arch flanked by black columns. In the 'predella' thirteen kneeling children. At the top, achievement and pairs of obelisks. – John Symons † 1763. Excellent big tablet of white and pink marble. Three cherubs' heads at the foot. – Thomas Symons † 1818. Still with an urn before an obelisk, i.e. conservative for its date. – Thomas Hampton Symons † 1831. Big classical tablet with pillars and arch, both filled with Greek key, i.e. ceasing to be correctly Grecian. – Richard Harcourt Symons † 1850. With a female figure seated on the ground below a weeping willow, a romantic conceit. – In the churchyard S of the porch Hudson Ludwyche † 1875 and wife. Fully High Victorian, with a cross encrusted with vine, flowers, fern, etc. A dove in the centre.

THE MYNDE. The house now appears Georgian. Its principal (E) front is of nine bays and two and a half storeys, rendered, and has a porch of two pairs of Tuscan columns. Behind are two wings sticking out far to the W. There seem at first to be few features of architectural interest; but in fact the house hides a long history. It belonged to the Pye family, then to two generations of Gorgeses in the first half of the C18 and then of Symonses. The E range was a hall of before the Reformation with short cross wings. The evidence for this is minor but enumerated by the RCHM. The wings were lengthened in the C16, and of this the parts remain visible which have the small oblong windows. They look as if they might have been towers. Then, between the wings (i.e. facing W), a widening or thickening took place behind the hall, *see* the doorway with the steep pediment and a thin rusticated surround. The wings also were again lengthened. But the main change is that which gave the hall its present façade – minus of course the early C19 porch. This change must belong to the Early Georgian moment, and it left the hall the finest room of its date in the county. It is five bays long and two storeys high, with a coved ceiling and giant Corinthian pilasters. Large panels between them with, above, little still-lifes of music, sculpture, architecture, and painting. Fine door surrounds, that to the entrance with a pediment. Above the doors medallions containing – a curious conceit rather ahead of its time – busts in profile of King Egbert, King Alfred, William the Conqueror, Edward III, Henry V, and another. Large military trophy above the (later) fireplace. On the ceiling a decorative roundel, and to its l. and r. an allegorical figure on clouds. The style is not easily dated. There are still many swags with thick bunches of flowers, but the door surrounds, the frieze, and other motifs do not allow a date earlier than about 1725. In the room behind the hall two Jacobean fireplaces formerly in the rooms to the N and S of the hall. They both have two tiers of the usual blank arches, but differ. In a room NW of the hall, panelling and two doorways of the date of the decoration of the hall. The staircase is SW of the hall. It has slender twisted balusters and carved tread-ends.

BRYNGWYN, ¾ m. SE. 1868. Tudor, stone, gabled, with an asymmetrical front, but all the same like a school or an institution.

MUCH MARCLE

St Bartholomew. An account of the church must start with the arcades. They are of *c.*1230–40. Four bays. Circular piers, circular abaci, double-chamfered arches. The capitals are moulded, except for the first pier from the W and the E responds. These have stiff-leaf as a band on only the upper half. Heads with branches sprouting out of the mouth and smaller heads appear, especially many on the NE respond. Noble clerestory of single lancets. Outside, strongly moulded corbels to support the nave roof. Traces of obliterated arcade arches further E, after a little blank wall, indicate that the present arcade was followed by a chancel arch and chancel chapels. The central tower, the most prominent feature of the church and one from the ground floor upward clearly Perp, removed them. But to continue the chronological order of events, the arcades must be followed by the S aisle doorway and windows, of the late C13 (fillets on the roll mouldings of the doorway, Y- and intersected tracery, a small W lancet) and the N aisle (one Y-window), and then the N chapel, rebuilt at the same time. At that time, then, the chancel must have been much lengthened. The chapel has two bays, circular piers, moulded capitals, circular abaci, and double-chamfered arches. The E window is of the typical Herefordshire variety of stepped lancet lights, i.e. again late C13. The chancel E wall has the same. From the E the chancel and the chapel with their two separate roofs appear indeed as twins. In the chancel a classical doorway was inserted early in the C18 with a segmental pediment on brackets. Dec S porch with ogee-headed side openings. Several Perp windows, especially the nave W window.

FURNISHINGS. COMMUNION RAIL. Late C17, with turned balusters. – SCULPTURE. 'Musica Celestis', relief in the style of Desiderio da Settignano and with a neo-Renaissance frame, carved by *Lady Feodora Gleichen* as a present to her sister Lady Valda and placed in the church by another sister, Lady Helena (of Hellens), *c.*1928. – PAINTING. Chancel, S wall. Venetian C16 Head of Christ. – STAINED GLASS. Much early glass by *Kempe*, namely E 1877, chancel S 1878, W 1882, N chapel E 1889 (the latter including a heraldic panel of 1628). – PLATE. Cover Paten, inscribed 1586; Cup, Cover Paten, and Flagon, 1638; Paten, 1641; Bowl, London, 1763. – MONUMENTS. Blanche Mortimer,

26

Lady Grandison, † 1347. She was the wife of Sir Peter, *see* Hereford Cathedral, p. 161. An outstandingly beautiful and interesting effigy. In a recess. The recess contains the tomb-chest, against which is cusped arcading with shields. The back wall has arcading too, and at the top coving with rather bare ribbing crossing at r. angles. Then a canopy cants forward. It has pendant arches and panels with shields over. The wavy cresting with putto heads is clearly not original. But now the effigy. The head is strikingly beautiful and realistic, eyes closed, lips slightly parted. Beautiful hands with long fingers. The monument provides, moreover, the most surprising demonstration of realism, i.e. the will to deceive – for all this was of course originally painted – in the way the train of the long skirt hangs down over the tomb-chest. Here is an English counterpart to the illusionism which occurs at the same time in Italian painting and German sculpture. – Effigy of a man of about 1360–70, of oak (s aisle, window sill). Bearded face. – Then two monuments in the Kyrle Chapel, i.e. the N chapel. Tomb-chest with two stone effigies of *c.*1400. She is again characterized with startling touches of realism, the slightly Chinese features, the *chic* clothes, and the puppies pulling her skirt between her feet. Feathered angels by her pillow. On the tomb-chest busts of angels in cusped fields and narrower panels with shields. – Sir John Kyrle appropriated the N chapel in 1628. He was buried in it in 1650. Tomb-chest of black and white marble. Fine cartouches with wreaths on the tomb-chest. Effigies well characterized and carved with care for the details of the clothes. – CHURCH-YARD CROSS. With steps, base, and stump of the shaft.

VICARAGE, E of the church. Dated 1703. Brick. Five bays, two storeys, quoins, hipped roof with three dormers. Doorway with an open segmental pediment. A very handsome specimen of a familiar type, unfortunately disfigured by a C19 bay window. The other side is almost identical, but the pediment is of the scrolly kind and the windows have mullion and transom crosses.

HOMME HOUSE. Essentially two parts, meeting at r. angles, one facing s, the other E. The former is of *c.*1500 and has a low tower with a canted oriel window and battlements. The window has arched lights. The attached gateway and turret seem to belong to the C19. The E front is Late Georgian, brick, of six bays and two storeys. Porch of two pairs of Tuscan columns. Round the corner, at the same time, a spacious canted bay window was made. In the entrance hall a panel of heraldic stained glass dated 1623. Handsome curved flying staircase with very restrained iron handrail. In the room to the l. of the entrance hall Late Jacobean panelling and a monumental wooden chimneypiece with paired Tuscan columns and, above, paired Ionic columns flanking a large field of strapwork, in the middle of which hangs a shield at an angle in front of drapery. Behind the Early Tudor part a Queen Anne range of brick with mullion-and-transom cross windows.

Above and behind the house a SUMMER HOUSE of stone, octagonal, with a staircase attachment. The oval windows of the latter in oblong panels indicate a date c.1670. The lower window, if anything, looks older, and the top doorway of the staircase has a four-centred arch. But the top windows are probably of the C18.

HELLENS. An uncommon thing in Herefordshire, a Jacobean brick house with mullioned and transomed windows. What we see now is clearly a fragment. It also seems to incorporate older parts, and to these the staircase tower at the back with the stone newel staircase may well belong. A second staircase is Jacobean and of wood, with sturdy balusters. In the staircase hall an overmantel with blank arches. In another ground-floor room a fine Jacobean plaster frieze. A room on the first floor has a big chimneypiece with coupled Ionic columns and smaller coupled Corinthian columns over. Strapwork in the middle. Another first-floor room has a ceiling with patterns of thin ribs and a pendant. The overmantel refers to Mary Tudor, and this would bear out the pre-Jacobean date of the house and be of interest, if the plaster ceiling turns out to belong to the 1550s as well.

To the N DOVECOTE of 1641, octagonal, of brick.

(MORTIMER'S CASTLE, N of the church. Motte and bailey. The motte is c. 50 yds in diameter and up to 21½ ft high above the bottom of the ditch. Inner bailey to the E, much altered and with a semicircular ditch. Outer bailey to the E and N, and beyond this, to the NE, a further enclosure. RCHM)

OLDBURY CAMP. An Iron Age hill-fort on Ridge Hill, 1½ m. W of the church. It consists of a roughly oval enclosure originally defended by a single bank and ditch with a second line of fortifications on the NW. The ramparts have been badly damaged by cultivation and have almost disappeared on the S.

MUNSLEY   6040

ST BARTHOLOMEW. Nave and chancel and bellcote. Early
Norman and Victorian (1863). The Early Norman contributions are the tiny E window, the equally small nave and
chancel N windows, the typical herringbone masonry above
the E window, and the unmoulded chancel arch. – SCULPTURE.
Stone slab in the S wall with an illegible inscription. Probably
Anglo-Saxon. – STAINED GLASS. Ancient bits in the Norman
nave window.

(MOUND, SW of the church. Only c. 6 ft high now. To the SW
remains of the moat probably of a bailey. RCHM)

MAINSTONE COURT, ¾ m. SSW. Built shortly after 1821. Red
ashlar. Five bays, two storeys, with a central bay window
made into a Tuscan porch on the ground floor. In the garden
wall a niche with a pointed-trefoiled head, no doubt re-set.

MUST MILL *see* KINGSLAND

MYNYDD-BRÎTH *see* DORSTONE

NASHEND FARMHOUSE *see* BOSBURY

NETHERTON FARM *see* PENCOYD

NETHERWOOD *see* COLLINGTON

NEW HOUSE *see* STRETTON GRANDISON

NEWHOUSE FARM *see* GOODRICH

NEWTON   3030

ST JOHN BAPTIST. 1842. Small W tower with W doorway. Nave
and short chancel. Lancet windows. – PULPIT. Of c.1660.
The panels are typical of such a date. – PLATE. Secular Bowl
with acanthus foliage in repoussé, 1682; Salver, London,
1805.

(CWARELAU, I m. SSW. Part of one wing is of the C15 and has
exposed crucks. RCHM)

NEWTON TUMP *see* CLIFFORD

NEW WEIR *see* KENCHESTER

NEW WESTON FARM *see* BREDWARDINE

NORTON CANON

St Nicholas. In the porch a Norman capital.* The NW tower belongs to the C13. Clasping buttresses below, unbuttressed above, pyramid roof. Nave, chancel, and transepts are of brick and were being built in 1716 (*Trans. Woolh. N.F.C.*, XXXV, 69). The brick is mostly but not consistently laid in Flemish bond. The remarkable thing is, however, that the architect of 1716 used the windows of the medieval church, carefully and without any solecisms. They are all of *c*.1300. The interior victorianized (1868 and 1876). – REREDOS and PULPIT with Jacobean materials. – COMMUNION RAIL. Early C17, with nicely turned balusters. – STAINED GLASS. Even the grisaille glass of *c*.1300 was re-used when the N transept window and the nave SW windows were re-erected. – PLATE. Silver-gilt Paten of *c*.1480, with the face of Christ in a sunk medallion; Chalice, Elizabethan.

NUN UPTON see LITTLE HEREFORD

OCLE PYCHARD

St James. Small W tower with recent copper-covered broach spire. Nave and chancel in one, probably early C14. Of the same date apparently the vestry. Few features of interest. Perp E window. The tower is narrower than the nave and projects into it – a very unusual arrangement. – PLATE. Cup and Cover, 1571.

(White House, 300 yds SE. Late C16, but with a re-used C14 door-head. RCHM)

At Livers Ocle, 1¼ m. W, was a small Benedictine cell, founded in 1100 and dependent on Lyre in Normandy. An outbuilding is known as the chapel, but has no features.

OFFA'S DYKE see KINGTON and LYONSHALL

OLD CASTLETON see CLIFFORD

ORCOP

St Mary. Broad W tower, the upper part of wood, i.e. a weatherboarded upper storey, a truncated pyramid roof, the bell-stage, and a spire. This structure necessitates an impressive timber structure inside, with big posts on big sleepers

* From a pillar piscina.

and very big scissor-braces on the N and s sides. E.E. N aisle, *see* the lancet windows and the low arcade of three bays with circular piers and double-chamfered arches. Much of the rest dates from the restoration of 1860 (*T. Nicholson*), e.g. the polygonal vestry. Nice wagon roof in the nave. – SCULPTURE. Top of a scalloped Norman pillar piscina (chancel). – PLATE. Elizabethan Cup; Cover Paten, inscribed 1576; Almsdish of the early C17 (?). – CHURCHYARD CROSS. With steps, base, and a stump of the shaft.

(CASTLE, ⅙ m. NNW, at Moat Farm. The castle lies at the bottom of the valley and covers 2 acres. The motte is large, 74 yds in diameter and 21 ft high above the bottom of the ditch. Kidney-shaped bailey to the N, entered originally probably from the N. RCHM)

ORLETON

4060

ST GEORGE. The w window of the Norman nave is now blocked by the w tower. Norman also a small piece of SCULP-TURE, a shaft with a dragon, now loose by the font. In the chancel, according to the RCHM perhaps re-set, a small round-arched doorway. This leads now into the vestry. In the tower, probably re-set, a round-arched w doorway of two continuous chamfers. This may be of *c.*1200. Early C13 chancel with lancet windows. In the E wall two of them, with a small niche inside between them. A little later the w tower. Arch towards the nave with two continuous chamfers. Pretty shingled broach spire. The nave windows (cusped-intersected and reticulated tracery) are early C14. Two big heads as supports for the former rood-beam. Tie-beam roof with kingposts and queenposts and also two-way struts. – FONT. An excellent late C12 piece, characteristic of the Hereford-shire school. Nine standing apostles under arches. The stringy folds are as typical as the long, jointless fingers, just like the folds. – PULPIT. Fine mid-C17 piece with broad blank arches and pairs of columns at the angles. Panels with flat strapwork above and below the arches. – CHESTS. Two dug-out chests of the C13 in the vestry. – (SCULPTURE. A 7 ft 6 in. figure of Death with a coffin in one hand, a spade in the other, was discovered about 1865 and destroyed. It dated from 1720. *See The Builder*, 1865.*) – STAINED GLASS. In the nave win-dows some original C14 fragments. – PLATE. Chalice made

* Quoted from Mr Ferriday's card index.

up of various pieces; Paten, Elizabethan; Flagon, Dublin, c.1780. – CHURCHYARD CROSS. Steps, base with a niche, and shaft; C14 or C15.

Pretty, winding street, with a number of black and white houses, e.g. LOWER HOUSE, 250 yds W, on the N side. A little further away, off the main street, 450 yds SW, the MANOR HOUSE, a very handsome front with close-set verticals, a big polygonal oriel, and a gabled porch.

(Just E of COMBERTON FARM, ½ m. NE, is a house with a gable decorated with curved diagonal struts and also cusped concave-sided lozenges. The window below has a projecting sill and the post below a figure of a man with an axe. RCHM)

PARK PALE see THORNBURY

PARTON see EARDISLEY

PEG'S FARM see WELLINGTON HEATH

PEMBRIDGE

3050

Pembridge is a small town, not a village, and one of the prettiest in the county for its black and white houses and cottages, hardly disturbed by Georgian brick, though disastrously disturbed by some recent filling stations. The Market Place is behind the main streets, the church lies up some steps, and half hidden from both the main street and the market place.

ST MARY. The only evidence of a Norman church is one small detached capital in the N porch. This church must have been big; for the chancel had the same width as the present chancel. Proof is afforded by the former N and S chapels whose date – the early C13 – can be deduced from the respond which remains on the S side. This has a round abacus and a capital with upright leaves. The rest of the church is all of the C14, and may date from c.1320–60. Chancel, transepts, nave and aisles; no W tower. The fact that the aisle arcades do not take the transepts into consideration may indicate that the latter go back to an earlier date, at least in their foundations. The nave is tall, the transepts are a little lower, the chancel is yet lower. The windows have mostly reticulation motifs (E and W four lights). The clerestory windows are circular and cinque-foiled with ogee foils. Two of them face E above the chancel roof. In the NE angle of the S transept pretty rood-stair turret with pinnacle. The N porch may be a little later than the rest.

It has windows with flowing tracery and a tierceron-star vault inside. Tall arcades of six bays between nave and aisles. Octagonal piers. Arches with two sunk-quadrant mouldings. The w walls of the transepts are continued by a rising half-arch which touches the apex of the last arcade arch but one. The details of the chancel arch probably a little earlier. In the chancel a low tomb recess, also with early C14 mouldings. The single-framed nave roof is of the C14 too, though much restored.

But the most remarkable part of the church has not so far been mentioned at all: the BELL-HOUSE. This is of a type[35b] more familiar from Essex than from the West Country, and structurally related to the stave-churches of Norway and the bell-houses of Sweden. Externally visible is a broad, low stone stage with chamfered corners, a high truncated pyramid roof on this, a vertical weatherboarded bell-stage, a truncated pyramid pent-roof, a further, yet smaller, vertical stage, and a little spire. Inside is a powerful and most impressive timber[35a] structure surrounded by an ambulatory, which is the part with the stone walls. Eight mighty posts form a square. They are braced scissor-fashion and horizontally and rise to the height of the high, lower truncated pyramid roof. The building is ascribed by the RCHM to the later C14.

FURNISHINGS. FONT. C13. Square stem with attached semicircular 'responds'. Bowl of the same form. – PULPIT. Jacobean. With the usual short blank arches and, below them, panels with dragons. – READER'S DESK and LECTERN. Also with Jacobean dragon panels. Specially pretty one with a dragon and a puppy. – COMMUNION RAIL. Jacobean or later. With flat, cut-out balusters. – DOOR. The N door is of the C14, with good big iron hinges with branches. – PAINTINGS. Wall painting in the s transept. White circles on red ground. – Two Miracles of Christ. Late C18; English (?). – STAINED GLASS. Small C14 fragments in the aisle w windows. – CHANDELIER. Of brass. Dated 1722. In the chancel. – PLATE. Chalice and Cover Paten, London, 1750. – MONUMENTS. Two pairs of effigies on simple tomb-chests, one of a Civilian and Lady, early C14, the other of a Knight and Lady, later C14. – In the chancel two tablets with flanking allegorical figures: Mrs William Sherborne † 1660 (s) and Mrs Essex Sherborne † 1668 (N). – Two larger tablets with twisted columns, very similar to one another: William Sherborne † 1671 and Thomas Trafford † 1685. All four have pairs of putti reclining at the top. – Henry Evans and others of the same family, the last † 1799. By *Sir R. Westmacott*. Simple tablet (s transept).

PERAMBULATION. The centre is the little MARKET PLACE with MARKET HOUSE, of the early C16. It formerly had an upper storey. The remaining ground stage is open and has eight carved posts. Immediately SW of the Market House is a house with a C14 core. Large square timber-framing and, in the roof inside, cusped principals and collar-beams. Also one surviving quatrefoiled wall-panel. A little further S, at the bend, COURT HOUSE FARM with handsome OUTBUILD-INGS. The N side of the Market Place is the NEW INN, early C17, with two identical projecting gabled wings to the S. To the E of the New Inn is the hub of Pembridge, the place where Bridge Street from the N meets the West-Street–East-Street axis. In BRIDGE STREET first on the l. DUPPA'S ALMSHOUSES, built probably in 1661. Then, nearer the river, CLAN ARROW COTTAGES of the C16 and BRIDGE COTTAGE with a C14 hall as its centre. This has original but mutilated cruck-trusses. The timbering of the solar-wing also looks original. Beyond the bridge, a little further out, CLEAR BROOK, a specially ornate house, with three identical gables, all decorated with cusped concave-sided lozenges. The brick chimneys with tall blank arches are late C17, while the rest of the house is probably of the early C17. (Staircase with shaped and pierced balusters and pierced and enriched newel posts. RCHM)

Facing Bridge Street at its S end, i.e. part of EAST STREET, is the SHOP, a fine big early C16 house with later additions. On the first floor a seven-light oriel. The gable above this has good bargeboards carved with fruit, flowers, and dragons. After that to the E the terrible filling stations already referred to. Then the GREYHOUND INN, early C16, with close-set upright timbers and an oversailing upper storey on shafted posts and carved brackets. Also door-head with big leaves. Then a terrace of timber-framed cottages. Opposite a C14 or C15 house with arched former doorway on the l. and cross-gable on the r. Then, opposite again, a detached house with a medieval core. (Inside, the central roof truss with arched braces and a collar-beam with foiled openings above. RCHM) At the exit of the town TRAFFORD'S ALMSHOUSES, founded in 1686.

Finally WEST STREET, with more enjoyable timber-framed

houses. (One house on the N side, opposite a detached house fronted in brick, has a cruck-truss inside. Cruck-trusses also in two others, some four or five houses on. RCHM) The last house is specially crooked and picturesque.

WESTON COURT FARMHOUSE, 2 m. SW. Cruck-trusses in a barn.

YEW TREE FARMHOUSE, see MARSTON, p. 250.

PEMBRIDGE CASTLE

4010

A relatively well-preserved smaller border castle. It dates essentially from the C13. The round TOWER in the NW corner appears to be the oldest piece. It may have been started before 1200. On its E side are the remains of a large chamfered arch which must have led into further apartments. The HALL now adjoining, however, is a C17 structure, though its outer wall is of course part of the C13 curtain wall. This wall seems to date from the same time, mid or late C13, as the monumental GATEHOUSE with its semicircular towers. The r. tower and the top of the l. are C20 restoration. The gatehouse is in the E corner. To the NE the castle forms an oblong with smaller round towers, not well preserved. The E angle tower is the more interesting. It is inside, high up, corbelled out. The N angle tower is close to the CHAPEL. The tunnel-vaulted under-croft of this is original. But the chapel itself is a C16 building, and the FURNISHINGS are all brought in. – SCREEN. From Essex. Simple, with one-light divisions. – BENCH END. With a poppy-head. – Top of a four-light wooden WINDOW with ogee-headed lights. – Heraldic STAINED GLASS of the C17. – BRASSES of a Knight and a Bishop, 14 in. long. They are not mentioned by the RCHM, and it is not known where they come from.

PENCOMBE

5050

ST JOHN. 1864–5 by *Thomas Nicholson* of Hereford. An odd conceit, meant to be Transitional or mixed Norman and E.E. This must have been conscious historicism. The s doorway e.g. has a Norman arch but E.E. stiff-leaf capitals. The nave is Norman, the chancel in the style of *c.*1300, the apse E.E. All details a little fussy. – PLATE. Cup, 1571; Paten on foot, London, 1691; Chalice, London, 1836.

(GRENDON COURT, 1¼ m. N. An outbuilding is said to have been a CHAPEL. RCHM)

LITTLE MARSTON, 2½ m. NW, at Marston Stannett. Timber-framed, with an impressive late C14 porch. Two-centred entrance arch. Oversailing upper floor on heavy brackets, also diagonal brackets. (Inside one heavy cruck-truss. RCHM)

PENCOYD

5020

ST DENNIS. A Dec church of little interest, with a chancel rebuilt in 1877–8. – PLATE. Cup and Cover Paten, 1636.

MANOR HOUSE. Jacobean. Of stone, H-shaped, with gabled wings.

(NETHERTON FARM, ⅔ m. E. The house contains a cruck-truss. Early C17 porch with pargetting on the side walls. RCHM)

PENLAN see HUNTINGTON

PENYARD CASTLE see WESTON-UNDER-PENYARD

PETERCHURCH

3030

ST PETER. A very well preserved, large Norman church, consisting of four parts, decreasing in height. The first is the nave, the fourth an apse, the third consequently the chancel. But what was the second? As it is pretty well square, it may well have carried a central tower. The internal sequence of the three arches is memorable. The first is very tall, and has saltire crosses on the abacus and a single-step arch. The second is of course the richest, with zigzag and zigzag at r. angles. The apse arch again has saltire crosses in the abacus and an undecorated single-step arch. Externally the apse has flat buttresses and a roll moulding below the window-line. Norman also the S doorway with one order of shafts and scalloped capitals. Zigzag arch. From the late C13 to the early C14 the W tower was built. It has diagonal buttresses with much-subdivided set-offs. The commanding recessed spire was alas largely taken down some thirteen years ago. It ought to be rebuilt. Large lucarnes at the foot of the remaining stump. A late C13 window in the S wall of the chancel as well. – FONT. Norman, of tub shape, with rope mouldings top and bottom and a frieze of nutmeg below the top rope. – DOOR. The S door is original, with long, not over-ornamented hinges. – PLATE. Cup and Cover Paten by *Hugh Roberts* of London, 1699.

WELLBROOK MANOR, ⅓ m. E. One of the best surviving

examples in the county of a C14 hall-house. The buttery wing has disappeared, but the solar wing remains. The house is stone but timber-framed inside. The hall has been horizontally subdivided, but the operative parts remain monumentally visible upstairs. Spere-truss at the l. end, central truss, E truss with decoration of the wall below. The central truss has crucks. All trusses have foiling. On the E wall, decorative pointed quatrefoils below the pointed trefoiled arches which brace the collar-beam. In the solar wing cusped wind-braces. Also several ogee-headed doorways in the angle between wall and solar wings, connected probably with a former staircase. Finally, in the actual solar a large stone chimneypiece with curious corbels with small panels of tracery. The original stone chimneyshaft survives too – which is very rare indeed.

URISHAY CHAPEL, 1½ m. SW. Simple oblong chapel, probably Norman, but with no securely dateable features. The chapel lies immediately N of the moat of URISHAY CASTLE. On the motte, which is *c.* 52 yds in diameter, now stand the ruins of a sizeable C17 and C18 house.

SNODHILL CASTLE, 1 m. SE of Dorstone. Earthworks of *c.*10 acres. At the E end the steep motte, with a roughly polygonal keep of *c.*1200. This has its gateway to the W, i.e. the bailey. Round towers l. and r. of the gateway. Of the bailey walls substantial fragments remain. They seem to be of the C14. Further earthworks to E as well as W.

SNODHILL COURT FARM, just SSE of the castle. Stone house of the C17. Nearly symmetrically N front, with two large and two small gables. The big stone brackets in the entrance hall and outside a side entrance may come from the castle.

LYNCHETS. ¼ m. WNW of the church is a group of three lynchets running NE across a field. Their date is unknown.

PETERSTOW

5020

ST PETER. On the N side, below a Norman window, some enormous stones. The RCHM calls them Anglo-Saxon. The other windows Dec. Inside, the chancel arch seems E.E., but the r. capital with its crude leaves is probably Perp. C14 nave roof with scissor-bracing. – PULPIT. With blank arches; Jacobean. – PLATE. Late C16 Cup and Cover Paten; Paten on foot by *Robert Timbrell*, 1713 (?).

LITTLE PETERSTOW has been demolished.

PEYTOE HALL *see* ADFORTON

PIPE AND LYDE

5040

St PETER. The earliest piece is the nave, *see* the s doorway with its still Transitional moulding. The long early C13 lancet proves that the nave came before the w tower, which must have been added almost immediately. Unbuttressed. Spire of 1874, by *Kempson*, with big broaches. The nave was largely rebuilt in 1874 (also by *Kempson*), the lancet arrangement being inspired by Acton Burnell. Late C13 chancel (Y-tracery, also the Herefordshire version of the three stepped lancet lights). Handsome chancel roof with collars on arched braces and a trefoiled opening above – a motif usual in the domestic field. – ROOD BEAM. A beautiful piece with two carved friezes of foliage. – PLATE. Chalice and Cover Paten by *Humphrey Payne* of London, 1716; also an early C16 CHALICE CASE of *cuir bouilli*, with shields, fleurs-de-lis, etc. (cf. Causton Norfolk, Moulton Norfolk, Swaffling Suffolk).★

PIXLEY

6030

St ANDREW. Nave and chancel in one. Victorian bell-turret with steep, shingled pyramid roof. The two lancet windows in the E wall of the chancel are original C13 work. Roof with tie-beams. The timber posts supporting the bell-turret are original too. – SCREEN. Very heavy timbers. Hardly early. – SOUTH DOOR. The large hinge is C13. – STAINED GLASS. The two figures in the E lancets probably date from the restoration of 1865, and are in style close to *Morris*.

PONTHENDRE *see* LONGTOWN

PONTRILAS

3020

PONTRILAS COURT. Gabled stone house of *c.*1630 with a gabled porch. Round-headed entrance arch. Inside, one room with a plaster ceiling with a geometrical pattern. Another plaster ceiling, on a smaller scale, in a room at the back. – Handsome, square, timber-framed DOVECOTE.

POSTON LODGE *see* VOWCHURCH

★ The chalice case is on loan to the Hereford City Museum.

PRESTON-ON-WYE 3040

ST LAWRENCE. Over-restored by *T. Nicholson* in 1883. Late
Norman s doorway. Trumpet-scallop capitals. Zigzag in the
arch. One Norman N window with a continuous roll moulding. N doorway Norman too, plain, converted by two red
sandstone blocks into a Dec shape. Over-restored chancel s
doorway of *c.*1300 with multi-cusped head. Dec the w tower
with diagonal buttresses, and Dec the N transept. The arch
towards the nave has the typical sunk-quadrant mouldings
and tripartite responds, but the responds have (already)
polygonal abaci. – PULPIT. Jacobean. Square, with panels
with specially tall blank arches. – BENCHES. The ends raw in
form and with a little Jacobean leaf decoration. – PLATE.
Chalice and Cover Paten by *Gabriel Sleath*, London, 1732. –
MONUMENTS. Nice slate tablets of *c.*1800 under the tower.

PRESTON WYNNE 5040

HOLY TRINITY. On no road. Built in 1727, but except for the
tower victorianized. The tower doorway has a segmental
head and pretty Baroque surround. Circular window over.
Arched bell-openings. Battlements and square pinnacles. The
small Gothic windows of nave and chancel were originally
large and arched. – PLATE. Cup and Cover Paten, 1576.

COURT FARM. Black and white, with a C14 centre extended in 32a
the C17. The higher cross-wing in its present form also C17.
In the C14 part remains of the original roof, including a
cruck-truss with a collar-beam halved into it, arched braces
forming a two-centred arch below the collar-beam, raking
struts forming a foiled opening above, and the spere-truss
with the spere-posts.

PUDLESTON 5050

ST PETER. The w tower is a mystery. The quoins and the rere-
arches of the windows, including the strangest of them,
visible from inside the nave, look decidedly Anglo-Saxon.
But within the latter is a typically Norman window which,
moreover, from its splay, seems to be a nave w window built
regardless of the tower. Also the w doorway is of course
Norman. It has zigzag in the arch and a hood-mould with
leaf decoration. The tower has a handsome spire consisting

of a truncated pyramid and a spire proper. C13 chancel with two S lancets. The E window is of 1857 (designed by *Woodyer*). Nave rebuilt in 1813, aisles added in 1851. – STAINED GLASS. According to Mrs Stanton's unpublished researches *Pugin* designed glass for Mr Chadwick of Pudleston Court in 1850–1. This must refer to the apostles and angels in the aisle windows (*see* the dedication in the S aisle W window). – The glass in the E window is by *Hardman* to *Woodyer*'s design.

OLD RECTORY, N of the church. Georgian, of five bays and two storeys with a pedimented doorway.

PUDLESTON COURT. Built shortly after 1846. Castellated and asymmetrical. Ambitious EAST GATES with castellated and turreted lodges.

FORD ABBEY, I m. SW. Timber-framed, with a two-storeyed porch to the N.

6030

PUTLEY

CHURCH. 1875 by *Thomas Blashill*, but for the Norman bits of shafts, capital, and zigzag re-used to block the N doorway, and some chancel details of the late C13 (fine piscina with shafts and strongly moulded pointed-trefoiled head, N lancet cusped). Some old parts in the nave are not worth recording. – Elaborate REREDOS of alabaster and mosaic; elaborate STALLS with tall traceried canopies, all lit by skylights in the chancel roof. – PULPIT and low SCREEN with re-used Jacobean blank arches and Ionic pilasters separating them. – PLATE. Secular Dish of 1662 with foliage in repoussé; Cover Paten inscribed 1679; Chalice, London, 1825. – CHURCHYARD CROSS. With steps, base, part of the shaft, and the badly preserved head. The Crucifixus, the Virgin, and two saints on the head.

THE BRAINGE, ⅓ m. NNE. A very fine house of 1703. Brick, five by three bays, with quoins and a hipped roof. Doorway with handsome open curly pediment. In the early C19 a porch with Greek Doric columns was put up in front of one of the short sides. The windows were given oddly shaped cement tops with voussoirs of red and black bricks (or is that Victorian?), and the staircase with twisted balusters was shifted to the new entrance.

PUTLEY COURT, 250 yds W of the church. Dated 1712, and a very different version of the same theme. Also five bays, also quoins, also a doorway with a pediment, but this time a curly segmental one. But two and a half storeys, which changes the proportions very much, and a parapet, a lower hipped roof, and a pretty glazed lantern on top. – (Behind the house an early C18 SUMMER HOUSE with four Tuscan columns and a pediment. RCHM)

OLD CASTLE, ⅝ m. NE. A house of *c.*1700 which was partly submerged by a recent addition. It must have had five bays and two storeys and a hipped roof. The windows have kept their wooden mullion-and-transom crosses.

(NEWTONS, 200 yds SSW of the church, has a BARN with cruck-trusses. Cruck construction also in THE LACONS, a cottage ⅙ m. NW of the church. RCHM)

RHYDSPENCE INN *see* BRILLEY

RICHARDS CASTLE

4060

ST BARTHOLOMEW. On a hill with wide views over the plain to the W and S. Very irregular group. Of buff and pale red sandstone. Short square separate bell-tower of *c.*1300 (Y-tracery). Pyramid roof. The church has a Norman nave (two N windows), a S aisle of the early C14 under a separate pitched roof (windows with Geometrical and intersected tracery, the latter with ample ballflower; doorway with filleted moulding), a Dec chancel and N transept (flowing tracery, in the straight-headed transept E window), and a Perp W window. The transept N window with the six-pointed star in its tracery is 46a curious and may be C17 work. Inside, the S arcade of three very wide bays belongs in date to the aisle. The piers have four polygonal projections, the capitals much ballflower. Double-chamfered arches. The N transept has to the S a two-bay arcade. The pier has the same shape, but all panels are slightly sunk, and the capitals are castellated and have fleuron decoration. Double-chamfered arches, also sunk. The date may be later than that of the aisle. In the N wall of the transept big damaged tomb recess. The chancel arch has castellated capitals too. – BOX PEWS, one with a date reading formerly 1688, FAMILY PEW with thin columns, and rising WEST PEW. – STAINED GLASS. Original figures and fragments in S aisle and chancel S windows, but the best is the transept E window. – PLATE. Two Patens on foot, 1694; Chalices, 1724 and 1729; Ewer, 1729. – MONUMENT. A coffin-lid of the C13 with a specially richly foliated cross in high relief.

ALL SAINTS, at Batchcott in Shropshire, *see The Buildings of England, Shropshire*, p. 69.

CASTLE, W of the church. Motte and bailey. In all probability this is Auretone, mentioned in Domesday as held by Osbern FitzRichard. Later Mortimer property. The motte is 65 yds wide at the base and rises to 60 ft above the bottom of the ditch. Kidney-shaped bailey to the E of the motte. Entrance to the bailey on the SE. Of the wall of the bailey fragments remain on the N, up to 12 ft high. Traces of an outer bailey enclosing the church and possibly the original village.

COURT HOUSE, ½ m. SE. Early C17. In the gable on the N side cusped concave-sided lozenges. (To the house belong a CIDER MILL of the early C17 and a DOVECOTE of stone, probably medieval. RCHM)

₃₀₆₀
RODD

RODD COURT. A stone house of c.1625 (one fireback dated 1629) with a brick front. Far-projecting r. wing. Gables. Mullioned and transomed wooden windows. Three-storeyed gabled porch. Inside, the best room is in the projecting wing on the first floor. This has a stucco ceiling with simple interlocked panels and fleurs-de-lis. Also an overmantel with coarse sculpture. Others in other rooms, and also in the library, which was added in 1953. Small staircase with flat balusters.

(LITTLE RODD, immediately N. With a medieval cruck-truss inside. RCHM)

UPPER NASH FARM, 1 m. W. Timber-framed. Medieval centre. An addition of the C16 with a gable. This has brackets on twisted shafts and below, for the first floor, a moulded bressumer and pendants and bracket. (Inside, two early C17 overmantels with blank arches. RCHM)

LITTLE BRAMPTON, 1⅜ m. SW. Timber-framed, very varied outside. The prettiest features are on the entrance side, where a gable and the adjoining recessed centre of the house have very thin baluster posts and carved brackets. Also a carved bressumer for the first floor below the gable. All this is given to the C16 by the RCHM.

(HIGHLAND, 1¼ m. SE. The E wing has a medieval cruck-truss. RCHM)

₆₀₂₀
ROSS-ON-WYE

ST MARY. The story of this large and interesting church begins with the arcades inside, provided one realizes at once that their present height dates from 1743. The whole of the lower parts did not exist before then, which of course changes the character of the interior completely. The s arcade comes first. Except for the E bay, this is of *c.*1200. Circular piers, circular abaci, double-chamfered arches. The w respond still has a trumpet-scallop capital. This is the restorer's work, but the NW respond is original. The N arcade on the other hand is a little later – *see* the octagonal abaci of the circular piers. The last pier on the s has the same feature, and the E responds are tripartite and filleted. So we are beyond 1200 here. The chancel arch has the same fillet down the responds. Now the windows appear in the picture; for much rebuilding went on in the late C13 and early C14. The tall N aisle windows with cusped lights and encircled quatrefoils, the bars having attached members circular in section, are a fine feature and obviously late C13. The N porch entrance has early C14 mouldings. The N aisle w window is of *c.*1300 or a little later (three pointed trefoils in the big top circle). The s aisle is again a little later – except for the s doorway, which must be re-set, as it has E.E. shafts and arch mouldings. Early C14 however the ballflower frieze which appears outside at the w end. The tall E arch in the aisle was a window whose tracery unfortunately has been destroyed. Early C14 also the s porch. Entrance with two continuous chamfers. Of the same date the w tower, ashlar-faced, with diagonal buttresses and a tall recessed spire. Only the oversized pinnacles are an unhappy restoration. The tower arch has three continuous sunk curves. Finally, adjoining the s porch immediately, the Perp Markye Chapel or outer s aisle. Two large Perp arches. Octagonal pier. Straight-headed windows.

FURNISHINGS. FONT. Of baluster type, late C17 (*see* the swags, which do not allow a later dating). – PULPIT. Late C17, plain. – COMMUNION RAIL. Late C17, with twisted balusters. – STAINED GLASS. In the E window four complete C15 figures. They come from the house of the Bishops of Hereford at Stretton Sugwas. – In a s aisle s window many bits. – PLATE. Cup and Cover Paten, 1661; Flagon, 1673; Paten on foot, 1706; Almsdish, 1711. – MONUMENTS. An exceptional number and of exceptional variety. They will be listed chronologically. William Rudhall, attorney general to Henry VIII, † 1530, and wife. Alabaster tomb-chest with very good effigies. Against the chest on one long side saints, and in the centre group of figures kneeling before the Trinity.

Against the other long side saints. Against the short side group of figures kneeling before the Annunciation (s aisle E). – William Rudhall † 1609. Big tablet. Both kneeling main figures missing. Only the prayer desk between them and the children in the 'predella' are left (s aisle E). – Nathaniel Hill † 1632. Small tablet with kneeling figure (chancel s). – John Rudhall † 1636. Sumptuous tomb-chest with black marble top. Alabaster effigies with elaborate rendering of the clothes. They are holding hands. Against the tomb-chest the children, including a babe on its side and a little girl propped up on her elbow (s aisle E). – Colonel William Rudhall † 1651. Like a statue in a public place. Standing figure in armour. On a square pedestal with military trophies, he oddly overlooks the other crowded monuments at the E end of the s aisle. – Elizabeth Markey † 1681. Tablet with inscription surrounded by drapes, skull above, big putto head below (Markye Chapel s). – G. Abrahall † 1729. Architectural tablet with coupled Corinthian pilasters (Markye Chapel w). – John Kyrle, the Man of Ross (*see* below). Erected in 1776. By *Marsh* of Ross. A very good piece. Open scrolly pediment above the inscription, and above that obelisk with portrait head in an oval medallion. Another oval medallion with two Virtues (chancel N). – John Partridge † 1810. With profile in medallion (N aisle). – Thomas Westfaling, 1817 by *William Theed Sen.* White marble. Free-standing bust on a high square plinth. Against this, relief of Charity, teaching children. Excellent. – CHURCHYARD CROSS. To the s of the chancel. The shaft is not old. Against the base the inscription Plague Ano Dom 1637 Burials 315 Libera nos Domine. – MISCELLANEA. The indoor plants climbing up in front of the N aisle E window are enchanting. They represent the tradition of John Kyrle's elms in the church. They are indeed trained round dead timber, but whether the original elms were planted inside the church or sprang from the roots of trees planted outside is not certain.

CHURCH, Hom Green (medieval dedication: The Paraclete). By *Bodley*, 1905–6. Nave and chancel and bellcote superficially like so many others, but in fact remarkably personal. There is a low screen in front of the w front and a low screen-like E vestry behind the altar wall. There are also most surprising tall octagonal piers along the centre of the building, dividing it into two naves. Yet there is a wagon roof over the whole. The E side is characterized by a tall chimney at one corner of the vestry and a buttress up the centre of the completely windowless E wall. The windows all have triangular heads to their lights.

BAPTIST CHAPEL, Broad Street. 1861, by *G. C. Haddon* of Hereford, and very terrible. Grey brick, in an Italianate which dithers between Romanesque and Renaissance.

FRIENDS' MEETING HOUSE, Brookend Street. *See* Perambulation, p. 282.

MARKET HALL. 1660–74. Of red sandstone. The ground floor, as usual, is open. It has two by six columns and arches. The upper windows have medallions and arched lights. Against one gable a good medallion of Charles II. Staircase with dumb-bell balusters. In the upper room along the axis four square tapering timber piers.

WILTON BRIDGE. Built in 1597, strengthened with reinforced concrete ties in 1914. A splendid bridge, though widened. Six round arches with ribs and massive cutwaters. On the parapet in the middle big early C18 SUNDIAL. It has an inscription:

> Esteem thy precious time
> Which pass so swift away
> Prepare thee for eternity
> And do not make delay.

PERAMBULATION. What distinguishes Ross from all other towns is initially due to John Kyrle, the Man of Ross. He was born in 1637 and died in 1724. He was wealthy, but simple in his habits, so as to be able to be charitable on a princely scale. Pope's praise of Kyrle is familiar. The most conspicuous monument to Kyrle's public-mindedness is the public garden S, W, and N of the church, called the PROSPECT. He leased the ground in 1693. The original layout does not survive, and the N part has been sold, but the south GATE remains, very dignified, like some college gate at Oxford, with its Corinthian pilasters, its pediment, and its cypher and date. The date is 1700. In the E wall is another gate with big vases on piers supported from l. and r. by volutes. This also is dated 1700. The prospect to the W is indeed delightful, including the most recent newcomer to the landscape, the stretch of the future Birmingham–South Wales MOTORWAY with the elegant arches of its bridge.*

---

* The bridge is 350 ft long, was completed in 1960, and is designed by *Scott & Wilson, Kirkpatrick & Partners*, with *Ansell & Bailey* as consultant architects.

The N part of the Prospect was handed over to private enterprise, as we would say now, in 1836. A new road was cut 'beneath the red cliffs' (as Thomas Roscoe writes in 1838). The ROYAL HOTEL, opened in 1837, was built in the typical style of the picturesque-minded of that time, i.e. white, with bargeboarded gables, much as if it were e.g. at Sidmouth. At the same time, although no exact date is, strangely enough, recorded, the neighbourhood of the new road and the hotel was thoroughly and expensively medievalized, i.e. red sandstone walls with arrow-slits and heavily corbelled-out oriels were built on the red rock to the N of the hotel and further N facing Wilton Road and Wye Street. A round tower was also built, big enough to become part of the prospect of Ross as one enters by Wilton Bridge. It all looks very genuine, and nearly every traveller approaching that way will be deceived by it and admire the survival of the town walls. In fact, there was at least one palpable reason for going so medieval in this place: the existence of a house of the bishops of Hereford. But nothing of it seems to be incorporated in the ambitious new works.

The approach can be by either of the two roads just named. On the upper we admire the rocks and the middle-agery, on the lower there are some houses to be noted. First villas in the style of the Royal Hotel, then No. 11 and its neighbour the BRITISH AND FOREIGN SCHOOL, built in 1837. The former is just a small Gothic sandstone house with four-centred heads to the windows, the latter a surprisingly tall building with a pedimental gable and windows of the same kind on the fourth, i.e. top, storey. The street then bends E, and normal houses begin: first VAGA HOUSE, Late Georgian, with giant pilasters, a Tuscan porch, and two canted bay windows, the whole curiously forming an obtuse angle. Then a low house of red stone with Gothic windows and battlements (an outbuilding of a house further N?), HOLLAND HOUSE with two canted bays, and a house (now MAN OF ROSS) with a Dutch gable. Is it C17? Opposite the CASTLE VAULTS, again Tudor with gables and bargeboards, and this time dated 1838.

From this corner we first turn N, into EDDE CROSS STREET; for the same character is here continued. The VALLEY HOTEL has a garden at the back with a polygonal tower, sandstone below, brick above,* and the MERTON HOTEL a

* It is believed originally to have belonged to Vaga House. In the garden wall is a date 1774.

summer house, said to have been built with materials from
Goodrich Castle but recently damaged by fire, a bit of sham
ruin, and, attached to the house, the room called the Chapel,
with a heavily panelled and traceried wooden vault. The house
is supposed to have belonged at the time to a Mr White, a
friend or acquaintance of Nelson.

Back to the Castle Vaults and up the HIGH STREET. On the r.
a red sandstone house with an Adamish doorway. Then first
up ST MARY'S STREET to see, at the church corner, where
the street turns to the Royal Hotel, the house called PALACE
POUND, late C17, with quoins and doorways with rusticated
surrounds. Then CHURCH ROW, with the former school
(now parish hall), red brick, entirely unadorned, two storeys,
six bays with doorways in the first and the last.* Down back
to the High Street by CHURCH STREET, where the RUDHALL
ALMSHOUSES, founded in 1575. Red sandstone, low, with
gables and small mullioned windows. The house opposite is
again late C17, though the doorcase is later. In the stretch of
the High Street thus bypassed is the KING'S HEAD, with an
early C19 front, whitewashed, with giant Ionic pilasters and
attic windows above them. Broad doorway with Ionic columns
and a broken pediment. Then further E the SARACEN'S
HEAD, black and white, with narrowly-set uprights and
ornamented bressumers.

So to the MARKET PLACE, a triangular space with the Market
House in the middle. To the S KYRLE'S HOUSE (No. 34),
again with narrowly-set uprights. Behind the house in the
garden a SUMMER HOUSE with a pretty symmetrical front of
red sandstone. Two steep gables with lancet windows below
and an entrance between. Nothing of interest inside, but the
winding path to the summer house crossed by three little
grotto arches is charming. The whole is on the smallest scale,
but, as Kyrle died in 1724, the date is remarkably early for
Picturesque garden furnishings.

The NW side of the Market Place is a nice Georgian curve of
brick houses. From the Market Place first for a moment to the
SE, i.e. down COPSE CROSS STREET, with the humble
WEBBE'S ALMSHOUSES, founded in 1603 but with pointed
windows probably of c.1800, and turning off the street to the
E on the return journey, in OLD GLOUCESTER ROAD, the
WALTER SCOTT CHARITY SCHOOL, founded as a Bluecoat

* The RECTORY, in Church Street to the E of the church, has been
replaced.

School in 1717 but given its present form in 1796–8. Brick, of seven bays, with large arched ground-floor windows, one schoolroom to the l., one to the r. Doorway with Tuscan columns and a pediment. The upper floor was probably living quarters.

Now from the Market Place down BROAD STREET, which winds gently. Nos 1–2 on the w side must be early C18, stuccoed, with quoins and segment-headed windows. Off into NEW STREET, where Nos 44–46 are a good Later Georgian group, the l. half five bays, two and a half storeys, red brick, with two single-storey bows, the r. half also five bays and two and a half storeys, but white and with a pretty porch with Adamish columns. This group is followed by the former PRISON. It is a square block, of red stone, and with lancet windows and a pyramid roof.

To continue in Broad Street, the NEW INN has an Early Victorian front with wide, tripartite, segment-headed windows. Broad Street continues as BROOKEND STREET, and at the top of this is the RAILWAY HOTEL, early C18, with quoins, segment-headed windows, and a hipped roof, and N of it BROOK HOUSE, of about the same date (doorway with round-arched hood), and then the FRIENDS' MEETING HOUSE. Dated 1804 on the façade, which is a blank wall of red stone with two arched openings, one of them blank.

ALTON COURT, ½ m. SE. Pretty gable to the NW, with closely-set uprights and herringbone bracing in the gable itself. C16. The rest much restored. Late C17 staircase with nice fat-bellied balusters.

CHASE WOOD CAMP. A univallate Iron Age hill-fort of roughly sub-rectangular plan lies in Chase Wood, 1 m. SSE of the church. An entrance cut through the rock on the NE is probably contemporary with the defences. Further entrances on the N and in the middle of the W side may be comparatively modern.

ROTHERWAS CHAPEL *see* DINEDOR

ROWLSTONE

3020

ST PETER. Unbuttressed, late W tower with pyramid roof. But the nave is Norman and has in its S doorway and chancel arch two of the very best and most characteristic pieces of the Herefordshire school of carvers. Both pieces are clearly the work of one man. His obsession was birds, especially cocks. Cocks are e.g. on the capitals of the one order of shafts of the s doorway. The abacus has intertwined trails. In the arch a thick roll moulding and a band of rosettes. But the tympanum is what really matters, a tympanum that helps much to reconstruct the all but lost one of Shobdon, of which Rowlstone is to all intents and purposes a copy. It represents Christ in Glory. The legs are placed in the typically Romanesque way, with knees wide apart and feet together. The folds have the tense, stringy parallel curves of the Herefordshire school. The figure is in a halo, not almond-shaped as usual, but with top and bottom rounded. Four angels hold the halo, and all four are represented flying head downwards. This allows the carver again to display his curved parallels. The composition is highly accomplished. What is against nature is in accordance with stylistic principles. In the capitals of the chancel arch there are again birds. The capitals 11b are of one piece with the outer adjoining panel of two small figures on each side. On the l. (N) they are an angel and a bishop, on the r. it is not so easy to recognize them, as they stand upside down. That does not seem quite so accomplished, and the most baffling fact is that the whole stone was not rejected. Such indulgence is attractive; it is instructive too. Many birds once more in the abaci. In the doorway arch a thick roll and an outer band of saltire crosses. Norman windows in nave and chancel. Several Perp windows, including the chancel E window. – CANDLE BRACKETS in the chancel, l. and r. of the altar space. Long iron brackets (each 4 ft 7 in. long), each for five candles. Decoration by small cocks (here too), swans, and fleurs-de-lis. Late medieval. – PLATE. Chalice, London, 1816.

(MOUND, NE of the church. About 15 ft high above the bottom of the ditch and about 40 yds in diameter at the base. RCHM)

RUDHALL HOUSE see BRAMPTON ABBOTTS

RUMNEY BUILDING see STANFORD BISHOP

RUXTON COURT see LLANGARRON

RYEFORD see WESTON-UNDER-PENYARD

ST DEVEREUX
4030

ST DUBRICIUS. Unbuttressed W tower, Dec above but older below. Late C13 nave, see the two tomb recesses inside and the lancet and the two-light windows with cusped lights and a quatrefoil in a circle above. Chancel Early Perp. E window of three lights. – PLATE. Elizabethan Cup, inscribed 1576; Cup and Cover Paten, said to come from Amsterdam, C17. – MONUMENTS. Thomas Goode † 1664. Very big ledger-stone standing upright. Nice floral border. – Ann Goode † 1668. Also a ledger-stone; also upright. With a rustic figure of the young girl and again a floral border. – Bits of other C17 monuments, e.g. small semi-reclining figures from the tops of pediments.

TRELOUGH, ½ m. W. Early C18. Brick, of five by three bays with a hipped roof.

(CASTLE, at Didley Court Farm, ¾ m. NE. Motte and bailey, the motte 26 yds in diameter and 17 ft high above the bottom of the ditch, the bailey crescent-shaped but badly preserved. RCHM)

3030

ST MARGARETS

ST MARGARET. By a farm, but otherwise far away from any traffic. Nave and chancel and weatherboarded bell-turret projecting a little to the W and ending in a pyramid roof. Plain Norman chancel arch. – ROOD SCREEN. This is one of the wonders of Herefordshire, deliciously carved and in extremely good preservation. It is really a loft whose coving rests on two posts. The posts are covered with delicate, lacy ornament and have two little niches near the top, for statuettes. The coving has ribs meeting at r. angles and with bosses at the junction. The arches are not really arches; they are horizontals with little quadrant curves, and they are set out with a frill of inverted cresting. Above, the loft parapet, and, below as well as above it, foliage friezes with inverted crestings below and proper crestings above. The screen is of c.1520 and of a specifically Welsh type (cf. e.g. Llangwm, Denbighshire, and Llanegryn, Merionethshire). – COMMUNION RAIL. Jacobean. – PLATE. Cup and Cover Paten, 1618.

WHITEHOUSE, see Turnastone, p. 301.

MOUND. ⅓ m. ENE of the church is a circular mound, about 50 ft in diameter and 10 ft high, which may be a Bronze Age round barrow.

4020

ST WEONARDS

ST WEONARD. This is a dedication unique in England. In the S wall of the nave two lancets with pointed-trefoiled heads, i.e. work of *c.*1300. The rest mostly Perp. w tower with diagonal buttresses, a tall arch to the nave, and a four-light window. Chancel with large E window. N aisle with a four-bay arcade whose two-centred arches however may well be re-used C13 material, as the RCHM suggested, and with straight-headed windows. The E window is of four lights. In the N wall a cusped niche and, above, the badly carved demi-figure of an angel supporting a bracket. In the (C19) S porch a stoup with a large face. – SCREENS. To chancel and N aisle E bay. Dado with linenfold panels. One-light divisions above. Elementary top frieze of leaf. – PULPIT. Jacobean, with the well-known blank arches and ornamental panels above. – BOX PEWS (N aisle E). – CHEST. A C13 'dug-out' (N aisle E). – STAINED GLASS. N aisle E by *Baillie & Mayer*, 1875, but incorporating substantial C15 remains. – One larger early C16 panel, probably German, in a nave S window. – PLATE. Cup on baluster stem, 1628; Almsdish, inscribed 1675; Chalice and Cover Paten by *Richard Bayley*, London, 1715; Flagon by *Edward Jay*, London, 1776. – MONUMENT. Robert Minors Gouge † 1765. With the usual obelisk and in front of it an urn with two cherubs' heads below.

TREAGO CASTLE. The castle belongs to a type with angle towers and an inner courtyard which is characteristic of the C14 (Bolton Castle, Bodiam, etc.). Yet the RCHM could not recognize any masonry earlier than the time of Henry VII. References to the castle go back to the late C13. It has been in the hands of the Mynors family ever since the early C14. Much was altered in the later C17, the C18, and finally in 1840. The sash windows are of the C18, the Tudor windows of 1840, based however on one three-light mullioned window with arched lights on the S side, close to the SE tower, which looks C16. The principal entrance is by a deep three-storeyed porch on the N side. The porch led into the screens passage and the hall (now the kitchen). Of the original hall roof timbers remain considered hammerbeams by the RCHM. This does not seem certain. At the end of the screens passage the stair-case which, with its twisted balusters, must be of *c.*1670. Of the same time the plaster ceiling in the room to the W of the hall. Two oblong panels with an oval wreath and sprigs of oak and rose. Some time before the later C18 the N side of the house was heightened by a sham storey so that the porch no longer runs higher than the rest of the façade. Perhaps at the same time the courtyard was roofed over and the area subdivided. The principal tower of Treago Castle is at the SE corner. It contained the original kitchen. Whether the evident heightening of the tower also belongs to the C18 is not certain. The new storey projects and has a conical roof.

ROUND BARROW. A Bronze Age round barrow, 130 ft in diameter and 14 ft high, lies 70 yds SSW of the church. Excavation in 1855 revealed two cremation burials without grave goods. The burials were covered with a primary mound of earth upon which stones were heaped. Traces of the surrounding ditch can be seen on the E side.

SALTMARSHE CASTLE see EDVIN LOACH

3050

SARNESFIELD

ST MARY. Norman W window in the nave, now looking into the tower. Very narrow S aisle. The small four-bay arcade of before 1200, with circular piers, scalloped capitals, square abaci, and slightly pointed double-chamfered arches. Unbuttressed W tower of c.1300 with battered base. Tower arch with sunk-quadrant moulding. All the windows are of c.1300. C14 S chapel of two bays with octagonal pier and double-chamfered arches. Fine C14 nave roof with tie-beams and one tier of pointed-trefoiled wind-braces. Timber also the C14 S porch. Cusped wind-braces and trefoils above the tie-beams. Perp chancel arch. – STAINED GLASS. In the S transept E window four tiny, very charming C14 figures and C15 fragments. – MONUMENT. In the churchyard, W of the S porch, plain tomb-chest to *John Abel*, the carpenter (see Introduction, p. 50). He died in 1674 aged 97.

(HELL MOAT, $\frac{7}{8}$ m. NW. With an irregular island. RCHM)

5020

SELLACK

ST TYSILIO. A dedication unique in England. Dec W tower with fine spire on very small broaches. The interior at first very confusing. It starts with a Norman arcade bay – only one. Short circular pier with circular scalloped capital and unmoulded round arch. Then follows a Victorian stretch, designed by an architect who did not know what bases would suit Perp foliage capitals. But after that the medieval work goes on, in an arch with characteristic E.E. responds. The Victorian work evidently obliterated the rest of the Norman arcade, and the bay further E is a chancel chapel. The chapel incidentally has a vault with diagonal and ridge-ribs (cf. King's Caple near by), and this is probably Perp. Perp of course also the four-light chancel E window. Externally, the w end of the aisle shows that the Norman aisle was much widened about 1300. – PULPIT. Jacobean, with the usual blank arches (but with the unusual feature of big Ionic capitals to the pilasters). The pulpit has its tester. – PANELLING of the altar space; Jacobean. – WEST GALLERY. With two tapering Jacobean posts. – STAINED GLASS. The E window is a complete composition of 1630, consisting of work of that date mixed with C15 and C16 fragments. The dominant colours are yellow, blue, and brown. – PLATE. Cup and Cover Paten, 1614; Flagon and Paten on foot, 1674; large Paten on foot, c.1674. – MONUMENTS. Helip Fox † 1678. Tablet with twisted columns. – William Powell † 1680. Fine, large white marble tablet with two putti opening the drapery of a baldacchino to reveal an urn. This is central in style, the former provincial. – Thomas Symonds † 1760. By *Symonds* of Hereford. Good large tablet with a profile in a garlanded oval medallion. Big architectural background with long inscription.

CARADOC COURT. Large house, partly black and white and of the C16, partly of stone, built c.1620 and much restored and altered. On the principal front, the bay window, porch, and shaped gables are Victorian. The bay window at the back, however, is original. The windows are mullioned and transomed. Painted C17 decoration in the room at the N end of the w wing: large flower scrolls and also landscapes. RCHM)

SHOBDON   3060

ST JOHN EVANGELIST. A priory was founded at Shobdon by Oliver de Merlimond, chief steward to Hugh Mortimer of Wigmore Castle. But the church had been begun a few years earlier. It was consecrated by Bishop Robert de Bethune of Hereford, who ruled from 1131 to 1148. Shortly after, the priory moved away, returned, and finally settled at Wigmore (*see* p. 321). What remains of the church has been renewed and converted into an eye-catcher (*see* below). The w tower of the present church seems to be of the C13. It is broad, short, and unbuttressed. But its entrance has a broad, jolly ogee arch and there is an odd trefoiled window above. Both betray a mid-C18 date and are in fact part of a rebuilding of the church undertaken by the Hon. Richard Bateman of Shobdon

Court in 1752–6. He was a friend of Horace Walpole and had embraced Gothicism on the example of Strawberry Hill. Horace Walpole was proud of having converted him 'from a Chinese to a Goth', i.e. from chinoiserie to the Gothick. The nave, transepts, and chancel are all his, of ashlar, with battlements and two-light and three-light windows which are ogee-headed and have ogee-headed lights.* The interior is delightful and ought to be kept in a state of high finish. The walls have Gothick stucco panels between the windows. The ceiling is coved and decorated with some sparse Gothick details. Chancel and transepts are separated from the nave by tripartite pendant ogee arches. The s transept was the family pew. It has a big fireplace. The n transept was the servants' pew. The FURNISHINGS are robust and thoroughly Gothick too. They are painted white, with a little light blue. – BENCHES with ends of a broad fancy profile. – Three-decker PULPIT, i.e. pulpit proper with elaborate sounding board and red velvet hangings, reader's desk with ends similar to the bench ends, and lectern – all big, in fact a little too big for the small church. – CHAIRS. Two, in the chancel, excellent Gothick work. – STAINED GLASS. Some of 1753 survives, heraldic and ornamental, with dominating red, brown, yellow, and blue. – PLATE. Two silver-gilt Chalices and Patens, London, 1753; Flagon, London, 1753. – Not belonging to the period of 1753 the following: FONT from the Norman church. Four sinister lions passant around the short stem. – MONUMENTS. Ann Chaplin, 1697. Tablet with thick foliage surround and a semicircular top. – John Viscount Bateman, 1804 by *Nollekens*. Putto with portrait medallion in front of an obelisk.

SHOBDON COURT. The house of the Batemans which stood close to the church has been pulled down. What remains is Georgian STABLES of brick, the octagonal brick DOVECOTE, and the fine GATEPIERS to the N, broad, with alternatingly blocked Doric columns, niches between, and pediments. They may be of *c*.1765, the date scratched into the simpler s gatepiers.

SHOBDON ARCHES, N of the house and church, but best reached from Uphampton. This is an eye-catcher erected when the church had been pulled down and incorporating the Norman chancel arch and, to its l. and r., the two Norman doorways and (separately) their tympana. It makes a cinque-

* Mr. Colvin has arguments to suggest *Flitcroft* as the architect.

partite composition and was given pinnacles, battlements, and a gable with a trefoil window. The sculpture is – or rather was – of great interest, nationally and not only regionally, but has been so completely ruined by exposure that it can only be appreciated in conjunction with the lithographs of 1852 by G. R. Lewis. The sculpture belonged to the doorways and the chancel arch. The former have two orders of shafts, the latter has three. All the shafts are closely decorated, but the decoration varies a great deal not only in motifs but also in character. Interlace of beaded bands, linked medallions inhabited by birds, dragons, etc. Viking dragons arranged in pairs and tiers, addorsed pairs of birds head-downwards, human figures in pairs and tiers, and also zigzag at r. angles to the wall surface. On the capitals are, besides ornamental motifs, angels, their wings standing like a shirt, an entwined dragon, a bird in profile, affronted lions, and groups of human figures. Even the bases are mostly decorated. The voussoirs of the arches are more lively in the doorways than the chancel arch, which has mainly zigzag. In the doorways there are again fat Viking dragons, and in addition radially-placed birds, beasts, and heads of beasts. In the middle of one order of the r. arch standing human figures, angels, and even a siren, appear instead. The two tympana represent The Harrowing of Hell and Christ in Glory, the *mandorla*, or almond-shaped 9a halo, in the latter held by four angels in precipitous positions and a little as if they were tumblers in action. All figures are very long and thin, and the folds of the clothes are close and parallel. These characteristics apply to the same stylistic moment, i.e. the 1130s, in major works in France as well, cf. e.g. the tympana of Autun and Vézelay. The long, spreading folds of Christ's skirt (one is inclined to call it) are particularly telling. When the construction of the priory had been started, Oliver de Merlimond went on a pilgrimage to Santiago de Compostela. It is tempting to connect the Shobdon sculpture therefore with the Puerta de las Platerias, which was completed before *c.*1140; but the style will not match.

SCHOOL, in the village, ½ m. SW of the church. Gothic, with two gables. By *E. B. Lamb.*

LEDICOT, 1 m. SE. Georgian, of five bays and two storeys, with a one-bay pediment and a hipped roof.

SNODHILL CASTLE *see* PETERCHURCH

6030   SOLLERS HOPE

St Michael. Nave and chancel and timber bell-turret with
straight spire. In the chancel Dec N and S windows and a
probably Dec chancel arch (two continuous chamfers), but a
Perp E window. In the nave Perp windows. – PULPIT. C17,
with panels with a raised lozenge in the centre and fluted
panels above them. – STAINED GLASS. Original bits in the
chancel N and S windows and the W window. – PLATE. Cup
and Cover Paten by *John Sutton*, 1696; Paten on stem, London,
1722. – (MONUMENT. Incised slab to a Knight, *c.*1225;
chancel S wall. Greenhill) – CHURCHYARD CROSS. With
the stump of the original shaft continued by a Victorian
shaft.

Court Farm, NNE of the church. Early C16, timber-framed.
To the S, gable with closely-set uprights and diagonal brick-
nogging between. Projecting first floor with lozenges within
lozenges. Along the long side also closely-set uprights. Also
two chimneys, one of them with a stepped base to the shafts,
then a band of trefoil-headed panels and polygonal shafts
with star-tops. Under the N gable again the close uprights.
Moulded bressumer.

6050   STANFORD BISHOP

St James. Quite on its own. Latest Norman to late C13. Latest
Norman the S doorway, with one order of shafts carrying
trumpet-scallop capitals. Keeled roll moulding. Hood-mould
on stiff-leaf stops. Very simple, chamfered N doorway.
Norman nave N window and chancel S window, the latter
according to the RCHM re-set. Short, broad W tower. The
windows Norman or E.E., the arch to the nave on Norman
imposts but pointed. Pyramid roof. The chancel E part late
C13 (cusped Y-tracery). The S porch is called C14 by the
RCHM, though it has a round-arched entrance. It must be
changed about. – PULPIT. Simple, Jacobean. – DOOR. With
good, large, original metal hinges. – CHAIR. Very simple,
medieval armchair. Posts and boards, elementarily slotted into
them. Said to be St Augustine's Chair used by him at a
conference in 603. – PLATE. Cup and Cover Paten, 1571.

Rumney Building, ⅜ m. WSW, facing the road crossing.
Plain oblong of stone, once a school. This was founded in
1731 and rebuilt in 1826.

STAPLETON   *3060*

CASTLE. The building, which is in ruins, dates from the C17. There is no earlier evidence except the motte and the traces of the ditch. The motte was the shaping of an existing hill. Outer bailey to the N.

CARTER'S CROFT, ¼ m. E. Inside parts of three cruck-trusses remain. The RCHM dates the house to the C13 or C14.

LUGG BRIDGE, now really inside Presteigne. Probably C17. Of three segmental arches with cutwaters.

STAUNTON-ON-ARROW   *3060*

ST PETER. 1856 by *Nicholson*. Quite big, with a W tower with higher stair-turret. Aisleless, but with transeptal chapels. – PLATE. Set, Sheffield, 1828–9.

OLD HALL, 300 yds NNW. Largish, black and white, of the C16–17. Nice, varied roof-line.

HIGHLAND, see Rodd, p. 276.

COURT OF NOKE. Early C18, of brick. Seven bays, two storeys, projecting angle piers, hipped roof. Three-bay pediment. Nice staircase with turned balusters and carved tread-ends.

MOUND, SW of the church. Diameter at the top c. 63 ft. Height above the bottom of the ditch up to 28 ft. Traces of one or more baileys.

STAUNTON-ON-WYE   *3040*

ST MARY. The church has a good view across the wide Wye valley to the S. Norman S doorway with one order of shafts. The capitals and the details of the arch point to the late C12. The blocked Norman N doorway is at the time of writing hidden by ivy. Unbuttressed W tower with big pyramid roof. The bell-openings are of *c.*1300, but in the W wall, above the Victorian doorway, is what could be a re-set doorway of *c.*1200. Mighty tower arch of three chamfers, i.e. again *c.*1300. Most windows of the church are renewed. But there is one genuine N lancet. The N side formerly had a two-bay arcade. This is called early C14 by the RCHM. But the round pier has a capital so enormous and so crude that it looks C11 more than anything. Irregular double-chamfered arches. The chancel was rebuilt in the C18, but is all victorianized. – PANELLING. Under the tower a large number of Jacobean panels and six medallions with heads in profile, typical 'Early Renaissance', i.e. Late Henry VIII. – COMMUNION RAIL (now under the tower arch). With turned balusters; C17. – PLATE. Chalice and Cover Paten, London, 1576. – MONUMENT. Stone effigy of a Lady under a cinquefoiled canopy; early C14. Much defaced. It is in the churchyard, about 30 ft s of the chancel.

STOCKTON BURY see KIMBOLTON

STOGBATCH see LEOMINSTER, p. 231

6040

STOKE EDITH

ST MARY. Tall Dec W tower with diagonal buttresses. Thin recessed needle spire. The body of the church was rebuilt by the Foleys of Stoke Edith Park in 1740–2. Five-bay nave of brick, stuccoed. In the first and last bays doorways with round windows over. Big arched windows between. Arched also the E window. Inside, the first bay and the altar room are separated by giant Tuscan columns. Metope frieze along the wall. Nice marbling of the altar room, and niches l. and r. of the altar. – FONT. Marble bowl, very small, on an iron stand. – COMMUNION RAILS. Of wrought iron, three-sided. – PEWS. Completely preserved, including the squire's pew and the parson's pew, the latter building up into a three-decker PULPIT. – STAINED GLASS. The E glass by *Warrington*, 1846, is highly unsuited for its place. – PLATE. Two Chalices, two Flagons, Almsdish, all by *Gurney & Co.* of London, 1742. – MONUMENTS. Alabaster effigy of a Lady, later C15. She wears a butterfly head-dress. Behind C18 wrought-iron railings. – Paul Foley † 1699. Large standing monument of veined and grey marble. Big sarcophagus supporting an urn. Top pediment; no figures. – Edward Foley † 1806. By *Blore*, but designed by *Tatham*. Equally big standing monument; without figures too. Severe and massive. Vaguely Grecian. Mostly inscription. – Henry Wolstenholme † 1738 and his wife † 1749. Two identical tablets by *Richard Broad* of Worcester.

RECTORY. Built about 1740. Red brick, five bays, two storeys, hipped roof. Doorway with very prettily carved corbels.

STOKE EDITH PARK was burned in 1927. The house was called by Celia Fiennes nearly completed in 1698. Its central hall had painted decoration by *Thornhill*. Of the outbuildings something remains. The grounds were laid out by *Repton* (*see* his *Sketches* of 1799).

WEST LODGE. Brick, octagonal, with projection in the main direction, Tuscan columns *in antis* in the direction of the approaching visitor, and a copper dome. – EAST LODGE. Simpler, with a pedimented one-bay centre and lower one-bay wings. The architect may have been *Tatham* or *William Wilkins*.★

STOKE LACY   6040

ST PETER AND ST PAUL. 1863 by *F. R. Kempson*; in the E.E. style. Specially ugly W tower, ugly in the mixture of rock-facing and smooth dressings and in the outline of the spire. Nave rock-faced too, chancel of different masonry. Inside, the chancel arch is Norman. Responds with scalloped capitals. Single-step arch. – SCREEN. Low, of one-light divisions. Top cornice with a running leaf-frieze. – PLATE. Cup, 1649.

STOKE PRIOR   5050

ST LUKE. 1863 by *George Colley* of London. Not small. With embattled W tower. – PLATE. Elizabethan Chalice; Cover Paten dated 1584.

THE PRIORY, 300 yds ENE. At the corner of the roads to Risbury and Steen's Bridge. A stone house. It has two blocked windows, probably of the C14.

ROMAN SETTLEMENT. Finds made in the NE part of the parish in the C18 and C19 include foundations of a hypocaust, human and animal bones, Samian and coarse wares, and coins.

STORRIDGE   7040

ST JOHN EVANGELIST. 1856 by *Frederick Preedy* of Worcester. In the style of the late C13. W tower with broach spire. – STAINED GLASS. E window designed by *Preedy*.

STRETFORD   4050

ST PETER. Small, of nave, aisle, and chancel all in one, and with a timber bell-turret. The great surprise is the interior, which explains certain features at first puzzling externally.

★ The authorship is problematic, as Mr Colvin explained to me.

The church consists of two naves and two chancels, or a nave and chancel treated exactly identically with the aisle and chancel chapel. The N part of the church is Norman, *see* the simple N doorway and one Norman window. The S part was added in the early or mid C13, *see* the arcade of two bays and the arch to its E. Pier and responds round with round abaci and simply and heavily moulded capitals. Double-chamfered pointed arches. See also the S lancets and the one N lancet. Lengthening to the E in the Dec style, *see* the low ogee-headed recess in the chancel and the E windows with Y- and intersected tracery but ogee apexes. Good, solid timber S porch dated by the RCHM to the C16 or early C17, but quite possibly earlier. Up to the early C16 the N part and the S part of the church had separate roofs. The furrow between is marked by the top of the wall above the arcade. Then, however, in a bold and wholly successful move, a roof was erected over the whole width of the two naves and chancels. It is this that adds grandeur to the whole. Heraldry dates the roof to *c.*1530. One tie-beam, otherwise arched braces up to collar-beams. Four tiers of cusped wind-braces.* The bell-turret stands on a platform projecting from the W part of the wall above the arcade. – FONT. Norman, undecorated, on an oddly crooked stem. – PULPIT. Jacobean. With blank arches. – SCREENS. Two identical ones across the division between naves and chancels. Rustic work of the early C16, with one-light divisions. – SHRINE. Built against the E respond of the E arch a straight-headed stone shrine with cresting. It dates from the late Middle Ages. Its sill is a fragment of a foliated coffin-lid of the C13. – SCULPTURE. In the S chancel capital of a Norman pillar piscina. – MONUMENTS. Two stone couples in two recesses in the N wall, that further E of *c.*1320–30, the other some twenty years later. Both have the Delabere arms.

STRETTON COURT *see* STRETTON SUGWAS

STRETTON GRANDISON

6040

ST LAWRENCE. All Dec, except the re-set roll moulding round the priest's doorway. W tower with tall double-chamfered arch (the arch dies into the imposts) and with a recessed spire. Nave and chancel with ogee-headed lancets and reticulation motifs in other windows. Easter Sepulchre in the

* Other two-naved C13 churches are at Caythorpe in Lincolnshire and Hannington in Northamptonshire.

chancel N wall. – FONT. Hexagonal, Perp, with quatrefoils, drastically re-cut. – PULPIT. Perp, with panels with top tracery and a cornice of running foliage. – WALL PAINTINGS. Figure of a lady, C14, above the S doorway. – Opposite defaced St Christopher. – ARMOUR. Sleeve and gauntlet below the Hopton monument. – PLATE. Chalice, Paten, and Flagon, c.1675. – MONUMENTS. Sir Edward Hopton † 1668 and wife. Tablet with twisted columns. – William Jauncey † 1797. By *King* of Bath. With a column broken in two parts.

TOWN END FARM, ¼ m. WSW. Of c.1700. Red brick, two storeys, but low, with projecting wings and a hipped roof. In the centre a pediment.

(NEW HOUSE, ¾ m. E. Built c.1600. Inside an overmantel of that date with blank arches and another of the mid C17. RCHM) The house was visited by Celia Fiennes, as it belonged to a relative of hers.

HOMEND, ½ m. E. Early C19. Of five bays and two storeys, but the three-bay centre of two and a half storeys. The ground-floor windows are arched. On the short sides one window each flanked by coupled Corinthian pilasters.

STRETTON SUGWAS   4040

ST MARY MAGDALENE. 1877–80 by *Cheiake*, who later emigrated to Canada. He used a large number of old pieces, especially timbers for the black and white tower, and also windows and doorways, and among them the superb tympanum of Samson and the Lion, by the carver of Brinsop 10 and the Castle Frome font. The long claws of the lion are unmistakable. The parallel folds, here taken over also for Samson's long hair, on the other hand are elements of the Herefordshire School in general. Samson rides the lion. The head of the lion has the Viking character of Kilpeck. He is just engaged in opening the beast's mouth and seems to concentrate on this with an intensity familiar from Castle Frome and Brinsop. Hood-mould on two heads. Rope moulding between them. Norman also the tower W doorway. The timber-framed upper parts of Cheiake's tower are inspired by Holmer. – TILES. In the vestry, C15, one with the date 1456 (cf. Croft). – PLATE. Cup on baluster stem, 1636. – MONUMENT. Splendidly incised slab to Richard Grevelhey and his wife who died in 1473. Smartly dressed. Under a broad canopy.

(BRIDGE, 1¼ m. NE. Small, of one segmental pointed arch.
Perhaps C14. RCHM)

SUGWAS COURT, ¾ m. SSW. 1792 (or 1809?). Of five bays and
two storeys. Brick. The broad segment-headed windows are
characteristic of the date. Round-arched centre window.
The house stands on the foundation of a house of the bishops
of Hereford. The remaining Norman archway, now in the
stables (single-chamfered, with hood-mould), belongs to the
wall of a range, probably the chapel, whose front had traceried
windows.

STRETTON COURT, ¾ m. NE. Simple Later Georgian brick
house. Inside two overmantels, one of the familiar Jacobean
type with caryatids – they hold strapwork shields – and blank
arches filled with big fleurs-de-lis and leafy branches, the
other more restrained and accomplished, with fluted flanking
pilasters and fluted pilasters for the blank arches. The latter
is dated 1598.

SUFTON *see* MORDIFORD

SUGWAS COURT *see* STRETTON SUGWAS

5040   SUTTON

ST NICHOLAS. Early C13 chancel arch on 'Norman' imposts
with a single-chamfered arch. Of the same date the lancet
windows with round rere-arches. Unbuttressed short C16
W tower with corbelled-out parapet. S transept opening in a
two-bay arcade to the nave. The arch mouldings are typical
of the early C14. Outside the transept two re-set C13 corbel-
heads. Nice early C14 piscinas with ballflower decoration in
nave and chancel. C14 timber-framed N porch. – PULPIT.
Jacobean two-decker; simple. – SCREEN. Also simple. One-
light divisions. Dado with two versions of linenfold panelling. – PLATE. Cup, 1636.

ST MICHAEL. Nave and chancel and bell-turret with pyramid
roof. But the arch in the W wall suggests the existence of a
W tower. The W buttresses are probably part of its N and S
walls. In the chancel on the N side and the E side small Norman
windows. In the nave on the N side a blocked Norman doorway. The chancel arch Norman too, but remodelled. Other
windows early C14. – FONTS. One is circular, tub-shaped,
Norman, with four busts of lions against the foot. – The other

is something very rare, a mid-C17, i.e. probably Commonwealth, font. It is very small, an urn of classical shape,
carried by the demi-figure of an angel holding a book. It is
now in the sill of a S window but was found below the E
window of the chancel. At the time the altar table stood in a
W–E position in the chancel. – PLATE. Chalice by *John
Scofield*, London, 1781. – MONUMENT. Elizabeth Cotton,
1654. Big for a tablet. The centre is the inscription. It is
flanked by standing allegorical figures. Above is an open
segmental pediment with reclining putti, below a corpse in a
shroud, and at the foot a putto head. The execution is rustic.
(IVY COTTAGE, E of St Nicholas. The house has a C14 hall.
The central roof-truss has arched braces, a collar-beam, and
a foiled opening above. RCHM)

SUTTON WALLS. An Iron Age hill-fort on a ridge overlooking
the flood plain of the Lugg, ¼ m. N of the church. The fort is
of univallate construction and irregular plan, the rampart
following the contours. Much of the interior of the fort has
been destroyed by quarrying, but the greater part of the
rampart on the N, S, and W is preserved. Recent excavations
have shown that the occupation of the site extended over a
considerable period. The earliest settlement precedes the
construction of the rampart but may have been associated
with a timber palisade. Connected with this occupation is
'duck-stamped' pottery of Iron Age B type. The second
phase is marked by the building of the rampart, material for
which was obtained partly from the ditch cut at the foot of the
slope, partly from shallow scoops at the rear of the rampart.
In these scoops huts were erected; Iron Age B pottery was
found in the occupation material from their floors. About
A.D. 25 the ramparts were raised in height and the revetment
at the W entrance was probably in part rebuilt. A number of
the huts were also reconstructed at this time. The end of this
period, which can be attributed to Belgic immigrants, and
the Roman occupation of the area is marked dramatically by a
large number of skeletons in the ditch, some decapitated and
others showing evidence of wounds – presumably the native
defenders. After this attack the rampart was allowed to fall
rapidly into decay, and some deliberate destruction may
have taken place. Settlement, in the form of huts similar to
the pre-Roman examples, did continue however, and in the
C2 a more solidly constructed dwelling with a stone-paved
floor was erected on the site. A stone-built corn-drying kiln

may also belong to this period. Finally the interior of the fort was given over to agriculture and continued to be ploughed well into the C 4.

SWANSTONE COURT *see* DILWYN

6040   TARRINGTON

ST PHILIP AND ST JAMES. The church is Norman, i.e. nave and chancel, and formerly an apse, the SW beginning of which was left exposed after excavation. Much of the Norman work is fully preserved. Both nave doorways have one order of shafts and decorated capitals. The man and horse however cannot be trusted. In the chancel N wall two windows whose arch blocks, made of one piece as usual, are decorated with arbitrary geometrical motifs not fitted to the place. Inside, three windows have a curious frieze of holes along the arch. Were they filled with some other material? Also inside, the tower arch, somewhat changed – *see* the N capital – and the jambs of the chancel arch are Norman. The capitals have scallops and also heads. The abacus is decorated. The hood-mould rests on the l. on two little men. Perp W tower with diagonal buttresses, twin bell-openings with a shaft, usually an earlier motif, and a parapet with blank arches. Perp chancel E and (very renewed) four-light S windows. N aisle of 1835. – FONT. Octagonal, with pretty cusped panels each an open tulip-shape of two ogee curves. – STAINED GLASS. In the chancel S window original fragments, including parts of figures; C14–15. – PLATE. Late C17 Cup and Cover Paten. – MONUMENTS. Coffin-lid with a plain cross and two rings hanging from the cross-bar. What can be its date and significance? – Effigy of a Lady of *c*.1360 in an early C14 tomb recess with buttresses and finial. Decorated with dog-tooth and ballflower. – CHURCHYARD CROSS. With steps and base, but only a sorry stump of the shaft.

FOLEY ARMS, on the main road. Late Georgian. Of red brick, three bays and two storeys. One-bay pediment. Porch with Tuscan columns.

(FOLEY COTTAGE, I m. SSE of the church, has cruck-trusses in the E and W walls. RCHM)

TEDGEWOOD *see* UPTON BISHOP

TEDSTONE DELAMERE   *6050*

St James. Nave and chancel and timber bell-turret with spire.
In the nave two Norman windows of tufa. The w quoins are
blocks of tufa too. One s lancet further E. The chancel 1856–7
by *Sir G. G. Scott*. – SCREEN. Simple, with one-light divisions. – HOUR GLASS. In the porch, l. of the doorway. –
STAINED GLASS. E window by *Hardman*, 1857 (TK). – Nave
N by *Kempe & Tower*, c.1905. – PLATE. Cup and Cover Paten,
1573; Flagon, London, 1715. – CHURCHYARD CROSS. Lower
part C14, upper part 1629. The C14 head now near the w
gate of the churchyard. On one face Crucifixus, on the other
Virgin and Child.

TEDSTONE WAFRE   *6050*

St Mary. Of the old church the w and part of the N walls
stand to about 6 ft. No features of interest. The new church
dates from 1873 and was designed by *Haycock*. It looks as if
it were made of old-fashioned children's building bricks.
Nave and chancel in one. Very tall roof of red and blue tiles.
Oversized bellcote. s chapel and s porch with useless buttresses.
(Of the medieval CHURCHYARD CROSS, the head in two
pieces is preserved in two trefoiled niches in the churchyard
wall.)
High Lane, 1 m. N. A stone house with an austere three-bay
s front. Wide bays, central canted bay, hipped roof.

THING HILL GRANGE *see* WITHINGTON

THORNBURY   *6050*

St Anne. Unbuttressed C13 w tower. Norman nave, chancel
of 1865 (by *Kempson*), but with re-set C13 lancet. In the nave
on the N side a Norman window (and one of c.1300) and a
Norman doorway. This has primitive capitals, one with
volutes. Arch with zigzag. On the s side remains of the
mid-C13 arcade to a s aisle. Circular piers, heavy moulded
capitals, double-chamfered arches. Simple (re-set) C13 s doorway. – FONT. Norman, of tub shape. With a frieze of lozenges
within lozenges. – PLATE. Chalice, London, 1571; Salver by
Hugh Roberts, London, 1703.
(Wooding Farm. One roof-truss of the C14 hall with arched
braces, collar, and foiled openings. RCHM)

NETHERWOOD, *see* Collington, p. 104.

(PARK PALE, surrounding Park Farm, ¾ m. from the church. The area enclosed is 97 acres. Rampart and external ditch. The pale probably separated the cultivated from the forest land. RCHM)

4030   THRUXTON

ST BARTHOLOMEW. Mostly Dec, *see* the bell-openings of the W tower, the chancel windows, except for the Early Perp E window, the nave windows, the timber S porch with its pointed-trefoiled wind-braces, and the scissor-braced nave roof. – FONT. Octagonal, with a small bowl on which panels with an inscription which reads: This fonte was made March 16th 1677. An inscription is on the foot as well: Baptismus est ablutio peccatorum. – STAINED GLASS. In the chancel on the S side in the tracery top a small but excellent Crucifixus of the early C14, with ample brown loin-cloth. – PLATE. Elizabethan Cover Paten, inscribed 1577; Cup on baluster stem, 1633.

MOUND. A possible Bronze Age round barrow, 126 ft in diameter, lies 100 yards W of the church. It is surrounded by a ditch and has a slight outer bank on the NW. Excavation in the C19 is said to have revealed a rough chamber of stones within the mound. There are no records of this excavation. The site may be a Bronze Age round barrow covering a large stone cist.

3060   TITLEY

ST PETER. 1868 by *E. Haycock Jun.* – PLATE. Chalice, London, 1569; Paten probably of the same time; Almsdish, London, 1712 by *Anthony Nelme*; Flagon, London, 1714; Chalice 1731 and Paten 1733 by *Richard Bayley*.

TITLEY COURT, ⅓ m. S. Victorian exterior, but inside a fine stucco ceiling of the later C17 and some Jacobean woodwork. The ceiling has panels enclosing wreaths. One overmantel comes from Upper Mowley near Staunton-on-Arrow and is dated 1625. Another is made up of a variety of disjointed pieces.

Titley also had a small CELL of the Order of Tiron, of which there were only four houses in England, the other three being in Hampshire.

TRASECH *see* HENTLAND

TREAGO CASTLE *see* ST WEONARDS

TREGATE CASTLE *see* LLANROTHAL

TRERIBBLE *see* LLANGARRON

TRETIRE   *5020*

ST MARY. Nave and chancel and thin polygonal stone bell-turret. Almost entirely of 1856. In the style of 1300.

RECTORY. Stone, with segment-headed windows. Built by a rector who died in 1722. (In the garden a round-headed Norman window. RCHM)

TUPSLEY *see* HEREFORD, p. 176

TURNASTONE   *3030*

ST MARY MAGDALENE. Small nave and chancel in one. Little bell-turret with pyramid roof. Late Norman S doorway with illiterate moulded capitals. Two nave windows of *c.*1300. Handsome ceiled wagon roof with bosses. – PULPIT. Simple; Jacobean. – PLATE. Chalice, London, 1611. – MONUMENTS. Incised slab to Thomas Aparri † 1522 and wife. Very enjoyable portraiture. To the l. of his head a little satyr with a big hat playing the pipe. – Mrs Traunter † 1685. Exuberantly but rustically decorated tablet with twisted columns, two allegorical figurines at the top, a cherub's head at the foot, and much foliage.

WHITEHOUSE, ¾ m. SW. L-shaped. One wing C17, gabled, with mullioned and transomed windows, the other of stone, Late Georgian, of three widely spaced bays and two storeys with a parapet and pointed windows. (Inside, an overmantel with blank arches in which paintings of a bust of a man with a globe and an inscription. The fireplaces come from a destroyed E wing. RCHM and information kindly given me by Mr A. S. Wood.)

TYBERTON   *3030*

ST MARY. In the grounds of Tyberton Court, which was built by *John Wood* of Bath, but has been pulled down. Wood appeared on the scene in 1728. But the church was built in

1719–21 and thus need not be Wood's design.* It is of brick. The w tower has arched windows and a top with urn pinnacles and four little pediments between. The windows of both nave and chancel were unfortunately converted into lancets in 1879 and filled with plate glass. s porch with arched doorway. Tunnel-vaulted ceiling inside. Oddly enough, the c18 client kept the Late Norman s doorway of the preceding church. It has one order of shafts with tall scalloped capitals. Almost perfectly preserved FURNISHINGS. The FONT has a fluted stem and a bowl with cherub heads. – The LECTERN is a kneeling angel. Specially pretty base. – The ROYAL ARMS have nicely carved decoration above the frame and are dated 1720. – BOX PEWS and simple two-decker PULPIT. – COMMUNION RAIL. With thin twisted balusters. Another communion rail with pierced flat balusters under the tower 58a (probably Jacobean). – But the finest thing is the PANELLING behind the altar, apsidal within the straight E end. This was indeed designed by *Wood*. It was designed in 1728 and completed in 1731. It has beautifully carved emblems like trophies, of God, of Christ, of the Passion, and others. – CANDLESTICKS. Two fluted Ionic columns. – PLATE. Set of two Chalices and Cover Patens, Flagon, and Salver, all 1720 by *Gabriel Sleath*. – MONUMENTS. William Brydges † 1668, with twisted columns. – Margaret Brydges † 1671, with two standing allegorical figures and two small ones at the top. – Mrs Anne Brydges † 1696 with two columns and a cartouche at the foot. – Francis Brydges † 1727 and his first wife † 1691, almost the same. – William Brydges † 1764. A putto flies down and holds a scroll with the inscription. By *Thomas King* of Bath. – Francis W. T. Brydges † 1793. With a draped urn. Also by *King* of Bath. The Brydges family lived at Tyberton Court. The Duke of Chandos, John Wood's early patron, was a Brydges. – CHURCHYARD CROSS. Complete with its head, with the Crucifixus on one side, the Virgin seated on the other.

TY MAWR *see* CLODOCK

5040

ULLINGSWICK

CHURCH. Nave and chancel and timber bell-turret with a pretty Victorian bell-stage (by *Kempson*). In the nave two Norman

---

* I owe much information on the church and its history to Mr Bruce Bailey.

windows and a lancet in the W wall. The church was probably
lengthened in the C13. The chancel windows point to the late
C13 or c.1300 and include the Herefordshire-Special of three
lights under one arch. – STAINED GLASS. In the E window
bust of the Virgin and Child; C15. In the other chancel
windows acceptable imitation C13 glass of c.1850–60. –
MONUMENTS. In the chancel on the N side C13 coffin-lid
with foliated cross adapted to re-use in 1699. – John Hill
† 1591. Painted on stone four kneeling figures l. and r. of the
effigy of John Hill recumbent on a tomb-chest.

LOWER COURT FARM. The house, described by the RCHM, is
now externally all weatherboarded. Inside, a Jacobean overmantel with a little stucco decoration of fleurs-de-lis and
pomegranates.

UPHAMPTON *see* SHOBDON

UPPER GOYTRE *see* WALTERSTONE

UPPER NASH FARM *see* RODD

UPPER SAPEY

6060

ST MICHAEL. Nave and chancel Norman. Norman N chancel
window, blocked N doorway with two orders of shafts carrying
capitals with elementary leaf and scroll decoration. Arch with
zigzag at r. angles to the wall. Similar S doorway. In the
chancel on the S side two windows of c.1300, one a low-side
window, the other of two lights with a transom (an unusual
detail). Short unbuttressed W tower of 1859 with a broached
truncated pyramid roof and a spire. Inside, the chancel arch
was shifted to become the tower arch. It has two orders of
shafts and capitals similar to those of the doorways. The
arch again has zigzag at r. angles and in addition a rare motif:
rows of pointed arches meeting along the edge of an arch
order, one row parallel with the wall, the other at r. angles to
it. – PULPIT and other woodwork carved by *John Kitchen*, a
carpenter who worked from c.1860 onwards. Some panels,
however, are supposed to be genuine. – BENCHES. Four plain
early C16 benches with straight-topped ends. They have
moulded edges and tops. – PLATE. Cup, 1571.

UPPER WYTHALL *see* WALFORD-ON-WYE

6020

UPTON BISHOP

ST JOHN BAPTIST. Blocked Early Norman N doorway. To this
nave a Late Norman S arcade of three bays was added.
Circular piers, capitals with trumpet scallops or upright
leaves, square abaci, but pointed double-chamfered arches.
The chancel was rebuilt early in the C13, *see* the two remaining
tall lancets in the E wall, part of a former group of three,
no doubt stepped. The middle one was replaced by a Dec
window. In the N wall one C13 lancet, and one Dec window
with a head in flat relief in the spandrel between the two lights.
The two E lancets are shafted inside. Big, grey Perp W tower
with diagonal buttresses. Restored by *Sir G. G. Scott* in 1862.
– FONT. Octagonal, Perp, with quatrefoils. – PULPIT.
Jacobean, with the usual blank arches. – SCULPTURE. Built
into the wall of the chancel is a Roman tombstone. The
surviving portion depicts the head and shoulders of a man
with right hand raised, inset in a round-headed recess. Alongside
this figure is a second fragment, again in a recess, and
now represented only by a fragment of the left hand. –
STAINED GLASS. Original bits in the S aisle windows. – Nave
N, by the pulpit, c.1855 by *Clayton & Bell*. – By the same a
chancel S window, c.1875. – In the chancel on the N one two-
light window by *Wailes*. – By *Hardman* the E window and,
c.1865, a S aisle window (Good Samaritan). – MONUMENT.
In a tomb recess in the S aisle effigy of a Civilian under a flat
ogee canopy, mid-C14. What is the square object he is
holding?
UPTON COURT, ¾ m. NE. A stone house of the C14 with
additions. Much remains of the C14 roof. Tie-beams and
collar-beams and foiled openings between them. Also the
tops of the principals, foiled, and pointed-trefoiled wind-
braces.
(TEDGEWOOD, ¾ m. E. Timber-framed, early C16, with, in the
E front, posts with attached shafts. RCHM)
FELHAMPTON, ⅗ m. SW. Timber-framed, and impressive to
look at. Gabled and with narrow uprights, big diagonals on
ground floor and first floor, and more and smaller diagonals
in the gable.

UPTON COURT *see* **LITTLE HEREFORD**
and **UPTON BISHOP**

URISHAY CASTLE *see* PETERCHURCH

VAULD FARM *see* MARDEN

VOWCHURCH   *3030*

ST BARTHOLOMEW.* Nave and chancel in one. Bell-turret of
timber, dateable *c.*1522 by a bequest. The rest mostly the
work which was consecrated in 1348.‡ The windows include
the typical Herefordshire three-light type, but there is also
one Norman s window. Dec again the s doorway with sunk-
quadrant mouldings. s porch with slim C17 balusters. The
interior provides the clue for this. It was largely re-equipped
in or *c.*1613. Roof on timber posts set inside the stone walls.
Tie-beams, queenposts, and collar-beams. Modest Jacobean
decoration. At the w end however the posts for the bell-turret
must be the original ones, even if they received some Jacobean
decoration. The posts incidentally are not braced by scissor-
bracing, as e.g. in Essex or at Pembridge. The chancel roof
also is medieval and probably of before 1348. Trusses with
cusped raking struts. Dec also the two recesses in the nave
N wall. – FONT. Norman, with fluted bowl. – SCREEN. Dated
1613. With sparse balusters and two funny caryatids (Adam
and Eve?). Top pediment. – STALLS. Two backs are dated
1636. – COMMUNION RAIL. Also C17, but rather *c.*1675. –
PLATE. Cup and Cover Paten, 1688; also a wooden C17 Cup
with baluster stem; Jacobean. – MONUMENT. Sir Edward
Boughton † 1794 (*see* below). With profile in a medallion
against an obelisk.

OLD VICARAGE, to the SE. Early C16, with narrowly-set
uprights. In the l. gable herringbone strutting.

POSTON LODGE (also Poston House), 1 m. N. Built *c.*1780 by
Sir William Chambers for Sir Edward Boughton as a shooting
box and still used as such about 1870. It is a real bijou, tucked
away in the woods and with a glorious view to the SE. Unfortunately it has been inflated by two Victorian wings.
Originally it consisted of a Tuscan portico with wooden
pediment, an entrance hall, and a domed circular room. This
still has its delicate, very restrained stucco decoration and
chimneypiece.

* Thus in Crockford.
‡ The Rev. J. C. Davies draws my attention to this date.

(TUMPS, less than ½ m. SSE. Two, on either side of the stream.
The larger is 64 yds in diameter, the smaller 46 by 40. RCHM).
(MOUND, 1¼ m. ENE. Oval, *c.* 60 by 52 yds. RCHM)

HILL-FORT. There is a multivallate rampart fort on a promontory 1 m. N of the church and 200 yards S of Poston
House. Excavations conducted between 1932 and 1937
revealed a number of structural alterations during the occupation of the site. The first earthwork, erected at the end of the
C1 B.C., consisted of a single rampart with outer ditch. Sherds
of Iron Age B pottery were recovered from hut sites of this
period immediately within the ramparts. The ditch of this
fort was soon allowed to silt up and huts were constructed
within it – a state of affairs which appears to have been
maintained until the middle of the C1 A.D. Then, probably as
a reaction against the Roman invasion of south-east Britain,
the area of the fort was extended and a second rampart and
ditch were constructed with a stone revetment at the entrance.
The huts of this period were of stone and had clay floors. A
third structural phase is marked by the provision of a third
rampart and ditch laid out between the two pre-existing
ramparts and the moving of the entrance through the outer
rampart to the E end of the fort. This final building period is
probably to be ascribed to the years of Frontinus's campaign
in the Welsh Marches. Occupation continued into the Roman
period and is marked by vessels of wheel-turned, Romano-
British coarse wares.

6050   WACTON

CHURCH. In 1932, when the volumes of the RCHM came out,
the walls still stood up to 5 ft. There is much less left now.

MOUND, NW of the church. Oval; small.

3070   WALFORD
                   1¼ m. SW of Leintwardine

COURT HOUSE. Inside, remains of a Jacobean plaster frieze.
Lozenge-shaped panels; one with a mermaid. (Also two
capitals, one C12, the other C13, probably from Wigmore
Abbey. RCHM)

ROUND BARROW, 270 yds S of the cross-roads at Walford. The
barrow is 94 ft in diameter and 9 ft high. An urn was found
in it in the C19.

WALFORD-ON-WYE

ST MICHAEL. Essentially of the C13, in the following order.
First the N arcade of four bays with round piers with round
capitals and abaci. One pier still has a trumpet-scallop capital,
the others a frieze of small upright stiff-leaf. The arches are
already pointed and double-chamfered. There is also the W
lancet window left. Then the chancel arch, with a fillet down
the semicircular responds, and the N chapel of three bays.
Circular piers with crudely moulded capitals and abaci. One
capital was left unmoulded. Of the same time the N tower,
which adjoins the N chapel. The bell-openings are small
lancets. Perp chancel E window, all renewed. – FONT. Octagonal, Perp, with quatrefoils on the bowl, and on the foot
pretty fleurons, leaf paterae, etc. – COMMUNION RAIL. Of
c.1700. – HELM. Funeral helm of c.1600 (above the chancel
arch). – PLATE. Chalice, London, 1692. – MONUMENTS.
Tablet to William Adams, 1681, and in the same style but
more ambitious, with allegorical figures l. and r., Edmund
Yerne † 1707 (both chancel E). – Stratford family (latest date
1709), with fluted Corinthian pilasters and two mourning
putti. – John Stratford † 1738. With skulls and cherubs' heads
at the foot.

UPPER WYTHALL, ¾ m. ENE, up Bull's Hill. Picturesque black
and white house of the early C16 to early C17. The front has
a variety of gables of different sizes and at different heights.

THE CEDARS, ¼ m. NE. Late Georgian, of four bays with a
two-bay pediment and a Greek Doric porch of four columns.

HILL COURT. A monumentally spreading symmetrical house
of red brick, first visible from the E down a long avenue. The
centre was built in 1698–1700. It is of seven bays and was
originally (see Buck's engraving of Goodrich Castle) of two
storeys with a big hipped roof on dormers. In the C18 a half
storey and a half-parapet–half-balustrade were added and
the roof lowered. The doorway to the garden with its open
scrolly pediment is original, that to the entrance is later C18,
though it seems to connect quite well with the window
above, which is distinguished by volutes down its sides. The
entrance side has a three-bay pediment beautifully carved
with cornucopias etc. and quoins for the angles of the three
bays as well as the angles of the façades. In 1732 one-bay
wings were added, connected by lower one-bay links. The
wings have pediments to E as well as W, and on the ground

floor Venetian windows. The windows of the centre were of course originally of the cross-type, i.e. not sashed. One such window survives on the N side of the centre block. Inside, the best room of *c*.1700 is the staircase hall. It has a plaster ceiling with a boldly detached wreath of fruit, flowers, etc., and the staircase itself has twisted balusters and carved tread-ends. On the first floor the middle room has marbled panelling. Excellent fireplace of *c*.1760 (not originally belonging to the house) in the Drawing Room in one of the wings. (Also one bedroom with late C17 chinoiserie painting. E. Croft-Murray) In front of the forecourt on the entrance side splendid GATEPIERS with splendid vases. The iron gates between are of 1933. – DOVECOTE, also of *c*.1700, also of brick, octagonal with a lantern.

(GREAT HOWLE, 1½ m. E of the church. Camp on the top of Howle Hill. Rectangular enclosure, the rampart up to 11½ ft high. RCHM).

ROMAN CAMP. 50 yds N of the church is the site of a camp of rectangular plan in which a hoard of nearly 18,000 Roman coins, contained in three urns, was found in the C19. The coins are nearly all of C 4 date.

3020

WALTERSTONE

ST MARY. Nave and chancel, with a big Victorian bellcote. No features of interest. – SCULPTURE. In the porch a stiff-leaf bracket not *in situ*. – STAINED GLASS. In the chancel on the S side a C17 piece with heraldry and foliage. – PLATE. Chalice and Cover Paten, inscribed 1718. – MONUMENTS. Slate tablets to members of the Price family, one of them († 1775) signed by *Aaron Brute*. – CHURCHYARD CROSS. The shaft is preserved.

CASTLE, W of the church. Motte and bailey. The motte rises 30 ft above the bottom of the ditch. The bailey is of kidney shape and lies to the E and SE.

UPPER GOYTRE, ¾ m. E. In one room a low ceiling with heavily moulded beams and stops of long flat leaf at the ends of the beams and the joints. Early Tudor no doubt.

ALLT-Y-YNYS, 1 m. SSW. In a room a plaster ceiling of *c*.1600 with thin ribs forming polygons, stars, etc., and small ornamental motifs between.

(COURT FARM, 350 yds SE. Inside, a cruck-truss forming a pointed arch. RCHM)

HILL-FORT, on a spur ½ m. E of the church. Probably of Iron
Age date, the site consists of a roughly circular area of about
10 acres enclosed by three concentric ramparts broken by
entrances on the SW and NE. Outside the ramparts on the NE
are a complex series of outworks, rectangular mounds, and
ditches. Their relationship to the fort is uncertain.

BARROW. 300 yds SW of the church is a possible Bronze Age
round barrow, 21 ft in diameter and 2½ ft high.

SETTLEMENT. A Roman settlement is attested by the finding of
a mosaic pavement in the C18. The exact location of the site
within the parish is uncertain.

WELLBROOK MANOR *see* PETERCHURCH

WELLINGTON   4040

ST MARGARET. Much of the church is Late Norman, and first
of all the curious W tower. It starts with rubble and ashlar
dressings, and broad flat buttresses, shafted. Some shafts
stand on corbels, others have extremely odd waist-bands.
The capitals are of the trumpet-type or have a head or
crockets. Some windows pierce the buttresses. The next
stage is rubble, and the buttresses stop some way up. The
next stage after that is ashlar-faced and resumes the motif of
the buttresses. It has single-chamfered bell-openings. Finally
the top stage, which is rubble and embattled. The tower arch
towards the nave is very simple, but not Norman any longer.
Its capitals and mouldings, however, are those of the chancel
arch, which is depressed rounded, i.e. purely Norman, whereas
the tower arch is pointed. Norman also a blocked nave S
window, the plain N and S doorways, and the moulding of the
head of the priest's doorway. There is no E.E. contribution,
except for one lancet and the beautiful little piscina in the
chancel which has a corbel with upright leaves. It should
however also be considered whether the double-hollow-
chamfered N arcade arches are not re-used C13 material. Dec
nave windows, Dec S porch (ballflower in the abaci of the
entrance, splendid roof with much-cusped timbers and foiled
wind-braces), Dec tomb recess in the chancel. Perp N transept
with big N window. Perp arcade to the N aisle with coarse
octagonal piers. The double-hollow-chamfered arches have
already been mentioned. A half-arch of the same moulding
rises as a division between aisle and transept. Fine N aisle
roof with two tiers of quatrefoiled wind-braces. Can it really 36

be Perp? Single-frame nave roof with tie-beams. – PULPIT. Jacobean, with the usual blank arches. – STAINED GLASS. In the chancel SE window some original fragments, including a head of a monk. – PLATE. Chalice and Cover Paten, London, 1702. – MONUMENT. Sir Herbert Perrot † 1683. Tablet with twisted columns. – CHURCHYARD CROSS. With tall polygonal shaft.

Several attractive buildings in the village, especially the octagonal brick DOVECOTE of a farm SW of the church, and the OLD VICARAGE, a little further W, which is black and white and dated 1636.

BRIDGE INN, ¼ m. E. A large Early Georgian inn, the façade of eight bays, three, three recessed, two. The windows are segment-headed. Broad angle pilasters.

ALMSHOUSES, S of the former. 1682, but almost entirely remodelled in 1887.

WELLINGTON HEATH

7040

CHRIST CHURCH. 1951, using parts of the church of 1840.

PEG'S FARM, ½ m. WNW. A C14 house in which the present owners have exemplarily exposed the original roof-trusses, the spere-truss as well as foiled openings above the collar-beams. This was done without removing the ceiling inserted in the early C16 to divide the hall horizontally. The ceiling has heavily moulded beams.

WOOD HOUSE FARM, 1½ m. WNW. Also probably of the C14, but the roof construction including the spere-truss, the central cruck-truss of the hall with a collar-beam halved in, and foiled raking struts not now visible.

BURTON'S FARM, ¾ m. SW. Early C16 and early C17. The former the closely-set uprights, the latter the square framing.

WELSH BICKNOR

5010

ST MARGARET. 1858–9 by *T. H. Rushforth* of London. Paid for by the rector and Stephen Allaway. A costly looking job. Externally a curious mixture of Norman and E.E., e.g. a Norman W wall with an E.E. W porch. SW tower with spire. Two-bay S arcade with a pier carrying a tremendous alabaster capital with heads at the angles. Heads also the motif of the stone FONT and the stone PULPIT. On the other hand plenty of birds round the chancel arch. – Good STAINED

GLASS in the chancel, in the style of the C13. – PLATE. Elizabethan Cup and Cover Paten, dated 1576. – MONUMENT. Excellent late C13 effigy of a Lady, the oddly boneless or jointless arms still in the tradition of Westminster and Wells, i.e. the mid C13. In the same tradition the many parallel angular folds down one leg. To the l. and r. of the head angels. – CHURCHYARD CROSS. A big, monumental piece; Victorian.

WELSH NEWTON

4010

ST MARY. Very thin w tower with small stone spire, yet attributed by the RCHM to the late C13. Nave and chancel in one, definitely of the C13, *see* e.g. the two w lancets. The most striking window is the Dec dormer window on the s side. The window itself is of two lights with a reticulation unit. The position explains itself inside. The window was intended to give light to the ROOD SCREEN, erected at the same time, and an important piece in that it is of stone and so early. Three bays. Octagonal shafts. Many-moulded arches. Hood-mould, and also top cornice with ballflower decoration. There is no structural division between nave and chancel. The ceiled wagon roof runs right through. At the junctions of the ribs – in fact rafters, purlins, braces, etc. – little bosses. – STONE SEAT in the chancel on the N side, the arms with stone knobs l. and r. of the back and at the end where the hands rest. Probably of the C13. – PLATE. Chalice (from Llanrothal), by *R.S.*, 1618; Cup and Cover Paten by *I.L.*, 1689. – MONUMENT. John Kemble, Catholic priest, executed in 1679. Tomb-slab inscribed: 'I.K. Dyed the 22 of August Anno Do 1679.' In the churchyard under the cross. – The church incidentally had a chantry founded in 1547. Is that the last in England?

WEOBLEY

4050

ST PETER AND ST PAUL. Set back from the street, and with views into the fields to the N. The showpiece of the church is the tall C14 NW tower with its commanding spire. But the building history of the church starts much earlier. The s doorway is Norman. Of the capitals of the shafts only one is left, with upright ribbed leaves. The arch has zigzag at r. angles to the wall surface. The chancel is of the later C13, *see* the chancel arch on tripartite shafts. They have fillets and stand on corbels. Of the chancel s windows one is of three stepped lancets, shafted inside, another has Y-tracery. The E window is Perp. Also of the later C13 the S transept, the piscina, pointed-trefoiled and also with dog-tooth and the (re-set?) hood-mould with dog-tooth above the E window. With the (five-bay) arcades we move into the C14. Octagonal piers, arches with chamfers with hollows. The NE arch has ball-flower enrichment, and so has the W doorway, inside and outside. The clerestory is contemporary too. It has windows of two lights with pre-ogee tracery. The N transept also belongs to the same campaign, and so does the curious recess to the S of the chancel arch. It has a cinquefoiled ogee head under a crocketed gable. The bracket for an image is carried by an excellent figure. The completion of all these works, which began late in the C13, may be indicated by a conse-cration of three altars in 1325. The tower followed next. Why it does not stand in line with the nave and the then narrower aisles cannot be said. The tower probably just touched the N aisle. A skew arch leads into it. The tower has clasping buttresses. On the ground stage are three-light windows with reticulated tracery. The l. and r. lights are blocked and have brackets for images. On the top are tall, square, panelled pinnacles with crocketed spirelets, connected by flying buttresses with the spire, the only example of this type in the county. A tier of lucarnes with Dec tracery starts right at the foot of the spire. They serve as bell-openings. Perp widening of the N aisle. – FONT. Octagonal, early C14, with arches demonstrating a variety of tracery motifs of that moment, i.e. the pre-ogee moment, as if they were taken from a pattern book. Flat relief. – PULPIT. Parts of a C14 stone pulpit with moulded sides are lying in the church. – SCREEN. Parts in the N aisle, including a post with a shield bearing the symbol of the Trinity. – STAINED GLASS. In the tracery of a N window, five figures of seraphim; C15. – PLATE. Elizabethan Chalice, 1595 (?); Chalice, London, 1636 (re-modelled); Plate and Flagon, London, 1747. – MONUMENTS. In the S aisle at the E end C13 coffin-lid with uncommonly fine foliated cross. It commemorates Hugo Bissop of Norton Canon. – So-called Sir William Devereux, c.1430. Alabaster effigy on a tomb-chest with shields in quatrefoils. – Dame Alice Crutwell and Sir John Marbury † 1437. Two alabaster effigies in a simple recess with ogee top. – Col. John Birch † 1691. White marble statue in armour pointing with his baton. Against a background of light and dark grey marble. Corinthian columns, open

pediment. – Ann Birch † 1846, by *R. Westmacott Jun.* Tablet
with a wheatsheaf and a sickle.

ST THOMAS OF HEREFORD (R.C.), Kington Road. 1834.
Small, of stone, with pointed windows. The adjoining priest's
house is higher and of brick.

CASTLE, ¼ m. S of the church and immediately W of Hereford
Street. Earthwork, much damaged on the W side. On the E a
semicircular bank, and S of this a deep double ditch. There
appear to have been C13 stone fortifications with round towers.
But of these nothing remains. The castle originally belonged
to the Lacys.

RURAL DISTRICT OFFICES, former Workhouse, ½ m. W. Red
brick, of the usual plan, and still in Latest-Georgian forms.
Probably *c.*1836.

PERAMBULATION. Weobley is uncommonly rich in early
timber-framed houses. Broad Street, the main street, runs 2a
N–S away from the church, with a W and NW branch at the N
end and W and E branches at the S end. Until a few years ago
the High Street had an island of houses in the middle of its
S part, but that was destroyed by fire and has been replaced
by some, rather self-conscious, planting and a bus shelter.
Walking S from the E end of the church one at once reaches
the RED LION. An outbuilding at its back has exposed crucks. 31
The Red Lion itself has a fine E cross-wing of the C14. Sturdy
angle-posts with moulded capitals. Square panels above.
Heads of two three-light windows with cusped ogee lights.
At the N end, ogee door-head. To the S heavy arched braces
l. and r. of the upper window. To the W on the S side of the
street a house of the C14 (TUDOR HOUSE), with large square
framing, cusped diagonal braces, and traceried bargeboards.
(Inside, it has the original roofs in the centre, i.e. the hall,
and the wings. Foiled openings above the collar-beams and
foiled wind-braces. RCHM) The r. neighbour of the house
has traceried bargeboards too. In MEADOW STREET, leading
N, the first old house on the E side is again C14 or C15. Timber-
framing in big squares. (A cruck-truss inside with an arch-
braced collar-beam and foiled raking struts above. *Arch. J.*,
CIX, 151) At the corner where Meadow Street turns W two
C15 or C16 houses with closely-set uprights.

Up BROAD STREET. At the corner facing the Red Lion a house
of the C14 or C15. Big square framing. Sturdy angle-post
with moulded capital. Then a whole group on the E side, and
specially one externally very perfect specimen with stone

ground floor and the C14 type of hall with higher gabled solar
wing and buttery wing. Arched braces l. and r. of the upper
window in one gable, cusped braces in the other. Late
Georgian porch with Tuscan columns. s of this some C18
brick houses, one with an arched recess above the doorway.
On the other side, facing the council planting, a C15 house
with coving in the hall range to bring the roof in line with the
gabled wings (so-called Wealden type). Original middle
window on the first floor. (Inside, two ogee-headed doorways.
RCHM)

Then into the HIGH STREET, and first to the SW. At the junction
of High Street and CHAMBER WALK a C14 house of which
one cross-wing has disappeared. Big square framing. In the
gable one pair of cusped braces. Near the l. end an original
mullioned window. On the other side a little further s a tall,
gaunt red brick house of five bays with arched windows. Each
arch has an outer band of blue vitrified bricks. The house was
a corn-mill and may well be as late as c.1840. Finally the E
part of the High Street, with the excellent C14 W part of the
UNICORN HOTEL. C14 gable with cusped diagonal braces.
Inside, an ogee-headed doorway. The part of the hotel to
the r. has the same coving as we have seen in Broad Street.
Round the corner into HEREFORD STREET. The house called
THE THRONE is of c.1600; its main window is not original.
So to the old GRAMMAR SCHOOL on the other side. This is
Jacobean, and has a symmetrical front with central porch.
Scrolly spandrels and brackets.

THE LEY, ¾ m. SW. Dated 1589. Timber-framed. The charm
of the house is the play of gables: gables of the wings, of the
centre, of the porch, and slightly lower gables of three bay
windows. The porch breaks the general symmetry. It is still,
in the medieval way, at the lower end of the central hall.

FENHAMPTON, 1¼ m. SW. Jacobean. E front with two gables
and a gabled porch.

(LITTLE SARNESFIELD, 1 m. W. Probably C14. Hall and two
cross-wings. In the s wing two original trusses, one with a
tie-beam on arched braces and foiled openings above, the
other with a collar-beam on arched braces and a trefoil
above. RCHM)

5040

WESTHIDE

ST BARTHOLOMEW. Short, unbuttressed late C12 W tower with
pyramid roof. The arch towards the nave has responds with

trumpet-scallop capitals. Broad pointed arch with two slight chamfers. Chancel and nave N side rebuilt in 1866–7. S aisle early C14 – *see* the S doorway (sunk-quadrant mouldings), the W doorway, the windows, including the E window which has reticulated tracery, and the arcade of two bays with octagonal pier and arches whose mouldings have one chamfer and one slight chamfer. Tomb recess in the S wall. The chancel arch is of a similar date. Head-brackets in the E walls of the chancel (re-set) and the S aisle. – PAINTING. Nice original red scroll-work in the soffit of the S aisle E window. – PLATE. Chalice, probably Elizabethan; Cover Paten, inscribed 1629; Paten by *John Ruslen* of London, 1709; Salver by *Gabriel Sleath* of London, 1725. – MONUMENTS. In the recess, effigy of a Civilian holding his heart in his hands, early C14. – Also in the S aisle fragmentary Elizabethan slab with two effigies, now standing on its side. – Alabaster slab with the incised figures of Richard Monyngton † 1524 and wife. Below, sixteen children. – CHURCHYARD CROSS. Steps, base, and stump of shaft.

WESTINGHOUSE COURT *see* GRENDON BISHOP

WESTON BEGGARD 5040

ST JOHN BAPTIST. S doorway of *c.*1200. Continuous roll and chamfer. Hood-mould on a head and a leaf knob. Also of *c.*1200 the chancel arch. One trumpet-scallop capital, one with simple flat upright leaves. Double-chamfered arch. W tower of the C14. Diagonal buttresses. Arch towards the nave of three continuous chamfers. The windows of the church all renewed (restoration 1881, *T. Nicholson*), but indicating the late C13 and early C14. The entrance of the S porch goes with that date. In the chancel on the S side an uncommonly sump-tuous tomb recess. It is not strictly pre-ogee, as there is one inconspicuous ogee there, but essentially it still represents the stage of *c.*1300–10. Cusped and subcusped arch, all spandrels with leaves and suspended shields. The gable also with much foliage. Short buttresses with broken finials, crockets up the sides of the gable, big finial on top. Opposite a much simpler tomb recess with ballflower decoration. – CHURCHYARD CROSS. On top of the base a tiny sundial of 1649.

HILL END FARMHOUSE, ⅓ m. WNW. One wing is of the early

C17. It is of stone and has four-light mullioned and transomed windows.

PIGEON HOUSE FARM, ½ m. NE. Of brick. Georgian, of seven bays with a pedimental gable. Octagonal C18 DOVECOTE, also of brick.

WESTON COURT FARMHOUSE
see PEMBRIDGE

6020

WESTON-UNDER-PENYARD

ST LAWRENCE. Late Norman N arcade with circular piers, shallow capitals with scallops or leaf, square abaci, and single-step arches. Hood-moulds on head-stops. The hood-moulds are decorated with billet. The N doorway is probably Norman too. E.E. chancel with three separate stepped lancets in the E wall. But most of the windows in the church are C19 or over-restored. (Restoration by *Street*, 1867.) Dec W tower with Perp W window. N porch of timber, C14 or C15. The nave roof is single-framed and scissor-braced. – PLATE. Chalice, 1637; Flagon, 1723; Chalice and two Salvers, 1824–5; all London-made.

BAPTIST CHAPEL, Ryeford. Red and grey stone. Three by four arched windows. Front with giant pilasters carrying a frieze which is interrupted in the middle bay. There, instead, is a large arched doorway and a large arched window reaching up into the pediment. Behind is the predecessor of the chapel (now school). Established in 1662. Completely plain, with pitched roof and normal windows.

WESTON HALL, ½ m. NW, the first larger house as one comes in from the W. Jacobean, of red sandstone, with a nearly symmetrical façade. L. and r. gables with canted bays under. Central gabled porch. Mullioned windows. Fine early C18 GATES to the road.

WYE HOTEL, to the E of the former. Late Georgian, of five bays and two storeys. Greek Doric porch, and on the short side two canted bay windows.

RECTORY, ½ m. NE. Late C17 stone house of seven bays and two storeys. The stone is supposed to have come from Penyard Castle. Hipped roof. Doorway with Tuscan pilasters and a segmental pediment. Above it a panel with an open book.

STREET HOUSE, ¼ m. N. Dated 1711. Stone, of five bays and

two storeys with wooden cross-windows, but not a hipped roof. Arched hood over the doorway.

BOLLITREE CASTLE, ¾ m. NNE. The house looks a perfectly normal late C17 building. Red stone, five bays, two storeys, hipped roof, three steeply gabled dormers. Altered doorway. But behind is the utter surprise of extensive Gothick out-buildings, judging by their style, of a date hardly after 1770. The ogee arches, quatrefoils, and other details prove that. The Gothick additions appear in a drawing of 1789 at the Hereford Library. So that is the *terminus ante quem*. The buildings have battlements and angle turrets and there are several of them, more or less completely gothicized. More-over, they incorporate genuine medieval material said to come from Penyard Castle and a church at Bristol. To this belongs the shaft on top of the main doorway into the largest building.

(HOWNHALL, Ryeford. 1914 by *Sir Patrick Abercrombie*. M. Whiffen)

PENYARD CASTLE, 1 m. SW. Even those parts which were described by the RCHM can no longer be inspected. The farmhouse has collapsed, and the C14 undercroft is filled with nettles and undergrowth. In the one end-gable of the farmhouse which stands up, a two-light window with pointed-trefoiled heads.

ROMAN SETTLEMENT. Possibly the site of the Roman town of ARICONIUM. Excavations in the C18 produced many sherds, bronze brooches, lamps, and coins. Foundations of buildings, including a possible granary and fragments of tessellated pavement, were also discovered. Finds in the C19 included a number of British gold and silver coins, including some of Cunobelin, numerous Roman coins ranging in date from the C1 to the C4 A.D., keys, rings, pins, and other objects of bronze. More recently, in 1921, excavations revealed the foundations of two rectangular buildings, one with a hypo-caust system. Finds from this excavation included early Samian ware, Rhenish ware, and imitation Samian. The large quantities of iron slag scattered over the area suggest smelting on the site in Roman times.

s of Ariconium a paved road 8 ft wide runs through the Forest of Dean to join the coastal road at Lydney. This road is rather narrower than the normal Roman road, but the kerbed edges and straight course suggest that it is of Roman date.

N of Ariconium a Roman road runs for 27 m. to Ashton,

near Leominster. Its course is traceable largely by the align-
ment of lanes and hedges with portions of the *agger* in some
places, notably near Risbury Camp.

WHARTON COURT *see* LEOMINSTER, p. 231

7050
WHITBOURNE

St John Baptist. Late Norman s doorway with one order of
shafts and trumpet-scallop capitals. Arch with various zigzags.
In the nave s wall one tall c13 lancet. The chancel windows
lancets with ogee tops, the e window Early Perp. n aisle of
1866 (by *Perkins* of Worcester). c14 w tower with diagonal
buttresses. The tower arch of three continuous chamfers. –
font. Circular, Norman, with interlocked rosettes. –
sculpture. Several corbel-heads re-set (e.g. above the s
doorway inside). – monuments. Several tablets, under the
tower, notably Bellingham Freeman † 1689, with good foliage
volutes and a cherub's head at the foot.

lychgate. Timber-framed, late medieval, on six posts.

Old Rectory, immediately to the w. Georgian, of three bays
with a hipped roof. Doorway arched, all the surrounding
windows of the Venetian type.

w of the rectory two nice black and white houses, one with
Early Tudor chimneyshafts decorated with zigzag and pellets.
(The rchm mentions a number of cottages and farmhouses
with cruck-trusses, i.e. the Ring of Bells, Fincher's
Farm, Bradbourne's Farm, and Lower Poswick and
its barn.)

Whitbourne Hall, 1¼ m. w. 1861–2 by *A. L. Roumieu* or
Elmslie. The attribution to Roumieu is most surprising. It is
based on a note in the obituary in *The Builder* (1877), which
however mentions additions to the house only. The tender
published in the same journal in 1860 (£21,500 – a very large
sum) gives as the architect Elmelic, which must be a misprint
for Elmslie of Elmslie, Franey & Haddon. The idea of copying
the details of the Erechtheum was the client's. Noble Ionic six-
column portico with pediment. One bay each side of it. Round
the corner a big one-storeyed bow window and the remains of a
large, once domed conservatory. The principal doorway is also
taken from the Erechtheum. Central hall with glazed ceiling.
Pillars and columns around carrying a gallery. The gallery
forms a bridge where the wide staircase rises behind the hall.

The staircase starts in one arm and returns in two. The details
are here in the mid-c19 Grecian of the École des Beaux Arts.
The Drawing Room on the other hand is Dixhuitième.

GAINES, 1 m. sw. Large red brick house with an irregular
eleven-bay front. Three-bay projection without pediment.
No special features outside, but inside fine later c18 decoration. One large room is in a very graceful early Gothic Revival,
others have stucco in the Adam style. Small staircase under an
oval glazed dome.

WHITCHURCH

ST DUBRICIUS. Immediately by the Wye. The chancel looks
Dec, with the reticulated tracery of the E window and the
continuous chamfers of the chancel arch. However, built into
the s wall and now revealed is the upper part of a circular c13
pier. It cannot be *in situ*, as the direction of a hole for some
beam proves. N aisle of 1860 (by *Terry*). Good single-framed
nave and chancel roofs. – FONT. Circular, Norman, with flat,
continuous round arcading. – PLATE. Cover Paten, inscribed
1609; Cup on baluster stem, *c.*1660–5; Paten, 1698; Chalice,
London, 1749.

OLD COURT, ¼ m. w. Quite large stone house of the c16 to c17,
in the form of an irregular E. Mullioned windows.

(BROOK HOUSE, ⅔ m. w. The house has a staircase with twisted
balusters; RCHM. The date must be the later c17.)

DOWARD HOTEL. Probably early c19. Five bays, two storeys.

(OBSERVATORY. On Doward Hill an observatory was built of
iron trellis-work. Does it still exist?)

SELLARSBROOKE, *see* Ganarew, p. 135.

ROMAN SETTLEMENT. On the boundary of the parishes of
Whitchurch and Ganarew a mosaic pavement and coins were
found in the c19.

WHITEHOUSE *see* LAYSTERS
and TURNASTONE

WHITFIELD

1½ m. ssw of Kingstone

A plain, sizeable Georgian brick house with prominent pairs
of bow windows towards the s as well as the N. The house was
built *c.*1755–60, but given more or less its present appearance
*c.*1775–80, except that the top storey was added only in the
c19. Large additions were made about 1850. They have

recently been removed (by *Philip Tilden*). Only the rustication of the windows of the N half remains from the changes of 1850. A fine fireplace of brown and white marble inside which looks 1755 rather than 1775.

WHITNEY

ST PETER AND ST PAUL. Most of the church was built in 1740 after a flood of the river Wye. But much of the old materials was re-used. Unbuttressed W tower with big battlements and a recessed pyramid roof. Nave and chancel. Georgian S doorway, arched and rusticated. Traces of arched Georgian windows. – PULPIT. With the usual Jacobean blank arches, but also openwork panels which look mid-C18. – REREDOS. With Jacobean panels, including an overmantel and a shield dated 1629. – WEST GALLERY and staircase. Turned balusters. If they are of *c.*1740, they are very conservative. – COMMUNION RAIL. With turned balusters. – PANELLING. Made of C17 pieces and also one door dated 1704. – PLATE. Chalice and Cover Paten, London, 1693. – MONUMENT. Tablet to Thomas Williams † 1698, with a nice garland at the foot.

BRIDGE. On wooden posts, built *c.*1820. Rough work.

WHITNEY COURT. 1898–1902, by *T. H. & A. M. Watson* of London. Large, neo-Tudor.

WICTON FARM *see* BREDENBURY

WIGMORE

A delightfully placed village in the hills, with a short main street rising towards the church, which lies, however, away from the street in an elevated position. The castle is some way further W again.

ST JAMES. Early Norman nave, *see* the herringbone masonry outside the N wall and one blocked S window visible inside. So the present nave width is that of the late C11 or C12. S aisle, nearly as wide as the nave, *c.*1300. Windows of three stepped lancet lights under one arch. Arcade of two bays with octagonal piers and double-chamfered arches. Chancel Dec, windows with details of the late C13 (cusped arches, quatrefoil in bar tracery) as well as Dec details (reticulation). The chancel arch Dec too. Of the C15 N aisle only one bay remains, and traces of the second. The arcade has the same motifs as the S arcade, but is smaller and shorter, and the details differ of course. The castellated capital is C19 (RCHM). Broad W tower of the C14, with small openings. Triple-chamfered arch towards the nave. C14 roof in the S aisle, C15 in the nave. The earlier wind-braces are foiled, the later cusped. The church was restored by *Bodley* in 1864. – STALLS. With traceried fronts and coarse poppy-heads. – PULPIT. Perp, with linen-fold panels. – STAINED GLASS. Eight small figures of apostles under canopies, one of them signed by *D. Evans* (of Shrewsbury), 1849. Strident colours. – PLATE. Elizabethan Chalice and Cover Paten, probably local; Paten on foot by *Thomas Tearle*, 1726; Chalice, London, 1754; Flagon, London, 1795. – MONUMENTS. Minor tablets, e.g. one by *Denman* († 1814) with weeping willows.

WIGMORE CASTLE, ¼ m. W of the church. One of the largest castles along the Welsh border, but badly preserved and badly looked after. Untold trees, bushes, bracken, nettles. According to Domesday Book it was built by William FitzOsbern, Earl of Hereford. It belonged then to Ralph de Mortimer, who is supposed to have been a kinsman of William the Conqueror and also became the founder of the great Marches dynasty of the Mortimers. The castle remained Mortimer property until the C15. Earthworks to the SE formerly the outer bailey. The inner bailey is surrounded by walls and towers of the late C13 to the C14. The S tower has two ogee-headed windows. The gatehouse is half-buried. At the NW end of the inner bailey the motte crowned by a roughly oval shell keep. A little of this seems to go back to the C12, but most of what remains is of the C14. The castle was called 'utterly decayed in lodging' about 1535–40, and in Buck's engraving of 1732 it appears about as ruinous as it is now.

WIGMORE HALL, at the S end of the village. Black and white; C16 and later. Eminently picturesque NE front with the gabled two-storeyed former porch in the middle.

HOUSES. The best houses in the village are one of brick, of the late C17, at the main street crossing, and one timber-framed, of the C17, in the main street, to the SE of the former.

WIGMORE ABBEY, 1⅜ m. N. Founded in 1179 by Hugh Mortimer for Augustinian Canons of St Victor of Paris who had first settled at Shobdon c.1140 (*see* p. 287), then moved to Aymestrey, back to Shobdon again, and finally to Wigmore. The abbey church was the burial place of the Mortimers. Of it, however, unfortunately no more remains than the gable wall of the s transept and lower parts of its w wall and the nave s wall. These parts dated from the late C12, and the nave was apparently vaulted in stone. The E parts were remodelled in the late C14, with transept E chapels and chancel N and s aisles. The main surviving building lies to the sw of the transept wall and represents the Abbot's Lodging, which projected w from the cloister w range. It consists of two parts. The E part, buttressed on the s side, has a two-light C14 window and a three-light C15 window with panel tracery, both to the s. Inside there are roof trusses of the C14 still in existence, alternatingly of tie-beams with kingposts and diagonal struts and of arched braces up to collar-beams. Cusping above the collars. Adjoining to the w a low part with a C14 gateway and a C14 timber-framed upper floor. The timbers, including diagonal struts, are very heavy. (Inside also remains of the C14 roofs.) To the NW along the road another building, also of the C14, with one small doorway.

CHAPEL FARM, see Lingen, p. 233.

LODGE FARM, see Letton, p. 232.

UPPER LIMEBROOK FARM, see Limebrook, p. 233.

WILLERSLEY
3040

St MARY MAGDALENE. Nave and chancel in one. Transparent Victorian timber bell-turret. Norman the s doorway. Very tiny lintel decorated quite arbitrarily with a variety of motifs. From l. to r. in vertical strips: small crowns in squares, interlocked rosettes, squares within squares, horizontal zigzags, a big rosette, interlocked rosettes. Rosettes on the soffit of the doorway, that is the underside of the lintel, as well. What can have moved the carver to do this as an adornment of the entrance to the church? In the N wall of the nave the remains of a former Norman window. In the chancel N wall a small early C13 lancet. – REREDOS and front BENCHES with some Jacobean panels. – PLATE. Two Patens on foot, both domestic, both London-made: 1765 and 1770; Chalice, London, 1808.

WILLERSLEY COURT, N of the church. The hall-house type with gabled solar and buttery wings, but refaced in brick and given Georgian windows. The rhythm is two–three–two. (Inside, a C17 chimneypiece with blank arches along the overmantel. RCHM)

WILTON BRIDGE see ROSS-ON-WYE

WILTON CASTLE *see* BRIDSTOW

WINFORTON   2040

ST MICHAEL. Unbuttressed W tower with a timber-framed
upper part (cf. Holmer). This is of the C16. Pyramid roof.
Nave and chancel. S doorway of the C13 with a continuous
roll moulding. Most of the windows renewed, in the style of
*c.*1300. – PULPIT. With some Jacobean panels, dated 1613. –
COMMUNION RAIL. With turned balusters and many knobs.
Given in 1701. It was originally three-sided. – ORGAN CASE.
Good, and apparently of the early C18. – PLATE. Elizabethan
Cup and Cover Paten, the latter inscribed 1599; two Plates
and a Flagon, London, 1809. – MONUMENT. Nice slate tablet
signed by *R. Powell* of Eardisley.
WINFORTON COURT, 250 yds W. Handsome black and white
house. The l. gable of the N front has gay diagonal bracing to
form lozenges within lozenges.
(OLD HOUSE FARM, W of the church, has some early C16
timber-framing with narrowly-set uprights. RCHM)
CROSS FARM, WNW of the church, has an exposed cruck-truss.

WINSLEY HOUSE
see HOPE-UNDER-DINMORE

WISTESTON COURT *see* MARDEN

WITHINGTON   5040

ST PETER. What will be remembered about the church is the
tall, slender, recessed spire with roll mouldings up the edges.
It stands on a late C13 tower with diagonal buttresses and an
arch with three continuous chamfers towards the nave. Two
simple Norman nave doorways, that on the N side blocked.
The windows are E.E., Dec, and Perp. The chancel is all
renewed. – SCREEN. One-light divisions, tracery with leaf
cusps. Moulded cornice and cresting. – STAINED GLASS.
Three-light S window by *Ward & Hughes*, 1892. – PLATE.
Chalice and Cover Paten, inscribed 1675; Paten on foot,
London, 1674; Paten by *Edw. Cornock*, London, 1726;
Flagon, London, 1726.
    LYCHGATE. It originally had only three posts, and the
beams supporting the roof were castellated.

BAPTIST CHAPEL, ½ m. S. 1821. Stone with hipped roof. The windows have four-centred heads.

WHITE STONE, E of the chapel, at the NW corner of the cross-roads. It was a wayside cross and was re-used in 1700 as a direction stone, pointing to Hereford, Worcester, Ledbury, and?

EAU WITHINGTON COURT, 1¼ m. W. Later C17, but the five-bay front later. Timber-framing with gable at the back. Nice staircase with turned balusters. (A small building W of the house has the date 1682. RCHM)

THING HILL GRANGE, 1½ m. NW. A C14 hall-house with solar and buttery wings. In the hall range the spere-truss remains, though on the ground floor one spere-post has been taken out. Close by two doorways into the buttery, one with a well-preserved ogee head. Above the collar-beam foiled opening. The former solar wing also has its original roof, tie-beams on arched braces and foiled openings above.

WOLFERLOW
6060

ST ANDREW. Mostly of 1863 (by *Kempson*) and 1890–4. The bell-turret with its broach spire, however, rests on medieval timbers, and there are some substantial genuine Norman survivals. The S doorway has a tympanum with upcurved bottom, the blocked N doorway one order of shafts with capitals of odd shape. Arch with outer band of saltire crosses. The chancel arch also is Norman. – MONUMENT. In the chancel an excellent late C13 stone effigy of a Lady. The large number of parallel folds, and especially the parallel row of angles down the legs, are all still in the C12 and earlier C13 tradition. Mantle hanging over the left arm. At the head two angels.
23a

COURT FARM, to the E, across a field. Timber-framed. Gabled wing with narrowly-set uprights.

WOODCROFT FARM *see* BISHOP'S FROME

WOOD HOUSE FARM
see WELLINGTON HEATH

WOOLHOPE
6030

ST GEORGE. Essentially a Norman church, as the one chancel window now giving on the vestry and the N arcade show. The part in question of the N arcade is of two bays. Circular pier and semicircular respond, multi-scalloped capitals, square abaci (the capitals by the Victorian restorer, but the decoration of the abaci correct), round single-step arch. Arch, not arches; for the second was changed to a pointed double-chamfered form when the arcade was lengthened about 1300. The piers are now octagonal. The S arcade is all Victorian. But the S doorway is correct and again of *c*.1300 or a little earlier. Of the same time the W tower (Y-tracery). Diagonal buttresses, parapet. – PLATE. Chalice and Cover Paten, London, 1670. – MONUMENT (N aisle, re-set upright). Effigy of the early C14, under a cusped canopy with some ballflower enrichment. Crossed hands. Part of the legs is missing. – Also two fragmentary but very interesting coffin-lids, one of the C13 (?) with a Lady in profile and odd objects, the other of the early C14 with two crosses and nobbly foliage sprouting between.

23b

WORMBRIDGE

4030

ST PETER. Unbuttressed W tower, of the C13 below – as the double-chamfered tower arch and the lancet windows show. Top stage and broach spire of 1851–9, when the church was violently restored. Of that date the chancel almost entirely. Nave N doorway of *c*.1200, round-arched, with a step and a slight chamfer. – WOODWORK. Bits under the tower and in three big composite panels in the nave. They were given to the church in 1870 and come from Newnham Paddox near Lutterworth in Leicestershire. The bits are English Jacobean, Netherlandish Mannerist (the caryatids in strapwork fetters), English Perp (the running vine trail of the top frieze), and Italian (?) C18 (the copies of paintings) – STAINED GLASS. Chancel N and S, all kinds of fragments. They include a series of small early C15 figures. – PLATE. Porringer with two handles and repoussé ornament, 1683; Salver by *Samuell Lea*, London, 1718. – MONUMENTS to the Clive family, including the two companion marble panels with large portrait busts to Lady Katharine Clive † 1882 and Charles Clive † 1883. She is in a Verrocchio-Leonardo style. They were carved by Miss *Mary Grant*, niece of Grant, the painter and P.R.A.

WORMBRIDGE COURT. Dignified brick farmhouse, with a symmetrical front with three gables. The façade is an overlay over Jacobean work (cf. the chimneypiece inside with Ionic

pilasters and caryatid statuettes in the overmantel; RCHM).
In the yard C18 DOVECOTE of brick.

WORMSLEY
4040

ST MARY. Norman nave and rebuilt chancel and late C13
bellcote. The S doorway is Norman and has a tympanum with
an incised trellis and lozenges. The lintel below is worn or cut
as if it also were part of a tympanum. The nave windows
and the original chancel windows are C13. So is the chancel
arch. – PULPIT. Two sides only. Jacobean. With blank arches
and arabesque panels. – PLATE. Cover Paten, London, 1571;
Chalice and Plate, London, 1825. – MONUMENTS. Sarcophagi
in the churchyard to Richard Payne Knight (*see* below and
Downton Castle, p. 117) and Thomas Andrew Knight (*see*
below and Elton Hall, p. 128). They had both lived in a
greater world or greater worlds but wanted to go home at
the end.

WORMSLEY GRANGE. A rather forbidding Early Georgian
stone house of five bays and two and a half storeys. The bay
windows are Victorian. Near by a battery of stone oasthouses.
The whole looks like a picture from the Peak or the Yorkshire
moors. It was here that Richard Payne Knight and Thomas
Andrew Knight were born. The planting of the estate may
well be theirs. To the E of Wormsley Grange lay Wormsley
Priory, founded for Augustinian Canons *c*.1216.

YARKHILL
6040

ST JOHN BAPTIST. Early C13 S doorway with foliated crocket
capitals. The foliage stops of the hood-mould look Victorian
renewals. Some of the timbers of the S porch, with their uncommon dog-tooth decoration, are of the C13 too, but late.
The rest of 1862 (by *Ainslie & Blashill*), except for the W
tower, which has an arch to the nave, Norman at least in its
jambs and imposts, even if the unmoulded pointed arch may
not be in order. C13 lancets, and the top stage probably of
1466. – FONTS. One of blackish stone, Norman, in the form
of a many-scalloped capital with a square abacus. – Another
font under the tower; C13. – Yet another with fluted bowl,
perhaps C17. – CHURCHYARD CROSS. The Crucifixion of
the head of a cross is set above the S doorway.

VICARAGE. 1855. Mildly Gothic, with gables. Red brick with

black diapers. By the doorway two trumpet-scallop capitals, evidence of a Norman stage of the church.

SCHOOL, ¾ m. NW. 1865. Also Gothic. One window is circular, and in it is very good early *Powell* glass, designed by *Casolani*. It was made in 1866.

YARPOLE   *4060*

ST LEONARD. One of the Herefordshire churches with a separate tower. It is square and has a truncated pyramid roof, then a vertical weatherboarded bell-stage with a pretty band of quatrefoils, and then a spire. Inside, the four massive main posts stand detached from the angles of the stone walls, and there is scissor-bracing. The church is of *c*.1300, but has a chancel rebuilt by *Scott* in 1864 and a N aisle added at the same time. The original work has windows with Geometrical tracery. Single-frame nave roof with tie-beams and kingposts. – FONT. Octagonal, Norman or C13, with blank arcading. – DOOR to the bell-tower, plain, with long iron hinges. This, as well as the tower itself, could be C13–14. – PLATE. Paten on foot, London, 1726; Chalice, *c*.1730.

Nice black and white houses immediately N, W, and SW of the church. The house to the SW has diagonal bracing. To the SE the MANOR HOUSE. To this belongs a stone gatehouse. The front archway may be altered. At the back a small chamfered archway and the jamb of a former, much larger one.

At BIRCHER, ¾ m. NNE, the GATEHOUSE, on the E side of the road, facing N, has a carving of a human head in an arched niche – all one stone – which may all be Norman or even Saxon.

YATTON   *6030*

ALL SAINTS. 1841 by *William Roberts* of Chepstow. Nave with bellcote, transepts, and short chancel lengthened in 1901–3 by a polygonal apse rib-vaulted in stone. The old parts received their wooden coved ceilings at the same time. They are attractively painted. – SCREEN. Only the posts and top rail and the traceried spandrels remain. – LECTERN. The stem is foreign late C17 work made for a different purpose. – SCULP-TURE. Flemish early C16 relief of Christ before Pilate. – Another of the Resurrection, also C16, but later, and also Continental.

OLD CHAPEL, by Chapel Farm, ½ m. w. Disused, and now displaying a corrugated iron roof. The s doorway is work of the Herefordshire School of C12 carvers, but a poor work, i.e. by a minor master of the group. In addition it is re-assembled and re-assembled badly. The capitals raw in their decoration and lacking all logic. The tree of life in the tympanum is more acceptable, but even there a comparison with the intensity and impact of Kilpeck is crushing.

YATTON COURT see AYMESTREY

4040

YAZOR

ST MARY. 1843 by *George Rowe*. In the E.E. style, with a thin w tower carrying a thin spire. Lancet windows and groups of three stepped lancets. Transepts and a polygonal apse. – STAINED GLASS. The glass of 1866 in the two chancel lancets is uncommonly good. – The apse windows are by *Warrington*, c.1845. – MONUMENTS. Several tablets to members of the Price family, e.g. Uvedale T. S. Price † 1844, a white marble slab with a brass cross and a representation of the church which he had been responsible for.

ST JOHN BAPTIST. In a field to the s. Only the s transept remains roofed. Also the s aisle arcade and the w tower, smothered in ivy. The arcade is Perp with octagonal piers and double-chamfered arches. The windows of the transept indicate a date c.1300.

FOXLEY. Foxley was the estate of Sir Uvedale Price (1747–1829), the most brilliant of the theorists of the English Picturesque. He lived in a square red brick house of 1717, of the Shropshire (Cound) or Smith-of-Warwick type, that is with giant pilasters and arched windows. The house has entirely disappeared, but of Sir Uvedale's planting much must remain.

GLOSSARY

ABACUS: flat slab on the top of a capital (q.v.).

ABUTMENT: solid masonry placed to resist the lateral pressure of a vault.

ACANTHUS: plant with thick fleshy and scalloped leaves used as part of the decoration of a Corinthian capital (q.v.) and in some types of leaf carving.

ACHIEVEMENT OF ARMS: in heraldry, a complete display of armorial bearings.

ACROTERION: foliage-carved block on the end or top of a classical pediment.

ADDORSED: two human figures, animals, or birds, etc., placed symmetrically so that they turn their backs to each other.

AEDICULE, AEDICULA: framing of a window or door by columns and a pediment (q.v.).

AFFRONTED: two human figures, animals, or birds, etc., placed symmetrically so that they face each other.

AGGER: Latin term for the built-up foundations of Roman roads; also sometimes applied to the banks of hill-forts or other earthworks.

AMBULATORY: semicircular or polygonal aisle enclosing an apse (q.v.).

ANNULET: *see* Shaft-ring.

ANSE DE PANIER: *see* Arch, Basket.

ANTEPENDIUM: covering of the front of an altar, usually by textiles or metalwork.

ANTIS, IN: *see* Portico.

APSE: vaulted semicircular or polygonal end of a chancel or a chapel.

ARABESQUE: light and fanciful surface decoration using combinations of flowing lines, tendrils, etc., interspersed with vases, animals, etc.

ARCADE: range of arches supported on piers or columns, free-standing: or, BLIND ARCADE, the same attached to a wall.

ARCH: round-headed, i.e. semicircular; pointed, i.e. consisting of two curves, each drawn from one centre, and meeting in a point at the top; segmental, i.e. in the form of a segment;

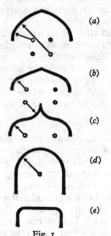

Fig. 1

pointed; four-centred (a Late Medieval form), *see* Fig. 1(a); Tudor (also a Late Medieval form), see Fig. 1(b); Ogee (introduced c.1300 and specially popular in the C14), see Fig. 1(c); Stilted, see Fig. 1(d); Basket, with lintel connected to the jambs by concave quadrant curves, see Fig. 1(e) for one example; Diaphragm, a transverse arch with solid spandrels carrying not a vault but a principal beam of a timber roof.

ARCHITRAVE: lowest of the three main parts of the entablature (q.v.) of an order (q.v.) (see Fig. 12).

ARCHIVOLT: under-surface of an arch (also called Soffit).

ARRIS: sharp edge at the meeting of two surfaces.

ASHLAR: masonry of large blocks wrought to even faces and square edges.

ATLANTES: male counterparts of caryatids (q.v.).

ATRIUM: inner court of a Roman house, also open court in front of a church.

ATTACHED: see Engaged.

ATTIC: topmost storey of a house, if distance from floor to ceiling is less than in the others.

AUMBRY: recess or cupboard to hold sacred vessels for Mass and Communion.

BAILEY: open space or court of a stone-built castle; see also Motte-and-Bailey.

BALDACCHINO: canopy supported on columns.

BALLFLOWER: globular flower of three petals enclosing a small ball. A decoration used in the first quarter of the C14.

BALUSTER: small pillar or column of fanciful outline.

BALUSTRADE: series of balusters

supporting a handrail or coping (q.v.).

BARBICAN: outwork defending the entrance to a castle.

BARGEBOARDS: projecting decorated boards placed against the incline of the gable of a building and hiding the horizontal roof timbers.

BARROW: see Bell, Bowl, Disc, Long, and Pond Barrow.

BASILICA: in medieval architecture an aisled church with a clerestory.

BASKET ARCH: see Arch (Fig. 1e).

BASTION: projection at the angle of a fortification.

BATTER: inclined face of a wall.

BATTLEMENT: parapet with a series of indentations or embrasures with raised portions or merlons between (also called Crenellation).

BAYS: internal compartments of a building; each divided from the other not by solid walls but by divisions only marked in the side walls (columns, pilasters, etc.) or the ceiling (beams, etc.). Also external divisions of a building by fenestration.

BAY-WINDOW: angular or curved projection of a house front with ample fenestration. If curved, also called bow-window: if on an upper floor only, also called oriel or oriel window.

BEAKER FOLK: Late New Stone Age warrior invaders from the Continent who buried their dead in round barrows and introduced the first metal tools and weapons to Britain.

BEAKHEAD: Norman ornamental motif consisting of a row of bird or beast heads with beaks biting usually into a roll moulding.

BELFRY: turret on a roof to hang bells in.

BELGAE: Aristocratic warrior bands who settled in Britain in two main waves in the C1 B.C. In Britain their culture is termed Iron Age C.

BELL BARROW: Early Bronze Age round barrow in which the mound is separated from its encircling ditch by a flat platform or berm (q.v.).

BELLCOTE: framework on a roof to hang bells from.

BERM: level area separating ditch from bank on a hill-fort or barrow.

BILLET FRIEZE: Norman ornamental motif made up of short raised rectangles placed at regular intervals.

BIVALLATE: Of a hill-fort: defended by two concentric banks and ditches.

BLOCK CAPITAL: Romanesque capital cut from a cube by hav-

Fig. 2

ing the lower angles rounded off to the circular shaft below (also called Cushion Capital) (Fig. 2).

BOND, ENGLISH or FLEMISH: see Brickwork.

BOSS: knob or projection usually placed to cover the intersection of ribs in a vault.

BOWL BARROW: round barrow surrounded by a quarry ditch. Introduced in Late Neolithic

times, the form continued until the Saxon period.

BOW-WINDOW: see Bay-Window.

BOX: A small country house, e.g. a shooting box. A convenient term to describe a compact minor dwelling, e.g. a rectory.

BOX PEW: pew with a high wooden enclosure.

BRACES: see Roof.

BRACKET: small supporting piece of stone, etc., to carry a projecting horizontal.

BRESSUMER: beam in a timber-framed building to support the, usually projecting, superstructure.

BRICKWORK: *Header:* brick laid so that the end only appears on the face of the wall. *Stretcher:* brick laid so that the side only appears on the face of the wall. *English Bond:* method of laying bricks so that alternate courses or layers on the face of the wall are composed of headers or stretchers only (Fig. 3*a*). *Flemish Bond:* method of laying

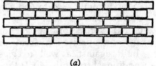

(*a*)

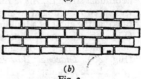

(*b*)
Fig. 3

bricks so that alternate headers and stretchers appear in each course on the face of the wall (Fig. 3*b*).

BROACH: *see* Spire.

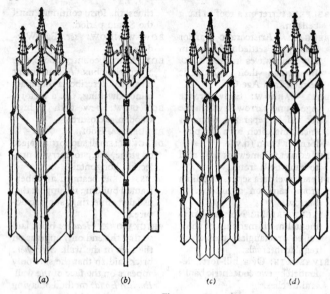

(a)   *(b)*   *(c)*   *(d)*

Fig. 4

BROKEN PEDIMENT: *see* Pediment.

BRONZE AGE: In Britain, the period from *c.*1800 to 600 B.C.

BUCRANIUM: ox skull.

BUTTRESS: mass of brickwork or masonry projecting from or built against a wall to give additional strength. *Angle Buttresses:* two meeting at an angle of 90° at the angle of a building (Fig. 4*a*). *Clasping Buttress:* one which encases the angle (Fig. 4*d*). *Diagonal Buttress:* one placed against the right angle formed by two walls, and more or less equiangular with both (Fig. 4*b*). *Flying Buttress:* arch or half arch transmitting the thrust of a vault or roof from the upper part of a wall to an outer support or buttress. *Setback Buttress:* angle buttress set slightly back from the angle (Fig. 4*c*).

CABLE MOULDING: Norman moulding imitating a twisted cord.

CAIRN: a mound of stones usually covering a burial.

CAMBER: slight rise or upward curve of an otherwise horizontal structure.

CAMPANILE: isolated bell tower.

CANOPY: projection or hood over an altar, pulpit, niche, statue, etc.

CAP: in a windmill the crowning feature.

CAPITAL: head or top part of a column.

CARTOUCHE: tablet with an ornate frame, usually enclosing an inscription.

CARYATID: whole female figure supporting an entablature or other similar member. *Termini Caryatids:* female busts or demi-figures or three-quarter figures supporting an entablature or other similar member and placed at the top of termini pilasters (q.v.). Cf. Atlantes.

CASTELLATED: decorated with battlements.

CELURE: panelled and adorned part of a wagon-roof above the rood or the altar.

CENSER: vessel for the burning of incense.

CENTERING: wooden framework used in arch and vault construction and removed when the mortar has set.

CHALICE: cup used in the Communion service or at Mass. *See also* Recusant Chalice.

CHAMBERED TOMB: burial mound of the New Stone Age having a stone-built chamber and entrance passage covered by an earthen barrow or stone cairn. The form was introduced to Britain from the Mediterranean.

CHAMFER: surface made by cutting across the square angle of a stone block, piece of wood, etc., usually at an angle of 45° to the other two surfaces.

CHANCEL: that part of the E end of a church in which the altar is placed, usually applied to the whole continuation of the nave E of the crossing.

CHANCEL ARCH: arch at the W end of the chancel.

CHANTRY CHAPEL: chapel attached to, or inside, a church, endowed for the saying of Masses for the soul of the founder or some other individual.

CHEVET: French term for the E end of a church (chancel, ambulatory, and radiating chapels).

CHEVRON: Norman moulding forming a zigzag.

CHOIR: that part of the church where divine service is sung.

CIBORIUM: a baldacchino.

CINQUEFOIL: *see* Foil.

CIST: stone-lined or slab-built grave. First appears in Late Neolithic times. It continued to be used in the Early Christian period.

CLAPPER BRIDGE: bridge made of large slabs of stone, some built up to make rough piers and other longer ones laid on top to make the roadway.

CLASSIC: here used to mean the moment of highest achievement of a style.

CLASSICAL: here used as the term for Greek and Roman architecture and any subsequent styles inspired by it.

CLERESTORY: upper storey of the nave walls of a church, pierced by windows.

COADE STONE: artificial (cast) stone made in the late C18 and the early C19 by Coade and Sealy in London.

COB: walling material made of mixed clay and straw.

COFFERING: decorating a ceiling with sunk square or polygonal ornamental panels.

COLLAR-BEAM: *see* Roof.

COLONNADE: range of columns.

COLONNETTE: small column.

COLUMNA ROSTRATA: column decorated with carved prows of ships to celebrate a naval victory.

COMPOSITE: *see* Order.

CONSOLE: bracket (q.v.) with a compound curved outline.

COPING: capping or covering to a wall.

CORBEL: block of stone projecting from a wall, supporting some feature on its horizontal top surface.

CORBEL TABLE: series of corbels, occurring just below the roof eaves externally or internally, often seen in Norman buildings.

CORINTHIAN: *see* Order.

CORNICE: in classical architecture the top section of the entablature (q.v.). Also for a projecting decorative feature along the top of a wall, arch, etc.

CORRIDOR VILLA: *see* Villa.

COUNTERSCARP BANK: small bank on the down-hill or outer side of a hill-fort ditch.

COURTYARD VILLA: *see* Villa.

COVE, COVING: concave undersurface in the nature of a hollow moulding but on a larger scale.

COVER PATEN: cover to a Communion cup, suitable for use as a paten or plate for the consecrated bread.

CRADLE ROOF: *see* Wagon roof.

CRENELLATION: *see* Battlement.

CREST, CRESTING: ornamental finish along the top of a screen, etc.

CRINKLE-CRANKLE WALL: undulating wall.

CROCKET, CROCKETING: decorative features placed on the sloping sides of spires, pinnacles, gables, etc., in Gothic architecture, carved in various leaf shapes and placed at regular intervals.

CROCKET CAPITAL: *see* Fig. 5. An Early Gothic form.

CROMLECH: word of Celtic origin still occasionally used of single free-standing stones ascribed to the Neolithic or Bronze Age periods.

Fig. 5

CROSSING: space at the intersection of nave, chancel, and transepts.

CROSS-WINDOWS: windows with one mullion and one transom.

CRUCK: big curved beam supporting both walls and roof of a cottage.

CRYPT: underground room usually below the E end of a church.

CUPOLA: small polygonal or circular domed turret crowning a roof.

CURTAIN WALL: connecting wall between the towers of a castle.

CUSHION CAPITAL: *see* Block Capital.

CUSP: projecting point between the foils in a foiled Gothic arch.

DADO: decorative covering of the lower part of a wall.

DAGGER: tracery motif of the Dec style. It is a lancet shape rounded or pointed at the head, pointed at the foot, and cusped inside (*see* Fig. 6).

Fig. 6

DAIS: raised platform at one end of a room.

DEC ('DECORATED'): historical division of English Gothic architecture covering the period from c.1290 to c.1350.

DEMI-COLUMNS: columns half sunk into a wall.

DIAPER WORK: surface decoration composed of square or lozenge shapes.

DIAPHRAGM ARCH: see Arch.

DISC BARROW: Bronze Age round barrow with inconspicuous central mound surrounded by bank and ditch.

DOGTOOTH: typical E.E. ornament consisting of a series of four-cornered stars placed diagonally and raised pyramidally (Fig. 7).

Fig. 7

DOMICAL VAULT: see Vault.

DONJON: see Keep.

DORIC: see Order.

DORMER (WINDOW): window placed vertically in the sloping plane of a roof.

DRIPSTONE: see Hood-mould.

DRUM: circular or polygonal vertical wall of a dome or cupola.

E.E. ('EARLY ENGLISH'): historical division of English Gothic architecture roughly covering the C13.

EASTER SEPULCHRE: recess with tomb-chest, usually in the wall of a chancel, the tomb-chest to receive an effigy of Christ for Easter celebrations.

EAVES: underpart of a sloping roof overhanging a wall.

EAVES CORNICE: cornice below the eaves of a roof.

ECHINUS: Convex or projecting moulding supporting the abacus of a Greek Doric capital, sometimes bearing an egg and dart pattern.

EMBATTLED: see Battlement.

EMBRASURE: small opening in the wall or parapet of a fortified building, usually splayed on the inside.

ENCAUSTIC TILES: earthenware glazed and decorated tiles used for paving.

ENGAGED COLUMNS: columns attached to, or partly sunk into, a wall.

ENGLISH BOND: see Brickwork.

ENTABLATURE: in classical architecture the whole of the horizontal members above a column (that is architrave, frieze, and cornice) (see Fig. 12).

ENTASIS: very slight convex deviation from a straight line; used on Greek columns and sometimes on spires to prevent an optical illusion of concavity.

ENTRESOL: see Mezzanine.

EPITAPH: hanging wall monument.

ESCUTCHEON: shield for armorial bearings.

EXEDRA: the apsidal end of a room. See Apse.

FAN-VAULT: see Vault.

FERETORY: place behind the

high altar where the chief shrine of a church is kept.

FESTOON: carved garland of flowers and fruit suspended at both ends.

FILLET: narrow flat band running down a shaft or along a roll moulding.

FINIAL: top of a canopy, gable, pinnacle.

FLAGON: vessel for the wine used in the Communion service.

FLAMBOYANT: properly the latest phase of French Gothic architecture where the window tracery takes on wavy undulating lines.

FLÈCHE: slender wooden spire on the centre of a roof (also called Spirelet).

FLEMISH BOND: see Brickwork.

FLEURON: decorative carved flower or leaf.

FLUSHWORK: decorative use of flint in conjunction with dressed stone so as to form patterns: tracery, initials, etc.

FLUTING: vertical channelling in the shaft of a column.

FLYING BUTTRESS: see Buttress.

FOIL: lobe formed by the cusping (q.v.) of a circle or an arch. Trefoil, quatrefoil, cinquefoil, multifoil, express the number of leaf shapes to be seen.

FOLIATED: carved with leaf shapes.

FOSSE: ditch.

FOUR-CENTRED ARCH: see Arch.

FRATER: refectory or dining hall of a monastery.

FRESCO: wall painting on wet plaster.

FRIEZE: middle division of a classical entablature (q.v.) (see Fig. 12).

FRONTAL: covering for the front of an altar.

GABLE: *Dutch gable:* A gable with curved sides crowned by a pediment, characteristic of *c.*1630–50 (Fig. 8*a*). *Shaped gable:* A gable with multi-curved sides characteristic of *c.*1600–50 (Fig. 8*b*).

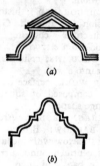

(a)

(b)

Fig. 8

GADROONED: enriched with a series of convex ridges, the opposite of fluting.

GALILEE: chapel or vestibule usually at the W end of a church enclosing the porch. Also called Narthex (q.v.).

GALLERY: in church architecture upper storey above an aisle, opened in arches to the nave. Also called Tribune and often erroneously Triforium (q.v.).

GALLERY GRAVE: chambered tomb (q.v.) in which there is little or no differentiation between the entrance passage and the actual burial chamber(s).

GARDEROBE: lavatory or privy in a medieval building.

GARGOYLE: water spout projecting from the parapet of a wall or tower; carved into a human or animal shape.

GAZEBO: lookout tower or raised

summer house in a picturesque garden.

'GEOMETRICAL': *see* Tracery.

'GIBBS SURROUND': of a doorway or window. An C18 motif consisting of a surround with alternating larger and smaller blocks of stone, quoin-wise, or intermittent large blocks, sometimes with a narrow raised band connecting them up the verticals and along the face of the arch (Fig. 9).

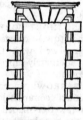

Fig. 9

GROIN: sharp edge at the meeting of two cells of a cross-vault.

GROIN-VAULT: *see* Vault.

GROTESQUE: fanciful ornamental decoration: *see* also Arabesque.

Hagioscope: *see* Squint.

HALF-TIMBERING: *see* Timber-Framing.

HALL CHURCH: church in which nave and aisles are of equal height or approximately so.

HAMMERBEAM: *see* Roof.

HANAP: large metal cup, generally made for domestic use, standing on an elaborate base and stem; with a very ornate cover frequently crowned with a little steeple.

HEADERS: *see* Brickwork.

HERRINGBONE WORK: brick, stone, or tile construction where the component blocks are laid diagonally instead of flat. Alternate courses lie in opposing directions to make a zigzag pattern up the face of the wall.

HEXASTYLE: having six detached columns.

HILL-FORT: Iron Age earthwork enclosed by a ditch and bank system; in the later part of the period the defences multiplied in size and complexity. They vary from about an acre to over 30 acres in area, and are usually built with careful regard to natural elevations or promontories.

HIPPED ROOF: *see* Roof.

HOOD-MOULD: projecting moulding above an arch or a lintel to throw off water (also called Dripstone or Label).

Iconography: the science of the subject matter of works of the visual arts.

IMPOST: bracket in a wall, usually formed of mouldings, on which the ends of an arch rest.

INDENT: shape chiselled out in a stone slab to receive a brass.

INGLENOOK: bench or seat built in beside a fireplace, sometimes covered by the chimneybreast, occasionally lit by small windows on each side of the fire.

INTERCOLUMNIATION: the space between columns.

IONIC: *see* Order (Fig. 12).

IRON AGE: in Britain the period from *c*. 600 B.C. to the coming of the Romans. The term is also used for those un-Roman-ized native communities which survived until the Saxon incursions.

JAMB: straight side of an archway, doorway, or window.

KEEL MOULDING: moulding whose outline is in section like that of the keel of a ship.

KEEP: massive tower of a Norman castle.

KEYSTONE: middle stone in an arch or a rib-vault.

KING-POST: see Roof (Fig. 14).

KNEELER: horizontal decorative projection at the base of a gable.

KNOP: a knob-like thickening in the stem of a chalice.

LABEL: see Hood-mould.

LABEL STOP: ornamental boss at the end of a hood-mould (q.v.).

LACED WINDOWS: windows pulled visually together by strips, usually in brick of a different colour, which continue vertically the lines of the vertical parts of the window surrounds. The motif is typical of c. 1720.

LANCET WINDOW: slender pointed-arched window.

LANTERN: in architecture, a small circular or polygonal turret with windows all round crowning a roof (see Cupola) or a dome.

LANTERN CROSS: churchyard cross with lantern-shaped top usually with sculptured representations on the sides of the top.

LEAN-TO ROOF: roof with one slope only, built against a higher wall.

LESENE or PILASTER STRIP: pilaster without base or capital.

LIERNE: see Vault (Fig. 21).

LINENFOLD: Tudor panelling ornamented with a conventional representation of a piece of linen laid in vertical folds. The piece is repeated in each panel.

LINTEL: horizontal beam or stone bridging an opening.

LOGGIA: recessed colonnade (q.v.).

LONG AND SHORT WORK: Saxon quoins (q.v.) consisting of stones placed with the long sides alternately upright and horizontal.

LONG BARROW: unchambered Neolithic communal burial mound, wedge-shaped in plan, with the burial and occasional other structures massed at the broader end, from which the mound itself tapers in height; quarry ditches flank the mound.

LOUVRE: opening, often with lantern (q.v.) over, in the roof of a room to let the smoke from a central hearth escape.

LOWER PALAEOLITHIC: see Palaeolithic.

LOZENGE: diamond shape.

LUCARNE: small opening to let light in.

LUNETTE: tympanum (q.v.) or semicircular opening.

LYCH GATE: wooden gate structure with a roof and open sides placed at the entrance to a churchyard to provide space for the reception of a coffin. The word lych is Saxon and means a corpse.

LYNCHET: long terraced strip of soil accumulating on the downward side of prehistoric and medieval fields due to soil creep from continuous ploughing along the contours.

MACHICOLATION: projecting gallery on brackets constructed on the outside of castle towers or walls. The gallery has holes in the floor to drop missiles through.

MAJOLICA: ornamented glazed earthenware.

MANSARD: *see* Roof.

MATHEMATICAL TILES: Small facing tiles the size of brick headers, applied to timber-framed walls to make them appear brick-built.

MEGALITHIC TOMB: stone-built burial chamber of the New Stone Age covered by an earth or stone mound. The form was introduced to Britain from the Mediterranean area.

MERLON: *see* Battlement.

MESOLITHIC: 'Middle Stone' Age; the post-glacial period of hunting and fishing communities dating in Britain from c.8000 B.C. to the arrival of Neolithic communities, with which they must have considerably overlapped.

METOPE: in classical architecture of the Doric order (q.v.) the space in the frieze between the triglyphs (Fig. 12).

MEZZANINE: low storey placed between two higher ones.

MISERERE: *see* Misericord.

MISERICORD: bracket placed on the underside of a hinged choir stall seat which, when turned up, provided the occupant of the seat with a support during long periods of standing (also called Miserere).

MODILLION: small bracket of which large numbers (modillion frieze) are often placed below a cornice (q.v.) in classical architecture.

MOTTE: steep mound forming the main feature of C11 and C12 castles.

MOTTE-AND-BAILEY: post-Roman and Norman defence system consisting of an earthen mound (the motte) topped with a wooden tower eccentrically placed within a bailey (q.v.), with enclosure ditch and palisade, and with the rare addition of an internal bank.

MOUCHETTE: tracery motif in curvilinear tracery, a curved dagger (q.v.), specially popular in the early C14 (Fig. 10).

Fig. 10

MULLIONS: vertical posts or uprights dividing a window into 'lights'.

MULTIVALLATE: Of a hill-fort: defended by three or more concentric banks and ditches.

MUNTIN: post as a rule moulded and part of a screen.

NAIL-HEAD: E.E. ornamental motif, consisting of small pyramids regularly repeated (Fig. 11).

Fig. 11

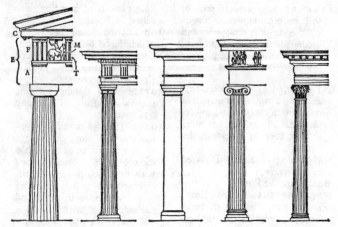

Fig. 12. Orders of Columns (Greek Doric, Roman Doric, Tuscan Doric, Ionic, Corinthian) E, Entablature; C, Cornice; F, Frieze; A, Architrave; M, Metope; T, Triglyph.

NARTHEX: enclosed vestibule or covered porch at the main entrance to a church (*see* Galilee).

NEOLITHIC: 'New Stone' Age, dating in Britain from the appearance from the Continent of the first settled farming communities *c.* 3500 B.C. until the introduction of the Bronze Age.

NEWEL: central post in a circular or winding staircase; also the principal post when a flight of stairs meets a landing.

NOOK-SHAFT: shaft set in the angle of a pier or respond or wall, or the angle of the jamb of a window or doorway.

NUTMEG MOULDING: consisting of a chain of tiny triangles placed obliquely.

OBELISK: lofty pillar of square section tapering at the top and ending pyramidally.

OGEE: *see* Arch (Fig. 1c).

ORATORY: small private chapel in a house.

ORDER: (1) *of a doorway or window:* series of concentric steps receding towards the opening; (2) *in classical architecture:* column with base, shaft, capital, and entablature (q.v.) according to one of the following styles: Greek Doric, Roman Doric, Tuscan Doric, Ionic, Corinthian, Composite. The established details are very elaborate, and some specialist architectural work should be consulted for further guidance (*see* Fig. 12).

ORIEL: *see* Bay-Window.

OVERHANG: projection of the upper storey of a house.

OVERSAILING COURSES: series of stone or brick courses, each one projecting beyond the one below it.

OVOLO: convex moulding.

PALAEOLITHIC: 'Old Stone' Age; the first period of human culture, commencing in the

Ice Age and immediately prior to the Mesolithic; the Lower Palaeolithic is the older phase, the Upper Palaeolithic the later.

PALIMPSEST: (1) *of a brass:* where a metal plate has been re-used by turning over and engraving on the back; (2) *of a wall painting:* where one overlaps and partly obscures an earlier one.

PALLADIAN: architecture following the ideas and principles of Andrea Palladio, 1518–80.

PANTILE: tile of curved S-shaped section.

PARAPET: low wall placed to protect any spot where there is a sudden drop, for example on a bridge, quay, hillside, housetop, etc.

PARGETTING: plaster work with patterns and ornaments either in relief or engraved on it.

PARVIS: term wrongly applied to a room over a church porch. These rooms were often used as a schoolroom or as a store room.

PATEN: plate to hold the bread at Communion or Mass.

PATERA: small flat circular or oval ornament in classical architecture.

PEDIMENT: low-pitched gable used in classical, Renaissance, and neo-classical architecture above a portico and above doors, windows, etc. It may be straight-sided or curved segmentally. *Broken Pediment:* one where the centre portion of the base is left open. *Open Pediment:* one where the centre portion of the sloping sides is left out.

PENDANT: boss (q.v.) elongated so that it seems to hang down.

PENDENTIF: concave triangular spandrel used to lead from the angle of two walls to the base of a circular dome. It is constructed as part of the hemisphere over a diameter the size of the diagonal of the basic square (Fig. 13).

Fig. 13

PERP (PERPENDICULAR): historical division of English Gothic architecture covering the period from c.1335–50 to c.1530.

PIANO NOBILE: principal storey of a house with the reception rooms; usually the first floor.

PIAZZA: open space surrounded by buildings; in C17 and C18 England sometimes used to mean a long colonnade or loggia.

PIER: strong, solid support, frequently square in section or of composite section (compound pier).

PIETRA DURA: ornamental or scenic inlay by means of thin slabs of stone.

PILASTER: shallow pier attached to a wall. *Termini Pilasters:* pilasters with sides tapering downwards.

PILLAR PISCINA: free-standing piscina on a pillar.

PINNACLE: ornamental form crowning a spire, tower, buttress, etc., usually of steep pyramidal, conical, or some similar shape.

PISCINA: basin for washing the Communion or Mass vessels, provided with a drain. Generally set in or against the wall to the S of an altar.

PLAISANCE: summer-house, pleasure house near a mansion.

PLATE TRACERY: *see* Tracery.

PLINTH: projecting base of a wall or column, generally chamfered (q.v.) or moulded at the top.

POND BARROW: rare type of Bronze Age barrow consisting of a circular depression, usually paved, and containing a number of cremation burials.

POPPYHEAD: ornament of leaf and flower type used to decorate the tops of bench- or stall-ends.

PORTCULLIS: gate constructed to rise and fall in vertical grooves; used in gateways of castles.

PORTE COCHÈRE: porch large enough to admit wheeled vehicles.

PORTICO: centre-piece of a house or a church with classical detached or attached columns and a pediment. A portico is called *prostyle* or *in antis* according to whether it projects from or recedes into a building. In a portico *in antis* the columns range with the side walls.

POSTERN: small gateway at the back of a building.

PREDELLA: in an altarpiece the horizontal strip below the main representation, often used for a number of subsidiary representations in a row.

PRESBYTERY: the part of the church lying E of the choir. It is the part where the altar is placed.

PRINCIPAL: *see* Roof (Fig. 14).

PRIORY: monastic house whose head is a prior or prioress, not an abbot or abbess.

PROSTYLE: with free-standing columns in a row.

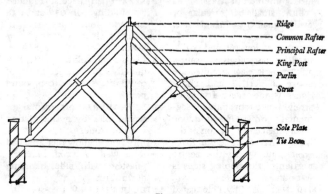

Ridge
Common Rafter
Principal Rafter
King Post
Purlin
Strut

Sole Plate
Tie Beam

Fig. 14

PULPITUM: stone screen in a major church provided to shut off the choir from the nave and also as a backing for the return choir stalls.

PULVINATED FRIEZE: frieze with a bold convex moulding.

PURLIN: see Roof (Figs. 14, 15).

PUTHOLE or PUTLOCK HOLE: putlocks are the short horizontal timbers on which during construction the boards of scaffolding rest. Putholes or putlock holes are the holes in the wall for putlocks, which often are not filled in after construction is complete.

PUTTO: small naked boy.

QUADRANGLE: inner courtyard in a large building.

QUARRY: in stained-glass work, a small diamond- or square-shaped piece of glass set diagonally.

QUATREFOIL: see Foil.

QUEEN-POSTS: see Roof (Fig. 15).

QUOINS: dressed stones at the angles of a building. Sometimes all the stones are of the same size; more often they are alternately large and small.

RADIATING CHAPELS: chapels projecting radially from an ambulatory or an apse.

RAFTER: see Roof.

RAMPART: stone wall or wall of earth surrounding a castle, fortress, or fortified city.

RAMPART-WALK: path along the inner face of a rampart.

REBATE: continuous rectangular notch cut on an edge.

REBUS: pun, a play on words. The literal translation and illustration of a name for artistic and heraldic purposes (Belton = bell, tun).

RECUSANT CHALICE: chalice made after the Reformation and before Catholic Emancipation for Roman Catholic use.

REEDING: decoration with parallel convex mouldings touching one another.

REFECTORY: dining hall; see Frater.

RENDERING: plastering of an outer wall.

REPOUSSÉ: decoration of metal work by relief designs, formed by beating the metal from the back.

REREDOS: structure behind and above an altar.

RESPOND: half-pier bonded into a wall and carrying one end of an arch.

RETABLE: altarpiece, a picture or piece of carving, standing behind and attached to an altar.

RETICULATION: see Tracery (Fig. 20e).

REVEAL: that part of a jamb (q.v.) which lies between the glass or door and the outer surface of the wall.

RIB-VAULT: see Vault.

ROCOCO: latest phase of the Baroque style, current in most Continental countries between c.1720 and c.1760.

ROLL MOULDING: moulding of semicircular or more than semicircular section.

ROMANESQUE: that style in architecture which was current in the C11 and C12 and preceded the Gothic style (in England often called Norman). (Some scholars extend the use of the term Romanesque back to the C10 or C9.)

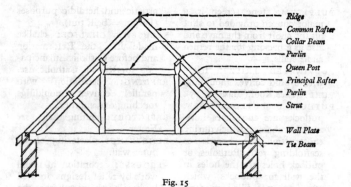

Ridge
Common Rafter
Collar Beam
Purlin
Queen Post
Principal Rafter
Purlin
Strut
Wall Plate
Tie Beam

Fig. 15

ROMANO-BRITISH: A some-
what vague term applied to the
period and cultural features of
Britain affected by the Roman
occupation of the C1–5 A.D.

ROOD: cross or crucifix.

ROOD LOFT: singing gallery on
the top of the rood screen,
often supported by a coving.

ROOD SCREEN: see Screen.

ROOD STAIRS: stairs to give
access to the rood loft.

ROOF: Single-framed: if consisting entirely of transverse
members (such as rafters with
or without braces, collars, tie-
beams, king-posts or queenposts, etc.) not tied together
longitudinally. Double-framed:
if longitudinal members (such
as a ridge beam and purlins)
are employed. As a rule in such
cases the rafters are divided
into stronger principals and
weaker subsidiary rafters.
Hipped: roof with sloped instead of vertical ends. Mansard:
roof with a double slope, the

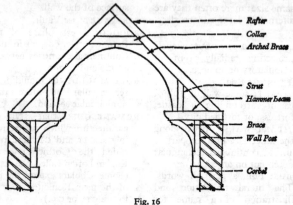

Rafter
Collar
Arched Brace
Strut
Hammer Beam
Brace
Wall Post
Corbel

Fig. 16

lower slope being larger and steeper than the upper. *Saddleback:* tower roof shaped like an ordinary gabled timber roof. The following members have special names: *Rafter:* roof-timber sloping up from the wall plate to the ridge. *Principal:* principal rafter, usually corresponding to the main bay divisions of the nave or chancel below. *Wall Plate:* timber laid longitudinally on the top of a wall. *Purlin:* longitudinal member laid parallel with wall plate and ridge beam some way up the slope of the roof. *Tie-beam:* beam connecting the two slopes of a roof across at its foot, usually at the height of the wall plate, to prevent the roof from spreading. *Collar-beam:* tie-beam applied higher up the slope of the roof. *Strut:* upright timber connecting the tie-beam with the rafter above it. *King-post:* upright timber connecting a tie-beam and collar-beam with the ridge beam. *Queen-posts:* two struts placed symmetrically on a tie-beam or collar-beam. *Braces:* inclined timbers inserted to strengthen others. Usually braces connect a collar-beam with the rafters below or a tie-beam with the wall below. Braces can be straight or curved (also called arched). *Hammer-beam:* beam projecting at right angles, usually from the top of a wall, to carry arched braces or struts and arched braces. (*See* Figs. 14, 15, 16.)

ROSE WINDOW (or WHEEL WINDOW): circular window with patterned tracery arranged to radiate from the centre.

ROTUNDA: building circular in plan.

RUBBLE: building stones, not square or hewn, nor laid in regular courses.

RUSTICATION: *rock-faced* if the surfaces of large blocks of ashlar stone are left rough like rock; *smooth* if the ashlar blocks are smooth and separated by V-joints; *banded* if the separation by V-joints applies only to the horizontals.

SADDLEBACK: *see* Roof.

SALTIRE CROSS: equal-limbed cross placed diagonally.

SANCTUARY: (1) area around the main altar of a church (*see* Presbytery); (2) sacred site consisting of wood or stone uprights enclosed by a circular bank and ditch. Beginning in the Neolithic, they were elaborated in the succeeding Bronze Age. The best known examples are Stonehenge and Avebury.

SARCOPHAGUS: elaborately carved coffin.

SCAGLIOLA: material composed of cement and colouring matter to imitate marble.

SCALLOPED CAPITAL: development of the block capital (q.v.) in which the single semicircular surface is elaborated into a series of truncated cones (Fig. 17).

Fig. 17

SCARP: artificial cutting away of the ground to form a steep slope.

SCREEN: *Parclose screen:* screen separating a chapel from the rest of a church. *Rood screen:* screen below the rood (q.v.), usually at the W end of a chancel.

SCREENS PASSAGE: passage between the entrances to kitchen, buttery, etc., and the screen behind which lies the hall of a medieval house.

SEDILIA: seats for the priests (usually three) on the S side of the chancel of a church.

SEGMENTAL ARCH: *see* Arch.

SET-OFF: *see* Weathering.

SEXPARTITE: *see* Vault.

SGRAFFITO: pattern incised into plaster so as to expose a dark surface underneath.

SHAFT-RING: motif of the C12 and C13 consisting of a ring round a circular pier or a shaft attached to a pier.

SHEILA-NA-GIG: fertility figure, usually with legs wide open.

SILL: lower horizontal part of the frame of a window.

SLATEHANGING: the covering of walls by overlapping rows of slates, on a timber substructure.

SOFFIT: underside of an arch, lintel, etc.

SOLAR: upper living-room of a medieval house.

SOPRAPORTE: painting above the door of a room, usual in the C17 and C18.

SOUNDING BOARD: horizontal board or canopy over a pulpit. Also called Tester.

SPANDREL: triangular surface between one side of an arch, the horizontal drawn from its apex, and the vertical drawn from its springer; also the surface between two arches.

SPERE-TRUSS: roof truss on two free-standing posts to mask the division between screens passage and hall. The screen itself, where a spere-truss exists, was originally movable.

SPIRE: tall pyramidal or conical pointed erection often built on top of a tower, turret, etc. *Broach Spire:* a broach is a sloping half-pyramid of masonry or wood introduced at the base of each of the four oblique faces of a tapering octagonal spire with the object of effecting the transition from the square to the octagon. The *splayed foot spire* is a variation of the broach form found principally in the south-eastern counties. In this form the four cardinal faces are splayed out near their base, to cover the corners, while the oblique (or intermediate) faces taper away to a point. *Needle Spire:* thin spire rising from the centre of a tower roof, well inside the parapet.

SPIRELET: *see* Flèche.

SPLAY: chamfer, usually of the jamb of a window.

SPRINGING: level at which an arch rises from its supports.

SQUINCH: arch or system of concentric arches thrown across the angle between two walls to support a superstructure, for example a dome (Fig. 18).

SQUINT: a hole cut in a wall or through a pier to allow a view of the main altar of a church from places whence it could not otherwise be seen (also called Hagioscope).

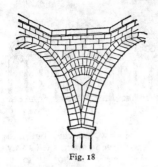

Fig. 18

STALL: carved seat, one of a row, made of wood or stone.

STAUNCHION: upright iron or steel member.

STEEPLE: the tower of a church together with a spire, cupola, etc.

STIFF-LEAF: E.E. type of foliage of many-lobed shapes (Fig. 19).

Fig. 19

STILTED: *see* Arch.

STOREY-POSTS: the principal posts of a timber-framed wall.

STOUP: vessel for the reception of holy water, usually placed near a door.

STRAINER ARCH: arch inserted across a room to prevent the walls from leaning.

STRAPWORK: C16 decoration consisting of interlaced bands, and forms similar to fretwork or cut and bent leather.

STRETCHER: *see* Brickwork.

STRING COURSE: projecting horizontal band or moulding set in the surface of a wall.

STRUT: *see* Roof.

STUCCO: plaster work.

STUDS: the subsidiary vertical timber members of a timber-framed wall.

SWAG: festoon formed by a carved piece of cloth suspended from both ends.

TABERNACLE: richly ornamented niche or free-standing canopy. Usually contains the Holy Sacrament.

TARSIA: inlay in various woods.

TAZZA: shallow bowl on a foot.

TERMINAL FIGURES (TERMS, TERMINI): upper part of a human figure growing out of a pier, pilaster, etc., which tapers towards the base. *See also* Caryatid, Pilaster.

TERRACOTTA: burnt clay, unglazed.

TESSELLATED PAVEMENT: mosaic flooring, particularly Roman, consisting of small 'tesserae' or cubes of glass, stone, or brick.

TESSERAE: *see* Tessellated Pavement.

TESTER: *see* Sounding Board.

TETRASTYLE: having four detached columns.

THREE-DECKER PULPIT: pulpit with Clerk's Stall below and Reading Desk below the Clerk's Stall.

TIE-BEAM: *see* Roof (Figs. 14, 15).

TIERCERON: *see* Vault (Fig. 21).

TILEHANGING: *see* Slatehanging.

TIMBER-FRAMING: method of construction where walls are built of timber framework with the spaces filled in by plaster

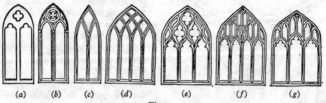

(a)   (b)   (c)   (d)   (e)   (f)   (g)

Fig. 20

or brickwork. Sometimes the timber is covered over with plaster or boarding laid horizontally.

TOMB-CHEST: chest-shaped stone coffin, the most usual medieval form of funeral monument.

TOUCH: soft black marble quarried near Tournai.

TOURELLE: turret corbelled out from the wall.

TRACERY: intersecting ribwork in the upper part of a window, or used decoratively in blank arches, on vaults, etc. *Plate tracery: see* Fig. 20(*a*). Early form of tracery where decoratively shaped openings are cut through the solid stone infilling in a window head. *Bar tracery:* a form introduced into England *c.*1250. Intersecting ribwork made up of slender shafts, continuing the lines of the mullions of windows up to a decorative mesh in the head of the window. *Geometrical tracery: see* Fig. 20(*b*). Tracery characteristic of *c.* 1250–1310 consisting chiefly of circles or foiled circles. *Y-tracery: see* Fig. 20(*c*). Tracery consisting of a mullion which branches into two forming a Y shape; typical of *c.* 1300. *Intersecting tracery: see* Fig. 20(*d*). Tracery in which each mullion of a window branches out into two curved bars in such a way that every one of them is drawn with the same radius from a different centre. The result is that every light of the window is a lancet and every two, three, four, etc., lights together form a pointed arch. This treatment also is typical of *c.* 1300. *Reticulated tracery: see* Fig. 20(*e*). Tracery typical of the early C14 consisting entirely of circles drawn at top and bottom into ogee shapes so that a net-like appearance results. *Panel tracery: see* Fig. 20(*f*) and (*g*). Perp tracery, which is formed of upright straight-sided panels above lights of a window.

TRANSEPT: transverse portion of a cross-shaped church.

TRANSOM: horizontal bar across the openings of a window.

TRANSVERSE ARCH: *see* Vault.

TRIBUNE: *see* Gallery.

TRICIPUT, SIGNUM TRICIPUT: sign of the Trinity expressed by three faces belonging to one head.

TRIFORIUM: arcaded wall passage or blank arcading facing the nave at the height of the aisle roof and below the clerestory (q.v.) windows. (*See* Gallery.)

TRIGLYPHS: blocks with vertical

grooves separating the metopes (q.v.) in the Doric frieze (Fig. 12).

TROPHY: sculptured group of arms or armour, used as a memorial of victory.

TRUMEAU: stone mullion (q.v.) supporting the tympanum (q.v.) of a wide doorway.

TUMULUS: *see* Barrow.

TURRET: very small tower, round or polygonal in plan.

TUSCAN: *see* Order.

TYMPANUM: space between the lintel of a doorway and the arch above it.

UNDERCROFT: vaulted room, sometimes underground, below a church or chapel.

UNIVALLATE: of a hill-fort: defended by a single bank and ditch.

UPPER PALAEOLITHIC: *see* Palaeolithic.

VAULT: *Barrel-vault: see* Tunnel-vault. *Cross-vault: see* Groin-vault. *Domical vault:* square or polygonal dome rising direct on a square or polygonal bay, the curved surfaces separated by groins (q.v.). *Fanvault:* late medieval vault where all ribs springing from one springer are of the same length, the same distance from the next, and the same curvature. *Groin-vault* or *Crossvault:* vault of two tunnelvaults of identical shape intersecting each other at r. angles. Chiefly Norman and Renaissance. *Lierne:* tertiary rib, that is, rib which does not spring either from one of the main springers or from the central boss. Introduced in the C14, continues to the C16. *Quadripartite vault:* one wherein one bay of vaulting is divided into four parts. *Rib-vault:* vault with diagonal ribs projecting along the groins. *Ridgerib:* rib along the longitudinal or transverse ridge of a vault. Introduced in the early C13. *Sexpartite vault:* one wherein one bay of quadripartite vaulting is divided into two parts transversely so that each bay of vaulting has six parts. *Tierceron:* secondary rib, that is, rib which issues from one of the main springers or the central boss and leads to a place on a ridge-rib. Introduced in the early C13. *Transverse arch:* arch separating one bay of a vault from the next. *Tunnelvault* or *Barrel-vault:* vault of semicircular or pointed section. Chiefly Norman and Renaissance. (*See* Fig. 21.)

VAULTING SHAFT: vertical member leading to the springer of a vault.

VENETIAN WINDOW: window with three openings, the central one arched and wider than the outside ones. Current in England chiefly in the C17–18.

VERANDA: open gallery or balcony with a roof on light, usually metal, supports.

VESICA: oval with pointed head and foot.

VESTIBULE: anteroom or entrance hall.

VILLA: (1) according to Gwilt (1842) 'a country house for the residence of opulent persons'; (2) Romano-British country houses cum farms, to which the description given in (1)

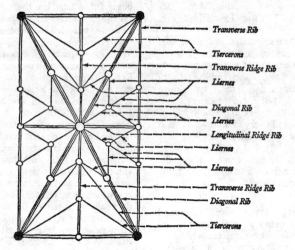

Transverse Rib

Tiercerons
Transverse Ridge Rib
Liernes

Diagonal Rib
Liernes
Longitudinal Ridge Rib
Liernes

Liernes

Transverse Ridge Rib
Diagonal Rib

Tiercerons

Fig. 21

more or less applies. They developed with the growth of urbanization. The basic type is the simple corridor pattern with rooms opening off a single passage; the next stage is the addition of wings. The courtyard villa fills a square plan with subsidiary buildings and an enclosure wall with a gate facing the main corridor block.

VITRIFIED: made similar to glass.

VITRUVIAN OPENING: A door or window which diminishes towards the top, as advocated by Vitruvius, bk. IV, chapter VI.

VOLUTE: spiral scroll, one of the component parts of an Ionic column (see Order).

VOUSSOIR: wedge-shaped stone used in arch construction.

WAGON ROOF: roof in which by closely set rafters with arched braces the appearance of the inside of a canvas tilt over a wagon is achieved. Wagon roofs can be panelled or plastered (ceiled) or left uncovered.

WAINSCOT: timber lining to walls.

WALL PLATE: see Roof.

WATERLEAF: leaf shape used in later C12 capitals. The waterleaf is a broad, unribbed, tapering leaf curving up towards the angle of the abacus and turned in at the top (Fig. 22).

Fig. 22

WEALDEN HOUSE: timber-framed house with the hall in the centre and wings projecting only slightly and only on the jutting upper floor. The roof, however, runs through without a break between wings and hall, and the eaves of the hall part are therefore exceptionally deep. They are supported by diagonal, usually curved, braces starting from the short inner sides of the overhanging wings and rising parallel with the front wall of the hall towards the centre of the eaves.

WEATHERBOARDING: overlapping horizontal boards, covering a timber-framed wall.

WEATHERING: sloped horizontal surface on sills, buttresses, etc., to throw off water.

WEEPERS: small figures placed in niches along the sides of some medieval tombs (also called Mourners).

WHEEL WINDOW: *see* Rose Window.

INDEX OF PLATES

For the 1982 reprint the photographs had to be reassembled (a task ably undertaken by Joanna Campbell); as a result, there are a few very minor changes. The abbreviation *N.M.R.* stands for National Monuments Record.

INDEX OF ARTISTS

INDEX OF PLACES

THE BUILDINGS OF ENGLAND

COMPLETE LIST OF TITLES

Middlesex *1st ed. 1951 Nikolaus Pevsner, revision in progress for incorporation into the above two titles*

Norfolk, North East, and Norwich *1st ed. 1962 Nikolaus Pevsner, revision in progress*

Norfolk, North West and South *1st ed. 1962 Nikolaus Pevsner, revision in progress*

Northamptonshire *1st ed. 1961 Nikolaus Pevsner, 2nd ed. 1973 revised Bridget Cherry*

Northumberland *1st ed. 1957 Nikolaus Pevsner with Ian A. Richmond, revision in progress*

Nottinghamshire *1st ed. 1951 Nikolaus Pevsner, 2nd ed. 1979 revised Elizabeth Williamson*

Oxfordshire *1st ed. 1974 Jennifer Sherwood and Nikolaus Pevsner*

Shropshire *1st ed. 1958 Nikolaus Pevsner*

Somerset, North, and Bristol *1st ed. 1958 Nikolaus Pevsner, revision in progress*

Somerset, South and West *1st ed. 1958 Nikolaus Pevsner*

Staffordshire *1st ed. 1974 Nikolaus Pevsner*

Suffolk *1st ed. 1961 Nikolaus Pevsner, 2nd ed. 1974 revised Enid Radcliffe*

Surrey *1st ed. 1962 Ian Nairn and Nikolaus Pevsner, 2nd ed. 1971 revised Bridget Cherry*

Sussex *1st ed. 1965 Ian Nairn and Nikolaus Pevsner, revision in progress*

Warwickshire *1st ed. 1966 Nikolaus Pevsner and Alexandra Wedgwood*

Wiltshire *1st ed. 1963 Nikolaus Pevsner, 2nd ed. 1975 revised Bridget Cherry*

Worcestershire *1st ed. 1968 Nikolaus Pevsner*

Yorkshire: The North Riding *1st ed. 1966 Nikolaus Pevsner*

Yorkshire: The West Riding *1st ed. 1959 Nikolaus Pevsner, 2nd ed. 1967 revised Enid Radcliffe*

Yorkshire: York and the East Riding *1st ed. 1972 Nikolaus Pevsner with John Hutchinson, revision in progress*